C000231634

# The Seres Agenda

R. Scott Lemriel
(AKA - R. Scott Rochek)

Special Fifth Edition
(Print & E-book - new original cover designs)
(E-book Special Techniques Section hyperlinks)
(Published April, 2019)

Copyright © R. Scott Lemriel (AKA - R. Scott Rochek)
All rights reserved
Special Fifth Edition
(Larger 6 X 9 format & new original cover)
(New E-book hyperlinks - Special Techniques Section)
(April, 2019)

Total Spectrum Publishing
Lake Forest, CA


Cover Design & Illustration by Michel Bohbot


ISBN 978-0-692-14386-5 (pbk)
ISBN 978-0-692-14387-2 (digital)


First originally published by Page Publishing, Inc. 2013


Printed in the United States
& at print-on-demand facilities worldwide.

# ACKNOWLEDGMENTS

The incredible journey of writing, editing, proofing and generally refining *The Seres Agenda* brings this current special 5th edition to you. This was a work in progress, like all of us on this temporarily backward planet Earth. The 5th edition includes a special techniques section added to the back for the uplifting, life-transforming benefit of readers, along with current professional editing and proofreading to present the work in its originally envisioned form by this author.

I would like to express deep thanks for the wonderful editing work done on the special techniques section through the donated time of editor Margaret E. Peiman (in Canada). She kindly donated her time to conduct the preliminary full edit of the entire special techniques section that first appeared in the 4th edition. Her efforts made the work of the primary editor I hired to prepare the 4th edition text a breeze and enabled her to go through this section so we could finalize it for publication.

Many thanks and great appreciation goes to Temi Ol of Temi Editing Services for her editing/proofreading work done on *The Seres Agenda* 4th edition. I have much gratitude for her editing skills.

*The Seres Agenda* special 5th edition (larger 6 X 9 size – new cover) is now published through my Total Spectrum Publishing company, along with the new Epub (E-book) formats containing the added hyperlinks in the Special Techniques section. In part, I have brought the 5th edition to this expanded form because of the work of these two past and recently acquired new editors. I consider myself fortunate to have crossed paths with them.

The extraordinary artistry of Michel Bohbot that went into designing the book cover for this newly published, larger 6 X 9 version – via my Total Spectrum Publishing company – deserves deep appreciation and gratitude.

He worked patiently and proficiently with the definitive descriptions in the book and from my clear visual directions to produce the accurate representation of two important and unique scenes. Michel Bohbot's remarkable artistry and book cover design work, among other professional artistry design services, are available at mbohbot.com.

My good buddy, Michael Kelly in New York, voluntarily went through *The Seres Agenda* and *The Emerald Doorway* (book one of The Parallel Time Trilogy) and found quite a few hard to see typos that three previously paid editors missed altogether. They are now fixed in The Seres Agenda 5th edition and The Emerald Doorway 2nd publication books that have new original cover designs. His efforts are much appreciated.

My mother in this lifetime has also been a rock of encouraging support from the day she finished reading the first manuscript of *The Seres Agenda* prior to its publication. While reading it, she discovered much about her son's extraordinary experiences while growing up that she never dreamed took place – to her great surprise. I never talked about all I was going through while growing up regarding contacts with highly evolved benevolent Master teachers and benevolent extraterrestrial beings from other worlds – many of them human – and explorations into higher dimensional realities until after the book was officially published.

I would also like to thank the many Master teachers and wonderful advanced, kind beings from other worlds whose paths I crossed, or vice versa, for their inspirational examples that encouraged me to go forward with revealing the deliberately hidden truths that are now contained in *The Seres Agenda*. I would also like to thank the omnipresent primordial, special first vibratory word or first Sound known as HU – imported to planet Earth from other worlds – and the new consciousness liberating Ray woven through it that originates from the source behind and supporting all that exists. The discovery of the new Ray, what it does, and how to use it has taken me many times far beyond good and evil and the petty bobbles of this physical world. My work is dedicated to assisting others to discover these deliberately hidden grand truths for themselves. From my direct experience, I can state there are new responsible, personal freedoms awaiting the adventuresome explorer who rides that rainbow home – while they are still alive here.

# CONTENTS

# PROLOGUE

# UNEXPECTED TRANSFORMATION

For the first time, *The Seres Agenda* journey uncovers what is soon coming to our planet Earth, something that no one will anticipate. The following chapters do not reveal a prediction of the end of the world, a foreboding Armageddon, or a doomed fate for our planet. However, it is the pronouncement of the coming of an event that has never happened before – an event that will transform the Earth. This coincides with the predictions of today's living Mayan leaders or Shamans regarding their Mayan calendar that ended on December 21, 2012. They proclaim what is coming will begin to occur during "the End Time" between 2007 and 2015, which they foresee will result one day in, "the ending of evil as an experiment on Earth." I have included this claim because of what I found during my deeper independent explorations beyond this insight, and what I subsequently discovered is coming to planet Earth in the near future to accomplish this great, worldwide change.

What has already begun that harmlessly passed through the end of the year 2012, and moved onward through and beyond 2015, will continue to expand for years into the future. This initially involved the critical juncture of planetary and solar system alignments that, otherwise, would have been destructive to the Earth. I have endeavored to share with people for quite a number of years that something very significant has changed in Earth's destiny, and we will begin to see the benevolent effects of this in the near future. At the right moment, it will become apparent to everyone that our world is beginning to go through something extraordinary. The destiny of our planet has changed

7

from a near future destructive direction to a coming unexpected worldwide event that will affect all life with an uplifting transformation.

Comprehensive understandings of purposefully hidden truths continued to surface during my extraterrestrial contact experiences and many ongoing out-of-body journeys from my early childhood onward. These explorations ventured into the primordial sound, omnipresent force, original word or first sound vibration sent out by the "Source" behind all life to develop, build, and maintain all creation. This first "Source" - predominantly referred to as the "Ancient One" or "Prime Creator" by very advanced extraterrestrial human beings who have a vast understanding of its nature - originated the very first sound or word that manifested the multi-dimensional universe. Extended from this center is an omnipresent, omniscient, and omnipotent conscious energy field that underlies, sustains, and supports all life everywhere.

The extraordinary experiences into the unknown universe I have encountered over this lifetime are all true. However, to paraphrase the statement made at the beginning of each episode of the old *Dragnet* detective drama television series, "The episode you are about to see is true, but the names of the characters and the locations where events took place have been changed to protect the innocent." Therefore, the unique story that unfolds throughout the pages of this book is based entirely on my direct true-life experiences. Some of you may understandably choose to view it as fiction to a degree. However, the wide panorama of events woven throughout this highly revealing account unveil the purposefully hidden truth suppressed in all of us long ago, and what is unexpectedly coming to liberate the people and change the face of the Earth. What will take place worldwide will constructively uplift all life on the planet. When the time is right all mankind will know, without a shadow of a doubt, that highly evolved benevolent human, humanoid, and other extraterrestrial beings actually exist, as well as many other parallel and higher dimensions.

Journey through the pages of *The Seres Agenda* and you will discover an ever-widening hidden truth beginning to surface within your own knowing imagination. Then you too will come to inherently understand, as I have, that the rate of vibration on this planet is in the beginning process of being greatly uplifted in quite dramatic, benevolent, and constructive ways.

You will come to know a new way is being prepared for us to gain the understanding, awareness, and insight to remain serenely balanced when this entirely unexpected worldwide transforming event takes place. Fortunately, the decision to finally implement this wondrous constructive change is irreversible.

Otherwise, our planet would most certainly be doomed.

While you travel further into the revealing depths of *The Seres Agenda* with the human being named "Mark Santfield," an adult in his mid-thirties, you will know how his entirely unexpected profound experiences forever transformed and expanded his understanding of the universe. He discovers a classified worldwide government, officially created after World War II, which soon came under the influential control of a diabolical, bipedal non-human, totalitarian extraterrestrial race. Then he unexpectedly awakens to the important key part he is to play to carry out a newly created vast extraterrestrial plan to safely retire evil as an experiment. He discovers a near future benevolent transformation is coming to our planet instead of its looming destruction.

As always, I wish all my fellow human beings living on Earth only the very best during the uplifting transforming days that lie ahead for all of us.

# CHAPTER ONE

# TAKEN BEYOND EARTH

$\mathcal{A}$ sleek, silvery, disc-shaped ship speeding through space, its entire circumference illumined with a pale-blue light, swiftly passed by the planet Mars and darted in a streak of light into the distant black void between countless stars. Minutes later, the slowing streak of light coming from a vast background star-field, gradually formed back into the mysterious spaceship as it passed by the moon, headed in the direction of Earth. It soon slowed to a stop, hovering above the cloud cover, moving in high above the west coast of North America.

Inside, a lone extraterrestrial pilot looked down and grinned with satisfaction at the blinking blue spherical crystal in the center of the rectangular paneled, half-octagon shaped control console.

***Good! The one the Galactic Council selected is located. He will help... he must,*** he thought to himself with some relief.

Silently reflecting on the purpose of his urgent arrival to Earth, the visitor reached down from waist-height and placed his right palm in the air with his fingers spread into the right illumined golden quartz crystal hand impression. It brightened the light passing through his translucent skin.

The rapidly descending spaceship passed down through the cloud layer and darted below it through a widening opening, sucking whirling, cloudy mists downward behind the hull. The ship stopped a second later to hover fifty-thousand-feet above a selected verdant-forested crest along part of the High Sierra Mountains of northern California.

The extraterrestrial's hand passed over the top of a green rectangular crystal, and a human male standing in a small clearing beside a two-man tent appeared on the wide vertical 3-D imaging screen projected a few feet above the control console. The extraterrestrial's eyes sparkled with anticipation as his left hand touched a smaller illumined red triangular crystal above the left guidance control hand impression, and a circle of red light appeared around the image of the man. The image began to zoom closer, bringing the Earthman into clarity.

The misty sprinkling of tiny warm raindrops hitting the man's upturned face at ground level was refreshing, and the mid-summer air was rich with the scent of Ozone.

*God, I needed this after all those months of madness in the city.*

Mark Santfield felt relieved by the thought as he peered deeper into his recollection of the past three months living under the smoggy skies of Los Angeles. That stint in the city was part of the research he was conducting for his new book about a suspected malevolent extraterrestrial presence operating behind a shadowy hidden government on Earth. He had already interviewed several dozen men, women, and a few children who had all claimed aliens abducted and mistreated them in some form or another before returning them to Earth with all memory of the experience repressed. That is, until deep hypnosis regression sessions brought back their clear memories.

"Yeah right!" he said aloud, smirking. But he did not feel an audible dialogue with himself on the subject was worth the effort, and so continued his reflections in silence.

*How the hell can all those people be abducted and have bizarre genetic experiments performed on them aboard some strange alien aircraft, and then be whisked back home with total amnesia, no proof, and nobody else ever witnessing a damned thing?*

He continued to muse over his reservations while he stood just outside his two-man tent below a cloudy but still warm mid-summer day in the mountains. He was trim, in his mid-thirties, just under six feet tall with short wavy brown hair, blue eyes, and a slight cleft chin. Although he never thought of himself as handsome compared to any famous men he knew of, his fiancée considered him to be good looking, or as she put it, "A real catch." He grinned as he recalled her charming ways and vivid green eyes. Then he looked down at the tiny water drops beginning to softly thud on the dry powdery dirt below his feet, and his smile widened with pleasure. He glanced up at the sky to appreciatively gaze across the forested mountaintops and verdant valleys that surrounded him. He took a deep breath of clean mountain air, and smiled like an imp as he started to sing — with childlike abandon — the cheerful lyrics to the old classic "The Song of The South."

"Zipadee-doo-dah, zipadee-a. My, oh my, what a wonderful day. Plenty of sunshine comin' my way. Zipadee-doo-dah, zipadee-a. Mr. Bluebird is on my shoulder. It's truth, it's actual, everything is satisfactual. Zipadee-doo-dah, Zipadee-a. My oh my, what a wonder . . . ful . . ."

He discovered nothing else would come out of his gaping open mouth. A shiver of energy ran down his spine as goose bumps sprang up on his exposed arms through his short-sleeved shirt. He slowly looked up to behold the clouds parting in a widening circle revealing a silvery disc-shaped extraterrestrial spaceship, surrounded by a pale-blue aura, silently hovering below the center of the opening.

*Oh . . . sh-sh-shit!*

The stuttered thought remained in silence as an ensuing indescribable rush of adrenaline and terror gripped him. His first impulse was to hightail it for the woods (he would have bolted) but a warm soothing glow began to emanate from his chest, and he discovered, amazed, that all fear had left him. A comforting mellow male voice clear as crystal then began speaking inside his head.

*Be at peace. You are not in any danger. My name is Mon-tlan and I am communicating to you telepathically mind-to-mind. I am also a human being just the same as you. However, I am not from Earth. My home planet circles a sun beyond what you call the Pleiades star group. I am in the ship you see above, and I have come to discuss with you a matter of extreme importance for all life on planet Earth. After you have personally experienced all that I have to reveal, you will understand the urgent nature that is behind my contacting you. Only then will I ask if you would be willing to assist a vast alliance of benevolent world systems to prevent the looming complete destruction of your planet. Will you allow me to bring you aboard the ship? I will respect your freewill response to my request.*

"Is this real?" Mark nervously blurted out.

*Yes Mark, it is,* Mon-tlan's kind voice replied firmly in his head.

Mark was beginning to experience the oddest sensation of calm familiarity with the being behind the voice.

"Um . . . if I agree, will it hurt?" he asked aloud.

Soft, kind laughter filled his head and the benevolent voice answered, *I promise the teleportation beam is completely safe and painless. Once you are aboard you will discover the experience was exhilarating. Mark, will you help us help your planet grow up and not be destroyed?*

Briefly spellbound by the astounding implications surrounding this monumental experience, Mark closed his eyes. Then he vigorously shook his head, rubbed his eyelids with the palms of his hands, and then took a deep calming breath. As he slowly opened his eyes he cautiously looked up to discover the alien spaceship was still there, but it had moved closer, and it was now hovering just a hundred feet above his head.

The same blue-white light was still enshrouding the silvery-gray metallic ship, and now he could make out more detail. Clearly defined on the bottom hull were three semispherical shaped pods, spaced six feet apart in a triangular position, pointing downward. A circular spiral of overlapping thin metal sheets, similar to a camera shutter, began to gradually become visible inside the triangular space between the pods. Mark looked back down at the ground to carefully consider the implications of what might happen next. Then he looked back up at the mysterious ship and shivered.

*Well, I did want to do more research for my second book.*

He pondered the thought further as he turned around to view the seeming security of the tent staked out on the ground. Then he looked back up at the ship and silently pondered another thought.

*Now that's just too damned ironic. I'm about to become one of those abducted people I interviewed; except, apparently I've been asked. Oh God, I hope I don't regret this. Well, here goes.*

"What did you say your name is?" he cautiously asked out loud.

*My name is Mon-tlan, but if you wish, just call me Monti.*

"Okay Monti but . . . uh . . . will I be gone a long time?"

*You will be exploring many truths for approximately three days or seventy-two Earth hours that have remained hidden from you and most other human beings on your planet. However, seven days will have elapsed by the time I return you to where you are standing by the tent. I will explain how this is possible once you arrive aboard the ship. Are you ready?*

Mark let his eyes caress the beautiful countryside surrounding his campsite one last time, before he focused back up at the ship.

"Well, I would like to help if I can."

The thin overlapping circle of camera shutter-like metal sheets on the bottom of the ship's hull began to spiral open. A transparent yellow-golden cone of light projected from inside the ship flowed down over Mark's entire body passing through every cell to create a soothing sensation, and an adventuresome spirit began to well up inside him.

He took one last look at the surrounding lush forested tree line and froze in his tracks. His eyes transfixed upon several moving sinister figures, just behind the tree line, dressed in dark black clothing with camouflaged hoods pulled down over their heads. The tallest of the three figures gazed through a pair of binoculars and motioned with a hand to the squatting man beside him to fire a shoulder-held, yard-long silvery cylindrical device pointed in his direction. For an unknown reason, Mark felt a presence silently direct him to hit the ground and he literally jumped forward landing face down in the dirt, just as a sizzling electrical sound split the air. A four-inch thick beam of solid white light burned across the top of his body, and Mark involuntarily threw both hands over the top of his head as a shield. The full force of the beam hit his tent a few feet away. The violent blast sent a heat wave backward that seared the tiny hairs on his hands, accompanied by a deafening roar like a jumbo jet taking off right next to him and a violent shuddering like an earthquake under his body. The tent and the ground surrounding it shredded in an instant into millions of blistering bits of dissipating golden light particles. Mark glanced up to see the last moments of a disintegrating fireball and smoke evaporating into nothing, leaving behind a round, black scorched circle of dirt where his tent had just been.

Mark looked toward the forest tree line to see the three men running in his direction over the several hundred yards between them, brandishing some kind of hand-held weapons pointed directly at him. Refracted sunlight passing through clear crystalline appearing barrels created an eerie full spectrum halo of light surrounding their black glove-covered hands. Adrenaline and terror rushed down his spine and Mark jumped to his feet to run for his life in the opposite direction. He glanced over his shoulder in time to see all three men simultaneously extend their arms aiming the guns. Then he heard the explosive energy discharge from their weapons split the air and leapt toward the ground in terror. To his astonishment, he was instantly suspended just above the dirt as tiny star-like sparkling points of golden light began dancing all over his body an instant before he simply vanished in a blinding whirl of golden energy.

The mysterious assailants stopped in their tracks with gaping mouths as their three pulsing red energy beams harmlessly passed through the empty air above the vanishing transparent molecules of Mark's body to hit a tree a hundred yards beyond him. A vertical four-feet section of the trunk just above the ground was dematerialized in an instant in a blinding explosive red light, and the remaining height of the giant fir tree dropped to the stump. The two-hundred-feet-high mighty bulk then started to fall over until it crashed with a thunderous roar to the ground. The three mysterious assassins looked up in time to see Monti's sleek Scout ship flash a brighter light around the hull before it shot straight upward and vanished from sight beyond the cloud cover. The taller enemy leader lifted a wrist communicator to his lips and spoke a command in a guttural alien language. A moment passed, and dancing yellow flecks of upward whirling light appeared around their bodies before they too vanished from sight.

Mark watched his hands reappear a moment later with the same tiny sparkling points of golden light dancing all over them before the energy faded away. He looked up still terrified to discover he was standing in front of a semicircular control console. Hundreds of various sized illumined crystal controls, producing a dazzling display of every imaginable color, spread out across the entire surface. The warm friendly smile of an extraterrestrial human-appearing male in his mid-thirties, with slightly curly blond shoulder-length hair and a matching short-cropped beard, was staring back at him. He was standing just three feet away behind the center of the console next to a sleek white chair. Mark immediately focused on the alien's striking clear sky-blue eyes and was spellbound as he gazed deeper into them. Then without the slightest bit of doubt, he just simply knew the mysterious being standing before him was human and quite benevolent. In fact, he was surprised he also understood this particular extraterrestrial was happy to greet an Earth person.

"Wow, that was incredible! I thought I was toast for sure down there. They were really trying to kill me," Mark blurted out, relieved but not realizing he just said it aloud with gusto. The sound of his own voice surprised him. "I mean . . . it's really true. Am I really aboard a spaceship?"

Monti chuckled, finding Mark's question a bit absurd and somewhat amusing, but replied this time using his vocal cords and a soothing baritone voice.

"The beings who were after you below are not human even though they may disguise themselves as such, and they most certainly would have killed you if they could. It seems I arrived in the nick-of-time, as I believe an old Earth expression states. Well Mark, now what do you think about how you arrived aboard?"

"Actually, I feel really good and kind of warm and tingling all over," he replied, a little breathless. "I've never been this clear-headed. I feel like Superman." Then Mark's smile dropped as he more somberly asked, "Why were they trying to kill me and who are they anyway?"

Monti sighed and answered, "They were sent to kill you by a rogue organization made up of mostly non-human tyrant beings called the Trilotew.

They are part of a totalitarian Alliance of worlds, and they have a deadly stake in Earth's future. This is the reason I contacted you at this time. You will understand more about this a little later. For now, welcome aboard."

Monti turned and placed both his palms with spread fingers into the luminous hand control impressions, and they brightened radiating light through the translucent skin of both hands.

The ship shot out of Earth's upper atmosphere at incredible speed and slowed in seconds to a stop to hover in space a hundred miles above the planet.

While Monti was talking, Mark had been steadily gazing more closely at him, noticing the single-piece knee-length light-blue gown he was wearing, which was belted at his trim waist with a dark-blue silken strip of material. It was tied off with a simple knot at his left side and the extra lengths were dangling down a foot over his hip. The top of the garment was designed with an open V-cut, which extended from the base of his neck to just above his solar plexus. Embroidered on the garment over his left chest was the symbol of a white gold-tipped pyramid, suspended above the center of a silvery galaxy with three blue stars in triangular position set above the pyramid's apex. The visitor's feet were clad in simple slip-on type blue silken shoes. He was completely human in appearance, firmly built, and stood perhaps six feet in height. He had smooth wrinkle-free lightly tanned skin and slightly sunken cheeks. Monti's cheerful eyes kept drawing back Mark's gaze because they appeared to be slightly larger eyes than most humans he had seen, and he could swear he was detecting a subtle glowing energy emanating from them. Then he recalled that he had experienced the phenomena three days before.

"Three days ago, a very unusual man calling himself Mr. Crystal mysteriously hinted I would soon meet someone very special, right after he introduced himself at the home of my fiancée's father," Mark stated. "No doubt he was referring to you, but he could not have known I would be attacked before then. Monti, I must know. Is he one of your people, as I suspect, and is our world already being run behind the scenes by the totalitarian extraterrestrial race you mentioned?"

"Yes, Mark," Monti replied, his smile vanishing. "Mr. Crystal is one of us. You cannot yet imagine how covertly and expertly the off-world totalitarian group has infiltrated your world. We caught them many times breaking a renewed treaty they resigned with the Galactic Inter-dimensional Alliance of Free Worlds in 1908 regarding Earth. By treaty agreement, many races from the stars secretly established observation and scientific study bases in hidden locations. The treaty forbade any of them to make direct contact with world leaders or the populace, but that has not worked. The previous cold war that took place between the United States and the former Soviet Union was influenced by an off-world treaty-breaking tyrant extraterrestrial race. A much larger and more dangerous cold war continues to this day that started 500,000 years ago between a vast organization of benevolent extraterrestrial races and a much smaller but highly technically advanced totalitarian race and its dominated allies, and Earth is caught right in the middle of it. The non-human race referred to here see all mankind as cattle, and your planet as just another resource-filled world to be dominated and added to their totalitarian imperial kingdom."

"I don't understand," replied Mark, mystified.

Monti thoughtfully paused, and then touched several controls on the console. A vertical projected view screen appeared above the console again, revealing the planet Saturn with its many rings and moons.

Monti pointed to it and stated, "Camouflaged within the rings circling this planet you call Saturn is one of our medium sized flagships. It's over a mile long."

He touched another control and the view screen changed to a close-up view of the central rings, revealing a large cylindrical spaceship stationed between the various sized icy-looking chunks that apparently comprised the rings. A ship just like Monti's was flying straight toward the central section of the massive ship as it began to fade from sight. The view screen changed to a closer image just as the vanishing ship completely disappeared a few feet from the central section of the parent vessel's glistening silvery hull. A moment later, it began to re-materialize inside a vast hangar bay that became briefly visible through the hull of the flagship. As the ship began to land beside eleven other identical ships, the hull returned to its normal non-transparent solid state.

"As you can see," continued Monti, "we don't require open launch bays to exit or enter the parent ships. Our technology allows us to take our spaceships into a parallel dimension by raising the molecular time rate of the ship's matter. Then the ship can harmlessly pass right through the solid hull of the mother ship. The Scout ship is then returned to the same molecular time rate as that of the parent ship and it can safely land inside the hangar bay." Monti steadily gazed at Mark and asked, "Will you come with me on the most revealing journey of your lifetime?"

"Everything you're telling me I've already dreamed about at night, and I had many visions about all of this while I was writing my first book," replied Mark, elated. "The confirmation you are providing is like giving fresh oxygen to a suffocating man. Yes Monti, I'd be honored to go with you, learn all I can, and help in some way."

Monti appeared pleased as he continued, "Then the people of your world may have a real chance to be taken off the quarantined status it is under per current treaty stipulations, and it could become a member of the Galactic Inter-dimensional Alliance of Free Worlds. When you return from this journey greatly changed for the better, you will be capable of carrying out the diplomatic mission it is your destiny to fulfill for the survival of your people and your planet. We have technology the rogue totalitarian factions do not know exists, and we are about to implement it to protect your world. We can monitor all hidden activity on Earth from the flagship.

"Yes, Mark, we know about the hidden government you wrote about in your first book and they are quite real. That group poses a deadly threat to three-fourths of the planet's population. With your permission, I will take you to the parent ship. From there, you can witness for yourself the very dire reality a certain non-human alien group and their allies are planning for the people of planet Earth. They already have a hypnotic control over the leaders of the secret world government.

"But Mark, you must also know we are not going to harm any of them to accomplish this great change. To do this we must first neutralize the implanted terrorizing controls in their subconscious minds. We can safely remove people from your world for a short time to get this done before we return them. This must occur before we will reveal our existence to all Earth inhabitants, and the truth about the existence of our entire Galactic Inter-dimensional Alliance of Free Worlds. Many millions of inhabited world systems make up our alliance, and many of them are human. We must act soon because the misuse of advanced waveform technology by the totalitarian race to subconsciously control the freewill of people all over your world is well underway. They want to make the people of Earth a compliant slave race, and they are continuing covert illegal operations on your world at this moment to advance their dominating endeavors. Because of this, the decision has recently finally been reached by all the Galactic Alliance members to utilize a recently acquired new benevolent tool. We can now stop the sinister plans of the diabolical race from reaching maturity. Otherwise, the complete annihilation of the Earth would likely be the result.

"For reasons that will become clear to you later, we cannot allow the destruction of your world to occur even accidentally. The repercussions of such an event would also create very harmful negative effects for hundreds of billions of advanced beings in the Alliance that live in numerous parallel dimensions where many other worlds like Earth exist. Great harm would also be caused to a vast number of other beings you know nothing about that inhabit some of the planets and moons within your own solar system."

Mark seriously pondered all Monti had just shared with him and then curiously inquired, "What exactly did you mean when you said I would be permanently changed for the better?"

"Certain elements of your DNA and the majority of mankind on Earth have been purposefully shut down or turned off entirely," replied Monti. "You should have a hundred percent use of your brain, be naturally telepathic, have a photographic memory, and your body should last for a thousand years or more without disease. This is your birthright heritage. Unfortunately, human beings on your planet were long ago genetically deprived of these abilities. I cannot go into the reasons for this here, but you can explore the truth about all this aboard the flagship."

Several thousand miles away, two enemy dark gray Trilotew Demon Scout Interceptors, with elongated triangular shaped hulls, tapered rounded ends, and three semispherical pods under the hulls surrounded by pale-red anti-gravity auras, were speeding parallel to each other when they shot out of Earth's upper atmosphere. They made several parallel ninety-degree curved turns and darted at increased speed in the direction of Monti's hovering ship. The red energy fields surrounding the ships intensified, and the rounded clear beam lens at the front end of each one, below a dark teardrop shaped cockpit window, simultaneously shot a basketball sized fiery-red weapon at tremendous speed toward Monti's ship.

Monti glanced at a blinking pink spherical control that lit up, emitting a shrill warning sound. He instinctively lunged for the rectangular emerald-green control beside it, tightly grasping it in his right hand. The view screen revealed there was now a clearly visible transparent blue energy shield wavering between the ship and the two rapidly approaching red fireball weapons. The two approaching enemy ships sped up again, just as the two fireballs exploded off the force field, violently rocking the ship from side to side.

Mark fell to the floor, but he jumped back up and yelled, "Monti what's wrong? What's happening?"

Monti was too busy to respond as he slapped both hands back into the hand impressions on the guidance control console.

The blue energy shield surrounding the ship's hull brightened as the ship darted into an open golden-violet energy tunnel that appeared directly in front of the hull. Two more red whirling fireball weapons shot right past the space where Monti's ship had just been as the energy vortex doorway dwindled to a point, then vanished with a swift sucking sound.

"That was too close," stated Monti from his seated position behind the console. "Those two ships are from the treaty breaking rogue worlds called Trilotew or the Righteous Illumined Over-Lords of the Empire Worlds. Their agents on the ground must have had hidden ships waiting nearby monitoring you when you were beamed aboard this ship, before they tracked us here. Fortunately, I was able to activate the protective energy shield in time or they would have destroyed us. We are safe from further pursuit . . . for now. Their ships are not able to follow us through the vortex because the Galactic Alliance controls and guards that particle opening. I will clarify how this works. Mark, we have just passed through what we call an inter-dimensional vortex tunnel. These natural openings exist throughout space between worlds and on the surface or in the atmosphere of many worlds like your planet.

"In fact, Earth is entirely unique in this manner because it has a geometrically located grid system of inter-dimensional portal openings surrounding the entire planet. These openings allow for travel into parallel dimensions, as well as swift travel to the far reaches of the galaxy. Different versions of your planet Earth exist in those parallel realities you are not able to normally perceive because the matter in them vibrates at a different molecular time or vibration rate. Another way of putting it is to state we can travel into a higher dimension that vibrates at a faster molecular time rate, traverse a short distance, and then come back down through another inter-dimensional opening to discover we have traveled across a vast expanse of interstellar space in the physical universe. This is possible because of the faster and slower molecular time rates between the two dimensions."

"I'm not sure I follow you but I'm beginning to visualize a wider picture of creation I never dreamed was possible before today," replied Mark, utterly fascinated. "I somehow seem to visualize what you're saying on multi-dimensional levels. What did you do to me?"

Monti smiled but did not answer as he touched another luminous control, and the three-dimensional view screen projected above the console changed again. Mark could see the spaceship he was aboard was passing through a kind of golden-violet hourglass shaped energy conduit that was gradually widening in the near distance. The planet Saturn, with its huge surrounding ring system and moons was clearly visible in the near distance of the black void of space on the other side. Then the ship suddenly shot through the opening, and the view screen changed, revealing the energy conduit fading before vanishing into the distance behind the ship.

"As you could see for yourself," continued Monti, "we just moved from a position high above the outer atmosphere of Earth to enter one of the inter-dimensional connective vortexes. This one opens into an area of outer space very close to the planet Saturn. We are now on course to rendezvous with the flagship. You can just make it out hovering in position between several of Saturn's foreground rings."

Mark leaned forward to see the image and the projected view screen changed again. He could now observe their fast approach to the giant mile-long parent ship looming larger. Then he began to recall the recent experience he had with his fiancée just three days before his departure for a long anticipated solo camping trip in the High Sierra Mountains. They were both en route to visit her father at his secluded mansion located near the top-most heights of Beverly Hills, California. Mark now discovered, amazed, he had the ability to clearly visualize the experience all over again, as if he was actually there, and a pleased smile unconsciously widened on his face.

# CHAPTER TWO

# WITH EYES WIDE OPEN

*Oh God, I can just hear her,* Mark thought hesitantly. ***She will hit the roof if I start down that road again. Damn it, I have to say something.***

"It's the beginning of the end of all things as we know it!" Mark Santfield finally blurted out to his slightly younger and shapely female companion, Janice Carter. He glanced down at the front-page headlines of *The Los Angeles Times* Sunday edition she had sitting on her lap. He paused for a moment to gaze passionately at her, a woman considered by many to be strikingly beautiful. She had emerald green eyes, long gently curled brunette hair, and a straight regal nose that curved ever so slightly upward at the end.

"This may be the beginning of what I've been predicting for years now," he continued with gusto. "The world is going through a transformation that will change the planet's entire surface. The proof is right in front of you. Just look at the stuff on that front page: tidal waves hit twelve coastlines of the world on the same day; violent earthquakes go off in seven locations at once; snow in the deserts; and three remote extinct volcanoes suddenly blow their tops. Good God, Janice, it's really about to happen."

She gazed at him smirking back obvious impatience with his seemingly never-ending negative attitude about everything.

"Go on then dummy and keep it up," she replied. "You'll just piss off everyone at the party, but I refuse to stand by your side this time to be embarrassed by your pontificating negative predictions."

"Oh okay, don't worry babe. After all it is your dad's party," he responded, motioning with his hand to relax. "I'm not really in the mood anyway. Oh, come on Janice honey, cheer up. I'm doing this for you. I promise I won't let you down."

He pulled the sleek late model blue four-door Jaguar over to the curb in front of the ornate wrought iron gate crested with the symbol of white-feathered eagle's wings with golden tips. Dozens of other very expensive cars had already parked along both sides of the long private drive leading up to the entry gates. The gentle half-moon curved driveway beyond it led fifty feet up to a twenty-thousand-square-feet Roman style mansion estate, built near the two-lane highway that ran along the mountain crest line high above Beverly Hills, California.

"Come on, let's have some fun," he impishly remarked.

He smiled widely at her, opened the door and jumped out, then hurried around the front of the vehicle to the passenger door and opened it wide.

"At your service, princess," he gallantly stated, bowing low with a wave of his arm.

She elegantly placed her hand in his as he helped her out of the vehicle. Then he surrounded her with his arms and kissed her passionately. She was blushing when they parted a few moments later, but before he could say anything she smartly straightened her blue silken dress and struck a very sexy modeling pose.

"Well, how do I look?" she inquired, expecting to receive the anticipated response.

"Like a goddess!" he exuberantly replied, surveying her radiant beauty and firm curves of her body. "Now we'll see if your dream was worth the humbling you endured to get me on your father's guest list."

"Lead on," she regally commanded, and gently placed her right hand on top of his offered open left palm.

She pushed the intercom buzzer set in the left brick gate pillar with her left forefinger.

"Yes," answered a husky older male voice.

"It's me, Daddy," she replied, and the gate began to swing open.

They stood back a few feet to let both gates swing back along each side of the entrance of the driveway. Then they nonchalantly walked hand-in-hand up the driveway toward the mansion. Well-trimmed healthy green grass and multi-colored rose flowerbeds in full bloom lined both sides of the driveway that continued around a circular water-filled courtyard. A beautiful female angel statue with spread wings stood in the center. Water was pouring from the palms of her open hands into a wide, curved blue granite bowl at her feet. They walked around the fountain to the double front doors and rang the bell. A moment passed, then the large ornate dark wood door on the right swung open. Standing stolid in the opening was a slightly balding gray-haired burly man in his late sixties with a brown mustache, wearing an expensive dinner jacket.

"Well daughter, it's about time you visited this house," he stated.

"Father, is that all you can say after the emotional marathon we went through last night?" she defiantly replied, placing her hands on her hips.

"Now daughter," he began backing off, "where's your usual sense of humor? So this is the young man you keep talking about. Are you treating my daughter well?" he inquired sternly, inspecting Mark from head to toe. "Damn well better be!" he hotly added, but quickly forced a pleased grin before his daughter could scold him. "Oh, don't mind me. I'm just exercising my fatherly rights."

Janice smiled, relieved and said, "Daddy this is Mark Santfield, and Mark, this is my father Ted."

Ted cordially extended his hand.

"Well Mr. Carter, I'm glad we finally get to meet," stated Mark as he smiled and firmly shook Ted's hand.

"Just call me Ted. Everyone else does," he replied as he stepped back inside the house just behind the open front door.

Hand-in-hand, the couple casually walked through the majestic entryway and the door closed silently behind them.

Already inside were six couples dressed in casual elegance standing around the wide oval entryway on the rich blue lapis lazuli bordered granite tiled floor. Several of them casually glanced at Mark and Janice and then resumed their conversations.

A very large, gold metal-framed crystal chandelier was hanging down eight feet from the white dome shaped ceiling like an upside down Christmas tree. It was glistening with reflected rainbow colors off a hundred teardrop-shaped crystals that gradually tapered down to one larger crystal at the bottom. Ten feet directly below the chandelier was another smaller winged female angel fountain with water also pouring from the open palms of her hands into the circular blue granite pool at her feet. Along each side of the fountain, twin polished oak staircases began which gradually curved around and upward behind it to open onto a long curved second level balcony, leading in both directions to many other rooms. Mark and Janice walked a few feet behind Ted as he approached the angel fountain and stopped to turn around and smile at them.

"You two can introduce yourselves to my guests. Most of them are already in the grand reception room through the open glass doors. I have something to attend to in my study. I'll join you in a few minutes."

He walked a few feet over to the left staircase and headed up to the second level balcony.

Mark looked concerned at Janice and asked, "Now what? I don't know what to say to this class of people."

"Oh don't worry, silly. I'll handle the introductions. I'm used to the formal chit-chat of this crowd." Raising her eyebrows, she playfully smiled and said, "Who knows, something interesting may turn up. Remember, that's why we're here."

Mark glanced at the quadruple-paneled French glass doors pulled back against each side of the entryway on recessed rails set below the stone floor. He could see beyond them was an expansive deep-blue lapis lazuli bordered granite tiled floor, inlaid with intricate mosaic hardwood patterns. Twelve Roman style gold-laced lapis lazuli stone columns encircled the entire room. Fifty couples merrily chatting away were standing around the circumference of the grand reception room beside a dozen exotic carved wood-trimmed glass-topped tables with matching intricately carved chairs, and several artfully placed luxurious couches.

Twenty feet up the wall surrounding the room were a dozen large horizontal oval-concave clear glass windows. Just above them stretched the long gentle oval-shaped curve of the huge white alabaster ceiling. A smaller oval section of the ceiling, built several inches down from the upper level, enclosed a bright recessed light source that illuminated everything below in the expansive room. A large green ornate granite fireplace at the far end of the room was fully alight with orange and blue-gold flames spiraling upward four feet from neatly stacked burning logs.

*Who's he kidding? This place is more like the royal ballroom of a king's palace. I wonder if Ted could be involved.*

Mark continued to silently ponder the very real danger that possibility represented since his first book was trying to expose a shadowy hidden government to the world's people that knew nothing about it. He was also growing a little hot under the collar at the gaudy spectacle of privilege and power the place represented to him. It smacked of unfettered greed, gained at the abusive expense of others, but he did not dare voice this to Janice. After all, he was not sure how her father had quite literally become the world's richest man with hundreds of billions under his control or how he made so much money in the first place, and he was curious to find out more.

He was not exactly poor himself, but knew he had made his money honestly after the sales of seventy-five million copies of his first research book revealing hidden truth. The characters' actual names were changed but what the pages revealed came entirely from a sinister covert plan he uncovered by personal experience while undertaking research for the book. He dug deeper and discovered that a small hidden group of powerful mega-billionaires devised a plan to financially control the world and its various governments from a hidden classified government. More importantly, some evidence had recently turned up that convinced him this elitist group of power-mad men had come under the control of a totalitarian extraterrestrial race who planned to eliminate a sizable portion of the population on Earth.

His last book had thrown him into enough controversy over the last two years and someone was monitoring his movements. Two days earlier, while he was leaving his house in Woodland Hills, California, he spotted several men in a late model black sedan parked across the street. The man sitting opposite the driver was snapping dozens of pictures of him with a long telephoto lens. When they knew he had seen them, they sped away. He was becoming more frustrated about the whole affair and this was delaying the release of his sequel book. It had been nearly ready for months and the publisher was pressuring him to cough up the draft. Yet he remained hesitant until he could find out more about the conspiracy he now knew was real beyond any doubt. He had not yet told Janice about everything he had uncovered that confirmed his suspicions, and he was not planning to tell her more any time soon. He knew he was heading into certain dangerous territory and wanted to find a way to shield her and himself from harm.

Meanwhile, Janice was gazing at him concerned and touched his cheek to draw him out of his reverie.

"Will you relax? I promise this night will be interesting. Come on, let's head inside and see what we can uncover."

Mark smiled at her self-assurance.

"Lead on lady. This night I'm all yours."

# CHAPTER THREE

## GUESTS FROM WAY OUT OF TOWN

*Mark* clasped her hand as she offered it to him, and hand-in-hand they strolled through the open entryway leading into the grand reception room. They had not taken two steps when they were simultaneously noticed by a middle-aged couple standing by one of the glass-topped tables near the left swung back louvered door. The man's regal goatee style beard and green eyes were striking, but what caught Mark's attention was the reflected overhead light glistening off the top of his mostly bald head. Then he briefly gazed at the lovely shapely woman with long black silken hair standing next to him wearing an expensive diamond and emerald necklace. It was hanging down over the front of her low-cut blue and black silken dress. They smiled at Janice and then at Mark as they approached.

"Well Janice dear," the woman began bitingly. Then, with an obviously phony smile and air of upper class distinction, "I see you finally decided to introduce your infamous controversial suitor to our little gathering."

"Oh Cynthia Piermont darling," replied Janice with a quick phony smile in return, "I see you still haven't quite got the knack of pulling back your snippy little nose when it's poking its unwanted way into other people's business."

Cynthia's smile dropped to a fuming frown.

"How dare you!"

She walked away in a huff, leaving behind her embarrassed consort looking all too apologetic for her behavior. He forced an appeasing smile at Mark and

Janice and extended a gracious welcoming hand to Mark.

"It's a pleasure to finally meet you, Mr. Santfield. I'm Mr. Carter's General Counsel, Henry Throckmorton."

Mark cordially nodded his head as they shook hands.

"Please excuse Cynthia," continued Henry. "I don't know what's got into her and believe me, I had no idea she was going to make a snide remark or I wouldn't have agreed to be her consort for this event. For my part, you should know I've read your book several times and find it utterly fascinating. Although I must also add that some of the people in this room were . . . well, how shall I put it . . . probably offended by some of the things you implied might personally be of concern to them. The snobs deserve it. They think they are above the basic law of the universe that tells us that every action creates an equal but directly opposite reaction."

Still miffed by Cynthia's snide remark, Janice interrupted, "Henry, you always were a level-headed guy. I could always count on you to be straightforward with me, so how on Earth did you get hooked up with that shrew?"

Embarrassed, Henry sighed before he glanced over his shoulder toward the fireplace in Cynthia's direction. She was already busily chatting away with several guests as if nothing had happened.

"Well, to answer your question, she is one of the wealthier members of this group directly involved with something your father is currently undertaking, something that could affect the whole world in some way. So far, that is about all I know. Your father insisted that I accept her invitation to escort her here after I politely bowed out the first time she asked me. Now, how could I refuse a request like that from your father?"

He winked at Janice, but she was not amused.

"Listen, Henry, we need to know what my father is about to do. I'm worried about him. My senses tell me he may be involved in something very politically incorrect and likely very illegal as far as our government or any government is concerned. If Mark is right about even half of what is revealed in his book, this little group is planning a very dismal future for the entire world. My father is just as tight-lipped about his business now as he was when I was a little girl and I can't get anything out of him."

Henry looked at Mark and started to say something but hesitated and sighed. He took Mark and Janice by their arms and herded them a few feet further toward the wall behind the table.

He looked around the room behind them to see if anyone was watching and then whispered, "I can't say too much here in this company. Hidden monitors line the entire room except in this one corner where a blind spot exists and the receivers cannot pick up any soft conversations. You must understand, the power represented in this room actually runs the world today behind the scenes of the elected governments. I could be in serious trouble just for saying that, and I am telling you this now only because in recent days I became concerned for my own safety. Let me explain. Yesterday, I came to the house to deliver a package addressed to your father that had obviously been delivered by mistake to my office since some of his business interests are listed as operating from there. I believed your father was still in England because he was supposed to be there. Yet, when I walked into his study to deliver the package, I accidentally interrupted a meeting between him and two very unusual looking men, if you can call them that. Several very odd things immediately came to my attention. I began to realize that neither your father nor his guests had arrived at the house by car or any other observable means I could discover. I could also swear that for a moment, right when the two tall strange men saw me open the door and enter the room, they were staring at me with malevolent intent through the red slits of vertical cat-like eyes. I glanced at your father and when I looked back, his guests' eyes suddenly changed to normal appearing human eyes, and their taller stature diminished in height. I can tell you their continued gaze at me sent shivers down my spine. Janice, your father's face was a mix of fear and consternation when he saw me standing in the open doorway. He jumped up from his chair and walked up to me, grabbed the parcel from my hand, grasped my arm and promptly escorted me from the room, closing the study door behind us. Then he gazed into my eyes and forced a smile."

"'Henry, my good man,' he said to me, trying to appear cordial. 'I should have told you I had to suddenly return from England. These two clients insisted on a personal meeting here. They demand absolute anonymity regarding our interests and you noticed they are very touchy about such matters. Well, there is no way you could have known, so no harm done. I'll straighten them out when I go back inside.'

"I was mystified by the whole experience and asked, 'Ted, what the devil is going on? I'm your Legal Counsel on most business matters but I've been left out of the loop on this one.'

"Your father placed a consoling hand on my shoulder and replied, 'It was necessary, but I'll have to explain more about that aspect of things later on. Everything is fine. Now trust me and head back to the office. I'll give you a call a little later.'

"'Okay then have a good meeting,' I reluctantly conceded, forcing my own smile. Then I got the hell out of there at a brisk pace. The further away I traveled from your father's house and his two odd guests, the better I felt."

Mark had his hand to his chin deep in thought after hearing all Henry had to say.

Then he looked at Henry and solemnly stated, "Thank you for trusting both of us. We will not betray your confidence. I must uncover the truth about the two tall strange men that met with Ted. If I am right, they don't come from anywhere around here. I mean from Earth, that is, and I don't believe their intentions for most of us on this planet are good. If it's all right with you, I'd like to coordinate our very discreet investigations through Janice, until we uncover the truth of this mystery. Then we can determine what, if anything, we can do about it because it could be very dangerous. Janice, I haven't told you about this, but you should know two days ago I caught several men taking pictures of me with a telephoto lens from a nearby car after I left my house. They sped away when they noticed I spotted them, and this was not the first time I noticed them tracking my movements. I am sure of one thing. This all has something to do with the success of my first book. Someone or something doesn't want the truth out there among the people."

"Why didn't you tell me ya' big lunkhead?" demanded Janice.

"Look Janice dear, I'm now concerned for your safety as well as my own and I didn't want to alarm you until I could find out more. Besides, I suspect your father is involved in all of this somehow and he may not even realize the danger he's in."

"What danger is he in?" she asked impatiently.

Mark placed both hands on her shoulders to calm her and fondly stared in her eyes then answered, "If my hunch is correct, your father is being used by beings from another world. They somehow convinced him and certain members of his worldwide group their business interests would best come to fruition if they cooperated with their hidden alien agenda for the future of our planet. I further suspect this arrangement has been going on now for many, many years."

Henry glanced over his shoulder and looked back appearing nervous and perplexed.

He quickly interrupted them with a big cheerful smile and grabbed both their arms then stated, "Well thank you, Janice, for introducing Mark and it's been a pleasure finally meeting you. I will look forward to reading your next book."

Just then, Cynthia and another couple walked by pretending to be engaged in conversation, but their attention was obviously focused with wide-open ears upon Mark, Janice, and Henry.

"Go on you two and enjoy the party," cheerfully continued Henry rolling his eyes in the direction of the three people who just walked by them.

He turned away and headed back into the room to engage in a conversation with another couple standing a dozen feet beyond them. Mark and Janice gazed briefly at each other, clasped hands, and then knowingly smiled as they started to walk across the large room toward the fireplace at the far end.

# CHAPTER FOUR

# THE MYSTERIOUS MR. CRYSTAL

The covert eyes of many of the couples standing around the huge room casually glanced in the direction of Mark and Janice nonchalantly walking across the center of the room towards the warm glow of the fire burning inside the big granite fireplace. Two well-kept women about Janice's age briskly walked by her left side and turned in unison to smile elatedly back at her. Jubilant with surprise, Janice instantly recognized them and they threw their arms around each other.

"Janice!" the taller woman stated with delight once they had parted. The shorter woman added, "You look beautiful."

"Mary and Joanne!" Janice responded with equal delight. "My father didn't tell me you two were coming to the party."

"This must be your mysterious boyfriend Mark," Mary stated—a skillful diversion—and both she and Joanne gave him an appreciated full-length gaze.

"Hello ladies," Mark said appreciatively.

"Janice dear, we have got to catch up on things. We should find a place where we can talk together quietly. Delighted to finally meet you Mark, but if you don't mind, can we borrow your fiancée for a few minutes?"

Janice snuggled his shoulder and happily announced, "Mark, these two ladies from my college days are my dearest friends. I won't be long."

Mark smiled wide back at her and her two friends and volunteered, "Go on ladies and have fun. I think I'll just hang here by the fire for a few minutes."

Janice kissed him on the cheek and the three women walked away already carrying on a very jovial conversation. As Mark turned toward the fireplace he was greeted by a clean-shaven man about his height in his thirties, who had the most interesting sky-blue eyes and shoulder-length golden blond hair. He was wearing an elegant dinner jacket, similar to Ted's, with an inch-long gold pin attached to the lapel. Its shape was like the fluid-form of some ancient Egyptian hieroglyphic symbol 🐝 or similar ancient caricature. Mark had never seen anything quite like it or the stranger's slightly larger than average appearing eyes, which seemed to emit a subtle glowing energy.

Mark was suddenly aware the stranger's smile was benevolent, while his intriguing eyes continued to gaze deeply back into his own. He was also amazed how completely unafraid and oddly uplifted he felt. Somehow, he just knew the man standing a few feet from him, with his right elbow comfortably resting upon the fireplace mantle, was emanating genuine friendliness. Mark smiled and extended his hand.

"My name is Mark Santfield. Perhaps you've heard of me."

The stranger's smile widened as he firmly shook Mark's hand and replied, "Yes Mark, I know about you, and that you're doing important work, far more important than you yet realize."

"Who are you really?" asked Mark suspiciously.

"I'm referred to as Mr. Crystal by people from very far out of town, if you know what I mean."

Contemplating the innuendo, Mark momentarily gazed into the stranger's compelling blue eyes not quite knowing how to respond, and then he simply understood.

"Yes Mr. Crystal, I believe I do understand what you mean. Please correct me if I'm wrong, but it's becoming clear to me now there are beings from locations way, way out of town who don't have your good intentions toward all of us living on good old planet Earth."

Mr. Crystal gave no answer, as Mark stepped up to the fireplace mantle to stand beside him for further conversation.

"Your insight into events taking place behind the surface appearance of things on Earth is accurate, but you don't yet know the full depth of what is hidden and what is being planned. For reasons you already understand concerning quite a number of the people who are gathered here, and many others around the world, I cannot reveal more now, other than to say you're on the right track. I believe the time has come for you to bring your fiancée and Henry, who you can trust, up to speed."

"Although your further explorations into the clandestine plans of these people and their controlling off-world allies will become increasingly more dangerous, there are also those from way out of town who are part of a vast alliance of free worlds systems that wish you well. Even now, they are watching over all three of you, and they will continue to do so from now on. An associate will contact you soon and if you are willing, he can show you the whole truth behind your suspicions and the wonders of the universe at the same time. Until then expect the unexpected and trust your own feelings regarding what is benevolent or malevolent in intent toward you. Now, I must be going. My time here is very limited before those with dominating designs on your world may detect my presence. It has been a pleasure meeting you, Mark. We will cross paths again. Farewell."

Mark reached to shake Mr. Crystal's hand, but the gold metal pin symbol on his suit lapel suddenly flashed a small pale-golden light and he vanished in a silent oval vapor of shimmering soft golden-white light that swiftly faded away. Astounded, Mark waved a hand across the air where the stranger had been, and a nearby couple curiously looked in his direction wondering what was wrong with him. Mark noticed their gaze and realized that somehow, neither they nor anyone else in the entire room had seen Mr. Crystal vanish—or perhaps they had never seen him standing there in the first place. Improvising a cover, he began pretending to be interested in the construction of the mantle by curiously looking it over from end to end. He fondly ran his fingers along its smooth surface and then turned smiling toward the observing couple. He gave them an approving nod and walked away in search of Janice.

# CHAPTER FIVE

# ARRIVING ABOARD THE MOTHER SHIP

*M*ark blinked several times as he came out of the reverie of events that led to the unexpected meeting with Mr. Crystal. He gazed at Monti, who was still sitting behind the control console looking at the image on the projected view screen of their approach to the massive mile-long flagship. Mark could see the Scout ship slowing its approach a few dozen feet away from the glistening silvery-white curved metal hull, midway along the parent ship's cylindrical length. Horizontally positioned along the central length of the entire hull as far as he could see in either direction, were a series of four-feet-wide transparent oval view-portals.

Monti reached out and touched a four-inch tall pyramid-shaped blue glowing control above the guidance controls, and the metal hull of the mother ship appeared to turn transparent.

In space, the Scout craft surrounded by its own pale-blue antigravity aura independent of the flagship was gradually becoming transparent a little at a time. It slowly passed right through the parent ship's hull on approach to land inside the launch bay.

"Monti, did we just pass right through the solid metal hull of the mother ship?" Mark inquired.

"You are exactly right, Mark," replied Monti. "The Scout ship is now operating at a higher molecular time rate within a slightly higher parallel dimension of the physical universe. Remember, I explained how we travel through natural warps or openings that exist on Earth and at various locations within the physical universe. We can travel a short distance within a parallel dimension operating at a different molecular time rate and then pass back down into the former reality to cover vast distances very quickly. Altering the Scout ship's molecular time rate in this way is often more expedient than locating and going through a natural opening in creation. Does this make sense to you now?"

Mark nodded he understood and looked back at the projected view screen to watch Monti's ship gently begin to lower toward several dozen identical Scout ships landed on the vast football field-sized hangar bay floor. He could also see several wider and taller Scout-type ships landed in the distance by a triangular opening that appeared to lead into the massive ship's interior. Glowing semispherical light sources in parallel rows lining both sides of the ceiling illuminated the long oval shaped launch bay with natural appearing light. Many personnel were busy carrying out their duties on top of, around, and underneath the Scout ships landed on the hangar bay floor. Not all of them appeared to be completely human and this immediately caught Mark's attention.

"Tell me something, Monti. Some of the human-like beings working around the launch bay are not exactly like human beings on Earth. Am I right?"

"Right again, Mark," answered Monti. "The personnel aboard this inter-dimensional Galaxy Class vessel represent over a hundred planets in the Galactic Alliance. As you can see, those maintenance personnel are of human stock with variations as to skin color and texture, forehead size, height, shape and color of the eyes, shape and position of the ears, and several other interesting differences.

"The beings you see working on the nearest Scout ship with the smooth pale-blue skin, pointed ears, slight gill slits up under the back of their chins that you cannot see, who you may think look like tall Elves, are from a planet called Oceana and they can breathe on land or under water. Their world actually exists in a slightly higher parallel dimension of the physical universe. In fact, they are one of the most ancient humanoid races in this galaxy. Their ancient ancestors' mentors called the Seres were the sponsoring benefactors of the entire Galactic Inter-dimensional Alliance of Free Worlds over five hundred thousand Earth years ago.

"Yet, even with their obvious differences, Oceana and Earth humans are capable of mating, and most of the humanoid species represented here originally came from the same ancestry long, long ago in Galactic history. Therefore, most of them are also capable of inter-marrying with Earth humans.

This explains why many of your ancient mythological historical records refer to mysterious ancient Gods who inter-married with Earth women. You should also know in a far more ancient Earth history the people of Earth know nothing about, women from other worlds have also inter-married with Earth men, but this was rare. What will amaze you even more is the fact that no human being ever originally evolved on Earth. They came to your planet during the different mostly scientific colonizing events that occurred over millions of years. Each colonizing event begins after the cyclic flipping of your planet's poles 180 degrees takes place overnight. This catastrophic event sinks much of the old mantle above sea level and quickly replaces it with a new one from the sea floor. You can experience the full realization of these natural facts for yourself in the security of this Galactic Alliance flagship."

Wide-eyed, Mark was astounded by this enlightening historic information, and he was about to excitedly ask a question when he was distracted by what he saw on the view screen. He could see the ship just touching down on the landing pad right next to the Scout ship with the crew from the planet Oceana working around, on top, and underneath it. The projected view screen vanished as Monti touched a control. He touched another thin rectangular green crystal, lighting it up, and a seam-like crack appeared in the hull directly behind Mark. He gazed at it curiously, because there was no indication the Scout ship's hull was anything but solid before. Then he watched fascinated as the widening seam formed into a vertical oval opening three feet wide and six feet high. Brighter light from the landing bay streamed inside the ship, and a ramp with steps appeared right below the opening, extending downward until it touched the smooth ivory white landing bay floor.

"Well Monti, now what?" asked Mark very intrigued.

"As promised, together we will explore many truths that have been hidden from you and the people on Earth. Then with your permission, we will remove the hypnotic programming that has kept you from knowing who you really are and where you came from. Mark, you have been the victim of a carefully orchestrated amnesia that was projected into your subconscious energy field. This was done right before your arrival on Earth, before you began to unconsciously operate a five-year-old male body."

"What?" blurted out Mark, mystified. "Someone actually suppressed all former memory of who I really am and where I came from before this lifetime?"

"I know it's hard to accept but don't worry about it for now. Everything will become clear to you soon. We should head inside the ship to meet several very important people who are anxious to meet you. Shall we go?"

Mark sadly shook his head as the deeper realization of Monti's words began to sink in. He sighed deeply, looked back up with a determined expression and replied, "Lead on Monti. Now I'm really ready to help you any way I can."

Monti nodded and placed a consoling hand on Mark's shoulder before he walked past him and headed out the opening and down the steps. Mark enthusiastically stopped at the opening to gaze briefly through it at the incredibly expansive alien launch bay. Then he hurried down the steps.

Only the Earthman's clothing appeared to be oddly out of place compared to Monti and the other human and humanoid personnel in the hangar bay, as they both walked a few feet away from the Scout ship. They stopped next to a two-way moving conveyor type walkway that was flush to the surface of the hangar bay floor. Mark glanced to his right to see the walkway ran in both directions from the triangular opening at the far right end of the landing bay across the center of the floor to an identical triangular opening at the far left end. Monti motioned to Mark to step onto the conveyor and they stepped on it together. Standing stoically side by side, the conveyor rapidly moved them between several dozen neatly landed rows of Scout-class spacecraft. It was taking them to the triangular opening at the base of the far left smooth ivory-textured wall another hundred feet in the distance.

Moments later, they came to the end of the conveyor and casually stepped off it onto the launch bay floor directly in front of the fifteen-feet-high triangular opening. The smooth wall surrounding it gradually curved upward high overhead, to become the long oval shaped hangar bay ceiling. Monti politely gestured with his right hand toward the opening and Mark enthusiastically stepped inside. He glanced at the unusual slanted walls as Monti stepped inside behind him and they quickened their pace together down the long triangular corridor.

# CHAPTER SIX

# THE
# GRAND DECEPTION

*A*fter another hundred feet, the triangular corridor opened into a larger chamber three-hundred-feet-wide and sixty-feet-high. Mark stopped just inside the chamber to gaze at the four-feet-long and three-feet-wide clear horizontal oval observation windows that lined the curved walls on opposite sides of the room. Gazing through the windows to his left, he could clearly see many varying sizes of ice-like crystals moving alongside the ship that apparently made up Saturn's relatively thin ring system. They extended into the distance well below and above the flagship that appeared to be moving in a synchronous orbit with the flow of the rings around the planet. Gazing through the oval windows to his right, Mark could also clearly see the vast layers of the enshrouding cloud cover moving across the massive gaseous world. Several of its small icy-looking moons were moving into view above the rings, high above the planet's left hemisphere. The largest orange-colored moon called Titan appeared to be slowly moving to the right high above the northeastern hemisphere. Monti stepped up behind Mark and stood by his right side. He smiled while he observed the astonished expression on Mark's face that clearly revealed he knew he was taking in a staggering sight most of his fellow human beings back on Earth had never experienced or imagined.

"Like any new discovery," encouraged Monti, "you get used to it after a while."

Mark remained speechless as he slowly turned to look at Monti to solemnly reply, "My God, Monti, it's going to take a long time for me to get used to this."

Still spellbound, he turned back to gaze through the oval windows at the expansive icy rings of Saturn, and then began to slowly look around the room to take in his surroundings.

Positioned directly below and in front of each oval window were several oval glass-topped tables with surrounding blue softly cushioned egg-shaped chairs. The carpeted floor had matching tightly woven blue material, and lights like those in the launch bay lined the curved ceiling in six parallel rows.

"So this room is some kind of observation area, right?" Mark asked.

"Yes Mark," replied Monti. "People come here to contemplate, talk together, or just gaze peacefully through the windows at the majesty of creation that extends in infinite directions outside the ship. Two dozen of these observation areas exist throughout the length of this vessel. As I mentioned before, several important people are anxious to meet you. If you can turn your gaze away from the rings of Saturn for a while, I will take you to meet them. Please follow me."

Mark came out of his fixation on the overpowering majesty of the scene before him and slowly turned his head toward Monti to nod his anxious consent. Monti started to walk the remaining fifty-feet distance to the far side of the observation chamber through another triangular entry hallway, and Mark followed close behind him. The second triangular hallway was shorter than the first and they had only walked fifteen feet before they passed through the opening on the other end to enter a geodesic dome-shaped chamber. It was a hundred feet across and fifty-feet-high. Twelve-feet-tall, three-sided ivory colored control consoles surrounded the walls of the room, which were lit up with hundreds of touch sensitive crystalline controls of different sizes and shapes. Many human and humanoid personnel with pastel colored skins varying from smooth ivory and tanned Caucasian tones through to smooth violet snake-like patterns, were sitting in chairs monitoring numerous projected view screens like the one on Monti's Scout class spaceship, but much larger. High overhead, a transparent fifteen-feet-wide convex domed canopy protruded from the center of the ceiling. A foot-thick vertical transparent tube extended from the top center of the clear convex dome to a matching convex dome centered in the chamber floor. The inside of the tube filled with powerful wavering pastel-blue static energy was in constant radiant motion from end to end. Surrounding the outer circumference of the bottom observation dome were a dozen more of the oval shaped tables and chairs.

Fifty-feet-long, horizoantal rectangular panels lined the half-octagon shaped control console that began just beyond the chairs. It was positioned along the gradual curve of the rounded end of the ship's hull, directly below twelve horizontal oval windows or view portals.

A panorama of stars was clearly visible through the windows in outer space, and the rings of Saturn below them extending into a vast distance as they gradually curved around the massive equator of the gas giant planet.

Mark and Monti approached a table centered in the room and Mark glanced down to see a human man and woman who appeared vibrantly healthy in their late-thirties standing up to greet them. They were wearing simple but elegantly designed single-piece slip-on silken blue uniforms belted at the waist with dark-blue leather-like material and matching slip-on silken shoes. The Galactic Alliance symbol of the white gold crowned pyramid superimposed over a silvery galaxy, with three blue stars positioned in a triangular formation above the pyramid's apex, were emblazoned and slightly raised on the right central chest area of their uniforms. Both of them were radiating warm friendliness toward Mark and Monti. The man's sky-blue eyes and the woman's emerald-green eyes were emanating the same subtle glow Mark experienced the first time he met Monti.

"This is Commander Jon-tral and next to him is his Second in Command wife, First Officer Sun-deema. They come from my home world beyond what your people call the Pleiades star system," stated Monti, as Commander Jon-tral extended a hand toward Mark.

As Mark shook his hand he had the same knowing experience that he was meeting two kind human beings, though considerably more advanced, and from another planetary system far from the quarantined planet Earth. The radiant and beautiful woman extended her hand, and as Mark shook her long slender fingers, he clearly heard her sweet mellow voice inside his head.

*You are most welcome aboard the deep exploration and reconnaissance flagship of the Galactic Inter-dimensional Alliance of Free Worlds. I have the privilege to be your guide during your short stay here, and during the implantation removal process that you will soon experience. If there are any questions you may have regarding this or any other area of interest at any time, please do not hesitate to ask and I will provide the answers.*

Mark was unconsciously smiling at his gracious hosts as he silently replied mind-to-mind just to see what would happen.

*Thank you, gracious Lady, for your welcoming words, and I thank you as well, Commander.*

They both smiled and nodded that they understood him.

"You mean you could both hear me mind-to-mind?" asked Mark surprised.

"Mark, remember when I first contacted you telepathically?" inquired Monti.

Mark nodded.

"Earth humans have the same telepathic capability. However, as I already mentioned it has been purposefully suppressed in Earth humans, and this truth is one of the primary reasons you were brought aboard my ship to journey here. If you wish to help us save Earth from a terrible fate no one on your world would invite if aware of it, you must be set free from what happened to you before you arrived on Earth. First, you must remember your true self, your true eternal spherical energy Atma form or what people on your planet call 'Soul.'"

"It's odd but now that you mention it, at one time somewhere in the past I was completely familiar with all of you and this inter-stellar space travel technology. Can you really help me remember everything that was taken from me?"

"Perhaps to start out it would be best if First Officer Sun-deema took you on a tour of the ship," replied Commander Jon-tral. "Then you can go with her to a special chamber that can facilitate the full recovery of who you are and where you came from that remains suppressed in the depths of your subconscious mind. After that, the extreme importance of the mission you agreed to carry out with us will become self-evident."

Mark glanced around the room and then looked at Commander Jon-tral and asked, "So, if I'm correct, this area must be the control and command center of your mile-long ship."

"Yes, that's very observant of you," answered Jon-tral, pleased with Mark's insight. "An identical command center is located on the opposite end of the ship. Because of this dual command capability and the ship's cylindrical shape, as well as other structural characteristics, we can direct the ship to travel into any number of inter-dimensional openings to traverse great distances in space many times far beyond what you call the speed of light. You will comprehend more about how this is possible after you regain full recall of all that was suppressed within you."

"Mark, listen closely," Jon-tral continued seriously. "As you already know, a great cyclic change is about to affect your solar system that normally reshapes Earth's entire mantle, and unfortunately, most of the life on the surface is destroyed in the process. After the extinction event of your dinosaur era long ago, many different extraterrestrial colonization events took place on Earth. They involved both human and non-human explorers over many millions of years the people of Earth are completely unaware existed at any time.

"The hidden, misdirected, elitist government members on your world have known for many years about this coming event but declared the information far above 'Top Secret' to keep humanity in the dark. They are planning to only save themselves by temporarily residing in secret underground bases and in several off-world colonies within your solar system. Their totalitarian off-world allies promised to assist them to escape the catastrophe. However, the Trilotew totalitarians have ulterior motives for pretending to offer genuine assistance. In reality, they want to dominate your world and make slaves of all humanity. When they finish using Earth's corrupted leaders, they will eliminate them and their families. If something unexpected destroyed Earth, the Trilotew would simply move on without remorse as they have done in the past. Then they would attempt to conquer some other world that is not yet a part of the Galactic Inter-dimensional Alliance of Free Worlds.

"As Mon-tlan explained on your way here, galactic history reveals the ultimate effect of any hidden totalitarian alien influence on a world like your Earth. The result is always the same. Eventually, one or more hidden leaders will unexpectedly set off a prized reverse-engineered extraterrestrial weapon that will disintegrate the entire planet. Should that happen, and it is likely, Earth would become just another orbiting asteroid belt like the one between Mars and Jupiter. The Galactic Alliance will not let that happen under any circumstance for reasons that go far beyond just Earth's survival. Therefore, the implementation of something recently brought into creation that is part of what we call *The Seres Agenda* will take place soon, regardless of whether or not the totalitarian faction wishes it. We will finally be able to prevent your planet from going through another destructive cyclic polar shift, and Earth humans can become enlightened space-faring members of the Galactic Alliance."

"But that's incredible!" Mark replied, elated. "This means the repressive governments will be gone, and the people of Earth will actually get to play among the stars."

"I believe you're catching on," confirmed Jon-tral, chuckling.

"Our immediate plan is to get you back home in time for you to effectively carry out your mission as the intermediary between the entire Galactic Inter-dimensional Alliance of Free Worlds and Earth's misdirected hidden government leaders, who are blindly heading your planet toward annihilation. For now, with your permission, please go with First Officer Sun-deema and Special Mission Officer Mon-tlan. They will begin your reorientation process so you can gain back your true self."

Mark enthusiastically nodded to Jon-tral and Sun-deema, and she smiled back as she headed toward the triangular exit on the opposite end of the room. Side by side, Mark and Monti headed toward the exit right behind her.

# CHAPTER SEVEN

# PARTING THE SUBCONSCIOUS VEIL

As they casually walked along another triangular corridor, Sun-deema began to explain to Mark how he had been unexpectedly captured en route to Earth, and how he was subsequently deprived of the entire memory of who he was, and where he came from, through a diabolical process involving an implanted terror-based amnesia.

"The way to suppress a person's true identity," Sun-deema began carefully, "and the wealth of natural understanding they have as an awakened sentient being, has been carried out on many worlds throughout galactic history by those who seek to dominate all life. This is a sad commentary on a tumultuous past between the forces that respect and appreciate all life, and those forces that seek only power at any cost to dominate all life."

Sun-deema kindly smiled and waited for Mark's further inquiry.

"I know exactly what you mean," replied Mark with a disappointed shake of his head. "Back on Earth, the more power men acquire, the more corrupt they seem to become. Now I begin to understand. Tyrants from other worlds have somehow orchestrated the destructive desire for power within certain families on Earth to believe they are elite over the rest of humankind. Based on everything I know now, they could not have naturally evolved to be as evil as they have become on their own without such an influence. Correct me if I am wrong, but it also seems to me they are in very grave danger themselves. The ulterior motives of the totalitarian alliance will likely include the eventual elimination of this hidden ruling class of people on Earth, when their overlords decide they no longer serve a purpose."

Pleased with Mark's insight, Sun-deema replied, "That's exactly what we discovered has taken place many, many times throughout galactic history on other worlds. This always happened after the citizens had been put through a covertly manipulated intrusion into their lives by a domineering race from outside their own world system."

Mark was now walking between Sun-deema on his right and Monti on his left, as they headed out of another triangular exit and stepped onto a transparent one-hundred-feet-in-diameter clear circular floor. He gazed through it and around the circumference of the curved ceiling to discover the circular floor equally bisected the top and bottom hemispheres of a huge spherical chamber. He estimated the amazing interior extended fifty-feet-above and fifty-feet-below the circular floor. Perfectly symmetrical clear, eight-inch long by four-inch-wide quartz crystals lined the entire surface of the spherical chamber. They were all pointing inward toward a smaller twenty-feet-tall spherical structure centered in the floor, made of twelve identical transparent pentagonal surfaces.

For some reason, the memory from a geometry class Mark had back in his college days came to mind. He recalled the spherical twelve-sided pentagon shape was referred to as a dodecahedron. As they approached closer, he could see inside the hallow chamber through its clear sides. Then he noticed a white cushioned chair on the floor in the middle of the chamber. Just outside the front of the chamber was a half-octagon shaped console like the one aboard Monti's ship but larger, supported by a green illumined four-feet-tall, eight-sided pedestal. Several dozen various sized controls covering the console were arranged in a different pattern than those on Monti's ship. He could see what looked like a clear quartz stairway descending below an opening in the floor at the left side of the console. It appeared to lead directly below the center of the dodecahedron and up into the back of the chamber to provide access to the chair centered inside. Sun-deema enthusiastically broke the silence.

"You can sit in the chair in this chamber and wear a clear crystal headset that extends around the forehead and temples. After activating the device, you will be able to recall any negative thought or emotion that has ever bothered you, such as the cause of the amnesia placed subconsciously in your electromagnetic field or aura. You will directly experience the controlling implant causing this buried in your mind at a frequency below your level of awareness, and then you will begin to remember everything. I consider it a privilege to be your guide through this process.

"For a long period of time now, Mark, we've been remarkably successful at freeing many other beings from such tyrannical subconscious controls. We have records of millions of human and humanoid beings dating back five hundred thousand years that went through this process in similar chambers throughout the Galactic Alliance. The Trilotew forced them to forget everything they once knew about themselves, where they came from, and everything they accomplished during numerous lifetimes spanning many millions of years. In some cases, this went back even further before we helped set them free of the implanted illusions. As former victims, they all experienced an astounding awakening that was both extremely uplifting and enlightening. To some degree the same has been true for any of us that were privileged at the time to observe the events."

Monti added, "Mark, you're actually about to go through this same extraordinary process to be set free from the subconscious programming that has kept you in the dark about your past. The official name for this device is the Frequency Harmonizing Mind-link Activator. To elaborate on what Sun-deema mentioned, this device has proven to be very effective in removing what we call implants. They are three-dimensional mental image pictures containing sight, sound, smell, motion, tactile sensations, and every possible emotion that will compel you to forget or behave in an abnormal manner for suppressive control purposes.

"In the past, entire planets have been enslaved in this manner by totalitarian invaders. The inhabitants and their leaders were so subtly manipulated they were unaware it was taking place, until after it was too late. Now your world is undergoing the same process. However, since the last Great War in our galaxy ended, we have monitored everything the totalitarian group has done. The Trilotew always covertly operate in direct violation of a treaty they signed with the Galactic Alliance just short of going to all-out war. Now, we are finally preparing to permanently suspend all their activities on your planet. In fact, implementation of *The Seres Agenda* that utilizes the implant removal process, from among its many other capabilities, is taking place elsewhere in the galaxy at this moment. This will ensure that this type of brainwashing will never take place again. Well, are you ready to begin?"

In wide-eyed awe, Mark breathed a sigh of relief and solemnly nodded his consent. Sun-deema smiled at him and gently grasped his hand. Then she led him down the stairs, while Monti walked over to the control console. Monti could see them reappear inside the chamber a few moments later as they walked up the stairs out of an opening that remained hidden from view behind the white chair. She nodded for him to take a seat. As he cautiously sat in the chair, the sides and back changed shape to comfortably conform to the size of his body. Mark appeared pleased by the effect as he glanced around at the transparent sides of the chamber. Then his gaze came to focus on Monti, who he could clearly see through the transparent pentagon shaped panel directly across from him. He was still standing behind the middle of the oval console in the outer chamber smiling back, giving an encouraging thumb up sign. Mark returned a thumb up sign as Sun-deema reached down behind the back of the chair and lifted up a four-inch-wide and inch-thick quartz crystal headset. As she placed it over his head, the three transparent long oval-shaped finger-sized prongs conformed to the shape of his forehead, across the top of his skull, and over his temples just above each ear.

"Wow, it's sending soothing sensations down my spine," Mark said, elated, as he leaned back in the comfortable chair.

Sun-deema stepped around in front of the chair to face him and kindly said, "I look forward to meeting you again after you remember who you are, and all that's been suppressed within you."

Then she respectfully nodded and walked back down the stairs. She reappeared a moment later by the control console and walked over to stand beside Monti.

Monti touched a blue diamond-shaped control and asked, "Mark, can you hear me clearly?"

He nodded, smiling through the clear pentagon panel directly in front of him.

"Okay then, Mark, we will begin," stated Sun-deema. "Monti and I will be guiding you through the session so you will understand what was done and how it affected you. Once a repressed memory surfaces, it also appears on the view screens and your true nature or true self returns to your awareness. We will then guide you to disintegrate the formerly subconscious implanted memories with a focused mental energy beam you will recall how to project."

She passed the palm of her right hand over a spherical green control, and all of the thousands of quartz crystals embedded in the walls surrounding the entire outer chamber started to glow with faint golden light. A low humming sound began softly pulsing through the room, and the clear pentagon panels surrounding Mark turned on, emitting a thin blue radiance. Then Mark heard Sun-deema's soothing voice again.

"Mark, concentrate on the thought that you want to know why you can't remember where you came from, and who you were before you arrived on Earth."

Mark closed his eyes but they immediately sprang back open. He was startled, staring at the clear panels surrounding him just as blurred images began to form and clear. Revealed before him, on the pentagon panels that turned on like TV screens, was a human man of similar build to him but with slightly larger eyes, dressed in similar attire to what Monti was wearing. The man was desperately struggling to get free. Two scaly green-skinned tall and muscular bi-pedal reptilian aliens with red, vertical cat-like pupils in oval violet eyes were tightly gripping his upper arms with long claw-like fingers. They were forcing the man through a transparent red energy shield that surrounded a high-backed black obsidian chair centered in the crude, dimly lit cavernous chamber. An invisible energy then forced the man back into the chair, and straps made of the same red energy appeared, binding his arms and legs to the chair's contours. The defiant man struggled with all his might to get free but to no avail, as the two reptilian beings stood back a few feet. The taller captor pointed a foot-long black rod tipped with a red sphere at the chair, and the crystal lit up, compelling the man to involuntarily close his eyes. He struggled, shaking his head to try to throw off the vision they were forcing him to see, and then he screamed in terror. Both reptilian captors gleamed in sadistic joy at the helpless predicament of their victim.

The images on the surrounding walls of the chamber suddenly changed in front of Mark. He was now objectively experiencing what the man on the screen was experiencing, as if he and the man were the same being. The first image Mark saw was the man when he was happy, dressed in a single form fitting silky-white diplomat's attire. Thousands of his fellow citizens joyfully waiting to greet him had lined up to shake his hand while he walked along a very advanced city street, surrounded by many tall crystalline buildings. Mark somehow knew he was witnessing the man on his home planet, far out in the galaxy.

The images changed again, revealing the same two reptilian captors pushing the man off a cliff headfirst. Mark watched the horrified man tumble down several hundred feet toward a volcanic inferno, and then screamed in terror with the man on the screen as his body burst into flames before it hit the explosive lava and sank.

The scene changed once again. The man was now sitting on an oval-shaped smooth blue rock. He was out in nature surrounded by tall tear drop-shaped trees lushly covered with broad silvery-green spoon shaped leaves, and long strands of interspersed star-shaped violet flowers emitting soft phosphorescent light. His happy eight and ten-year-old children, a boy and a girl, were sitting on his lap giggling while he playfully bounced them up and down. His beautiful green-eyed wife with long golden blond hair, who was wearing a soft white dress shimmering like a moonstone, walked up behind them and joyfully wrapped her arms around his neck.

The scene on the surrounding panels changed once more. The man was now standing spread-eagled, tied with thick ropes to several crude wooden posts in a prehistoric alien jungle setting. The same two reptilian captors approached him brandishing long curved double-edged swords and crude jagged-edged saws. They were laughing at the man's dire dilemma as their long, forked tongues dripping with sticky saliva zipped in and out of their mouths to sadistically lick the sides of his cheeks. The man convulsed and vomited from the stench of reptilian breath.

Mark squirmed in his chair as he heard the taller captor say in a deep guttural voice with hellish glee, "Which part shall we eat first? Should it be the eyes? Oh yes, the eyes are very tasty."

"I'm going to rip off your arm, human, and eat it in front of your fragile face," added the other captor. "But first let me remind you, puny thing, if you attempt to remember again who you are, this is what will happen to you."

The taller reptilian bi-pedal demon dropped the double-edged sword and jagged-edged saw, and then thrust both his long green arms forward with five-fingered razor-sharp claws and ripped out the man's eyes. Then he sucked them down his throat off the ends of his bloody fingertips. The tortured man and Mark sitting in the chair simultaneously screamed in agony as if Mark was actually going through the torture along with the man imaged on the screens around him. The slightly shorter alien dropped his weapons. He smiled viciously, and then thrust forward his long sharp-nailed hands and ripped the man's right arm from its socket. Then he quickly chomped and crunched the entire arm down his wide throat through his gaping mouth with two rows of upper and lower razor-sharp teeth until the fingers disappeared. Screams of utter agony vibrated the air and the man's and Mark's heads fell forward together as he passed into unconsciousness.

"Mark, it's over," Sun-deema stated loudly. "You uncovered the main implants they forced upon you. Now quickly look up at the screens."

Mark reluctantly opened one eye and then the other to see if the terror might still be there. Instead, he was again seeing the original scene of his own former highly evolved life as a happily married human man on another world with his two children playing upon his knees. All the joy of his enlightened awareness as a highly evolved human being from that other world started streaming back into his consciousness, and he sighed deeply. Then he started to cry uncontrollably, but they were not tears of sorrow or pain. He was experiencing indescribable, blissful relief as he began to recall all that was taken from him long ago.

"How long has it been?" he asked.

"The terrible events you witnessed took place aboard one of the reptilian battle cruisers," responded Monti's kindly voice. "Your Scout ship was intercepted as it entered Earth's atmosphere thirty-one years ago. You were to carry out a long-planned diplomatic mission to Earth's top hidden leaders. They were seeking to be free from their reptilian overlords already in control of Earth's secret second government. You were sent to help free them from the mind control that is now twisting their thoughts, and then prepare them for a large-scale arrival of the Galactic Alliance fleet in the near future. Since then, something most extraordinary has happened. What is now coming to Earth goes far beyond only revealing an open Galactic Alliance presence, something designed to permanently alter Earth's destructive direction. It will become an uplifted benevolent world and we will invite the populous to join the entire Galactic Alliance. Earth will be taken off the quarantined status, and the people can then freely play among the stars."

"I will make them pay for what they did to me," stated Mark, angrily determined.

Both Sun-deema and Monti blanched at his angry emotions, but they also wisely understood the pain he was still experiencing.

"Mark, listen to me," said Sun-deema with a calming voice. "This was just the beginning of your full recollection. Do you remember your true name?"

Mark was forlorn and tired as he tried with all his might to recall what was still lurking just beneath the surface of his awareness.

A moment passed, and then his eyes widened, "I'm a diplomat called Shon-ral from the planet Norexilam in the Starborn cluster, beyond what the people of Earth call the Pleiades star group. Dear Prime Creator, how long have I been imprisoned in this body?"

Sun-deema answered, compassionately looking on, "In Earth time thirty-one years have elapsed, but only one year has gone by on your home planet because of the space-time differential that occurred when your ship passed through the Blue Star Meridian vortex. That one is high in the Earth's atmosphere above Mt. Shasta in northern California. After your ship entered the planet's ionosphere, a large Trilotew spaceship intercepted and captured your Scout ship. Do you remember that now?"

Mark was blank-faced at first. Then his eyes opened wider as an angry scowl formed across his face and he bitterly answered, "Yes, now it's all coming back to me. They have been a thorn in the side of the entire Galactic Alliance for over five hundred thousand years. They have broken the treaty so many times we signed with them so long ago, it's amazing we haven't gone back to their home world and destroyed their totalitarian madness for all time."

"My friend, you still have much to remember or you would know the way of revenge is not our way," replied Monti. "The Trilotew were inflicted with their insidious totalitarian subconscious lust for violence, and eating the flesh of highly evolved beings, by their white-winged faction over half a million years ago. The more vile winged reptilians enslaved their conquered relatives after finally winning a hundred-year-old interplanetary war. During the course of many thousands of generations that followed, the subconscious programming drove the reptilian races to carry on their demented behavior wherever and whenever they could get away with it. To this day, they are still unaware they have not been in control of their behavior for over five hundred thousand years. They were not always this way. When you recall more of your true self, you will be able to understand how implementation of the new process that is part of what we call *The Seres Agenda* also involves the eventual deprogramming of the entire Imperial Trilotew race."

"Yes," replied Mark, astounded. "Somehow, I'm beginning to understand."

"I will continue, and you will recall more. Trilotew agents intercepted your secret mission. We now know a spy must be among our secret ranks on Earth and perhaps even somewhere highly placed within the entire Galactic Inter-dimensional Alliance of Free Worlds. That was how you were so easily captured. They removed your real true self or 'Atma' from your body, what Earth people call the 'Soul,' using an ancient device outlawed by treaty agreement. Then they implanted the hidden command for you to enter a five-year-old orphaned boy's body, after they forced out its occupant. The Trilotew would also implant a command for you to compulsively reincarnate on Earth as their prized political prisoner with no memory of your past. We know your foster parents raised you after that before they died in that tragic automobile accident fifteen years later."

Mark was now speechless, as more of his former enlightened human state began to surface. Then he remembered his wife back on his home planet and tears began to well up in his eyes again.

"Is she…" he began to ask hopefully, gazing at Monti. "I mean my wife … is she all right? And my children?"

"Yes Mark," replied Sun-deema. "Your wife Lorun-eral, son Shan-dreal, and daughter Taluna-tala are fine. Of course they miss you, but they also know we found you alive."

"You should know about one other problem," added Monti, not smiling this time.

Mark gazed back at him apprehensively and waited.

"After your ship was captured," he began hesitantly, "you were suspended in a powerful electromagnetic field. Your Trilotew captors compelled you to unconsciously enter a selected five-year-old orphaned boy's body with all former memory suppressed. After that was accomplished, they destroyed your adult human body or devoured it. I'm sorry to tell you this but the body you now have is the only one you have left."

Mark was crestfallen, and his head sadly lowered as he began to remember the lovely face of his wife and two children, and he dismally thought, *How can I ever return to them now?*

*We have a plan to reunite you with your family,* answered Sun-deema telepathically.

Mark looked up hopeful, and breathlessly waited.

"Good . . . good," continued Monti aloud. "Now your telepathic ability is starting to come back as well. Welcome back Mark, or I should say, Ambassador Shon-ral."

Still dismal, Mark did not respond.

Sun-deema smiled sweetly and added, "Once all the implants have been removed from your subconscious mind, we will significantly alter the DNA of your Earthly human body. We can reshape it to become the Pleiades body you lost. We can restore your former body by utilizing its more complex DNA structure that was stored back on your home world. But Shon-ral, we have been instructed to ask if you would be willing to temporarily play the part of Mark Santfield for a little while longer. Our adversaries on and off Earth are unaware we have the ability to fully remove their implants, and they will never suspect we can restore you to full Galactic Inter-dimensional Alliance status in a DNA-restricted body. If you don't look like your former self for now, we can go forward with you in the body you have to carry out your diplomatic mission to the leaders of Earth's hidden government."

Monti and Sun-deema patiently waited for Shon-ral's response, while he contemplated this unexpected turn of events.

"Are you sure you can eventually transform this body to the advanced home world body?" he inquired hopefully, looking up at them.

Monti and Sun-deema nodded.

"Can you make the brain of this body function as it should at one hundred percent?" he inquired, beginning to smile.

They both nodded again.

"And the lifespan?" he inquired further, now as Shon-ral smiling through Mark's body. His physical eyes appeared to suddenly grow just a little bit larger.

"It can be increased to that of our own," answered Monti happily. "Well over one thousand years or more if need be. However, first we must get your memory fully rehabilitated. Then we must promptly send you back to Earth so that suspicions are not raised among others, and you do have a fiancée waiting."

The Mark Santfield part of Shon-ral surfaced as he recalled he also loved and had committed to marry an Earth woman, and his smile faded.

"How can I go forward with Janice now?" he inquired, once again forlorn. "I already have a wife and children back home I dearly treasure."

"We have already contacted your wife to update her on all that happened. Lorun-eral wants you to go forward with the mission," encouraged Sun-deema. "You should also know your current fiancée is actually one of us. Can you recall what happened to your cousin Moon-teran?"

Mark squinted his eyes as he struggled to recall something all too familiar, but it was just out of reach. Then his eyes opened wide with sadness.

"Oh Ancient One, Prime Creator of all, what have I done?" he replied fearfully as he simultaneously remembered that most of the Galactic Alliance members respectfully referred to the primary cause behind all life in this manner. Mark lowered his head again and very reluctantly confirmed, "She is my cousin. I was informed right before I left for Earth she had mysteriously disappeared there just before finishing her six-month scientific mission. She was studying the culture, and monitoring Earth's dangerously increasing radioactive atmospheric and deep water table pollution levels. Now it's all coming back to me."

"Shon-ral, do not be ashamed," encouraged Sun-deema again. "That feeling is just one of many negative emotions implanted in most Earth humans. Before your trip to this ship, we had only recently discovered that Trilotew agents secretly operating on Earth behind certain government leaders had captured her. Six months before your ill-fated arrival to the planet, they had already compelled her to forget her former life. Then they destroyed her original adult body from her home planet and forced her into a captured young female body. During your full deprogramming, we will arrange to secretly bring her aboard this flagship and she can go through the same process. Then she can also help you with our overall mission objectives to turn Earth around, to save it from being destroyed or completely enslaved by the Trilotew.

"In other words, since both your former home world human bodies no longer exist, each of you could cleverly pose as a married couple until we complete our mission and free Earth's enslaved people. Then you can both go through the biological transformation process before returning to your own families on your home world. Your cousin, Moon-teran, also has a husband and three children back on your home planet, but you will remember that soon enough. Mark, I must now ask under these circumstances if you would be willing to go forward with your mission?"

He pondered the request as he began to recall how fervently he had committed himself to the grand plan to free the people of Earth from the negative drives implanted in them. Then he recalled the larger plan. It also involved the permanent removal of the evil subconscious drives that continued to compel the Imperialistic Trilotew Alliance to make living in the Milky Way Galaxy a traumatic experience for everyone who must put up with their terror campaigns.

"Very well," replied Mark more at peace. "For now, just refer to me as Mark Santfield, and that reminds me about a famous English fictional detective back on Earth named Sherlock Holmes who would say to his assistant before each investigation, 'Watson, my good man, the game is afoot.'"

His smile widened with newfound courage and a sense of freedom now that he had finally remembered who he really was.

"Well then, Mark Santfield, are you ready to get rid of the rest of that awful Trilotew subconscious garbage?" inquired Monti quite pleased, smiling back at him with Sun-deema.

"Indeed I am," he eagerly replied and asked, "But how does *The Seres Agenda* create this coming dramatic change?"

"As you know," answered Sun-deema, "the Seres race seeded all humanoid life in the galaxies before they vanished long ago. They very recently reconnected with their first blue-skinned Oceanan progeny to present them with a new tool, a consciousness-freeing Ray, then announced to the entire Galactic Alliance Council they are returning to the galaxy."

The good news deeply moved Mark as he pondered her statement. Then he smiled with a profound new realization and nodded he was ready to continue the deprogramming session.

# CHAPTER EIGHT

# ESCAPE FROM REPTILIAN CLAWS

*J*anice was frantic with worry after she learned that Mark had not returned from his camping trip after the weekend, and she filed a missing person report with the Beverly Hills police.

The ensuing police investigation discovered only a few obliterated tiny shreds of what had once been his tent, and the black burnt circle of dirt where it had stood. They also discovered the giant fallen tree near its sheered off stump in the distance behind it, but that had only expanded the mystery further because there was no sign of the missing section of the tree. Her concern deepened after the 7:00 p.m. prime-time newscaster on channel seven announced that a forensic team had arrived on the scene. After investigating the bizarre circumstances, they discovered something else very unusual. They concluded that some kind of unknown energy had disintegrated a four-feet section of the tree's trunk because there were no indications of any chainsaw markings or marks from any other type of cutting tool. The following scientific analysis of the splintered shreds from the sheered-off tree stump and the end of the fallen tree revealed a non-analyzable chemical residue in the seared wood fibers.

Janice knew her father had the resources to find things out that she had no way to discover, and she went to his mansion three days after Mark's disappearance to seek his assistance. Actually showing concern, which surprised her, he told her he would make several inquiring phone calls and hurried upstairs to his private study. She anxiously waited on a chair next to the entryway doors and ten minutes later someone rang the front doorbell. She cautiously opened the door to find standing before her two tall odd-looking strangers staring back at her with penetrating hypnotic gazes, and she immediately felt very uncomfortable. The taller man forced an obviously phony smile as he politely asked if Mr. Carter was at home, and she called upstairs to his study. A moment later, Ted appeared at the top of the twin staircases and gazed down with concerned alarm at the two men. Then he hurried down the right staircase to meet them. Janice stood aside as her father walked by to shake their hands, and the taller man whispered something in his ear.

Ted's face blanched as he looked up to briefly gaze into each man's eyes and then seriously stated, "Come up to my study. We can discuss this in private."

Both tall men turned in unison and gave Janice a chilling, mistrustful gaze that Ted observed very closely. To Janice, the growing concern on her father's face was obvious.

Ted gazed at his daughter with a reassuring smile and calmly said, "Janice, dear, I have to meet privately upstairs for a few minutes with my clients. Perhaps then I will have more news regarding what may have happened to Mark. They know he is alive but not where he went. They are attempting to track his location. Don't worry, we'll find him. Please wait for me here in the entryway and I'll join you in a few minutes."

He bent forward and kissed Janice on the forehead. He noticed her rather miffed expression and did a double take before he hurriedly headed back up the right side staircase with his two tall guests trailing right behind him. Janice carefully stepped toward the left staircase in time to catch a glimpse of his two taller guests staring with wide-eyed sadistic glee at the back of her father's head all the way up the stairs. Ted waved his hand for them to proceed into his study ahead of him, and then he pretended to smile down at his daughter. As he turned away, Janice noticed his forced smile became a fearful scowl before he entered his study and closed the door behind him. Then he forcefully locked the dead bolt with a loud. . . *clink*. . . which she could hear all the way downstairs.

A claustrophobic feeling began to creep over her, and she quietly opened the front door and stepped outside. She pulled a cell phone from her purse, hit a speed dial number, and a moment later a man's voice said, "Hello."

"Henry, is that you?" she asked and winced. "Oh thank God, you're there. Listen, we have serious problems. The two strange men you told Mark and I about when you attempted to deliver the package to my father's study just showed up here. I asked my father to use his resources to locate Mark and he made a phone call from his study. Ten minutes later, both tall men arrived to inform him they know Mark is alive, but his location was unknown and they were trying to track him. Henry, I think his life is in danger."

***Mark is safe and unhurt,*** stated a soothing kind man's voice from somewhere behind her.

Startled and with her hand over her heart, Janice spun around, but there was no one there.

"Who's there with you?" asked Henry's concerned voice back through her phone.

"I don't know," she nervously replied, "I can't see anyone. Henry, I must leave now. Someone may be watching me. I'll call you just as soon as I can. Take care."

She turned off the phone, opened the front door, stealthily re-entered the house, quietly closed the door behind her, and then glanced around the entryway for any spies.

When she turned back around to open the front door again to run from the house as fast as possible, she heard the mysterious stranger firmly state again, ***Janice, Mark is safe. My associates rescued him from certain death. You must trust me.***

She fearfully spun back around to confront the voice only to discover she was staring into the kindest human male eyes she had ever seen. A soft golden light briefly flashed off the strange looking pin symbol he was wearing on his right lapel, and she discovered her apprehension and fear had dissolved away. More than that, she now felt uplifted and refreshed while she gazed back at the six-feet-tall, clean-shaven man standing before her. He had the most captivating slightly larger than average sky-blue eyes and shoulder length golden-blond silken hair she had ever seen. He was wearing blue jeans, a white shirt, leather shoes, and a blue leather jacket with a gold pin attached to the lapel. She began to ponder how the pin looked like an inch-long fluid form of some kind of ancient Egyptian hieroglyphic symbol or ancient caricature. She had never seen anything quite like it, or the stranger's eyes that seemed to emit a subtle glowing radiance.

"Who are you, and how did you get here?" she inquired unconsciously smiling back at him. "Did you come in before my father and his two strange guests?"

"Pardon me, Janice. I am Mr. Crystal. My telepathic comments may have startled you but that was not my intent. I believe Mark told you about me. There's little time left to safely take you to him."

"Oh thank God," she spouted, relieved. "Yes, Mark told me all about you before he left on the camping trip. You're really from . . . well, you know . . . from out there?"

"Yes, Janice, I am," replied Mr. Crystal. "Mark is safe, but the two men meeting with your father right now and their associates tried to kill him. One of my people rescued him just in time. Now he's off-world going through a process to free him from the subconsciously implanted programming he was subjected to before he came to Earth."

"What do you mean . . . when he came to Earth? What's going on?" asked Janice becoming fearful again.

"You must trust me and quickly, before those two meeting with your father detect my presence here. If you are willing, I will take you to Mark and you will understand everything for yourself. Will you come with me?"

"How will we get there?" she asked with certain trepidation.

Mr. Crystal touched the pin on his lapel again and it emitted a brief flash. The churning apprehensive feeling in the pit of her stomach suddenly vanished.

She looked back at him confidently, relieved and pleased.

"We'll be teleported directly to a hidden base located within a mountain cavern inside Mt. Shasta in northern California. From there, we can safely proceed to where Mark is located. You will be pleased to know he learned much more about his quest to discover the truth regarding extraterrestrial life in the universe. Would you like to join him?"

"Yes, Mr. Crystal," anxiously replied Janice. "I will go with you now. When those two creeps upstairs looked at me, chills went down my spine. They gave me the willies. I'm very worried that my father is mixed up in something dreadful. Will you be able to help him too?"

"You'll have answers to your questions soon," answered Mr. Crystal with an urgent tone. "But we must leave now. Those two men are about to head back down the stairs, and if they catch us here you would not wish to be alive."

Janice winced again at the thought of their creepy eyes and remarked, "Just having those two look upon me once is all the experience I want of them for the rest of my life. Mr. Crystal, what are we waiting for?" she confidently inquired. "Let's get the hell out of here."

Mr. Crystal smiled and touched the golden symbol on his lapel three times. Just as the door to Ted's study opened, they both vanished in a silent oval vapor of shimmering pastel golden-white light that swiftly faded away.

Both tall angry men ran out of the study brandishing the same type of handgun weapons the camouflaged men in black used to try to kill Mark by his tent in the mountains. Ted fearfully came up behind them, grimacing for his daughter's safety. All three stopped at the railing by the head of the left staircase to gaze below at the vacant entryway. Ted's furious strange guests ran down the stairs lurching with weapons pointing in every direction in the vain hope of finding their intended targets. Ted ran up between them in a panic and stopped, not knowing what to do next, just as both aliens slowly turned around to face him. One was now standing in front of Ted and the other directly behind him as sweat began to bead up on his forehead. A growing fear etched across his face as he watched both intimidating guests reach into their suit coats and touch something. The energy shield illusion surrounding their bodies wavered and faded away revealing their true taller bipedal reptilian statures. Ted could not hide his revulsion, as he watched drool drip from their foot-long purple-red forked tongues, darting several times in and out of their elongated green scale-covered mouths between two rows of sharp fanged teeth. They now appeared to be quite tall, green scale-covered reptilian males, wearing a single-piece body suit made of a silver-gray looking metallic fabric belted at the waist with a blue oval buckle. Embossed upon their upper chests were upside-down black obsidian pyramids. The point of a wide vertical curved silver sword touched the middle of the pyramid's square flat shiny bottom, and two double-headed green snakes wound like a braid upward around the double-edged blade. Their four heads arched inward toward each other above the mother-of-pearl appearing handle, and their forked tongues extended through long fanged open mouths touched together at the space centered between the heads.

Both aliens were more muscular and solidly built than most weight lifters on Earth. The strong five fingers on each of their hands ended in long razor-sharp extendable curved nails. Centered within their large pastel-violet oval eyes were vertical cat-like fiery-red pupils. Their reptilian ear holes were located on each side of their heads where human ears would have been.

Sadistically grinning, they both pointed their hand-held weapons at Ted and licked their lips with their long darting forked tongues.

The taller one leaned close to Ted's grimacing face and stated, "It is very lucky for you, Earth human, that we are not hungry now. You told us this Mark Santfield was going to be at his camping location in the mountains, but failed to tell us soon enough. The Alliance forces now have him, and we must make other plans. Do not fail us again, Earthman. We can find another lead collaborator among your fellow rulers that will be more responsive to our requests. Do not forget that we agreed to leave you and your co-conspirators in charge of this planet when we finish helping you possess it. Otherwise, you would end up just like most of the other human cattle on this pathetic world, and do not forget that we would not then choose to save your daughter from extinction as well."

The slightly shorter reptilian sent his long, forked tongue out to Ted's face and slowly licked the side of his cheek. Ted nervously quivered with revulsion but forced a condescending grin.

"Now, now gentlemen, don't be hasty," he gingerly replied, mocking up some courage so as not to trigger a more vicious animalistic response from his alien collaborators that could end his life on the spot. "Look, we're allies, right?"

Both reptilians snickered and sneered a repulsive response, then gazed at each other to share in a private artificially created electronic telepathic communication Ted could not hear. The slightly taller leader sent his silent communication to his associate through a thought amplification transfer device on his belt.

*Are you thinking what I am thinking, Gorsapis?*

Gorsapis returned a widening toothy grin before he returned the thought, *Zushsmat, I sure am. If we were not under orders, I would rip off his arms right now and crunch them down my throat while he watched and slowly died.*

*Exactly,* Gorsapis replied mentally, drooling back at him. *I would rip out his beady human eyes, pop them in my mouth, and then rip off one of his legs and chomp it down before he would have time to fall over screaming. I just hate having to pretend we regard any of them with respect or honor because of that stupid agreement our predecessors made with their former weakling leaders. What a miserable little planet of food stock. I wish we were back home.*

Ted looked on helpless to do anything other than bide his time to find a way out of the predicament.

Gorsapis then backed off, smiling at Ted, and said aloud appearing apologetic, "Oh, don't mind us. We were having a bit of fun at your expense, but it was childish, and we apologize."

"Well, it wasn't one damned bit funny," Ted replied angrily, frowning as he let out a relieved sigh. "We are supposed to be helping each other and I do not like being threatened. Why is this Mark such a threat to your people anyway? He has no political power here, and most people just think of him and many others like him to be nothing but fascinating crackpots. Besides, he will soon marry my daughter. Can't you just let him be?"

Both reptilian aliens grimaced at Ted's request and started to become angry again, but then just managed to control themselves.

"He's already been more trouble than he's worth," replied Zushsmat to Gorsapis, mocking up an appeasing smile. "What do you think? Should we back off the hunt?"

"Well, we don't exactly have orders to kill this human," pondered Gorsapis, "but we will have to ascertain what he knows and if he's working with our enemies. Mr. Carter, you must let us know if Mark Santfield returns to see you or your daughter. Our entire plan could be in jeopardy if that nosy Galactic Alliance finds a way to intervene with the hidden leaders of your world to end their association with us. Meanwhile, we will use all our resources to discover how he managed to escape our trap. Now we must leave."

Gorsapis touched the sword handle symbol on his belt buckle, and they faded away in an upward whirling golden-white teleportation beam that sped up around their bodies and vanished. Ted looked on fuming about what he just went through at the hands of his reptilian alien associates. Then he spun around and marched angrily back up the right staircase to his study to make one more very important phone call.

He stopped in front of his desk, quickly grabbed the phone, and punched in a quick series of numbers.

He impatiently paused to wait for a familiar voice to answer and commanded, "Henry, get your ass over here right now. We have some very serious things to discuss, and we don't have much time." The voice on the other end asked something and Ted barked back, "Never mind all that now. Just get here, and I'll fill you in."

He slammed down the phone and started to pace back and forth in front of his desk nervously rubbing his hands together.

# CHAPTER NINE

# THE SECRET MOUNTAIN BASE

*J*anice and Mr. Crystal rematerialized inside a vast mountain cavern chamber, and she grabbed her arms and felt them to make certain she was still in one piece. Then she looked up both amazed and terrified at the sudden change in surroundings, desperately trying to emotionally adjust to her now greatly altered understanding of reality. Her eyes first focused five hundred feet away toward the back of the huge cavern upon a three-hundred-feet-long cigar or cylindrical shaped silvery metallic spaceship. A faintly detectable wavering blue anti-gravitational energy field enshrouded the mighty ship, while it hovered in a stationary position a dozen feet above the flat green granite cavern floor. Clear convex oval windows perhaps six feet apart spread horizontally along the upper half of the hull and appeared to surround the massive vessel.

Mr. Crystal was standing a few feet to her right, calmly observing her facial reactions as she came face-to-face with a totally unexpected alien environment. She slowly turned to face him with wide-eyed bewilderment.

"Stay calm, Janice. You're completely safe now and no longer in any danger," stated Mr. Crystal kindly, and he gave her a warm friendly smile.

Still too stunned to voice a question, she continued to let her eyes naturally rove around the giant carved out cavern taking in more detail. She could see the long spaceship moored to a ten-feet-wide walkway ramp with waist-high polished silver handrails. The ramp extended twenty feet to an oval opening in the ship's midsection from a massive rectangular building made of hundreds of transparent octagon wall panels and windows. Overall, it was twice the width, height, and length of the ship. Hundreds of human and humanoid men and women, with varying skin textures and sizes, were moving in many directions on twelve floor levels within the building. Several more were casually walking along the ramp's clear rectangular floor headed in the direction of the opening leading inside the ship.

She looked up at the center of the domed cavern chamber three hundred feet overhead to behold a four-hundred-feet-wide closed circular door, divided in half. She mused it must be able to be opened for the ships to come and go on their missions. Set in widening concentric circles around the circular door and covering the rest of the top of the entire curved dome ceiling were one-feet-wide, oval-shaped lights radiating an evenly dispersed natural appearing warm sunlight throughout the cavern.

She and Mr. Crystal were standing in the center of a gigantic thousand-feet-in-diameter cavern chamber. She thought some incomprehensible alien technology had carved out the mountain's interior and smoothly polished it. The walls also appeared to be laced with what she thought must be quartz and gold ore veins. Clusters of emerald crystals glittering from reflected light were also located in sporadic pockets throughout the cavern walls. Beyond each end of the long cigar-shaped ship, landed in two groups near the far wall of the cavern, were two dozen much smaller disc-shaped silvery metallic spaceships. From her perspective, they appeared to be perhaps thirty-feet-in-diameter, lined up in parallel rows on individually marked circular landing pads. She could see three semispherical pods set in triangular formations pointing downward from the bottom of their hulls.

An unusual sound drew her attention away toward a rapidly approaching teardrop-shaped transport vehicle with no wheels. It had just exited an oval opening in the back wall of the cavern beyond the massive cylindrical ship. As the six-feet-long open-topped vehicle silently sped in their direction, she could see a human male and a female sitting inside it near the front of its wide rounded teardrop-shaped front end. The car quickly slowed just six feet from where she and Mr. Crystal were standing. The two humans riding inside now appeared to be vibrantly healthy and trim in their late-thirties, dressed in familiar casual attire similar to what Mr. Crystal was wearing. The antigravity powered hover car stopped and lowered to the ground as a side door automatically opened. Both occupants stood up smiling in their direction, and then stepped out onto the cavern floor. They walked the few remaining feet up to Janice and Mr. Crystal, and then respectfully nodded their heads with their right hands held across their chests over the heart.

For some reason all trepidation and fear vanished from Janice and she found herself returning a genuinely warm friendly smile. Then she gazed, puzzled, at Mr. Crystal.

"Mr. Crystal," she asked hesitantly, "What . . . Where . . . Where are we?"

"Please let them explain," he gently replied, and turned to introduce the man and woman patiently standing before them.

"This is Commander Tam-lure. He is the planetary Commander of all twelve of our secret bases on Earth, and Una-mala is his wife and Second in Command or First Officer."

They smiled at Janice.

Tam-lure cordially began, "This station is one of a dozen bases we have located in secret locations on your planet. We built this one over one-hundred-years ago deep inside the upper portion of this Mt. Shasta Mountain in Northern California underneath the extinct volcanic cap. This particular type of research facility is here to observe and discreetly encourage the ongoing safe advancement of your people while you head toward space travel capability. The facility also functions as a policing or monitoring station to make certain the treaty the Galactic Inter-dimensional Alliance of Free Worlds signed with another totalitarian alliance of worlds is not broken. However, when this treaty was updated or resigned back in the Earth year of 1908, our diplomats knew the totalitarian alliance would likely sign it with the ulterior motive to covertly try to gain dominance over your world. They have done the same thing on other worlds in our Galactic history.

"By treaty agreement, many races from other planets were allowed to secretly come here for benevolent non-interfering scientific purposes only, and they were strictly forbidden to make contact with any of your people for some time to come. The situation on and off your world has changed much since then. The off-world totalitarian alliance spies have been caught many times conducting increasing systematic covert operations on your planet over the last sixty years. Their treaty breaking illegal contact, and subsequent influential control of your world leaders and people, has altered many things."

"You mean those two strange men back at my father's mansion have my father under their control?" asked Janice apprehensively.

"Janice, this may be hard for you to understand at first," interjected Una-mala kindly, "but your father and the group of men he works with are being manipulated to self-righteously and systematically take over control of all governments on your world. Mark has also been suffering all his life under a type of subconscious hypnotic programming. He has been struggling in his own way to get free from it by writing about his insights. This despicable deed occurred after his capture on his approach to Earth, when the body he now occupies was five years of age. Janice dear, things are not as they seem. They also trapped you six months after your arrival on Earth thirty-one years ago."

Janice blanched, and her face turned pink with embarrassment.

"But how can that be?" she asked, frightened and shaking.

"Janice, please tell us how you're feeling right now," asked Una-mala compassionately.

Janice was now squirming uncomfortably and fidgeting with her fingers as she glanced around the cavern in hopes of finding an escape from the tormenting question.

"I . . . I'm frightened. Oh God, no, I'm terrified, and a cold chill is running down my spine," she stated with chattering teeth, shaking from head to toe. "What's happening to me?"

"Be at peace, Janice," Una-mala answered gently. "We're going to free you from the subconscious burden of guilt and fear you've felt all your life whenever you tried to remember what seemed to be just out of reach."

Forlorn and frowning, Janice suddenly looked at them, embarrassed, as a new realization surfaced in her awareness.

She hesitantly asked, "You mean my father isn't really my father?"

"He is your Earth father," Una-mala stated gently as she approached and placed a consoling hand upon her shoulder. "He and your departed mother bore your body, then loved and raised you, but they were unaware you were not originally from Earth. You were on a scientific mission to this world when Trilotew agents captured you. They somehow discovered your hidden location, and then tracked you when you went out into the world disguised. After that, they reprogrammed your subconscious mind to make it possible to eventually get to your father and his wealthy powerful associates without your being aware of it. When they had finished with you, they compelled your true self, what Earth people call Soul, to enter the child's body at about two years of age. Then through your subconscious mind, they invaded your father's dream state at night without either of you being aware of it. Eventually, they gained a type of hypnotic control over him. However, he is now beginning to see through their masquerade, and he is starting to believe they are going to betray all that he and his associates have worked to accomplish. This was discovered when we intercepted a phone call he recently made to his General Counsel Henry. Now he's trying to find a way to extricate himself from their clutches through Henry, but he's up against his own associates who are already dominated by the Trilotew."

"Excuse me, but who are these Trilotew, and do you mean to tell me this is not my real body?" asked Janice, now confused.

"Allow me to elaborate," requested Tam-lure, kindly smiling. "After you were captured they forced your Atma or Soul from your body to place it in a suspended heavy gravity field by misusing another stolen waveform technology they acquired long ago from their ruling overseers. After that, they compelled you to enter the girl's body your parents bore when it was two years of age, after first forcing its former occupant to leave it to seek another one.

"These tyrants call themselves the Righteous Illumined Lords of The Empire Worlds or Trilotew for short," continued Tam-lure, "and they are a very deranged group. Their ancestors were involved in a war over five hundred thousand years ago with even more despicable beings from a parallel dimension that were genetically similar except they were white and had wings. This white-winged bi-pedal reptilian race called the Trilon-Kal had previously acquired mind-deprogramming technology designed for healing from a conquered world. Then they perverted it to win that earlier war with their green non-winged and non-carnivorous cousins by first gaining control of their leaders subconsciously.

"The Trilon-Kal overseers considered themselves superior over all other races, and they subconsciously programmed their captives with deeply aberrant compulsive behavior patterns they could control. These new tyrant Masters could then remain secretly hidden in the background to use their captured relatives as remorseless weapons to embark on many terror campaigns, aimed at taking over benevolent world systems. They have done this to the reptilian, and the short and tall Gray extraterrestrials you may have heard of, and to several human races. They indiscriminately killed many humanoids and other races without a thought of remorse. Sometimes they even ate their human captives alive or destroyed entire planets if they could not get their way. They acquired most of their current advanced technology through raids back then to become more technologically powerful. However, they are not as truly telepathic as they pretend to be. They now use technology to peer into other beings' minds to reprogram their subconscious to bend them to their will."

Una-mala continued, "The Trilotew overseers were finally defeated in a conflict with the Galactic Alliance with the secret help we obtained from friends that inhabit our nearest galactic neighbor your people named Andromeda. With their assistance, the winged reptilian overseers were defeated and forced back into their own parallel dimension, then permanently sealed inside. That war was very devastating to countless worlds, and the remaining reptilian race signed a treaty to avoid further conflict. That gave us time to rebuild the Galactic Alliance. Eventually, we will have to deprogram the entire Trilotew military and their tyrant leaders on their home world systems in order to end their terror campaigns for all time.

"Wait . . . wait . . . I don't feel good," interrupted Janice, now completely mystified.

Mr. Crystal touched the pin on his lapel again and she relaxed, breathed deep, and smiled.

"Janice, you will soon clearly understand what I'm telling you now. Please listen patiently while I help you remember what was taken from you," continued Una-mala. "We have already made inroads to neutralize the Trilotew's vicious behavior by utilizing a technology that is unknown and unusable by them. What is now underway will change the course of Earth from its certain destructive future direction. First, we must secure the planet from the attempted Trilotew takeover because that outcome would likely lead to the planet's unexpected destruction, like it has on other worlds they infiltrated."

"For reasons you will become aware of soon," added Tam-lure, "the destruction of your world would not just cause the loss of all human and other life on Earth. Great harm would also come to hundreds of billions of sentient beings living on planets in many parallel dimensions you know nothing about. That would further cause a great imbalance to occur in this galaxy, and the Galactic Alliance will not allow that to occur under any circumstance. Therefore, although we're normally reluctant to intervene in other worlds or their choices, in this case it's well justified because Earth leaders and the general populous no longer have the freewill they think they have."

Janice was worried and still shaking as Una-mala kindly commented, "I know this is a lot to take in right now, but once your full memory is restored all that is being imparted to you will make perfect sense. Janice, you must understand the Trilotew agents are still after your fiancé. Since his safe rescue, you became the next best thing to try to capture to use as bait. They will kill or recapture Mark if they can to put him back under their control. For now, if you want to help him and yourself, please go with Boun-tama or Mr. Crystal as he is known to you, and he will take you safely to Mark."

Mr. Crystal kindly smiled at her and cordially offered his arm. Her shaking suddenly subsided, her tense shoulders slowly relaxed, and she cracked a little smile as she placed her arm through his.

Commander Tam-lure and Second Commander Una-mala kindly nodded goodbye, and then Tam-lure benevolently stated, "We will be waiting here for you and Mark when you return. Then if you wish, you can assist us to carry out a great uplifting change for this planet and its people, a change that has never happened before. In fact, what is about to come to Earth has never happened in the history of this galaxy. A Scout ship has been prepared for your departure, so do not be concerned. From this base, we can get you to Mark without interference from any Trilotew agents or ships. What we call Prime Creator or the underlying conscious energy presence behind and supporting all life will go with you on your journey. Be at peace."

Janice smiled at them, and then she and Boun-tama began to casually walk across the cavern floor headed toward the closest Scout class ship. She could see it landed in the far background beside many other identical ships near the much larger cylindrical spacecraft. Tam-lure and Una-mala fondly watched them as they approached and then entered the ship.

The Scout ship lit up a few moments later surrounded by the thin layer of blue anti-gravity light, emitting a soft low frequency hum. It lifted straight up toward the top of the cavern as the two closed semicircular launch doors centered in the top of the cavern ceiling started to part. Revealed beyond them was the clear view of a rich star-filled night sky over the mysterious Mt. Shasta. The Scout ship sped up through the opening and paused just on the other side. A brighter blue light pulsed from the hull, and the ship darted straight up at tremendous speed to disappear within the myriad of glittering stars of outer space.

Like dutiful parents, Tam-lure and Una-mala lovingly smiled at each other in reflection of their meeting with Janice. They clasped hands and turned around to casually walk away, headed toward the wide clear octagon window sided administration building beside the large cylindrical starship.

# CHAPTER TEN

# DESTINED REUNION

With utter fascination, Janice watched the incomprehensible majesty of the wide panorama of stars in outer space displayed upon the projected view screen aboard the Scout ship. Boun-tama was sitting in the white tall-backed chair behind the control console with the palms of both hands depressed into the lit gold quartz guidance controls. The ship was speeding through space the normal way on approach to the gas giant planet Saturn, looming ever larger, surrounded by its wide ring system.

He looked up at Janice and commented, "We have not taken the more swift direct way of arriving here through an inter-dimensional portal this time because I wanted you to behold the beauty of outer space during our short journey to Saturn."

Janice was spellbound in childlike awe, unable to take her eyes off the wide rectangular projected view screen, and just nodded a response. Then she slowly forced herself to look away to see Boun-tama kindly gazing up at her.

"How did we get here so fast?" she asked, amazed. "We've only been traveling for maybe an hour, and isn't that the planet Saturn we're approaching?"

Pleased with her astute observations, and that she was keeping her wits about her, Boun-tama replied, "You're correct. That is the planet Saturn, and your estimation of our elapsed travel time is just about right. However, this ship is also capable of travel far beyond the speed of light. An energy field created around the hull forms an energy conduit in front of the hull that literally draws the ship forward through a higher parallel dimension. We can then travel through a parallel universe where the molecular particle flow or time-rate is faster than here. In other words, the ship travels through a higher vibratory reality for a relatively short distance that translates to traversing a vast distance when we lower the ship's vibration or molecular time-rate back again. The ship actually travels inside a continuously created whirling electromagnetic vortex void formed in front of and around the hull. To borrow an old Earth culture analogy, one might say this is like pulling yourself up with your own suspenders, except in this case, the suspenders create a type of anti-magnetic vacuum in front of the hull that continuously draws the ship forward into it. The intensity of the field created determines the speed of the craft relative to the gravitational focus of our intended destination."

Janice just stared back at him blank-faced and shook her head to clear her boggled mind and attempted to comprehend what he was imparting to her.

She finally sighed and exclaimed, "Wow! I mean . . . WOW! Well, actually I don't pretend to actually understand what you just told me, so I'll just accept you know what you're talking about."

Then she gazed back at the view screen to observe the ship on approach to the mile-long cylindrical flagship stealthily positioned inside Saturn's ring system and asked, "Oh, good heavens, it's gigantic. Mark's aboard that thing?"

"That is one of three interstellar mile-long Emerald Star class flagships stationed in this sector of the galaxy. Several hundred identical and much larger ships are scheduled to arrive around and on Earth in the near future that make up just a small part of a very vast fleet. After creating the proper conditions, this unprecedented event will take place to bring about a non-destructive benevolent worldwide disclosure of our existence to the entire Earth population. You will understand how this will be possible after we free you from the terrorizing subconscious programming that was forced upon you."

"I can't wait to see Mark's expression when he sees me walking towards him," she fondly stated, gazing dreamy-eyed into an imaginative near future.

Boun-tama smiled up at her.

"You will both discover much that was suppressed from your conscious awareness and will be greatly changed for the better. Know that I wish you only the greatest goodwill."

He looked back up at the projected view screen, just as Janice stepped up behind him to observe the landing.

She watched their Scout ship slow several dozen feet away from the central section of the flagship, as the massive hull appeared to become transparent, and their Scout ship harmlessly passed right through the transparent metallic side of the parent vessel. Still in awe, Janice continued to gaze at the view screen as it switched to reveal the flagship hull turn solid again behind the Scout ship.

The ship drastically slowed inside the hangar bay and moments later it gently touched down on a vacant circular landing pad next to eleven other Scout craft already landed in two parallel rows.

Like a child in wonderland, Janice stepped through the hatch opening and stopped at the top of the lowered ramp to gaze around the huge hangar bay. Boun-tama stepped up behind her and stood to her left side to calmly observe her reaction.

"I am a . . . well, I don't know what I am anymore," she breathlessly exclaimed, somewhat intimidated by the obviously very advanced technological surroundings. "Mr. Crystal . . . oh pardon me, I mean Boun-tama, when will I see Mark?"

Boun-tama wisely paused to consider how much he should disclose before she fully recovered her true-identity and then he replied upbeat, "He's currently undergoing a final therapy session to rid himself of all lingering subconscious Trilotew programming. If you wish, you can see him after that, but wouldn't it be better if you first go on your own experiential journey to recover the suppressed memory of who you are and where you came from?"

"What exactly will happen to me when I go through it?" she inquired, not smiling at the prospect.

Boun-tama gave her a cheery smile and answered, "In the first five minutes or so, you'll remember a great deal about what was suppressed below your level of awareness, and this will startle you at first. I assure you, the experience will also be very uplifting and relieving. There is no need to be afraid. You will not be harmed in any way."

He touched the strange hieroglyphic gold pin symbol on his lapel and it softly flashed gold light once. Janice shook her head and took a deep breath, then smiled with the discovery that any apprehensive fear she was experiencing had somehow vanished again.

"What does that pin you touch do to me?" she curiously inquired.

"Among other things," replied Boun-tama, "it can be used to trigger our teleportation to safety. You just recently experienced that. It can also temporarily emit an energy that can keep your negative subconscious programming from controlling your nervous system. This allows you to be more yourself regarding important decisions you may make for your own benefit. Otherwise, the Trilotew programming implanted in your subconscious would likely keep you from accepting the opportunity to be set free of it."

"Well Boun-tama," she confidently began, "it certainly does work wonders. I believe I'm ready now. Please lead the way. I want to be free from this nervous system trauma nonsense forever."

He gestured toward the ramp, and they walked down it and over to the moving by-directional floor conveyor. They stepped together on it and rapidly moved toward the same triangular entry hallway Mark had previously entered.

A short time later, they both walked out of another triangular hallway exit and stepped onto the transparent floor of the wide spherical chamber with the quartz crystal-lined walls. Janice stopped to stare at a human woman, appearing to be in her late-thirties, kindly gazing back at her. She was standing next to the control console in front of the transparent pentagon-sided dodecahedron chamber.

"Oh good heavens!" exclaimed Janice, smiling from ear to ear like an excited little girl. Then she began to recall the space observation lounge room she just passed through with Boun-tama and commented, "Boun-tama, perhaps I was just too speechless to say it before, but I never dreamed I'd actually see outer space and Saturn's rings through the windows of this flagship from right inside it. That was just fantastic."

She returned her gaze with renewed awe at the quartz crystal lined spherical walls. As she glanced down through the transparent floor, a sudden shaking from head to foot took hold, accompanied by waves of nauseous fear. Cold tingling nervous spasms were running up and down her spine and she started to collapse, but Boun-tama caught her arms and held her up. He could see she was going into unconsciousness as her eyes started to roll up behind her eyelids beyond the sockets, and he gently laid her down on the floor. He stood back up and touched a spot on the back of the special gold pin on his lapel. A wave of visible golden energy shot from it in one quick pulse across her body that was starting to convulse in an epileptic-like seizure. The golden energy quickly vanished into her skin, and her body went completely limp. Her breathing instantly returned to comfortable normal inhalations and she opened her eyes to behold Boun-tama and the woman gazing down at her.

"What am I doing on the floor?" she asked, mystified that she was lying on a cold floor.

As they helped her stand up, Boun-tama calmly answered, "You were experiencing another subconscious program triggered to take control of your nervous system in an attempt to keep you from this chamber. It's just an old trick of your former captors. However, the technique I used for your benefit will only last for an hour before you may be vulnerable to experiencing another episode, but there is no need for concern. Sun-deema and I will soon have you free of it. Do you feel strong enough to be rid of that madness?"

"Yes, I believe so," she softly answered.

"This is Sun-deema, wife of Commander Jon-tral," continued Boun-tama. "She will be overseeing your session today."

She weakly nodded and stated, "Oh my God, Boun-tama, I have never felt so terrible before in all my life. As soon as we entered the room, I started having uncontrollable visions of having my clothes torn off, and oh God I know those two reptilian beings were torturing me to death. The pain was unbearable."

Janice angrily winced and grimaced with newfound determination as she firmly grabbed Boun-tama's upper arm and demanded, "You've got to get me into that chamber now. I don't want to experience that insanity ever again."

He calmly removed the firm grip of the fingers she was unconsciously digging into his skin and gently tucked her arm through his own. He waved his other hand toward the clear-sided chamber in the center of the room. A few minutes later, she was sitting down in the chair. It began to conform to her body shape and size and she smiled. He placed the crystal headset over her head and it conformed to her cranium as a comfortable feeling came over her body.

"Well Janice," he encouraged, "are you ready for Sun-deema to begin the session?"

She nodded, and Sun-deema extended the palm of her right hand over several controls. The quartz crystals lining the spherical walls in the outer chamber began softly glowing with golden light, and the transparent pentagon panels surrounding her turned on. She was seeing a beautiful human female sitting happily upon four-inch-tall grass, snuggled together with a handsome human male. Three children, two girls and a boy ages eleven, nine, and seven respectively, were playfully giggling while they stood in the near background in a triangular pattern ten feet apart. They were tossing a transparent blue ball to each other. One child threw it underhanded into the air and it darted upward under its own power another fifty feet then stopped, while spinning suspended in place radiating a bright blue light. Then it darted down to the intended child emitting a pleasant tubular bell tone and a blur of rainbow colors behind it. It stopped again inches from the child who grabbed it and tossed it back upward. When a child tossed the ball again, it would stop to emit a different steady color before it darted to the next child emitting another stream of rainbow colors and a different tone.

The children's parents, appearing to be in their mid-thirties, were remarkably trim and fit. Janice noticed they were all casually dressed in beautiful spring blue and green form-fitting silken attire similar to what the personnel wore that she observed coming and going aboard the flagship.

Surrounding the family was a hundred-feet-wide grass-covered glade encircled by gigantic forest trees covered with spoon-shaped emerald-green leaves. The outer edge of each leaf was emitting a type of self-luminous phosphorescent light, clearly visible even in the radiance of the twin setting suns. One radiant orb was higher in the sky, several degrees apart from the second orb. They were gradually descending to set behind the distant snow-clad mountain range that visibly extended across the horizon under a light emerald-green sky.

Janice delightfully gasped as she suddenly recalled she was in fact the alien human woman on the grass, and she started to say something when the images surrounding her suddenly changed.

She could now see the same woman, standing upright spread eagled, with coal-colored chains clasped around her ankles and wrists to a crude cavern wall. Lit fiery red torches, stuck into spiked metal holders attached along the hard rock wall, were casting an eerie shadowy glow that danced across her naked body. Two tall reptilian captors slowly approached her from opposite directions with their sharp-clawed fingers sadistically grasping toward her. She screamed in terror as their long, forked tongues licked her torso and face emitting an appalling stench.

Janice was now also shaking with fear, and her forehead was dripping with sweat, as her terrified eyes watched the impending doom of the helpless woman that she was experiencing as herself.

Both Janice and the woman chained to the wall on the surrounding view screens suddenly wretched together in disgust. Then they violently jerked their hands and feet to somehow get free, while the taller reptilian began to nastily whisper in the woman's left ear.

"Go on and scream dainty morsel. No one will ever hear you in here. Remember well, useless human female, what will happen to you if you should try and recall what your fate in our hands is going to be here today."

Her reptilian captors suddenly lurched forward with long arms ending with sharp five-fingered grasping claws. The taller one ripped open her abdomen from her crotch to her throat with one long knife-like forefinger, while the other one stuffed her right hand all the way down his throat up to her elbow and viciously ripped it off with two rows of sharp fanged teeth. Janice and the chained woman screamed together in utter agony and dropped their heads forward into unconsciousness, just as the torture images vanished from the surrounding view screens.

"Janice, it's alright now," announced Sun-deema's loud voice through the intercom system. "You're safe aboard the flagship. The worst part of their subconscious implanted nightmare is now over."

Janice suddenly discovered she felt safe and relieved as warm glowing energy began to radiate throughout her body. She slowly opened her eyes to observe she was still sitting in the comfortable chair. Then she apprehensively lifted her head up to see Boun-tama and Sun-deema compassionately gazing back at her through the transparent pentagon panels. He had joined her, and they were patiently standing behind the control console in the outer spherical chamber. Janice sighed, greatly relieved.

"Oh God in heaven, Boun-tama, I remember. I experienced that at their hands more than thirty years ago." Tears of sadness welled up in her eyes and she hesitantly asked, "Oh dear Prime Creator, I remember everything. Did they . . . actually do that to my former home world body?"

Boun-tama thoughtfully replied, "We don't know if that was the eventual fate of your body. However, we do know they implanted the images and feelings of that nightmare into your subconscious energy field to control you. As you can understand now, any attempt by you to remember this terror would cause your nervous system to replay the event across your conscious awareness as if you were actually going through it, but with no visual and sound memory of what was causing it. In this way, it would be sheer torture for you to try to recall who or what you were or what you were doing before the time of the implant. Are you clear about this now?"

"Yes, I am," she sadly answered. "I was a scientist and happily married with children back on my home world. I am unable to recall exactly when they captured me, but I do remember it was near the end of my six-month scientific study mission at one of our hidden Galactic Alliance bases in South America, high up in the mountains of Peru. Oh dear Prime Creator, what has become of my husband and children? Boun-tama will I ever see them again?"

"Fortunately, they are quite safe back on your home planet," he compassionately replied. "To them, it has only been a year and a half since your disappearance. This time differential occurs because you arrived in less than a day aboard a ship that swiftly traversed vast distances of interstellar space by traveling through a parallel time vortex or inter-dimensional portal. In this way, you could carry out your six-month scientific mission on Earth and return after only having left your family on your home world two weeks earlier. Your ongoing family life would then continue with little interruption.

"Your husband Donum-tuma, daughters Yoral-telan and Vera-tima, and your son Danim-tama know you are alive. They also know your former body from home was likely destroyed or devoured after the Trilotew agents forced you from it to imprison you in a strong electromagnetic field. After they implanted their control images into your subconscious, they compelled you, the Atma or Soul, into the young two-year-old female body on Earth. That was how you came to replace the daughter of your Earth parents without you or them ever suspecting a thing. They likely accomplished this by capturing your Earth parents' female child hours earlier to force the being out of it. That being is now in a higher reality. Then they forced you to enter her body with her implanted memories, unconscious of your true identity. You were returned in the little girl's body to her unaware parents in a way that would not cause them to suspect anything had happened."

"I'm beginning to remember everything," stated Janice, dismally forlorn. "My real name is Moon-teran. With my original advanced human body destroyed, how will I ever be reunited with my family now?"

"We have a way," assured Boun-tama. "Your original body's four-stranded human DNA is stored back on your home world, as is the DNA of your current fiancé, who is actually your cousin. All Galactic Alliance citizens are protected in this way before they are given the privilege to go out into the universe on a mission."

Her face turned red with the shocking realization she was about to marry her own cousin, and Boun-tama could see her sadness becoming unbearable as she began to sob uncontrollably.

"Quickly Moon-teran, look back up at the view screens," he urgently commanded, and she slowly looked up with tears running down her cheeks to see new images surround her on every panel.

She now experienced being back in her specially built six-thousand-square-feet dome-shaped home, swimming with her husband, two daughters, and son in a wide oval pool centered under a transparent oval canopy the width of the pool. The fiber-optic light source, hidden under three overlapping concentric white coverings surrounding the transparent curved dome, was illuminating the pool with natural appearing light like the twin suns high in the light-green sky.

She suddenly recalled they lived in a beautifully lush country setting not far from a central governing building complex on her home world of Norexilam. She also recalled that it circled one of the many suns in the Starborn Cluster beyond what Earth people call the Pleiades star group. Then her awareness suddenly expanded with a joy she never knew in her Earth life as Janice, and all her fear vanished.

Boun-tama let go of concern for her safety with a sigh and with a smile continued, "You will be reunited with them soon, Moon-teran. In their time, only a year and a half will have passed when we return you to them. However, thirty-one and a half years went by while you were growing up on Earth. Moon-teran, the Galactic Council asked me to inquire if you would be willing to play the part of Mark's fiancée to complete a much greater mission the Alliance has initiated for the recovery of Earth's people. They are being entrenched under Trilotew control. Know that Mark, or rather Ambassador Shon-ral, remembers his true self again and he has already agreed to our request. He would like you to join him to help carry out the greater implementation of *The Seres Agenda*."

Expressionless, Boun-tama and Sun-deema patiently waited for the hoped for response as Janice closed her eyes to think it over.

"I must be free of all Trilotew implants," she firmly stated, opening her eyes. "And be fully recovered from their terrible effects before I could do such a thing. Also, what about some form of protection for both of us when we are returned to Earth? I mean, don't they know Mark was rescued from their evil clutches?"

Boun-tama thoughtfully gazed at Sun-deema, and she confidently answered, "Both of you will be provided with a very unique form of protection that cannot be penetrated by any Trilotew agent or weapon. Once they discover it, we must proceed very carefully because revenge upon others will likely dominate their ongoing covert efforts after that."

*I would dearly love to see those lizards roasted alive for what they have done to me, and to many others over such a long period in our Galactic history,* thought Janice, scowling.

Boun-tama appeared concerned after overhearing Moon-teran's telepathic anger for the first time, but he sent back the encouraging thought, *Oh . . . that is good. Since you are already recovering your telepathic ability you may also recall that no Galactic Alliance citizen would ever consider acting out of revenge like the subconsciously perverted Trilotew.*

Delightfully surprised, Moon-teran's mouth dropped open and she gasped aloud, "Oh my heavens, you heard me. I wondered if you would get the thought. Somehow, I just knew I could do it, and of course, you're right. Now I remember the Trilotew are following out their evil designs, compelled by a similar despicable subconscious programming they received a very long time ago. They weren't always like they are now." She thoughtfully paused and then continued with courageous gusto, "I will definitely help any way I can. We must prevent the populace of Earth from coming under their direct tyrannical control. Earth would become a hellish playground for their madness and we must not let that happen under any circumstances. We should get this deprogramming done. I want to see Mark, I mean my cousin Shon-ral, as soon as possible."

Pleased with her newfound confidence, Boun-tama smiled wide at her, and Sun-deema happily encouraged, "Okay, then let's get this done. It shouldn't take more than another hour to get you fully recovered," and she touched two controls on the console.

Meanwhile, Shon-ral was in one of the two command and control centers located inside each end of the gigantic flagship. He was now dressed in comfortable silken attire similar to what the ship's personnel wore, sitting next to Monti in one of four comfortable white leather-like chairs positioned around a clear blue oval topped, metal conference table. Sitting in one of the two chairs on the other side of the table was Commander Jon-tral.

Beyond the oval tables was the front of the rectangular paneled, half-octagon-shaped control console, which curved around the end of the hull directly below the twelve oval windows or view portals. Sitting on chairs or standing up were a half dozen other ships' personnel, monitoring hundreds of the illumined controls.

The spectacular panorama of stars was still clearly visible through the windows in outer space, along with the rings of Saturn below them which extended into the vast distance around the massive equator of the giant planet.

The dozen wide transparent view screens linked together along their vertical rectangular sides across the length of the console were now displaying unknown star systems, beautiful multi-colored nebulae, and two land and water-covered worlds with vast blue-green oceans similar to Earth's. A close up of both worlds displayed on the far left view screen panel revealed pastel green and light pink-colored clouds moving high above the surfaces of both spheres, slowly turning on their axes. Another view screen on the right was displaying the chart of a dozen naturally occurring whirling energy doorways or vortexes mapped out across the solar system containing the labeled planet Earth. One of the whirling vortexes was located in space near the labeled planet Saturn.

Displayed on the middle view screen close-up of Earth were a dozen similar but smaller vortexes located at various points on the planet's surface—in its atmosphere at varying heights, at two locations at the bottom of the Atlantic and Pacific oceans, one in the Himalayan mountains, and a dozen more just above the planet's outer atmosphere in space.

Red luminous dots indicated the vortexes' locations around the Earth, and projected English words beside each dot describing them. One was marked above the infamous Bermuda Triangle area southeast of Florida. Another one was just outside the planet's atmosphere positioned directly above Mt. Shasta in Northern California. Another was over the big island of Hawaii in the upper atmosphere directly above the active volcano. Another was depicted somewhere in the mountains of Peru in South America. One was marked in the lower atmosphere above the Mesa airport in Sedona, Arizona. Another was indicated near ground level in the middle of Russia's Siberian wilderness. One was marked at Land's End in Cornwall, England. One was in the atmosphere a mile above the great pyramids of Egypt. Another was in the deepest region of the Himalayan Mountains between Tibet, India, and Pakistan. There was one marked centered on the bottom of the Pacific Ocean, and another marked centered on the bottom of the Atlantic Ocean. The one Mark went through aboard Monti's ship was marked a hundred miles in space directly over a specific section of the High Sierra Mountain range in central California.

Other vortexes were also indicated, but they were labeled in an extraterrestrial language depicting the following locations: Spain's Pyrenees Mountains, Russia's Ural Mountains; in the atmosphere over the Gobi Desert; at a mountain location on the southern New Zealand island; and one at ground level in the vast desert in the very center of Australia.

"When can I see my fiancée, Janice, I mean my cousin Moon-teran?" asked Mark, looking at Commander Jon-tral. "Oh . . . do forgive me. I guess you can see old habits tend to die hard" and he laughed to shake off the absurdity of all that had happened to him.

"Boun-tama, or who you know as Mr. Crystal, just reported to us that Moon-teran has successfully gone through her first deprogramming session," replied Commander Jon-tral. "We should continue to refer to her as Janice to keep things in line with your original but now quite expanded Ambassadorial mission to Earth. She has come out of her most terrorizing repressive implant control session. Now she remembers her own husband and three children back home, and she will soon be ready to join us here."

"Well that should prove most interesting," replied Mark with a hesitant smile. "Even if she knows what I now know to be true about our past, we were still intimate together, and we were going to be married. I've heard of kissing cousins, but this whole thing has already gone way beyond the absurd. It will likely take some time for us to get used to pretending to be engaged to be married to implement *The Seres Agenda* on planet Earth."

Jon-tral smiled at him with kind patient eyes and encouraged, "You will both be surprised at how naturally you return to your true selves. The love and respect you have for each other will remain, but each of you will no longer feel an intimate attraction to each other. You should begin to realize your Trilotew captors also artificially programmed that attraction into you and Janice. They did this in order to keep you unconsciously trapped, too close to each other and too unconsciously guilt ridden to ever discover what had been done to you." Jon-tral leaned forward and seriously continued, "Because of what happened to you, we now know a hidden spy is operating somewhere within the Galactic Alliance itself and we believe we know who it is. This spy would have informed Trilotew agents about your cousin's arrival with a scientific expedition to Earth and the location of her hidden base, as well as your secretly planned arrival six months later. By discreetly watching the base from a distance, they would have eventually tracked her leaving its protection on a disguised journey among Earth's people. After capturing her, they must have probed her mind to confirm when your scheduled diplomatic mission to Earth's hidden leaders was to take place. They then carefully planned to capture you alive during your arrival to Earth.

"They could have simply destroyed your ship but that would likely cause an all-out war with the Galactic Alliance, and that would devastate them all the way back to their home worlds. Instead, they suppressed your former existence, masked your energy signature, and then forced you into another body on Earth to stop you from successfully carrying out your mission. We didn't detect what happened to you until after we explored the publication of your first book. Then we knew. They rightfully fear your mission could possibly not only topple all their evil plans for Earth and its people, but also end their ongoing existence as sinister beings in the Galaxy. We only recently discovered the spy was highly placed in the Galactic Alliance. He compromised your secret mission, after Trilotew agents captured his wife and children during a return space flight back to him on their home world. The Trilotew covertly blackmailed him into cooperating if he ever wanted to see his loved ones alive again."

"It has to be someone in the Galactic Alliance governing council itself," stated Monti frowning. "They would have been the only ones other than Shon-ral that would have known about his secret Ambassadorial mission, and its very delicate timing."

"That's exactly what we discovered," replied Jon-tral.

"You and Janice are going to be in grave danger of assassination or torture when you return to Earth," commented Monti, "and we are going to provide you both with a very special unique form of protection that no Trilotew agent or weapon can penetrate. When Janice, Boun-tama, and Sun-deema arrive here in a few minutes, Jon-tral and Sun-deema plan to reveal to both of you something most extraordinary that has never occurred in the entire history of creation itself; something that will end evil as an experiment in the lower worlds and on Earth forever."

"It's about damn time the Galactic Alliance showed a little backbone to those tyrannical Trilotew demons," stated Mark, gazing at Commander Jon-tral. "Whether we like it or not, if we don't stop them now, someday there will be another massive interstellar war with them like the one that took place over half a million years ago. I know it's not been our way to interfere, but there must be a method to neutralize their evil subconscious drives without killing them or going to war."

"We now have the way to accomplish exactly that," replied Jon-tral enthusiastically.

"Do you mean we can end their reign of terror in the galaxy for good?" shot back Mark, unsure he had really heard such good news.

"You heard me correctly," replied Jon-tral. "Before I elaborate, let's wait for Janice to arrive."

"Mark!" exclaimed the excited voice of Janice from the background.

Mark swung around to behold his cousin with tears of joy streaming down her face, standing beside Boun-tama and Sun-deema twenty feet away from the triangular hallway entryway to the command module.

"Janice!" he excitedly replied and jumped to his feet.

They ran toward each other and she threw her arms around him. He swung her around in several circles before they came to a stop, but this time they did not kiss.

He held her at arm's length, and they fondly gazed into each other's eyes as Boun-tama walked up behind them, followed by Commanders Jon-tral and Sun-deema.

"Well cousin," she began to say, deeply relieved, and then started to giggle.

"Good to see you again too cousin," replied Mark, equally relieved, and he started to giggle with her.

***Shon-ral, I remember everything***, she telepathically sent to him with an affectionate smile.

***Dear Moon-teran,*** he replied, ***I too remember everything. Maybe now we can do something together that will change the course of galactic history.***

He gallantly took her hand and kissed it.

"Well, I believe we're all glad to see you two have recovered your natural telepathic abilities," encouraged Second Commander Sun-deema, smiling at them. "That will make carrying out *The Seres Agenda* a little easier from now on."

"Please walk over toward the command console," requested Jon-tral, "and we will reveal what the entire Galactic Inter-dimensional Alliance of Free Worlds has begun to implement. After that, you will both clearly understand why what we respectfully call *The Seres Agenda* is finally moving forward."

As they approached the console, Jon-tral smiled at a very attractive young female technician standing near its center and politely said, "Jin-trean, I would say it's time we put *The Seres Agenda* program on the screen for our visitors."

"The program is ready, Commander," she happily replied as she reached down and touched a violet pyramid-shaped control.

A large rectangular projected view screen directly above and behind the console flashed on, revealing a massive golden-colored metallic pyramid illumined by a closely encompassing pastel-blue layer of antigravity light. It appeared to be floating in a fixed position somewhere in a mysterious void of outer space, surrounded by a background abundance of radiant blue-white stars.

Jin-trean touched the control again and the image zoomed to a close up of the entire structure. Another mile-long cylindrical ship identical to their flagship was stationary in space alongside the base of the giant pyramid's side directly facing the view screen. In comparison, the towering luminous structure appeared to be twelve times taller and three times wider than the mile-long ship hovering in a stationary position alongside it.

A Scout class ship, encompassed by its own blue light, began to gradually appear, slowly flying right out of the solid golden metallic side of the massive pyramid through a briefly appearing horizontal oval opening. It slowly flew down and hovered above the parent vessel, turning transparent before it entered the landing bay within the central hull.

"As you can see," continued Jon-tral, pointing to the pyramid on the screen, "one of our sister flagships is stationed by this transformational pyramid transmitter. It channels a very special energy from a dimension well beyond what the Trilotew know about, which is not part of the dual nature of the physical universe. No positive or negative force, weapon, or being, can alter or affect these pyramids in any way whatsoever. They are now beginning to radiate out into the universe in every direction. I'll put an overview of the pyramid network on the screens so you will have a better understanding of the comprehensive nature of what they are capable of creating."

He leaned forward and touched a control next to Jin-trean, and the pyramid and flagship images on the view screens began to rapidly zoom into the background until several different stars appeared in a triangular grid pattern. Identical radiant golden pyramid devices could now be seen positioned in between each of them. The image continued to zoom further into the background until an entire quarter quadrant of the Milky Way galaxy came into focus with countless golden dots present between vast numbers of stars. The image again zoomed further into the background until the entire galaxy appeared filled with millions of the pyramid structures radiating as tiny golden lights, positioned equidistant between the stars.

"What you're seeing depicted here is now taking place all over the entire physical universe within countless billions of galaxies," continued Sun-deema. "These pyramids are not comprised of any material known to exist anywhere within the physical universes, and we did not build them. I will explain more about this fact. These pyramids conduct or transmit a type of omnipresent energy that can only uplift life in a constructive manner. This energy is something entirely new in creation. It exists for one purpose, and that is to retire evil as an experiment in the same way dinosaurs outlived their usefulness 65.5 million years ago at the end of the Cretaceous prehistoric period of planet Earth's ancient history. You will also soon recall that dinosaurs did not originate on Earth.

"Every living sentient being, every animal, and all matter everywhere are about to be permanently transformed, starting with the most endangered planet Earth, because this energy is now undoing what was created billions of years ago. In other words, evil as an experiment is being permanently retired from creation because something wonderful is beginning to take its place to carry the now expanding creation forward into the infinite future.

"When we return you both to Earth, on your way there you will notice something new added in outer space. Out in the asteroid belt between Mars and Jupiter, you will discover one of these massive golden pyramids hovering in space. Utilizing a special device aboard Monti's ship, you will also be able to see the new pulsing waves emanating from all four sides, and from the top and bottom of the pyramid. They will look very similar to repeating pulsating emanations of expanding concentric or circular golden-white energy waves. More of these pyramids are spontaneously coming into existence all the time and they immediately begin to emanate continuous pulsing waves outward in all directions. They eventually interconnect or interlace with the same waves sent in every direction from identical pyramids. An energy grid system is created when they interpenetrate each other. Anyone or anything passing through this normally invisible field of energy will instantly begin to experience an uplifting expansion in their awareness, even the Trilotew.

"A visual radiant sphere then instantly forms outside their conscious being containing all implants, aberrations, and engrams of any negative nature that have been driving their actions from within their subconscious minds. Once this is accomplished, the vibrant living omnipresent force emanating directly from Prime Creator will offer the one experiencing the phenomena the opportunity to permanently have the subconscious nonsense dissolved forever.

"When any Atma or Soul is freed from this karma or subconscious madness, they return to a naturally benevolent state of awareness, and they become aware they have always been a part of Prime Creator or the source behind and supporting all creation or what many people on Earth refer to as The Supreme Being."

"You mean this energy field could really change the course of Earth's destructive destiny?" asked Shon-ral intrigued.

"That's exactly what it will do," replied Jon-tral, and he smiled. "This expanding universal grid system is about to be turned on all around Earth, and the Trilotew will not expect this or see it coming. No being or technology in the lower dimensions of time and space can reverse this process. You might say that Prime Creator itself has awoken to a new way to operate the entire creation in a far more advanced benevolent manner, to train all sentient beings to become truly free conscious co-creators with it. In other words, the reign of evil as a motivating teacher is being forever retired because a far more advanced way to train sentient beings to attain higher states of consciousness recently manifested in creation. It's now beginning to be implemented within the omnipresent, omniscient, and omnipotent force that underlies and supports all life and all creation everywhere, starting with this galaxy that Earth people call the Milky Way."

Moon-teran's eyes widened, and she found it hard to respond at first to such unexpected and startling revelations.

"Is this real?" she finally inquired, gathering her wits about her. "Can you really do it? Those pyramids represent a direct threat to the Trilotew totalitarian control of many worlds, and they will try to annihilate them."

"You should both begin to understand the depth of what is being revealed to you," Sun-deema replied patiently. "This coming change in creation is beyond any race, force, or science known anywhere by any group throughout the lower multi-dimensional universe. Some people on Earth refer to these dimensions as ever more refined realities ranging upward from the physical through the astral, causal, mental, and etheric or ethereal planes of existence. However, this very recently created force brought into existence as a new directive came down from the much higher pure dimensional realm of Prime Creator. That center of creation exists well beyond the lower world systems. As we both stated, nothing in the lower worlds can affect the pyramids or the energy they emanate."

"It's true," confirmed Jon-tral, "and in fact if any force, weapon, or thought were negatively projected at one of these pyramids, the energy would be directly reflected back upon the perpetrator to instantly dissolve or neutralize their weaponry and suspend their subconscious negative drives outside their awareness. They would quite literally become part of the solution instead of an evil-oriented problem-causing source. After that, they too would become carriers of this same emanation wherever they went, and those that ordered them to carry out such attacks would then go through the same process."

"Unbelievably amazing!" exclaimed Mark after letting out a deep breath. "It's truly just fantastic. Are you telling us that we will become vehicles or channels of such a powerful transforming energy presence during our mission on Earth?"

Boun-tama answered, "You will both know much more because a smaller version of one of these pyramids suddenly appeared within this ship not long ago, and everyone aboard went through a transformation into a new expanded state of awareness. We will escort you to a special chamber where you can stand before this radiant energy field to experience this wondrous change for yourselves. When we return you to Earth, you will carry this new liberating energy within you, and it will radiate outward in all directions through your renewed physical bodies. You will also be wearing special gold emblems hung from gold chains around your necks. They will warn you of any pending attack or approach by those intending you harm, and a new perceptive telepathic knowing instinct will begin to operate within each of you, twenty-four hours a day. Intuitively, you will both know how to effectively deal with every circumstance that confronts you, while you carry out the diplomatic mission to Earth's hidden leaders and people."

"But we must also proceed very cautiously," interjected Jon-tral, "because Trilotew agents have now infiltrated all levels of Earth governments, including the ranks of their top military personnel. They will seek to find ways to maintain their expanding covert control of the planet at any cost. As they have done in the past, if push comes to shove, the Trilotew will likely attempt to destroy the Earth if they are eventually forced to retreat back to their home planets. In fact, that's exactly what we're counting on."

"If I'm understanding you clearly," began Mark with a sudden realization, "every attempted attack the Trilotew initiate to stop this new energy emanation from going forward will result in a benevolent reversed or mirrored effect upon them. They will transform back to their original naturally benevolent natures, and then when they return to their totalitarian home planets their leaders become transformed in the same way. Is that accurate?"

"Now you're beginning to see the bigger picture that everyone aboard this ship only recently experienced," answered Monti, quite pleased. "Well, we must get you two fully awakened to prepare you to receive the impenetrable protection."

Janice was now giddy and giggled, "Oh dear Prime Creator, I . . . oh my heavens, do you mean to tell me that Earth will become a normal human planet like our home world?"

"That's exactly right," replied Sun-deema happily, "and that will only be the beginning of many vast uplifting creative changes that will continue to come to Earth and this Milky Way galaxy. Earth and its people are about to be reborn. Then we will invite them to join the Galactic Inter-dimensional Alliance of Free worlds. If both of you will go with Boun-tama now, he will take you to the chamber where one of these pyramid devices is even now radiating the new energy waves throughout this ship. There you will experience a greatly expanded state of awareness and like each of us on-board, you will become more deeply committed to carry out your mission for the benefit of all life. You too will know with certainty what is about to take place on Earth, in the galaxy, and throughout all creation."

Boun-tama motioned with his arm toward the triangular hallway exit from the control room. Mark and Janice gladly stepped up beside him and together they casually walked twenty feet up to the exit. They stopped to turn around to smile gratefully back at Jon-tral, Sun-deema, and Monti standing beside the control console smiling back at them like proud parents. Then Mark and Janice anxiously entered the hallway with Boun-tama in the lead.

# CHAPTER ELEVEN

# THE CHAMBER OF PRIME CREATOR

*R*adiant golden energy waves were emanating outward in expanding concentric circles from all four sides of the fifteen-feet-tall gold pyramid, centered in the circular floor of the chamber. Boun-tama, followed by Mark and Janice, entered the room from another triangular hallway and stopped. One after the other, expanding doughnut-shaped light waves rapidly vibrating their clothing, harmlessly passed through their bodies to continue unobstructed through the glistening curved ivory walls of the chamber. Their hair was flowing behind their heads as if a mild wind was blowing through the room, and uplifted expressions of pleasure spread across their faces.

Boun-tama turned his head to watch Mark and Janice expressing profound childlike amazement with their mouths unconsciously wide open. Their eyes were glancing back and forth following the energy waves emanating from the pyramid as they passed through their bodies without resistance to vanish through the circumference of the curved walls behind them. The golden light started to emanate from the pores of their skin until an oval halo of light formed around their entire bodies. Then it quickly receded back inside their flesh, and their eyes brightened with a profound new realization.

***Well, now do you two understand how this new conscious wave is beginning to radiate out into all creation, and what it does?*** inquired Boun-tama telepathically.

***Yes,*** they replied, and laughed.

They turned their heads with bright smiles of awareness toward Boun-tama in thanks for his guiding them to the experience, and he nodded. Then he calmly turned to leave the chamber and they knowingly followed behind him.

A short time later, they were back inside the main Command Bridge control room on the same end of the flagship standing before Jon-tral and Sun-deema.

*I see you two are now back to your old selves with something new added*, remarked Jon-tral, and he winked at Mark and Janice.

*It's amazing*, replied Mark. *We simply understand, don't we Moon-teran?*

Janice looked at him and said aloud, "Yes, now we understand everything." Then she solemnly said, "But I do dearly miss my family back home even though I know they are fully behind me continuing with the mission. I can feel their radiations of love across time and space. Shon-ral told me he's experiencing the same thing from his family," and she fondly gazed at him.

"Yes, it's true," confirmed Shon-ral aloud, fondly gazing back at her. I do miss them dearly, and they too stand behind me. Although, we now have the opportunity to make a real difference in this universe and on Earth, and we both think it's high time we got started."

He looked toward Jon-tral and Sun-deema for their approval, but it was not necessary.

They appeared quite pleased and Commander Jon-tral stated, "I hadn't told you about this before, but you should know two of these very special massive pyramids now rest at the bottom of two of Earth's deepest oceans, and another one is hidden inside a particular Himalayan mountain. They are radiating uplifting and transforming energy waves down into the planet's core and upward through the crust. When the waves from the pyramid stationed in the asteroid belt between Mars and Jupiter, and the waves from the pyramids on Earth's ocean floor and in that Himalayan Mountain, interlace with each other, we will have a very real opportunity to permanently change the destructive destiny of Earth's people. Earth will finally become a normal human planet."

"The gift of this new Prime Creator energy Ray, passed down to us by the mighty Seres race Ambassador, is now with both of you," added Sun-deema humbly. "Therefore, we have arranged for your immediate transport back to Earth. You will be dropped off at separate locations to minimize drawing any unwanted attention to your return."

"I'll have the honor of escorting you two back to Earth," remarked Boun-tama as he stepped between them and regally bowed. "I hope that will be acceptable."

Mark and Janice curiously gazed at him and Mark asked, "That will be greatly appreciated, but what happened to Monti?"

"He was sent back to Earth while you two were in the pyramid chamber," replied Boun-tama, "and he's already managed to beam Henry aboard his ship to enlighten him about our presence in the universe. They did manage to get a message through to your father without tipping their hand in any suspicious manner to Trilotew agents. When you two get back home, he and I will fill you in on how we plan to help you extricate your father from his predicament, and then the entire hidden government personnel from their trap. Well Shon-ral, are you ready to follow through with your newly expanded diplomatic mission to Earth, and Moon-teran are you ready to help him?"

"Yes, Mr. Mark Santfield, I will marry you," she said gazing playfully at Mark. She laughed.

"Yes, Janice Carter, I believe I will marry you too," Mark playfully confirmed, and he laughed with her. "You know, Boun-tama, I believe we are ready to pull this off. Lead the way."

"If you will follow me," continued Boun-tama, "I will get both of you back home in the most expedient manner."

"Before you two go," inserted Jon-tral, "we promised to give you a very special gift that will provide you both with a way to contact us here aboard the flagship if things get desperate. In the days ahead, you will need to do just that because we will be gradually moving things forward toward the day when our presence in the universe will be openly disclosed to all the people on Earth."

Sun-deema lifted up her right arm from behind her back and clenched in her grasp were two gold chains hanging down one-foot to each side of her hand. Two round gold pendant symbols hanging from the ends of both chains depicted an embossed white alabaster pyramid with the hieroglyphic or caricature symbol above the apex that Boun-tama always wore. She walked up to Mark with a radiant smile and held one of the chains open with the forefingers and thumbs of both hands to place it around his neck. Mark lowered his head to receive it, and she repeated this with Janice before stepping back to stand beside Jon-tral.

Mark and Janice picked up the gold emblem hanging from the chains and curiously looked them over.

"You'll be pleased to know," continued Jon-tral, "these special symbol devices act as telepathic amplifiers that are secretly connected to myself and Sun-deema in a unique way that no Trilotew can penetrate or perceive with any technology they possess. The pendants operate on an unknown frequency within the new Ray that's being emanated from the pyramid aboard this ship, and from all those that are continuing to appear throughout this and other galaxies."

"From this ship, we will be able to perceive ahead of time any threat you may encounter," encouraged Sun-deema. "However, you should also both know there will be much dangerous ground to walk over because the Trilotew will try every trick, and use any device they have in their arsenal, to entrap you one way or the other. If they cannot get to you, they will try to trap and use those who may be dear to you in order to force you to comply with their wishes. However, do not be concerned, for we will be monitoring their movements around the clock."

"As Sun-deema said," confirmed Jon-tral, "this new universe-changing wave that comes directly from Prime Creator is with both of you now. You can go forward with courage and strength of conviction to carry out the full extent of your mission on Earth. Although the survival of the planet and every living thing on it is at stake, know that several hundred billion of your fellow beings living upon hundreds of millions of worlds within the entire Galactic Inter-dimensional Alliance of Free Worlds in this galaxy are committed and actively involved in supporting this effort.

"Also, the one you know as Mr. Crystal or Boun-tama, and of course Monti or Mon-tlan, as well as Sun-deema and I will be available twenty-four hours a day, Earth time, if you need our assistance. In addition, we have a dozen monitoring Scout ships stationed at various secret bases on Earth, and another dozen patrolling in orbits around the planet for any emergency backup assistance you may require. Go in peace with Boun-tama, and know our friendship and love goes with you. For now, farewell."

He and Sun-deema respectfully placed a right hand over their hearts and nodded, and Mark and Janice returned the gesture. Then Boun-tama gracefully motioned with a hand toward the triangular hallway exit from the bridge.

Jon-tral and Sun-deema gazed benevolently at Mark and Janice as they walked away behind Boun-tama and disappeared down the triangular hallway headed toward the hangar bay to embark on their trip back to Earth.

# CHAPTER TWELVE

# ATTACKED
# FROM
# TWO DIRECTIONS

Janice's concerned thoughts were focused on her father's safety back home on Earth, while she fondly reflected on how he had taken such good care of her all her life. She and Mark were standing behind Boun-tama, who was sitting at the control console aboard the Scout ship as it lifted off the landing pad inside the flagship's launch bay.

The ship turned transparent and passed through the wall of the landing bay to enter outer space while Janice asked, "It was mentioned that my Earth father was secretly contacted by Henry and Monti while we've been away, but what does Henry know about any of this, and will my Earth father be kept safe?"

"As you know, Henry was aboard Mon-tlan's ship while you two were still aboard the flagship," assured Boun-tama, as he looked up from the console. "He now knows extraterrestrials exist and about the Trilotew threat to your father and Earth. He was only able to send your father the encouraging message that help was on the way because Trilotew agents are now constantly monitoring him. I understand your concern, but we are carefully monitoring them. If either of them are threatened with any serious danger they will be teleported aboard Mon-tlan's ship or sent to one of the hidden mountain bases."

Listening with his hand to his chin, Mark silently pondered, *How can we be returned to Earth without being asked questions we can't answer about where we've been?*

Boun-tama stood up and passed his hand over a spherical control. This time the projected view screen appeared above the entire control console. Images began to whirl into focus revealing the forested High Sierra mountain range in Northern California where Monti took Mark off world. The image was continuously magnified until a forested area near a small mountain valley town located at the base of the range came into focus, followed by a quaint white cottage next to a nearby clearing surrounded by dense evergreen trees.

Boun-tama pointed to the image and stated, "This is my home away from home on planet Earth. I live with my wife Lean-tala, also known as Mary Allison Crystal on Earth, disguised as a married couple in this country cottage. It provides good cover for any mission we embark on across the face of the planet. Both of us can be teleported at any time of day or night to any designated target on Earth, either from a shielded room within the cottage or from the secret Mt. Shasta base. No Earth military establishments or Trilotew agents are able to detect us. Now that you both understand this, I can answer the question that is foremost in your minds. When we arrive on Earth, I will land the ship in a special hangar near the cottage that is invisible to any outside detection. Then you will both be safely sent to a location where you can prepare to carry out your missions."

Janice winced as if she was in pain and asked, "I don't understand how that will work. My father on Earth and the Trilotew know I escaped. Surely, Trilotew agents will be after us again as soon as we arrive."

"Yes, and my situation is even more unbelievable," interjected Mark. "I've been gone an entire week."

Unconcerned, Boun-tama grinned and remarked, "Janice, on Earth three days will have transpired by the time you meet Henry, and that includes all the time you spent aboard the flagship, as well as travel time to get there and back again. This is due to a round trip time displacement phenomenon that occurs every time we travel through one of the inter-dimensional doorways like the ones near Earth and the planet Saturn. I believe you both recall how this works."

They both nodded.

"Let me explain further," continued Boun-tama. "A short time after we enter the Saturn vortex opening, you will both experience for yourselves the massive golden pyramid stationed hidden in the asteroid belt between Mars and Jupiter. Something extraordinarily new came into creation since the sabotage of your original missions to Earth. The Galactic Alliance Council wants you to see the special energy waves it now emanates. Mark, as you recall, Monti brought you to the flagship by entering Earth's high atmosphere vortex that is connected to the vortex opening near Saturn."

Mark nodded.

"As you also know, seven days will have elapsed by the time we return you to Earth and land this ship in the hidden hangar, but I have an ideal cover story that will explain your long absence. My wife and I will report to the authorities that we found you wandering along a road near our house dehydrated with memory loss, and we offered you shelter. We will further state that after three days of rest and proper nourishment you began to recall what happened. When asked, tell the authorities lightning struck the ground a few feet from where you were standing throwing you twenty feet through the air, knocking you out. When you awoke some hours later, you could not remember your name, where you had come from, or anything else about your former life. After spending the rest of the cold night and another two days disoriented by your destroyed campsite, you finally wandered down the mountainside and through the woods to where we found you on our road. When news channel reporters, local police, and any government agents interview you, just relay this story to them. Of course, both state and federal authorities will examine you in a hospital for several days, but don't worry. We'll make certain you are protected from Trilotew agents until your safe release a few days later can be arranged by highly-placed top government officials, who are secretly working for our cause to save Earth."

*I know we can do this if we work together. Are you with me?* Shon-ral asked telepathically.

Moon-teran replied, smiling, *Mark, I really miss my family and I know you miss yours. However, we must succeed and swiftly, before we can return to our homes to rejoin them, and enjoy the many years of our true lives watching our children grow up.*

The pain on Mark's face was unmistakable as he lowered his head to visualize his own loving wife and children back on their world. Then he suddenly remembered the critical nature of their mission, shook off the depressing feeling, and looked back up at her.

*Dear cousin Moon-teran, I could not have said it any better. However, we should find out what we can accomplish as a pretend married couple back on Earth. Both of us know with certainty the citizens on vast numbers of Galactic Alliance worlds will benefit if the Earth people finally join us or they will suffer the repercussions along with the inhabitants of the planet if it is destroyed. We will not fail.*

She smiled in agreement, and he turned to Boun-tama patiently listening to their telepathic conversations.

"Looks like we're all in for quite a ride from here on out," stated Boun-tama, "but I'm confident with full Galactic Alliance support we can succeed far beyond our original missions. Together we can bring about a new destiny for the Galactic Alliance and the people of Earth." He paused thoughtfully and added, "However, I must remind you again that once we arrive, you two in particular must be very cautious because agents from Earth's hidden military industrial establishment and the Trilotew will be after you in full force. They will know Mark's cover story is phony. That's when the real struggle will begin—to finally free our fellow human beings on Earth from their covert clutches, or we will watch the planet go down in flames of annihilation."

"Sounds like quite a plan, Boun-tama," remarked Janice, still uneasy. "Pardon me, I must remember to call you Mr. Crystal and that reminds me, may I ask what your first name is on Earth?"

"It's Dan," he stated, smiling. "But you two can call me Dan or Mr. Crystal as long as it doesn't make things more confusing than they are already."

He chuckled at his own comment, and they joined him.

Janice then thoughtfully inquired, "Even though only three days will have elapsed for me when we arrive, how will I explain my sudden disappearance from my father's house?"

"Just tell your father you ran out of the house to look for Mark because you received a phone call with information about his whereabouts. He will know better because the brief coded message Henry sent him let him know you are safe, and that discrete contact between you two will occur very soon. Will that suffice for both of you for now?"

Mark and Janice gazed at each other and then nodded.

"Very well then," he continued, "we're about to pass through the Saturn vortex that will get us very quickly back to Earth. I will change the view screen so you can see what the ship is doing. After we enter the inter-dimensional opening, we will travel just a short distance, and then exit out of another inter-dimensional opening to enter a parallel dimension. It vibrates at a slightly higher molecular time-rate frequency than this reality where the planet Earth exists. From this slightly higher parallel dimension, you will be able to observe the pyramid in operation, and you will begin to understand the reason why it is not detectable, for now, by anyone in your parallel reality."

"The currently invisible waves it emits are moving into the parallel dimension of Earth from its hidden location to interlace with those waves coming from the pyramids at the bottom of Earth's deepest oceans, and from one hidden in the Himalayan mountains. All the pyramids are currently invisible because they operate in a higher parallel physical dimension that co-exists alongside the Earth planet. Temporary energy shields not only protect them from any possible detection by Earth's military or secret forces, but also from any Trilotew technology that could detect them under normal circumstances.

"Like us, the Trilotew have the ability to travel between numerous parallel dimensions in the normal course of traversing vast distances of outer space. Nevertheless, when they eventually discover them, they will subsequently also discover they are not capable of harming or affecting them in any way, but if they have the opportunity, they will try."

Boun-tama passed his hand over a control, and the view screen image changed revealing the whirling vortex opening in space near the planet Saturn. The view screen changed again revealing the planet Saturn and its ring system quickly fading into the background distance of space.

The ship darted into the opening heading into the long whirling inter-dimensional violet tunnel. Boun-tama touched several controls, and a view in the distance ahead of the ship appeared, revealing the vortex separated at a junction point into two gradually diverging tunnel directions. The ship passed into the right tunnel and a moment later it popped out through another whirling opening. It continued a short distance and stopped to hover near a massive golden pyramid hovering in space, glowing with a thin blue layer of light.

Boun-tama passed his hand over another control, and the screen changed to a close-up of the pyramid. They could now see it was clearly hovering in its stationary position in space between two massive stable asteroids. The pyramid was emitting wave after wave of concentric circles of white-golden light traveling at incredible speed away from the top, bottom, and all four of its golden sides. The waves were swiftly fading away in the vast distances of outer space.

"As you can see," continued Boun-tama, "this pyramid is already sending out pulses of uplifting consciousness transforming waves. After they pass beyond the asteroid field, they enter the atmosphere of another Earth-type planet in a parallel dimension that circles the third planet around its sun, in exactly the same way Earth circles its own sun. Several of these Earth-like worlds are now able to support the larger part of humans living on Earth today. They will be relocated to them after the threat to Earth has been neutralized."

Mark and Janice glanced at each other, then Mark inquired, "Then this pyramid has to be a larger version of the one we both experienced back on the flagship. Is that right?"

"Exactly correct," replied Boun-tama.

Janice was now gazing away deep in reflection about her family back home beyond what Earth people call the Pleiades star group. She snapped out of it and eagerly asked, "Are these pyramids transmitting the same new uplifting awareness that we both experienced aboard the flagship? Will evil as an experiment actually be permanently retired from creation?"

"Correct again," replied Boun-tama. "I can see you two have just about returned to your normal selves. I also assume you now recall most of the worlds in the Galactic Alliance can harmoniously only support about five hundred million inhabitants, and planet Earth has nearly seven billion living on the surface. Therefore, the world in this parallel dimension, and several similar Earth-like planets in close parallel dimensions, are being prepared to resolve the planet's overpopulation and pollution problems that are beginning to destroy its ability to support life."

Mark and Janice continued to watch in solemn silence. They both understood what Boun-tama had said as he passed his hand over another control. The view screen revealed the ship as it headed back into the vortex opening, and then it darted far beyond light-speed into the depths of the whirling violet tunnel.

The ship popped out of the other end of the tunnel a few minutes later through another whirling vortex opening and it was soon hovering in a geosynchronous orbit just outside of Earth's atmosphere high above the northwestern United States. The ship's luminous blue hull brightly pulsed, and the ship darted in a long downward arc to disappear in a large cumulus cloud.

In less than a minute, it was already slowing its descent on approach to land in a circular clearing by the lone white cottage. A lovely blond-haired and blue-eyed woman in her mid-thirties, wearing a simple country dress, was standing on the cottage porch looking up into the sky with an expectant smile.

The occupants of the ship gazed at the view screen and could clearly see the cottage looming closer. The small town appeared to be located about a mile beyond the forest tree line near the base of a certain part of the High Sierra mountain range in Northern California.

If any people were covertly gazing at the scene from the tree line at ground level, they would most certainly have been quite astonished. However, only the woman on the porch knew what to expect, and she smiled as the ship slowly became visible to her. It stopped to hover thirty feet above the center of the circular field near the cottage, just as slightly brighter light than daylight began to pour upward out of two invisible widening rectangular openings. The ship slowly lowered down into the stealthy building, gradually disappearing inside it as the two invisible doors closed again.

The woman walked down the cottage steps and hurried at a quick pace into the tall grass of the circular field. She stopped a third of the way into it, reached out with her forefinger, and then touched an invisible spot at eye level. A triangular opening began to appear as an invisible triangular door slid sideways inside an invisible wall, sending slightly brighter light streaming out into the field. Her body vanished from view as she walked inside the structure, and the triangular opening dwindled and vanished as the door slid closed, once again leaving the appearance of a vacant field.

Boun-tama's ship was just touching down inside the octagon-shaped building as the blond woman stopped several feet away from the closed triangular door directly behind her. Four widening concentric circles of brightly lit circular lights surrounded the overhead rectangular launch doors centered in the top of the gradually curved silvery metallic ceiling. The illumination from them was casting an even, natural appearing sunlight around the entire octagon-walled building. The vertical oval door appeared in the side of the Scout ship and Boun-tama stepped through it. He hurried down the steps and into the waiting arms of his loving wife. They kissed and then stood side by side to face Mark and Janice as they appeared in the doorway and headed down the steps.

Boun-tama gestured with his left hand toward the elegant woman by his side and happily stated, "This is my wife Lean-tala, also known on Earth by the cover name Mary Allison Crystal."

She smiled at Mark and Janice as she placed the palm of her right hand over her heart and respectfully nodded to them.

"You are both most welcome to our home away from home here on Earth," she happily stated and courteously gestured with a sweep of her hand toward the closed triangular door behind her. "Please follow us out of the shielded Scout ship hangar and be welcomed with refreshments inside our humble home. We can get to know one another better, while we enjoy a prepared meal to celebrate the beginning of your official missions to finally free the people of this planet from tyranny."

She turned with her husband and they soon passed out through the triangular doorway opening, stepping into bright midday sunlight. Mark and Janice followed closely behind them.

Outside, it was a beautiful mid-summer day near noon, and sweet songbirds were merrily chatting away in the surrounding forest trees. Hummingbirds, bees, and butterflies were busily flying from violet flower to violet flower that covered the tall bushes surrounding all four sides of the cottage. To any casual observer who might happen to walk by the pleasant scene, this setting would appear to be an ideal dreamlike fantasy wonderland.

Mark and Janice were soon taking their seats around a wide oval glass-topped table in a spacious dinning room. Just beyond their two extraterrestrial human hosts seated opposite them was the open doorway to a large modern kitchen.

While those inside the cottage were beginning to sip their tea, two elongated triangular, slightly bat-wing shaped, Trilotew Scout ships radiating a thin red light around their hulls shot into view and abruptly stopped, hovering sixty-feet above the cottage in stealthy silence.

Boun-tama's golden pin on his lapel began to emit a pulsing golden glow. He clutched the pin in his fist as he and Lean-tala jumped in alarm to their feet.

A golden transparent spherical energy shield instantly surrounded them as he shouted out through it, "Quickly, you two, clasp hands. We're under attack."

Mark and Janice nervously jumped to their feet clasping hands just as both pendants around their necks under their clothes began to glow with a similar pulsing golden light. The light expanded to instantly radiate an upward spiraling golden energy field that surrounded their vanishing bodies.

They rematerialized from the spiraling light aboard Monti's ship that just happened to be hovering at that moment stationary in space high above the northwestern United States, they could see imaged on the view screen. Monti appeared jovial behind the control console as they gazed bewildered back at him. Then he got up from the chair and walked around the console to embrace them both with a jolly hug.

"Welcome to safety you two. That was a close one, but those two necklaces you are wearing worked perfectly. As you recall, they detect danger ahead of time and send you to safety. In this case you were sent to my ship because it was the closest place you could be teleported in time."

"What just happened?" asked Mark with a shake of his head.

"Yeah, what did we miss?" chimed in Janice.

"The cottage is being attacked by Trilotew ships," replied Monti. "I'll change the view screen."

Back down near the surface of the planet, the transparent rounded front ends of the Trilotew spacecraft simultaneously pulsed brightly and two whirling foot-wide red spherical energy weapons darted from them down at the cottage. The widening dome wave explosion briefly bent back the surrounding forest trees as the entire cottage turned to brilliant white light. The ensuing blaze of searing heat melted every detail of the cottage into a vapor that roared with a deafening hiss, before it simply faded and vanished.

The red aura surrounding the attacking craft pulsed brighter and they sped away above the treetops toward the mountains. Two similar blue tracking energy ball weapons suddenly appeared, darting in a blur toward them from the air directly above the invisibly camouflaged launch bay in the nearby field. The two ships darted apart in an attempt to outmaneuver the weapons that matched their maneuver and hit them, one after the other, exploding both enemy ships into blinding disintegrating golden-blue molecular energy. Only a fine fiery mist of tiny metallic particles remained to briefly rain down on the ground near the base of the mountain to tell the story of their former existence.

"As you both witnessed," continued Monti, "the cottage was completely disintegrated, but I assure you Boun-tama and Lean-tala escaped any harm. I was prepared to act swiftly if help was needed but they handled everything very well."

Boun-tama and Lean-tala remained unhurt back on the ground where their cottage home once stood. They were still standing holding hands on a small non-burnt patch of remaining ground near the center of the scorched blackened circle of dirt. He let go of the gold pin on his shirt and the protective transparent energy shield surrounding them vanished. They turned and gazed into each other's eyes with concerned telepathic knowing, and then looked away to the nearby grass field.

Boun-tama turned his gaze toward the mountainside, looked back at his wife, and then said relieved, "The hangar's automated defense system worked flawlessly. This time we were spared certain death."

"Yes dear husband, but the authorities of this world will be here soon," Lean-tala remarked cautiously.

He hugged her and held her at arm's length by the shoulders then encouraged, "Yes, it's certain they detected the explosions, but we can straighten out the mess once we board the ship. They will want to investigate the UFO phenomena and interview any town people who may have witnessed what happened to the enemy ships."

She nodded solemnly and they took off running side by side out into the circular field on the once tall grass now flattened by the concussive explosion.

They stopped a third of the way into the field and this time Boun-tama touched a place in the air at eye level. The triangular door appeared again, sliding inside the invisible hangar bay wall and they raced inside. The door vanished as it closed behind them.

They entered the landed Scout ship and Boun-tama placed both palms over two blue controls to turn them on, and two connected projected view screens came to life. The burnt circle where their cottage had stood at the edge of the flattened grass field appeared across them and Boun-tama touched a violet crystal.

The violet beam sent from the disc-shaped front edge of the ship's hull harmlessly passed through the hangar bay wall.

From outside the invisible hangar, the beam appeared to be coming from a spot in thin air at eye level focused on the burnt circle. It began to expand along the ground in a widening circumference until it covered the entire burned area where the cottage had been. Then from the ground up the vaporized cottage began to reappear, layer by molecular layer, as the surrounding air scintillating with a rushing hissing sound glittered in rainbow colors around it like a small tornado. Within a minute their entire cottage, the songbirds, hummingbirds, bees, butterflies, and all the tall violet flowering bushes were back in place as if nothing had ever happened.

Back inside the ship, Lean-tala noticed a blinking control on the console and pointed to it.

"Husband, they are already here," she calmly stated.

Boun-tama glanced at it, turned to her and whispered, "We must be completely silent until they pass far enough away for us to safely take the ship out of the hangar without being detected."

Two unmarked Black Hawk military helicopters outfitted with full armament and making almost no sound, whooshed over the top of their land. Both of them swung back around several times in wide loops to inspect every inch of the area. Finding nothing after a minute, they raced away toward the town at the base of the mountain range. A moment later two F-22 Raptor fighter jets passed overhead with a booming roar at a slightly higher elevation headed toward the town.

"It looks like Trilotew agents entrenched in their midst tipped them off," whispered Boun-tama to his wife. "They would also have told them what to look for. It won't be long before they discover the tiny bits of extraterrestrial metal strewn along the mountainside."

"But surely our hangar still remains undetectable," Lean-tala said seriously, "as long as the shielding remains intact in the next higher parallel dimension."

"They won't find it," he assured her and thoughtfully paused before adding, "Now it's also clear to me those Trilotew ships don't have the ability to detect our hangar or they would have targeted it as well."

"You're right, husband, but we must act quickly."

Boun-tama kissed her cheek and said, "We should leave the area for a while before this country's black-ops personnel arrive here. If they attempt to search the house, they will not be able to find anyone home or the shielded teleportation device hidden inside. Not even Trilotew operatives know how that shielding works."

She smiled at his confidence and remarked, "We must visit the Mt. Shasta base again and report what happened here. From there we can plan a new strategy."

Some minutes later, the roar of jet engines were fading into the far distance away from the cottage and field, while the two helicopters remained hovering back and forth like tiny specks along the line of the lower mountainside. Boun-tama's Scout ship slowly appeared rising in the air above the opening invisible launch bay doors, just as its sleek saucer shape began to quickly fade from visibility. The brighter light gleaming upward into the air below it coming from the stealthy hangar rapidly diminished and disappeared as the launch bay doors re-closed. Only the faintly visible transparent outline of the hull remained when the ship briefly stopped to hover fifty feet above the flattened grass field. A widening cone of transparent white light appeared, emanating from the center of the bottom hull swept over the circular field and the flattened grass instantly stood back up as if nothing had ever occurred. The beam shut off, and the radiant pale-blue aura surrounding the hull brightly pulsed as the ship began to fade into complete invisibility. Then it darted in a long upward arc away from the direction of the mountainside and prying eyes.

# CHAPTER THIRTEEN

# DEADLY GOVERNMENT ALLIANCE

In thoughtful reverie, the President of the United States, Martin McCoy, was impatiently pacing back and forth in front of the Oval Office desk with his hand to his chin. He was partially African American in heritage, fifty years of age, and many people considered his appearance youthfully handsome. However, on this day the stress revealed by his wrinkled forehead and worried gaze could not be hidden from Secretary of Defense Daniel Samuelson, a trim Caucasian man about his age with thick black wavy hair and glasses, as he walked into the office and stopped to await the President's pleasure.

"Daniel, what the hell took you so long? I ordered you here over an hour ago," demanded the President.

The berating he received from the President this time did not faze Daniel because he already had news that would ease his concern, and he remained calm, staring unblinkingly back at the Commander in Chief.

"Mr. President, we now know what happened out there in California," began Daniel.

"Go on man, out with it," barked back the President.

"It looks like the Galactic Alliance that the Trilotew warned us about is beginning to intervene more directly," he mysteriously replied, holding back more about the issue.

"Well, what did you find out?" the President impatiently shot back.

"That dangerous author Mark Santfield was apparently rescued by a known Galactic Alliance ship just before our joint Trilotew and black ops team could

102

eliminate him."

"Damn it!" shouted the President, turning red in the face as he angrily continued, "How the hell is that possible? We took every precaution. How did they find out about our operation?"

Daniel gazed uncomfortably down at the symbol of the presidential eagle seal woven into the carpet, but then confidently looked back up and answered, "It appears this Galactic Alliance, whatever they are, may have become very interested in Mr. Santfield after the successful release of his first book. It's now apparent they have been monitoring him while he was gradually uncovering bits and pieces of information about our secret worldwide government circle."

Before the President could respond with another sound scolding of the Secretary of Defense, a small whirling vortex of sparkling golden light appeared between them, and a moment later a tall man with very penetrating large green eyes materialized. He was not smiling when he turned to face the President, holding out a small-elongated triangular transparent weapon.

Then he pointed it directly at the President's head and commanded, "Tell me now how you failed."

President McCoy hotly shot back, "I'm the President of the United States and I don't take orders from you, Ambassador Grotzil, or any other Trilotew diplomat. Now put that damned thing away or one second from now the particle beams hidden in these walls will reduce you to a pile of ashes."

Ambassador Grotzil forced a grin as he lowered his arm and stuffed the device in his suit pocket.

"Oh do forgive my little prank, Mr. President," he cordially responded. "I was ordered to test you to see if you are ready to take out any Galactic Alliance spy if they appear, before they could take you out."

"From the stunt you just pulled," replied the President angrily, "it would appear your people have a very sick sense of humor, and I'm becoming increasingly more stressed by the treaty we signed with your Imperial Alliance so many years ago. What assurances do I have you will keep your word when the secret governing Council I receive special orders from announces their existence to the people of this planet?"

With a sinister grin, Grotzil shook his head and the illusion of his tall human characteristics vanished. He was now standing before the President of the United States in his true form, a tall dark scaly green skinned bipedal reptilian. Vertical red cat-like slits centered in his violet eyeballs, along with receding rows of upper and lower teeth and his nine-feet-height made his appearance ominous.

His long, forked tongue darted once out of his mouth with a hiss and he calmly stated back to the President, "Have we not been allies for the last sixty years after your predecessors signed the treaty with us? Didn't we provide your military industrial complex with advanced off-world technology and weaponry to put you in the most powerful position on your world?"

"That is basically true," replied the President not smiling, "but you also agreed to take off-planet only a few dozen people from around the world to conduct your bizarre genetic experiments. You were to return them unharmed with no memory of what happened. However, by our latest count you and your associates have now covertly taken six million unsuspecting citizens off-world. To date, you returned fewer than half with psychological damage and now they are all starting to remember. Your group has already broken the terms of our treaty many times, and reports are starting to come in from all over the planet concerning intimidation tactics your Trilotew associates are starting to use in an attempt to control our secret inner government members. I want to know what happened to the rest of those people, damn it, and I want to know right now."

Grotzil smiled with a wide sweep of the long, green sharp nails of his left fingertips and diplomatically bowed, then replied, "We will return them right after their training is finished on our home world. If you recall, it was also stipulated there should be an exchange program to orient some of your people to our culture and our ways."

"Ambassador Grotzil, were they killed?" inquired the undeterred President, still frowning.

Grotzil's phony smile faded, "Are you now calling the Supreme Illumined High Lord Ambassador Grotzil of the Righteous Imperial Lords of the Empire Worlds a liar?"

"I want to know what happened to millions of Earth citizens still missing and I want that answer now," shot back the President.

Grotzil shoved his long green fingers into his suit pocket and appeared to press something. The President's eyes suddenly softened, and then he began to relax into a light-hearted state. Daniel was still stoically standing behind Grotzil, observing the President shake his head, and then he suddenly appeared to be quite pleased to see the Ambassador standing between them.

"You were saying, Mr. President?" inquired Grotzil, sweetly.

President McCoy blinked several times and replied, "Oh, that's right. There was an exchange program. May I ask when our citizens will be returning to us?"

Grotzil nodded his head and cordially replied, "They should all be returned to their homes in approximately one year from now. Will that do?"

"Yes, yes of course, sounds fine," replied the President, and he shook his head again as if he was trying to recall a now faded memory.

Daniel walked up to the Ambassador's side and cheerfully stated, "It's good to see you again, Ambassador Grotzil. How was your trip?"

Grotzil turned his reptilian head down toward Daniel and answered, "It was quite pleasant, Mr. Secretary. Thank you for asking. How's the wife and kids?"

"Oh, they're just fine," replied Daniel, "although they would like to see their dad more often," he smiled.

"What brings you to the Oval Office this time?" asked President McCoy.

"We want to confirm your new security weapons system hidden in these walls is adequate to protect you from any Galactic Alliance threat. They are on the move now, and they will try to make inroads into your secret worldwide governing members to convince them their intentions for your world are benevolent. However, in reality they still want to dominate this planet and make slaves out of all of you. As you recall, we stated to you they had done it before in similar ways on a number of planets that once belonged to our Empire Worlds. Now you, your superiors, and your special forces must be very cautious."

"We'll be ready," replied President McCoy. "Our reverse engineered spacecrafts are now weapons updated, and with the support of your space fleet we will succeed at neutralizing their plans." He looked at the Secretary of Defense and asked, "Daniel, what have our forces on the back side of the moon, and from the orbiting space platform and ground bases of Mars detected?"

"As we speak," Daniel replied proudly, "they are observing Galactic Alliance ships in increasing numbers in our solar system, and we recently monitored a number of Galactic Alliance Scout ships patrolling our planet's atmosphere. Several Trilotew ships tried to destroy the one that rescued Mark Santfield but it escaped through one of those inter-dimensional portals. We think it arrived at another location in the solar system but we are not yet certain where. Our Earth-based Scout ships are now ready to launch from our underground city bases, and a squadron is now on constant patrol within our atmosphere. We'll be ready for them if they try to come at us with any numbers."

"Excellent," replied Martin, now strangely upbeat. "Let me know the moment anything develops."

"Yes, Mr. President," replied Daniel, and he walked out of the oval office.

Grotzil silently mused to himself as he turned to confront the President,

*Oh, I can't wait to devour this puny human leader when the time comes. My Imperial Lords back home must have had quite a delightful time devouring some of those stupid human captives.* With a subtle snide grin he then stated aloud to the President, "I look forward to my next visit with you one year from today. Then I will have a few surprises for you and the people of Earth which will considerably alter your perceptions about many things."

"Well, that sounds like good news, Ambassador Grotzil," replied the President, now apparently quite satisfied with the meeting. "Please give my regards to your leaders and thank them again for me for all their help over the last sixty years."

"As you wish, Mr. President," replied Grotzil forcing a smile.

The Trilotew Ambassador appeared to press something inside his pocket again, and the same whirling spiral of light surrounded his vanishing body to teleport him away.

Martin's smile faded as he glanced down at the eagle symbol on the carpet. Then he looked up puzzled and walked around the desk to stop and gaze out through the glass panes at the White House lawn. A nagging concern about something important he could no longer recall spread across his face.

# CHAPTER FOURTEEN

# THE SERES AGENDA UNFOLDS

*M*onti was pleased with himself, while he mused about how lucky they had all been to escape the covert vile clutches of the disguised Trilotew agents mixed with Earth's misguided secret black ops Special Forces. He was also gratefully appreciating the fact that he, Mark, Janice, Boun-tama and his wife Lean-tala had survived the attacks because of careful Galactic Alliance preparation, and somewhat superior technology that was, for now, still unknown to the Trilotew. His smile faded as he pondered the thought of what things would be like in the future if somehow the Trilotew were to one day discover how to use any of the slightly superior technological advantages the Galactic Alliance secretly possessed. He knew if they ever succeeded, the result would once again be great destruction to many worlds.

At that moment, Monti, Mark, and Janice were watching the view screen, observing the Scout ship touching down on one of the landing pads inside the secret hidden Mt. Shasta base. They could see Commander Tam-lure and his Second in Command wife Una-mala casually walking side by side toward their Scout ship, headed away from the clear octagon sided administration and command building. The cylindrical Medium Transport ship that had been hovering in a stationary position in front of it was now gone, as were all the Scout class ships that had landed on the pads behind and beside Monti's landing ship.

"What happened to the large Transport Carrier that was hovering there?" inquired Mark.

"That's what I was wondering," added Janice, "and what happened to all the other Scout ships that landed here?"

Monti passed his hand over another control and the oval opening leading outside the ship appeared behind them.

"I believe they are all out on patrol, invisibly shielded, of course. Things are heating up now on Earth between the many disguised Trilotew infiltrators and the entire Galactic Alliance. We must move fast to avoid a major catastrophe on your world. If things get worse, it will be your planet and its people that suffer. Let's go out and meet Tam-lure and Una-mala. They will update us."

Mark and Janice nodded respectfully and headed down the ramp behind him.

Commander Tam-lure and Una-mala stood on the cavern floor and greeted them with their right palms held over their hearts. Then Tam-lure exuberantly clasped forearms with Mark and Janice, and Una-mala embraced them.

"Well, you have both experienced direct assaults from the Trilotew and survived," stated Tam-lure. "That is no longer an easy thing to do these days. They are very cunning and vicious."

"They can't help themselves," added Una-mala with a compassionate shake of her head. "As you both know, they are all suffering from a command program that was forced into the collective subconscious minds of their entire race by their once dominating white-winged reptilian overseers. You know this too, but it bears repeating. With the secret help of our very advanced friends from the Andromeda galaxy, the Galactic Alliance defeated the Trilon-Kal, and then drove them back out of this dimension and permanently sealed them in their hellish parallel reality. They cannot return. Even though that occurred five hundred thousand years ago, their remaining non-winged Trilotew cousins still arrogantly attempt to carry out that deranged programming as they covertly go about the galaxy terrorizing less advanced species. When the Trilotew soldiers operate disguised as humans, they must hide a barely suppressible lust to devour alive any race they consider inferior. Their lack of respect is far less than how most people on Earth regard cattle, and they place humans in that category. This one thing gives them away."

She paused to gaze respectfully at her Commander husband, who was staring thoughtfully at Monti and then back and forth between Mark and Janice before he firmly stated, "We must now proceed with caution and split-second timing. The Trilotew and secret United States forces will want to kill you two any way they can, or try to use you and your friends against each other."

"What about my Earth father, Ted?" Janice blurted out. "They are already controlling him, and he'll most likely end up as bait to catch us."

"We are monitoring him twenty-four hours a day," replied Tam-lure, "and we have been in touch with Henry, who is now ready to fully cooperate with our efforts to save your planet. First, we must get you both back into Earth society under camouflaged surveillance at all times. Mark, you are once again the official Galactic Alliance Ambassador to Earth and the President of the United States - he most certainly needs your help now more than ever before. Because of current treaty agreements, we could not prevent the Trilotew Ambassador from paying a recent visit to him in the Oval Office. We secretly monitored the meeting, but had no authorization at the time to directly intervene. However, now we do, and I can tell you the Trilotew were planning a horrifying future for your world and all humanity."

Una-mala graciously interjected, "It will be far more comfortable and expeditious to move ahead with *The Seres Agenda* from inside the command center. Boun-tama and Lean-tala will arrive in their Scout ship in a few minutes and they will join us."

She and Commander Tam-lure turned together and started to walk toward the command center. Monti looked at Mark and Janice and encouraged, "Everything will turn out alright because we now have a way to neutralize the Trilotew threat for all time. When the moment finally arrives, this will take place without war or destruction. After you," he motioned with a hand toward the command center.

Mark and Janice glanced at each other and headed toward Tam-lure and Una-mala, who were already nearing the command center. Monti paused to briefly reflect upon all the suffering he knew they had been through, and then smiled at their newfound courage as he stepped in place behind them. The co-base Commanders walked into the triangular opening at the base of the command center, and Mark, Janice, and Monti walked through it a few moments later.

A clear oval tubular shaft just inside the entrance whisked them upward utilizing an unseen anti-gravitational force. Their upright bodies quickly slowed to a stop as a transparent oval floor appeared beneath their feet in front of another triangular exit.

They gazed for a moment out through the opening to behold a vast chamber sixty-feet-high, a hundred-feet-wide, and a thousand-feet-long. The silvery metallic octagon framework high over their heads, and that surrounded them on all sides, held in place the large transparent octagon windows lining the entire circumference of the elongated room. They were now inside the top floor of the third section of the command building structure. Two other sections or six more floors were now below their feet. Hundreds of human and humanoid personnel from many other world cultures were busy around the room monitoring ten-feet-wide and four-feet-high projected view screens surrounding the tops of twenty-four rectangular paneled, octagon shaped control consoles. All the workstations were at waist level, a dozen feet apart, and extended in two parallel rows down the length of the entire oval chamber.

They walked through the triangular opening and headed along the middle of the oval floor toward one of the control consoles that had an open space facing them for entry and exit. Hundreds of lit controls covered the entire surface surrounding a middle-aged humanoid technician seated behind one of seven surrounding projected view screens. His high cheekbones, smooth pale-green skin, ivory-white eyes with red pupils, and long pastel violet hair that draped down behind his protruding long pointed ears to his shoulders, gave him a uniquely handsome appearance.

The two commanders, along with Mark, Janice, and Monti at each side of them, walked up and stopped at the console by the technician. He looked away from the screens and respectfully stood up to greet them. He placed his right hand over his heart and nodded to his superior Commanders, who returned the gesture.

"Greetings, Lieutenant Elon-tal," began Commander Tam-lure. "What's the status of the Trilotew war ships hiding above each pole of the planet?"

"Greetings, Commanders," replied the Lieutenant calmly. "They remain unmoved in their orbital positions. However, a dozen of their Demon Scout fighters left the two command carriers an hour ago. They took up positions in the upper atmosphere directly above the Arizona desert where one of the secret government underground bases is located. They're about to start something."

"Well done, Lieutenant," replied Tam-lure. "Order the fleet ships to approach and surround the planet camouflaged in a higher parallel frequency. Instruct the Captains to send out four squadrons of camouflaged Scout ships to surround their Demon Scout fighters and have them wait for my signal."

"Yes, Commander," replied Elon-tal, as he sat back down at the station and touched two lit controls that began to pulse.

"Things will speed up significantly from this point onward," stated Second Commander Una-mala looking at Mark and Janice. "The Trilotew know we are massing ships throughout your solar system because we wanted them to. However, they don't know we are about to directly intervene in Earth affairs on a massive planetary scale for the first time in galactic history."

Just then, Boun-tama and his wife Lean-tala walked up behind them and Boun-tama happily stated, "Well now, we're all back together again without Trilotew interference."

"Yes, and perhaps one day we'll actually get to have that casual meal and really good cup of tea we talked about before they rudely obliterated our cottage," commented Lean-tala smiling back at her husband. "Nevertheless, it's good to see we're all in one piece."

Pleased with his wife's upbeat disposition, Boun-tama threw an arm around her shoulder and hugged her close.

"Mon-tlan, why don't you fill them in," requested Tam-lure, "while Una-mala and I attend to those two Trilotew battle cruisers operating outside Earth's atmosphere."

"It would be my pleasure, Commander," replied Monti with a playful bow.

The two base Commanders walked away toward another background control station, and then Monti began to fill them in.

"The plan is simple at any rate. You, Mark, Boun-tama, and Lean-tala will be sent back to the teleportation room secretly shielded inside the cottage home."

Lean-tala continued, "Then I'll call the local police to let them know we found you, Mark, walking around in a daze with amnesia. They will come to the cottage right away, and you must then convince them to accept the cover story."

"It'll work," confidently stated Mark. "After all, I did almost get annihilated with their beam weapons, and to that end the story I tell them will be partially true."

"What about me," asked Janice, "I've been gone for three days, and may I ask exactly how I'm to convince anyone where I've been all that time is believable?"

"We've already worked that out with Henry," Lean-tala answered kindly. "Monti will take you to rendezvous with him at his estate in Santa Barbara. From there, he will have you contact your father. You will then let him know you rushed terrified away from his home to Henry's home three days ago because of the two odd threatening men you met there seeking his help to find Mark. Henry was able to secretly get a message to your father with Monti's help. He will know what you say is actually a coded message that lets him know you are safe and not in Trilotew hands. After that, Henry will arrange to get you both together. At that point, you will have to be more alert because the Trilotew will have access to you. But don't forget, my dear, you're now wearing a very special pendant that will shield you from any harm, and the Commander and his wife will be watching over you."

Janice was not smiling as she grabbed the pendant hanging from the gold chain around her neck, but it lit up startling her. She held it up to look at it more closely and a warm field of energy shot from it into her heart center. Her smile widened as an apprehensive feeling melted away.

"Oh-h," gasped Janice with pleasure. "That's most intriguing. Now I am truly ready to go forward with Mark to carry out *The Seres Agenda* mission."

"Well then, cousin, let's get on with this pretend marriage engagement so we can go back home to our own families."

"Oh, you said it, pretend future husband," shot back Janice, and they all laughed at the absurd situation.

"I think it's time we go to the teleportation room and get back to our cottage," remarked Boun-tama. "Janice, you will go with Monti. He will definitely get you places quickly and that's certain."

"If you will follow me," requested Monti, "I can have you back with Henry in about an hour."

Janice hugged Mark, and then she and Monti headed toward the triangular opening leading away from the command center. She turned and waved goodbye before they entered the opening. Then Boun-tama, Lean-tala, and Mark headed in the opposite direction toward another triangular exit on the opposite side of the control room.

Monti and Janice were soon aboard his Scout ship on the floor of the hidden cavernous Mt. Shasta base. He touched several small controls in succession, and then looked up to Janice standing beside him.

"I've just set up a link to Henry's phone. He's at his house in the Santa Barbara hills. We will hear it ring just as if I were using a phone to call him."

They could hear his phone ringing and Henry answered, "Hello, who's calling?"

"Henry, my good man, Monti and Janice are on the other end," replied Monti.

"Oh, thank God, you finally got back in touch with me. I have been pacing the floor for hours. Well, don't keep me waiting. What's our next move?"

"Hello, dear friend Henry," interjected Janice.

"Oh, dear Janice, I'm so glad to hear your voice. Is everything going as planned?"

"Yes, old friend, we're on our way to you now."

"Well that is relieving news," he shot back.

"Listen, Henry," continued Monti, "we will arrive at your estate one hour from now. After I drop off Janice, contact Ted and take her to meet him at the designated location, and Henry, thanks for your courage. We will need your help to move the plan forward."

"Those are certainly kind words indeed," replied Henry not expecting a compliment. "All I want is for this sinister covert nonsense to end for all time. I really like Earth, and I don't want to be eaten by one of those overgrown reptiles, if you know what I mean."

"Indeed I do, Henry," replied Monti chuckling. "Take care, and we'll make contact again when we arrive. Goodbye for now."

"See you soon, Henry," added Janice, and Monti touched the control to disconnect the line. They confidently glanced at each other, and then Monti placed his hands down into the guidance control hand impressions.

The ship began to glow pale-blue, emitting its usual gentle low-frequency hum, and it swiftly lifted straight up and out of the opening launch doors at the top of the cavern ceiling. It faded into transparency as it stopped to hover fifty feet above the extinct Mt. Shasta volcano in the crisp noon air. The blue light around the hull flashed brighter and the ship shot upward then vanished in the upper atmosphere in the twinkling of an eye.

# CHAPTER FIFTEEN

# MISGUIDED
# SECRET AGENTS

$\mathcal{M}$ark was soon standing with Boun-tama and Lean-tala at each side of him on a ten-feet-wide, circular transparent teleportation platform. The oval entry opening to the platform chamber across from them was part of a fifteen-feet-tall by twenty-five-feet-in-diameter transparent domed enclosure. Three semicircular, inch-thick clear quartz steps surrounding half the platform led down to the smooth ivory-textured floor. A lovely young female technician with pale blue skin and long silken black hair was standing by the left side of the first step behind a waist-high half-moon-shaped teleportation console covered with luminous controls.

The technician looked up and joyfully remarked, "Safe journey to you Captain Boun-tama, Captain Lean-tala, and Mark Santfield. Oh, pardon me, I meant to say Ambassador Shon-ral. The teleportation coordinates are locked onto the higher frequency coordinates of your shielded unit at the back of your cottage home."

"Thank you, Trel-una, we're ready. You may begin the teleportation cycle," instructed Boun-tama, smiling at her.

She touched a pastel-violet octagon spherical control and the chamber was instantly enveloped in golden-white light and the occupants faded away.

They rematerialized from another whirling light that appeared on an identical circular platform. Surrounding it was a twenty-feet-square room with satin-smooth white walls. They stepped off the platform and down another set of three quartz steps to stop beside an identical control console. However, no technician was operating it. The pastel-violet control in the center of the console shut off, and Boun-tama followed by Lean-tala and then Mark, headed for the wooden door at the back of the room.

Boun-tama stopped at the door, turned to Mark and stated, "The closet room on the other side of this chamber acts as a transformer to lower our molecular frequency down a little, to match the time rate frequency of your Earth's parallel dimension. Once we pass through this door you will feel a little light-headed at first but that will quickly dissipate. Okay then, let's go in."

He opened the door, revealing a simple rectangular closet on the other side with clothes hung on hangers from wooden poles lining both sides of the room. They entered inside, and Lean-tala closed the door behind them. The room instantly filled with a faint white luminance that faded away, and Mark shook his head.

"Whoa . . . that was strange!" he exclaimed. "I did feel very dizzy but only for a moment. How is it that if anyone else entered the closet they would not be able see the door on the other side, and then find this chamber?"

"Mark, look behind you," replied Lean-tala.

He turned to observe the door simply fade from view and try as he might, he could not feel or find anything other than a smooth plaster wall where the door had just been.

"Now that's the way to hide something," he remarked, pleased as he turned back around. "I suppose in time I will remember how it's done. It sure seems familiar like I should already know it."

"This room is shielded," remarked Boun-tama. "It's really part of the teleportation chamber designed to look like a simple closet. If a Trilotew or Special Forces team entered here none of their detection equipment would locate it. Once the frequency modulators inside these walls lower the molecular time rate of our bodies to a slightly slower time rate frequency, the room instantly transforms into a simple closet. It becomes a very real part of the cottage in this reality or parallel dimension on Earth. The room can only be reactivated by myself or Lean-tala after we enter, because it's programmed to respond only to our unique life-force-energy signatures."

"Oh, now I remember," stated Mark, suddenly elated. He let out a relieved sigh. "It's all coming back to me. Dear friends, lead the way. Let's move *The Seres Agenda* forward."

Boun-tama opened the outer closet door revealing the back of their country cottage living room and the front door on the opposite side of the room. They headed inside, Lean-tala walked over to a low glass-topped oval table, picked up the phone handset, and dialed 911.

A male voice responding on the other end and she calmly stated, "Hello Sheriff. This is Mrs. Mary Allison Crystal out on Starlight Lane." There was a pause and she answered, "That's right, the cottage home not far from town. I wish to report that my husband and I found a man walking on our property three days ago dehydrated and starving with amnesia." She paused to listen, and then answered, "No, no. He had no ID on him and he was unable to explain that. Although, he did say he thought his wallet might have fallen out of his back pocket when a lightning bolt knocked him backward through the air. He needed our immediate help to survive, and we took him in to hydrate and feed him. After he cleaned himself up, we gave him a set of my husband's clothes to wear. He was so exhausted after that he fell asleep on the couch. He finally woke up two days later with his memory apparently fully recovered. Then he told us his name is Mark Santfield, and he had quite a story to relate to us. That was yesterday." She paused to listen to the Sheriff, and then replied with pretend surprise, "Oh he has, for a week? Well that fits with what we know." Then she listened again and answered, "Well, he said he was standing near his tent when a bolt of lightning struck it, and the force of the charge threw him backward a dozen feet knocking him out cold. He believes he became conscious again two days after that with no memory of who he was or how he got there. He said he found a circle of black scorched ground but did not recall at the time his tent had been there. He also discovered the burnt stump of a tree not far from where the lightning threw him, and the entire giant tree lying on the ground beside it. After the bizarre disorienting circumstances, he remained on the mountain for two more days before he finally wandered down the mountainside and through the woods outside of town. When he walked dazed out of the trees onto our field three days ago, we discovered him and took him in otherwise he would not have survived. He may need further medical attention but appears unharmed as far as we can tell. Would you send a car over to pick him up?" She paused again, and then reaffirmed, "Right then, in about ten minutes. We will be waiting. Goodbye." She hung up the phone and stated, "They're on their way."

"Mark, you know what to tell them," encouraged Boun-tama. "From here on out you will be on your own. However, Lean-tala and I will also carefully monitor you from our hidden hangar bay in the field, and several invisibly camouflaged Scout ships will also constantly track your movements. Oh, and don't forget about that special pendant you're wearing. Keep it hidden under your shirt and no harm will come to you."

Mark tucked the gold-chained amulet down inside his shirt, took a breath, smiling, and remarked, "You know, Lean-tala, if you don't mind, this time I would actually like to have a really good cup of tea before some other unexpected bizarre thing happens."

"Coming right up, Mr. Ambassador," she gladly stated and headed into the kitchen to prepare the tea.

"I wouldn't be surprised if more than the local police show up here," cautioned Boun-tama. "I'd better contact the ships scheduled to monitor your movements to alert them to watch over this property for the next hour."

He touched the special gold hieroglyphic pin symbol on his lapel and it flashed three times. Boun-tama smiled at Mark and faded from view, just as his wife came back into the living room holding a tray with a steaming teapot, a milk dispenser, three cups, and several forms of sweeteners.

"Now where did Boun-tama go to?" she asked.

"As a precaution, he just beamed up to one of the Scout support ships to get them ready in case more than just the local police arrive here."

"A wise move. My husband always looking ahead has saved our lives many times." She started to pour the tea into a cup for Mark and added, "We've learned to always expect the unexpected in our dealings with the Trilotew and their minions. Other arrangements have also been made to provide security after the police take you away for questioning."

Mark sat down beside her on the comfortable white couch and started to drink his tea when they heard three hard knocks on the front door. Lean-tala got up and opened the door. A middle-aged Sheriff and much younger Deputy were standing in the doorway.

"Hello, Mrs. Crystal. I'm Sheriff Pat Donyfield, the one you talked with on the phone, and this is Deputy Alec Johansson."

She invited them in, and they very curiously gazed at Mark sitting on the couch.

"Is he really alright?" inquired the Sheriff. "We'll need to question him. Do you think he's up for it?"

"Officers, I assure you I'm fit as a fiddle and ready for your questions. I seem to be no worse for the wear, but a local hospital will no doubt want to run some tests to be sure. Ask me anything you like and I'll tell you what happened."

They approached Mark and the Deputy lifted up a note pad he had in his hand, pulled out the pen stuck into the spiral binding, and placed the point on the paper. The Sheriff began a long list of questions starting with what happened to Mark after the lightning struck his tent.

Ten minutes later, Boun-tama came walking up the steps to the porch and entered the house. The Sheriff and the Deputy now seated in chairs to each side of Mark stood up, and Sheriff Donyfield asked, "I presume you're Mr. Crystal?"

"Yes Sheriff, I'm Dan Crystal." After the Sheriff introduced himself and the Deputy, they shook hands and Boun-tama continued, "I was just out walking around the circumference of our field to relax from all that's happened when I saw your squad car arrive, and I hurried over. I'm certainly glad you're here." He gave Mark a supportive smile and asked, "Well Mark, do you feel ready to get back to your normal life again?"

"Indeed I do, Mr. Crystal, and I thank you and Mrs. Crystal again for all your kind hospitality. I wouldn't have survived without you two."

"It's alright, Mr. Santfield," stated the Sheriff, "we can continue the inquiry back at the station."

He nodded toward the Sheriff and Deputy, and then got up to follow them out the front door onto the porch. Boun-tama and Lean-tala followed right behind him. They stopped by the squad car, and just as Mark was hugging his hosts two unmarked gray four-door sport utility vehicles appeared speeding up the dirt road leading to the cottage. They came to an abrupt sliding stop in the dirt, sending clouds of dust into the air. Two well-dressed men wearing dark-blue suits and shades jumped out of each car and quickly surrounded Mark at gunpoint. One immediately grabbed one of Mark's hands, then the other one, and roughly handcuffed them behind his back.

As the suspicious Sheriff and Deputy began to draw their own guns, one of the agents pointed his magnum at the Sheriff's head and hotly demanded, "Back off. He's now under federal jurisdiction." Then he reached into his suit coat with his other hand, pulled out a black wallet and flipped it open, held up his National Security Agency identification card in the Sheriff's face and ordered, "He's wanted for questioning regarding a very serious national security matter. He must come with us now."

"But we need to get him to a hospital to have him checked to see if the lightning strike caused any harm," shot back Sheriff Donyfield.

"That won't be necessary Sheriff. We will take him to a medical facility where he will receive the best medical care available. We can question him there, and release him after we are satisfied. Now please step aside and let us do our jobs."

The Sheriff threw up his hands.

"Go ahead and take him. He would have wound up in our local hospital at any rate, and I'm quite certain the press would have a field day with him there. At least this way he may get some rest."

The agent that revealed his NSA identification turned and firmly gripped Mark's upper arm. Then he began to rudely pull him toward the closest SUV. The other three Agents followed right behind them in a triangular position with their guns drawn pointed at the back of Mark's head.

Boun-tama and Lean-tala were now quietly watching the whole episode from the bottom steps leading up to the cottage. Boun-tama discreetly reached up and tapped the strange gold pin on his lapel. It blinked once.

The Agent gripping Mark's arm let go and grabbed the car door handle, threw open the door, and then started to rudely shove Mark's head down to force him into the back seat. Just then, three Galactic Alliance Scout ships darted into view and stopped to hover discreetly fifty-feet directly overhead. Faint auras of blue light surrounded their silver-gray metallic hulls were emitting a low frequency humming sound. The Agent holding Mark's arm shoved the gun in his other hand back into the shoulder holster inside his suit coat. Then he reached into an inner pocket and pulled out an elongated transparent handgun. The other Agents began firing their guns at the ships, but the bullets just ricocheted off the blue energy shields surrounding them. The Agent who had held Mark's arm pointed his alien weapon up at the lead ship with both hands and slowly squeezed the trigger. The lead ship at the front of their triangular formation flashed a brilliant golden-white energy beam from the front edge of the hull down over all four Agents, instantly sending them away in a whirling teleportation light. A moment later, much more powerful pulsating green beams sent from all three ships intersected to form one thicker beam that struck both sport utility vehicles. They literally melted into oblivion in an instant, accompanied by a quickly dissipating hissing and drafts of fiery vapor. Brighter blue light pulsed from the hulls of the three ships and they darted away in a blur of light. Mark's handcuffs mysteriously uncoupled themselves from his wrists and dropped to the ground.

The Sheriff and Deputy were now both speechless and petrified, and they unconsciously began to draw their guns without really knowing where to point them. Boun-tama and Lean-tala hurried over to Mark, just as two more unmarked gray four-door sport utility vehicles raced into view coming down the dirt road. They too slammed on their brakes bringing the cars to a screeching halt that threw more clouds of dust into the air. Four more agents wearing suits and dark sunglasses jumped out of the vehicles, but they cautiously began walking toward Mark without drawing weapons.

"Mark, it's alright!" shouted Lean-tala. "We requested these men from the NSA for added protection to escort you from here with the local peace officers. Those other men were probably from a hidden faction of the NSA controlled by the Trilotew. They must have monitored my phone call and raced here first."

Boun-tama looked over at the Sheriff and Deputy. Then he touched the gold pin on his lapel two times and it blinked twice. The terror on the faces of both peace officers simply melted away. Without realizing why, they slowly put their guns back into their holsters, shook their heads as if they were coming out of a trance, and simply relaxed.

One of the four benevolent Agents approached the peace officers and said sincerely, "Thank you Sheriff, and you Deputy, for your assistance with holding Mr. Santfield here until we arrived. The United States government will take over from here."

He then vigorously shook hands with both peace officers, who now appeared quite pleased with themselves, for they no longer had any memory of the alien spacecraft or the four previous malevolent Agents and their cars. They nodded a farewell to Mark, Boun-tama, and Lean-tala, got back into their squad car, and slowly drove away.

"What happened to the other four Trilotew controlled NSA Agents?" asked Mark, turning toward Boun-tama.

"Oh, don't worry about them. They were not harmed, but they won't be getting their two vehicles back," replied Boun-tama with a mischievous grin. "Those four misguided men are being taken to the flagship to undergo deprogramming that will remove all Trilotew subconscious brainwashing. After that is completed, they will return to continue as NSA Agents who will actually begin to protect the United States as new associates of the Galactic Alliance. They will want to after they find out just how deeply duped they have been.

Each of the other three benevolent NSA Agents approached Mark and shook his hand. Then, the lead agent gave him a friendly smile and said, "Mr. Santfield, I'm Special Agent Jacobson. If you are willing, we will safely escort you to an undisclosed hospital location where you will only undergo a simple pretend debriefing and medical inspection for the sake of the news media. In addition, our secret faction of the NSA is aware you are the true Galactic Alliance Ambassador to our planet, and we are very grateful you finally arrived. You can provide your cover story to the press concerning your week-long disappearance at the hospital, and you will receive maximum protection from your people and from us. Will that do for now?"

"Indeed it will, Agent Jacobson," replied Mark, very pleased. "I am grateful for your help. Lead the way."

Mark turned and hugged Boun-tama and Lean-tala, gave them a grateful smile, and then climbed into the back seat of the closest sport utility vehicle. Both cars slowly drove away.

Lean-tala affectionately smiled at her husband, took his hand and said, "I've been wondering how Monti and Janice are getting on with her part of the mission."

"I've been wondering the same thing," replied Boun-tama. "Let's get to the hangar bay and monitor things from there. Come on, I'll race you."

He shot off running out into the field and she darted after him giggling. They both stopped beside each other a third of the way out in the tall brown grass and she touched an invisible spot chest-high in the air in front of her. The triangular opening to the hangar silently slid open, and he took her hand as they walked inside. The triangular door silently slid closed behind them and vanished, leaving behind the now empty circular five-acre field. The tops of the tall brown grass slightly bent over by the gentle summer breeze, pointed toward the snow-crowned mountain range that towered above the evergreen forest trees.

# CHAPTER SIXTEEN

# THE
# HIDDEN GOVERNMENT
# AWAKENS

*M*onti touched a control, and the projected view screen appeared above the console. A tiny image in the center of the surrounding blank screen zoomed forward to reveal a clear overview of Henry Throckmorton's mansion estate in Santa Barbara from a hundred feet in the air.

"Well Mon-tlan, it'll be interesting to see how Henry changed now that he knows about us from other worlds," remarked Janice.

Monti touched another control and said through the transceiver, "Henry, this is Monti. Please respond."

A moment passed, and Henry's voice replied back through the transceiver, "Oh thank God, Monti. I have been so worried. Is everyone all right? Is Janice with you?"

"Not to worry, Henry," replied Monti smiling. "She is here standing beside me aboard my ship. It's actually hovering above your mansion as we speak, but you won't be able to see it yet."

Henry was nervously pacing back and forth on the solid oak entryway floor inside his mansion by the double front doors. He was holding a transceiver communicator near his ear disguised as a normal Timex watch strapped around his wrist. A scintillating rainbow of sunlight was coming through the twin full-body-length stained glass windows. They were set within the surrounding twin ornately carved solid oak doorframe. Depicted in the glass were two elegant white swans standing facing each other in a still water river eddy by a riverbank underneath the overhanging branches of a weeping willow tree.

"If you come outside," continued Monti's muted voice through the wristwatch communicator, "things will become quite clear to you in just a few moments."

Henry held the transceiver watch near his mouth and excitedly replied, "I'm on my way out the front door right now."

Aboard the ship, Monti and Janice could hear the opening and slamming of the mansion's front door through Henry's transceiver, and Monti touched several other illumined controls. From the changing perspective of the mansion on the view screen, Janice could see the ship was now slowly moving in a long downward arc toward the rectangular acre of well-manicured green grass lawn in front of Henry's mansion estate. Beautiful multicolored rose gardens lined both sides of the long driveway that ran through the center of the grounds. As the ship touched down on the grass on the left side of the driveway, she could see it was now level with the rectangular two-story Roman style mansion another fifty feet further away. Twin green granite columns supported the long curved-rectangular glass roof of the entry walkway that led to the twin stained glass front oak doors. Henry was jogging down the six wide blue granite steps leading away from the long entryway. He continued across the circular driveway and walked a short way on the grass then stopped to speak into the wrist communicator again.

They could hear him ask a little breathlessly through the transceiver, "When will you arrive? I'm outside waiting at the edge of the grass."

To Janice, Monti's mischievous smile was unmistakable as he touched a small blue spherical control.

Henry's mouth dropped open as he watched the sleek silver-gray disc shaped Scout ship, which was surrounded by a thin blue aura emitting a low hum, slowly materialize into full visibility. It had landed only a dozen feet further out in the grass from where he stood.

"Is that soon enough for you, Henry?" he heard Monti's cheerful voice ask through his wristwatch transceiver.

"Fantastic!" shouted Henry through the device. "That was just fantastic, and welcome to my home."

He impatiently watched as the oval door in the side of the ship appeared and the ramp slid out below it to the ground. Monti and Janice appeared in the opening and headed down the ramp to the grass. Monti touched a spot on the hull beside the upper ramp, and the ship faded from sight. As they started to walk toward him, Henry was already expressing childlike wonder as he darted off running to greet them.

Monti smiled and respectfully nodded at the excited attorney with his right palm held over his heart, just as Henry stopped in his tracks a few feet away to reflect on the gesture, and then he quickly mimicked the cordial salute. He excitedly hugged Janice with his right arm and clasped forearms with Monti with his other arm.

"I'm so relieved to see you two here," he stated, a little out of breath.

"Dear Henry," began Janice smiling back at him, "I could always rely on you to calm me down when my father remained stubbornly aloof to answer my questions about his strange visitors and odd business dealings."

Henry appeared deeply worried as he looked away and concurred, "He always remained tight lipped even with me about any association he had with the hidden second government or their devilish Trilotew sponsors. All those years you were growing up I was never certain about what I suspected, but now I know how dangerously ensnared he's become in their web of deceit." He shook his head, and then looked back at Monti and remarked, "I don't know if you can get him free from all this now. Those two Trilotew agents watch over him like a pair of eagles watch over a mouse they can't wait to grasp and devour."

"I think you and Janice should leave that to us in the Galactic Alliance for now," Monti encouraged. "He is being discreetly monitored, and we will not let anything happen to him. I must leave you now so that I can continue to do my part to carry out this mission. Janice, go with Henry back to his house and phone your father to let him know you are safe. That will be his cue to meet you at the designated time and neutral location right after Henry drops you off there. For now, farewell to you both."

He smiled and nodded with his right palm held over his heart again, and then began to walk back toward the ship.

Janice and Henry gazed into each other's eyes, and then Henry boldly stated, "Let's get this done so we can send those Trilotew monsters off planet Earth for good."

"Now you're talking," she replied with equal zeal, and they headed at a hurried clip back toward his house.

They stopped at the top of the granite steps just under the clear canopy walkway to turn around and watch Monti place his right palm on a waist-high spot in the air, and the ship reappeared. He walked up inside it and the ramp withdrew. The vertical oval door closed and the seam vanished. The hull lit up with a familiar transparent pale blue aura and the sleek Scout craft lifted off the ground. Then it shot straight up sixty feet and stopped to hover as it faded back into invisibility. Janice and Henry eagerly glanced at each other and hurried along the long entry walkway to enter the large house.

Henry walked over to the phone sitting on the expensive looking glass-topped cherry wood living room table, picked up the handset, and handed it to Janice.

She quickly dialed a number and listened for an answer, then stated relieved, "Daddy, it's me and I'm alright."

"Thank God," replied Ted in a muted voice. He waited to hear her anticipated message.

"I stayed away from you for the last three days at Henry's home because of those two strange men you associate with that sent chills down my spine the moment I saw them. I was worried about Mark and had no one else I could trust. The situation is better now. I'll be seeing you soon."

"Understood dear daughter, I love you," she heard him reply on the other end a little choked-up. With tears rolling down his cheeks that she couldn't see, he added, "I don't know what I'd have done if I lost you."

"I love you too, Daddy. Goodbye for now," she replied, and hung up the phone.

"We better get on the move," stated Henry. "I will drop you off at the Griffith Observatory on the Hollywood hilltop overlooking Los Angeles in just under—" he glanced down at his wristwatch then continued, "—two hours. That should give us plenty of time if we leave now."

They headed across the large living room toward the six-car garage attached to the left side of the ten-thousand-square-feet mansion.

Ted placed the phone receiver in the cradle on his desk. Then he took in a deep relieving breath and wiped tears from his eyes and cheeks. He started to walk toward the open doorway leading out of his office study, but a bright flash of scintillating light coming from behind him raised the hair on the back of his head and he turned around. Standing before him were the same two menacing Trilotew overseers, Gorsapis and Zushsmat, who had tried to kill his daughter just one week earlier when she came to see him. Both Trilotew were expressing a subtle growling sneer at him. The taller one pulled a three-inch round black disc device from an inside pocket in his brown leather uniform. Glowering with sadistic glee, he held it up in one hand in front of Ted's face. He reached up with the long sharp-nailed index finger of his other hand and depressed one of the twelve buttons arranged in a circular pattern near the outer circumference of the top surface of the disc.

Ted instantly discovered that he was unable to move. The Trilotew inquisitor darted his long, forked tongue out of his mouth between his sharp fanged teeth and slowly licked the side of Ted's face. Ted grimaced with revulsion from the stench of reptilian breath. The shorter Trilotew stood close to Ted, stuck his long, forked tongue into Ted's left ear, and then licked the back of his neck. "Now, human, you will tell us who just called and what was said," demanded the taller Trilotew senior officer Gorsapis with obvious revulsion of the human he had pretended to respect for so many prior years.

Ted was spellbound by the device, but he was also much stronger willed than either Trilotew suspected. He struggled to disclose only a partial truth to them, nervously stuttering, "It . . . it . . . w-was Henry, my General Business Counsel. He . . .he said my daughter went to see him three days ago because she was terrified after she saw both of you the last time she came here. Where else could she go and who could she trust after she realized I was somehow covertly involved with both of you? It was you two that compelled her to seek Henry's help instead of mine to locate Mark."

"Yes-s-s," hissed Gorsapis, "she should be frightened of us-s-s-s. We would have had our way with her by now if she was not your daughter, and that nosy Galactic Alliance spy had not interfered. Now, what else will you tell Zushsmat and I, human?" he asked, expressing great disgust at the human he had mistakenly thought was completely under his control.

Ted pretended to hesitate, and both Trilotew hissed in his face until he finally added, "She will visit with me here soon, Gorsapis, after she hears any news concerning Mark."

"Very well," continued the drooling Trilotew interrogator. "After we leave here, order Henry to tell you anything he hears or discovers about Mark Santfield's location. You will then report what you find out to us immediately. Is that understood?"

"Yes, yes I understand," Ted replied nervously.

Gorsapis sneered at Ted one last time, and then depressed another button on the disc device held in his hand. Ted instantly discovered he was free from the effect and he rubbed the back of his aching neck.

"Remember this day," Gorsapis added angrily as he touched the center of the disc.

A moment passed, and they both vanished in the bright whirling teleportation light. Ted felt drained as he staggered up against his desk. He reached into his sport coat jacket and pulled out a handkerchief then nervously wiped the sweat from his brow with a shaking hand. He shook his head to clear his mind, and then angrily grimaced renewed determination as he turned and hurried out of his study. He raced down the right staircase and headed across the entryway toward the ten-car garage.

When Henry and Janice finally arrived in his expensive late model Mercedes Benz four-door sedan at the Griffith Observatory public parking area, he drove the car to the front of the lot and parked it near the entrance walkway and shut off the engine. It happened to be a slow day and only seven other parked cars were in the lot. Henry took her left hand and gave it a squeeze.

"Are you sure about this?" he asked, a little nervous.

"Dear friend Henry," she fondly began, "thank you for your genuine concern for my welfare. I always knew I could trust you. Don't worry about me. I'll be fine. Besides, I have a special protection those two Trilotew reptilians spying on my father know nothing about."

"Well then, my dear, take special care to watch out for those two because they can disguise themselves as humans, and they are deadly dangerous. If you need me for anything, just call my cell phone."

She fondly smiled at him again, squeezed his hand, opened the door then stepped out of the car. Henry waved at her as he drove away, and she watched his car until it disappeared further down the road beyond the parking lot. A few moments later, she noticed her father's gold Rolls Royce convertible turning into the parking lot. He drove the big vehicle up beside her, placed it in park with the motor still running, and jumped out to throw his arms around her.

"Janice dear, I'm so glad you're safe."

"Well maybe now we can start to be honest with each other about many things," she replied. "I know about the hidden government and the Trilotew threat. What on Earth were you and your associates thinking? Why did you let those monsters begin to control this world?"

Ted's eyes were now downcast. His saddened expression of guilt and shame was unmistakable, and her compassionate nature took over.

"Father, do you know who I really am?" she quietly asked.

He gave no answer as he continued staring sadly at the ground.

"Father, I know your hidden secret government may have started down a covert road more than sixty years ago for what appeared to be good reasons, but you were all duped. The price this planet may pay, just so you and your greedy members could get your hands on off-world technology none of you are morally or spiritually ready to cope with, may result in the destruction of the entire world. The Trilotew will betray and kill you all in the end. They would then use up this planet's resources, while they have an all-you-can-eat human buffet."

"Yes, dear daughter, I know who you really are," he sadly began, lifting his head. "An hour after those two vicious Trilotew overseers left my house the other day, Henry and Monti transported to my location in the backyard beside the pool. I was startled but Henry assured me they were there to try to get me out of the mess I was in for cooperating with the Trilotew. Then a moment later Monti transported us aboard his ship that was invisibly hovering above the house. There I learned the truth about the Trilotew threat to Earth, and now I understand the extent of the damage many people and their families suffered because we secretly signed a treaty with them. The Trilotew took advantage of our predecessor's lust for power by flattering their huge egos. Those of us that comprise the secret government today inherited our positions from them, and for that I am now truly sorry."

Janice reached up and lovingly lifted his chin a little higher so his sad eyes could meet her loving gaze.

Then she hugged him, and rested her head on his shoulder and said, "Oh, my dear father, you are the only father I've known most of my life until recently, and you have taken very good care of me." She pulled away to look at him directly and continued, "My true home is located on another planet and I have a family waiting there for my return. Remember, you are my Earth father. Know that I will always love you. Now help us to correct this great tragedy before it's too late for all the people of Earth."

"What happened to my own little girl so long ago?" he sadly inquired.

"She was forced from this body by the Trilotew who captured me when I secretly went out among the Earth populous. They also forced me from my own adult body, suppressed the memories of all I had been, and then projected the memories of your little girl into my subconscious mind, along with their own hidden terrorizing implants. After that, they forced me into this body before they returned me unconscious within it to you and mother that same day. After that, they destroyed my adult extraterrestrial human body, and your daughter's true essence or Spirit would have moved on to a higher reality. Father, their purpose for this was to work through my unconscious mind to influence you. They also did this on a larger scale to infiltrate your inner government members after they gained their confidence. They provided only a secret limited exchange of their less advanced off-world technology for the right to experiment on randomly selected members of Earth's populous they claimed would not be harmed. They have actually conducted many damaging genetic experiments on many human beings they had other extraterrestrial races under their control abduct for them. Some they returned, but many others taken off the planet against their will were likely killed or devoured alive. A few others used as controlled slaves may still be alive.

"To be fair, your reluctant predecessors would have suspected something was wrong with the treaty offer, but the Trilotew blackmailed them into signing it. They inferred it would give them an advantage over other governments like the former Soviet Union during the Cold War. However, what your predecessors did not know was the Trilotew were also already in Moscow blackmailing them with the very same offer at the same time. After signing the secret treaty, the Trilotew started to implement a direct takeover of certain members inside your secret government military industrial complex. They gained control of a few others like yourself through the subtle manipulation of your subconscious minds with devices they carry. You, dear father, were a stronger individual than they thought, because you recently began to suspect something was wrong. Now that you know the truth we need your help to get the other remaining members out of this trap before it's too late."

For the first time he looked at her to see who she really was, and his eyes gradually brightened with the realization of what he must do next.

"Janice, I've got an idea. It's dangerous and a long shot, but if your friends are willing to help maybe we can rescue the situation in time. We must get back to my house as soon as possible. From there I can take you directly to one of our secret industrial military complex cities we have underground in the Arizona desert. With the added protection of your off-world benevolent friends, we must awaken the secret government members from this trap. Will you come with me?"

"Yes, of course I'll come with you. Let's get going," she confidently replied, and they jumped into the Rolls Royce and drove away from the famous Griffith Observatory parking lot.

In little over an hour they entered the open garage at Ted's sequestered house off Mulholland Drive high above Beverly Hills, California. They hurried up the twin staircase along the right side of the angel fountain and entered his office study.

"Janice, I never told you about this before because I've sworn an oath to my own organization and the Trilotew to keep it secret. I have a Trilotew teleportation device hidden behind the wall of my study. I plan to teleport us directly to the underground location where an annual worldwide meeting of some of our members is about to take place. They have me scheduled to update them there. That will be a perfect time for you to reveal the elements of the Trilotew betrayal to them. We can only attempt this if your Galactic Alliance friends will help. Otherwise, we would be foolish to show up together. Trilotew agents will also be present, and our lives will be in jeopardy."

She rolled her eyes with a relieved sigh and remarked, "Well that explains how you were able to show up here with those sadistic reptilian agents when you were supposed to be in England. It also explains many other unanswered questions I've had about you all my life."

She reached up and touched the pendant hidden under her blouse, and it emitted a quick flash of gold light.

"What was that?" asked Ted, noticing the brief glow.

"It was confirmation we have help, and that we are to proceed. Now, let's get there and get this done."

Ted smiled proudly at the self-assured woman standing before him and placed his hands upon her shoulders and tenderly kissed her forehead. They walked around his desk and stopped in front of the bookcase shelves on the back wall. He started to reach for a particular book but froze with fear of the familiar flash of golden-white light behind them. He spun around to confront Gorsapis and Zushsmat. They finished materializing in their tall, non-camouflaged Trilotew bodies, holding two elongated triangular handgun weapons pointed at them. Gorsapis sadistically sneered, and they both pulled the triggers. The two-inch-thick green beams ricocheted off a thin golden energy shield that instantly appeared emanating from the glowing pendant under Janice's white blouse, and both beams struck the Trilotew agents in the chest. The expressions of terror and shock on their faces lasted but a second as their bodies disintegrated into vanishing white dust, along with their fading echoing screams. The glowing energy emanating from the pendant shut off, and the protective energy shield surrounding them vanished.

"Oh my God," gasped Ted. "That was too close. We could have been killed."

"And we would have been if it hadn't been for the protective pendant I'm wearing," she stated in grateful recollection. "It was Commander Jon-tral and Sun-deema, his Second in Command wife from the Galactic Alliance flagship, who gave me the gift before I was returned to Earth."

"Well now, that gives me more confidence to go forward with this plan. But what happened to those two monsters?"

"They were destroyed by their actions toward us. The new Ray coming from the pendant reflected their exact intent and weapons back upon them. It could have simply spared their lives and neutralized their weapons. However, in their case in particular maybe it decided to remove their bodies, and then send them into another incarnation to experience what it's like to be on the other side of their evil natures."

"You mean you're telling me those two monsters are now permanently removed from ever intimidating me again?" he asked.

"Yes Father, they are," she solemnly replied. "But it wouldn't have been my choice to kill their bodies. That decision was way out of my hands."

Ted shook his head and shoulders to throw off the emotionally frightening experience. Then he reached toward the bookcase and grabbed a book that was partially sticking out between two others. A moment later, the appearance of a wall lined with bookshelves vanished revealing a short hallway leading to a strange smooth blue-metal door with no handles. They walked up to the door and Ted placed his right palm with spread fingers on the center of the door and removed it, leaving behind his luminous hand impression on its surface, which faded as the door silently slid open inside the left wall. The fifteen-feet-in-diameter dome shaped room beyond the opening was made of polished silver metal. Different colored illumined semispherical controls covered the top of a waist-high semicircular control console centered in the room. Ted indicated to Janice to walk around the console and stand on the six-feet-wide circular platform. As she stepped up onto it, Ted touched the largest semispherical control centered on the console surface and it lit up blinking. Then he hurried around the console and stepped onto the circular platform next to her. The control stopped blinking and brightened, and they both dematerialized into an upward whirling golden-white light that swiftly faded away.

They rematerialized inside another whirling light standing on an identical circular platform next to another control console. They stepped off the platform, down three steps, and onto the smooth milky-white quartz-rich granite floor. Janice stopped to look around; amazed at what she thought must be a huge hangar bay the size of an enclosed football field. A few feet to their left was another three steps leading up to a longer platform. A six-feet-in-diameter transparent tube with a rounded end filled with radiant turquoise-blue light began a dozen feet from the far end of the platform. It continued into the distance along the smooth rock floor another five-hundred-feet before it entered a round opening in the center of the back wall of the huge hangar bay.

Fifty feet directly overhead were two massive closed polished silver metal doors, centered on the long curved rectangular solid rock cavern ceiling. Bright halogen lights lining both sides of the metal doors extended in six parallel rows across the entire ceiling to illuminate the interior of the hangar bay. The light was also curiously reflecting off the dark-gray metal surfaces of four Trilotew triangular Demon Scout ships landed just twenty-five-feet further away from where they were standing.

"Be cautious about what you say here, Janice. We're being met," stated Ted, and he looked toward the far end of the cavern along the length of the luminous blue tube.

She began to hear a soft low humming that was gradually growing louder. She looked to see a very sleek double-ended transport vehicle (tapered to a point on each end like a double terminated gem) speeding inside the tube toward them out of a round opening in the bottom center of the far wall. Both pointed ends of the vehicle were rapidly changing color from red, to blue, and to green every few seconds. It appeared to be about twelve-feet-long as it sped down the length of the tube and dramatically slowed revealing two human occupants riding inside. Janice surmised that some type of very advanced anti-gravity or gravity suspension propulsion must have been powering the transport vehicle. She could now see it had traveled down its entire length suspended inside the radiant blue light of the tube without touching the inner circumference of the tube's wall. It came to an abrupt stop at the end of the tube, and the blue light illuminating the tube's interior vanished. The rounded tube end silently swung open upward, and the double-terminated vehicle slowly moved forward until its entire length was alongside the platform. Janice could now clearly see the human passengers were actually two U.S. Air Force military police sitting in the two front seats under the transparent teardrop-shaped canopy. The canopy opened upward from the side of the car facing them, and the two MPs jumped out and stood at attention.

Ted grabbed his daughter's hand and they briskly walked up the three steps to the blue-granite platform then along its length to the waiting car and the two MPs.

"Good evening, Mr. Chairman," stated the taller MP, and both men formally saluted Ted in military fashion.

Ted saluted them back and replied, "Thanks for your prompt arrival Lieutenant Thomas, and you too, Sergeant Walker."

"We've been expecting you for over an hour," continued the Lieutenant. "We came as soon as we detected your teleportation arrival, but our orders were to pick up you only."

"Gentlemen, this is my daughter Janice. She has no security clearance, but I will personally vouch for her this time because she just brought to my attention important critical information the Council must know about at once."

She gave both MPs a courteous smile, but artfully hid her mystified curiosity as she whispered into her father's right ear, "Mr. Chairman? Chairman of what, may I ask?"

"It's a long story, Janice dear," he replied softly, "but here I'm the Chairman of the second hidden government that runs this planet in some ways that direct the President of the United States to make certain decisions, and take certain actions, apart from his usual duties. However, do not be concerned with that now. We have far more important critical matters to address at this time."

"Yes, of course you are right, Mr. Chairman," she acknowledged respectfully, for the sake of the two service members looking on in wonder of what they were discussing.

"Has the Council started the session?" inquired Ted.

"They are now all gathered together awaiting your arrival."

"Okay Lieutenant, we're ready to be taken directly to the central Council chamber. My daughter and I will address the members as soon as we arrive."

The Lieutenant grabbed a walkie-talkie clipped on the side of his belt, lifted it to his lips and said, "This is Lieutenant Thomas. The Chairman and his daughter have arrived. Please have your security people waiting at the lobby elevator to escort them inside the main Council chambers. We should arrive there in a few minutes."

"Acknowledged," replied a female voice.

The Lieutenant placed the communicator back on his belt, and both MPs saluted the Chairman. They assisted Ted and Janice to step into the back of the hovering transport car and securely strapped them into the two leather-lined seats. The MPs then jumped into the front seats and buckled up. The canopy closed and sealed them in with a swift sucking sound, and the transport car slowly moved back inside the open tube. The rounded tube end swung down and closed with a swift air-removing *s-s-sip,* and the entire inside length of the tube instantly lit up with the same turquoise-blue luminescence. The car suddenly shot away in a blur at tremendous speed to vanish back inside the round tunnel opening at the far end of the hangar.

A short time later, the transport car came out of another round opening already slowing on approach to another long blue rectangular granite platform. It also had three wide steps leading from it down to a smaller platform level. As the car came to a stop, the blue radiance within the tube turned off and the rounded tube end opened upward. The MPs stood up as the teardrop shaped canopy swung open, and they both hopped out to assist Ted and Janice step out of the car onto the platform landing. The MPs then stepped behind Ted and his daughter as they headed down the few steps to the smaller platform and up a few more steps to a much larger blue granite platform. A ten-feet-high rectangular structure that looked like an elevator made of transparent walls with opened doors was at the center of the platform floor a few feet further away. They walked over to it and headed inside. The doors closed, and a blue luminance began to emanate from underneath it as it silently lifted up several inches above the floor. Then it silently moved smoothly sideways a dozen feet towards the end of the platform. It slowed and came to a stop inside a rectangular opening below an enclosed clear rectangular elevator shaft that continued twenty feet up through the curved rectangular green granite ceiling. The elevator swiftly sped up the shaft and vanished beyond the ceiling.

The elevator slowed to a stop at the top of the shaft several floors above the hangar bay and transport tube station. Before exiting the elevator, Janice could see they were about to enter a short hallway with polished green granite floors. Her first impression was that it looked very much like the elevator hallway of a modern hotel. As they walked out of the elevator, she noticed the hallway actually lead to a main lobby area just as two men wearing expensive Italian suits walked up to them and nodded, and the MPs walked away.

"Welcome, Mr. Chairman," stated the taller man. "I was instructed to meet you here and take you directly to the central Council chamber, but no one else has been cleared to come here with you."

Both men dubiously eyed Janice because her presence there was certainly a breach of protocol. Janice sternly stared back at both men with her hands defiantly on her hips, and the men took a cautious step backward.

"You have questioned her presence here and both of you are precisely following correct protocols, but there is no need for concern. That was well done. I will put in a good word for each of you. This is my daughter, Janice. I brought her here to speak directly to the entire World Council to deliver new critical information for our survival. Now, please lead us to the main Council chamber."

The two men nodded compliance to the Chairman's wishes, and then headed into an adjacent carpeted hallway. They had not gone far when they came upon a set of large golden doors. Centered on both doors was the symbol of a radiant eye over a white alabaster pyramid. To Janice it looked very similar to the symbol that is on the back of a one-dollar bill. The taller man opened the doors and they walked inside. The eyes of a hundred men dressed in expensive suits varying in age from thirty-five to eighty years old turned to stare unsmiling at Ted and Janice. Angry scowls immediately appeared on their faces for her presence among them. Ted protectively took her hand, and they boldly began to walk together down the lush blue-green carpeted aisle between the austere men. He remained confident staring straight ahead while he walked up the three steps that led to a podium centered on a small stage area. Then he turned around with Janice at his side to face the secret government Councilmen. They were all sitting in lush brown leather chairs as he began to address them in a serious somber tone through the flexible microphone attached to the top of the podium.

"Fellow Council members, and any Trilotew associates that may be present, I came here today to inform you of some very critical information that has come to my attention from my daughter Janice. I brought her here without going through normal security clearance procedures due to the very stark nature of what I just learned. I will now give the floor to her, and she will enlighten you so that each one of you can make new constructive choices that will alter the direction we've set for the future of this planet."

The men now appeared quite nervous as they restlessly stirred in their chairs not quite knowing what to make of Ted's comments. Several tall men in the back seats suddenly jumped to their feet, just as Janice approached the podium to speak into the microphone. One of them pulled out a small device from his suit pocket hidden in his palm and put it to his lips. Both men appeared to be very nervously anxious about something as he lowered the device and stuck his hand back in his suit pocket. Then he appeared to firmly grab something else tightening his grip around it, and an angry sadistic sneer formed on his face.

Janice calmly looked over all the men in the chamber with the certain knowledge she was among a den of vultures ready to pounce on her and tear her to pieces. Their actions did not deter her as she reached up and touched the pendant hanging from its gold chain around her neck hidden inside her blouse.

She let her hand go and firmly stated, "Gentlemen, if I can call you and your predecessors that, you have all been lied to for more than sixty years."

The following uproar in the room was deafening as the members stood up shouting their indignation at her.

"What the hell is she doing here Chairman?" yelled one elderly rotund bald man.

"How dare you address us in that tone insolent child!" shouted another middle-aged man.

"Young lady, do you know who you're talking to?" yelled another angry younger man.

Another yelled out, "What does your daughter have to do with our plans, and how does she know what we're planning?"

Ted stepped between her and the microphone and sternly shouted, "All of you shut up! She may just save all your lives today, and that of your families from a fate worse than death."

They remained standing, but quiet, still fuming as she calmly continued.

"The treaty your predecessors signed with the Trilotew to gain certain off-world technologies is a fraud. They promised them the power to rule this world, but they are merely using all of you to take over this planet. When they determine your usefulness to them is over, you and your families will be sadistically tortured to death or devoured alive. Then Trilotew agents disguised to look like you will take your places. Each man in this room who still has his own human wits about him has suspected for some time that several of your other members no longer act quite like their normal selves. After Trilotew agents succeed at taking over all your positions worldwide, they will use all humankind as either slaves or a food source. Even now, the secret waveform transmitters they carry in their coat pockets are subconsciously influencing all of you. I suspect Trilotew agents disguised as two of your former human Council members are the two taller men standing at the very back of this room. If I am right, they just contacted their ships and they will arrive here soon to annihilate this place. They will do everything that they can to cover up any evidence of their breaking of the treaty they signed with the entire Galactic Inter-dimensional Alliance of Free Worlds."

The two tall men at the back of the room angrily grimaced and darted down the aisle toward the podium. They reached inside their suit jackets and pulled out short triangular handgun weapons and pointed them at Janice and Ted. Two undisguised Trilotew agents wearing their own off-world tight-fitting brown leather uniforms, with the symbol of a white-winged bipedal reptilian emblazoned upon their chests, suddenly materialized in the back of the room. They were holding elongated transparent rifle weapons pointing them in sweeping maneuvers at all the men gathered there. The startled Council members were aghast with disbelief upon seeing their supposed off-world Trilotew reptilian allies pointing weapons at them, expressing menacing sadistic sneers on their green scaly faces.

Janice grabbed the pendant hidden under her blouse again in her closed fist, and it flashed to life brilliantly lighting the room through her clenched fingers. Ted instinctively threw her to the floor and covered her with his arms, just as two sizzling beams of green radiant energy blasted a round hole in the wall directly behind the podium with fiery disintegrating atoms of green light. The energy emission coming from her pendant instantly expanded into the room with a thousand rainbow colors that harmlessly passed right through the bodies of everyone to continue in every direction through the walls, floor, and ceiling of the chamber. All four Trilotew agents were suddenly stopped in their tracks, and they fearfully discovered they could no longer move except for their eyes that gazed down to see their weapons harmlessly drop from their limp hands to the carpeted floor. The human illusion disguises covering the two Trilotew agents wearing suits melted away in quick puffs of vanishing smoke, openly revealing their true bipedal reptilian nature. For the first time, oval violet eyes with cat-like vertical red pupils of all four reptilians were expressing real terror.

Ted helped Janice to her feet, while she remained clutching the glowing pendant. Then she approached the podium again and calmly continued, "This new energy Ray that was recently given to the Galactic Alliance comes from a higher realm that is many dimensions far above the entire physical universes. No force utilized by beings residing in the lower dimensions can stop it, and no type of weapon can affect it in any way. This new energy Ray is not here to harm any of you. As you feel it penetrate your chests, you will also begin to perceive a projected transparent white sphere of light above your heads filled with all the negative terrorizing control images implanted deep inside your subconscious minds. Then you will once again know the truth about your original celestial natures as exhilarated loving beings, filled with the passion to create new things and new ways of living for the well-being of all life everywhere. All of you please take your seats. Then make the right choice. Determine right here and now to have those awful, false torturous memories dissolved forever, and this new gift Ray will erase them. You will finally be set free once again to live as you were always meant to live, in harmony with all life."

The force that was holding the four Trilotew from any movement vanished, and they shook their heads. Then they cautiously picked up their weapons, but did not point them at Ted and Janice. All hardened expressions on the faces of the power-mad men in the chamber, and the sinister expressions of sadistic glee on the four Trilotew agents began to soften. Expressions of childlike wonder and real joy gradually took their place for the first time in their lives. One by one, transparent white spheres appeared above all their heads filled with images of horror, torture, suppression, sadistic cruelty, and every other imaginable demented type of experience. As each individual in the room silently made the correct freewill inner decision for the first time, all the horrifying scenes inside the spheres dissolved into pure white light and faded away. Many astonished childlike murmurs began to come from the mouths of the Council members.

"Oh dear God, at last!" one cried out, greatly relieved.

"This is unbelievable! I am finally free of this terror," said another breathlessly, as tears began to pour from his eyes.

"I didn't know. I just didn't know," lamented another older man, and then he began to smile from the warm expansive feeling he was beginning to experience.

The most senior representative gasped with a new realization and asked, "Oh my heavens, what have we done to our people and our planet? Oh no, no, no we must turn this around."

Then many more uplifted expressions of sublime surprise continued to come from all of them.

The facial features of the four Trilotew had now completely changed. Their coarse reptilian scales had morphed into beautiful smooth green skin. Humble smiles now appeared on their faces, and their eyes began to emanate a kindly nature. Their true selves genetically buried below their level of awareness had surfaced for the first time. Slowly, they began to walk together toward the podium, respectfully holding their arms extended away from their chests with open palms up toward Janice and Ted, while repeatedly bowing their heads.

Their mystified leader stopped a few feet away and humbly asked, "You set us free. Why would you do this for us?" Before now, we would have gladly tortured you to death, ravenously eating your bodies."

"You couldn't have stopped yourselves before if you had tried," replied Janice kindly.

"Before today, the subconscious control implants genetically placed inside your ancient ancestors by their former ruthless white-winged conquerors was continuing to drive your negative passions. The Great War we had with your ancient winged overlords ended over five hundred thousand years ago, after our secret allies forced them back into that hellish parallel dimension from which they came. However, your ancient ancestors had to deal with us to end all hostilities. We only recently discovered a long past genetic programming is still controlling your entire ancient race and your current Emperor. Even now, he continues to order you to terrorize and conquer other races through deception, blackmail, and sadistic intimidation. This is how you have covertly operated to avoid another open war. The Galactic Inter-dimensional Alliance of Free Worlds did notice your many attempts to disguise your covert breaking of the treaty. I can see in your eyes that all four of you now know this to be the truth."

The Trilotew leader nodded humbly, and she continued, "I presume you are the senior officer of the other three Trilotew agents." He nodded again, and she inquired, "May I ask your name?"

He lowered his now saddening eyes and replied, "I am First Officer Zorbok, but I'm unworthy to gaze upon one such as you. You set us all free from this terrible curse, and we will be eternally grateful to you and the entire Galactic Alliance for this miraculous change."

"First Officer Zorbok of the Trilotew, I did not bring about this change. Even now, this Ray emanating to everyone here is continuing to accomplish that miracle. I must also tell you this process of changing you back to your true original natures is irreversible. From now on, no Imperial Trilotew technology or any other technology will be able to negatively affect or control you ever again. After you return to your ships, each one of you will discover you have awakened the innate desire to help change the course of history in only benevolent ways. You will actually become consciously aware contributing conduits to all life with this new gift Ray. Eventually, this uplifting transformation will spread to all your people on all the Trilotew dominated worlds, including to your Emperor. You will be the first Trilotew to begin to repair all the damage your combined races have caused over the last five hundred thousand years. Be at peace, for each of you are no longer considered enemies of the Galactic Alliance, and I can now call you friends."

The four Trilotew soldiers began to grin uncontrollably from the effect of her completely unexpected kind comments, and utter relief began to show on their astonished faces.

Zorbok nodded, smiling widely and replied, "I will signal our ship to beam us back aboard. Know this Janice and Chairman Carter, we will always fondly remember and treasure this momentous day."

She boldly walked down the steps and extended her forearm to the Trilotew officer. He looked even more amazed back at her entirely unexpected friendly gesture, and then gladly but gently grasped her hand. She graciously shook it, and then repeated the gesture to the other three Trilotew. Then Ted did the same, giving each one a warm genuine smile.

Zorbok reached into a pouch strapped to the side of his brown leather uniform and pulled out a thin triangular ruby-red device. He was about to touch a concave depression in its center with his thumb when the back wall of the council chamber suddenly exploded sending debris flying through the room.

A warning bell began to loudly clang, and the panicked Council members raced for the nearest exits located on each side of the chamber. Two-dozen more Trilotew soldiers carrying the elongated triangular rifles rushed into the chamber through the wide gaping hole in the back wall, just as heavily armored defending base soldiers raced into the chamber from both side exits pointing similar rifles back at the Trilotew.

"Council members hit the floor," yelled the squadron Commander, as the Trilotew infantry opened fire at many of the fleeing Council members and their defense infantry.

The radiant green beams, shot from the tips of their weapons, vanished several feet away in the neutralizing power of the new Ray radiating throughout the room. The military soldiers returned fire, but the new Ray also neutralized those sizzling light beams. The opposing forces desperately tried several more times to open fire at each other with the same effect, and they gradually began to recover from the immediate shock of the ineffectiveness of their weapons. The Trilotew infantry standing behind the four Trilotew nearest Ted and Janice tried to open fire at them again, but the green beams also vanished inches away from the tips of their weapons. The bewildered Trilotew frantically shook the rifles and then pulled the triggers repeatedly with the same result.

Janice grabbed the glowing pendant under her blouse with her fist, and this time Commander Tam-lure and Una-mala from the hidden Mt. Shasta base materialized directly behind her and Ted. They just simply appeared without the necessity of getting there by the energy vortex of a teleportation beam. A protective transparent golden bubble instantly formed around all four of them, and the angered Trilotew soldiers opened fire again. The green beams ricocheting off the protective energy sphere instantly dissolved several feet away in the neutralizing rainbow colored energy still radiating throughout the room.

The Trilotew and base security forces finally began to relax their fear, but remained nervously pointing their weapons at each other. Then Commander Tam-lure began to speak to them through the protective transparent barrier.

"Cease all hostilities," he commanded kindly. "I promise, no harm will come to any of you."

As they reluctantly began to lower their weapons, one of the Trilotew soldiers standing hidden behind several others lifted a wrist communicator to his reptilian jaws to quietly warn his fleet about the events taking place in the chamber.

"I am Commander Tam-lure, and this is my Second Commander wife Una-mala of the Galactic Inter-dimensional Alliance of Free Worlds. We wish you no harm. You must realize by now any weapons used here will be completely ineffective."

THE HIDDEN GOVERNMENT AWAKENS

Una-mala then kindly added, "You will each begin to experience a change in consciousness from the effect of the new energy Ray emanating in this room, and you will soon discover your suppressed original benevolent natures will resurface as the deranged terror implants that were programmed into your ancestor's genetic codes so long ago are removed."

All of the soldier's faces on both sides suddenly began to soften and morph into non-aggressive kindness while they continued to gaze amazed at each other. Each of them began to look up to behold transparent golden-white energy spheres appearing above their heads. Upon seeing images of terror, torture, and sadistic vengeance appear inside them, they all started to fearfully back away. A moment later, the images dissolved and the spheres vanished. The soldiers on both sides then began to gaze for the first time at a former enemy with humble respect and awe.

"If you wish," continued Tam-lure, "all the Trilotew here may go back with us to our Mt. Shasta base to undergo a full deprogramming. You will become what your ancient ancestors were before they were perverted by their white-winged overseers. They were then highly intelligent benevolent beings, non-carnivorous, and at one time long ago they were very giving constructive members of the Galactic Alliance. After we return you to your own ships secretly stationed around Earth a day later, you will discover this new Ray will continue to emanate through each of you toward your fellow Trilotew. Then they too will begin to experience the awareness that your long conflict between us is now headed toward a permanent peace."

The one who had tipped off his superiors by lifting a wrist communicator to his lips was now also gratefully smiling back at the humans standing on the stage, and he reached to touch the same button on the communicator again but thoughtfully hesitated.

Showing concern, he loudly stated to Tam-lure, "I am Second Officer Razjewl, and right before the transformation I contacted my superiors to tell them of your presence here in this base. They will want immediate revenge."

Commander Tam-lure smiled and nodded his thanks for the information.

"We will be ready for them, and you all need to know they will not be harmed if we can help it," he replied gazing back at Zorbok.

Then he looked over the two-dozen other Trilotew soldiers and asked, "Will you let us help return you to your true selves?"

All the Trilotew soldiers looked toward their comrades for confirmation, and then Zorbok answered deeply relieved, "We are all tired of this conflict. We will go with you now."

Tam-lure smiled at each one of them, touched a small golden symbol attached to his right sleeve three times, and all the Trilotew present in the room vanished from sight before the astounded eyes of the Council members and the perplexed base soldiers guarding them.

The protective transparent bubble surrounding the four humans on the stage vanished, and the relieved Council members began to stand back up with astounded dazed expressions. Then they began to move closer together toward the center of the room like bees drawn to flowers.

"Each one of you in this secret government knows the truth about what happened to your predecessors and to you," kindly continued Tam-lure. "The vicious covert control over you is now gone. If you wish, we can send you all to our secret Mt. Shasta base. There you can also experience a more complete deprogramming of any other subconscious implants that remain in the way of a full re-awakening to your original highly intelligent benevolent natures. After we return all of you back here a day later, you will have one great task. You will be inspired to benevolently utilize your control of the military industrial complex, and the hidden wealth you have stolen from the world's hardworking populous, to right all the past wrongs. You will have help to correct what your predecessors, you, and the Trilotew have done. We understand there are many other prominent men belonging to your organization who are not present here at this meeting. They will need your help before we can implement the full disclosure of our presence to all the people of Earth. Know that when you contact your fellow members worldwide or their Trilotew overseers, this new uplifting and transforming Ray will begin to operate through you. It will help them make the same transition back to their true benevolent natures. In the near future, many of our representatives in every field of endeavor will be coming to Earth to advise and assist you all with this transitional process. Then all humanity on Earth will have the opportunity to become a full member of the entire Galactic Inter-dimensional Alliance of Free Worlds. Will you and those soldiers who are present here come with us?"

The one hundred former members of a hidden world government on Earth, finally liberated from the sub-conscious effects of the black disc devices used by their former Trilotew overseers, were now smiling with childlike wonder for the first time in their lives. Previously, they had blindly followed the orders of their superiors, who they had mistakenly thought were official representatives of the elected leaders of the United States government. They were also beginning to experience a rapidly expanding conscious awakening back to their original benevolent natures, and each one wanted more. They all nodded their approval to Tam-lure, and he touched an identical small golden symbol attached to his other sleeve three times. All one hundred Council members, along with the several dozen soldiers guarding them, vanished from the room in an upward whirling light. A moment later, a soft beeping sound coming from his wrist communicator interrupted Tam-lure.

He lifted the device to his ear to hear an urgent young adult male voice state, "Commander, the two dozen Demon Scout fighters launched from those two Trilotew battle cruisers are now moving swiftly toward your underground location. What are your orders?"

Tam-lure put the device to his lips and replied, "They know we're on to them. They will very likely attempt to destroy all evidence of their treaty-breaking covert influence on this planet, starting with this hidden government base. Lieutenant Dun-tal, I believe the time has come for us to reveal to all the Trilotew the beginning phase of *The Seres Agenda*. Have they detected our fleet in orbit?"

"No Commander," replied Dun-tal back through the transceiver. "They show no signs they are able to detect our ships while we're operating in the higher parallel frequency. We remain invisible to them."

"Before the Trilotew ships arrive above this hidden underground location, order our four medium cruisers stationed in the upper atmosphere to descend and hold their positions higher in the atmosphere, frequency-fazed to render them undetectable. Have them prepared to neutralize all power aboard the Trilotew medium destroyers. Then have them launch four Scout fighter squadrons also frequency-fazed to remain undetectable. When the Trilotew Demon Scout fighters attempt to launch their matter annihilator weapons, have our Scout squadrons surround and neutralize them as well. Do it quickly and keep me updated."

"Yes Commander. I'm already on it," replied the young Lieutenant.

Ted's face had now also softened, and he was smiling with joy at the new state of consciousness he was experiencing from the energy emanations that continued passing through his body, coming from his daughter's off-world pendant. For the first time, he began to experience concern for the fate of the monstrous Trilotew without regard for his own safety.

He found himself silently musing, *After all, they could not have stopped what they were doing. Subconscious programming implanted in them by their sadistic winged overlords was driving their sadistic behavior.*

Ted came out of his reverie and asked Una-mala, "What happens now?"

"That's what I'd like to know," added Janice.

"A battle is coming," Una-mala replied, "the first battle that may be openly witnessed by average Earth citizens, and the Trilotew will not be able to cover up the truth about their covert involvement with Earth's secret leaders for much longer. There are other powerful people in hidden bases like this one around the world that are also a part of the hidden secret government cover-up, and their controlling Trilotew overseers could still destroy this planet out of sheer meanness, if they believe their plans for Earth are about to be neutralized. However, for the first time I am very optimistic about the eventual outcome. All four of us should now beam back to the base to help with the full deprogramming of all those just sent there. Then we will see what tomorrow brings."

Commander Tam-lure smiled at his wife, and then turned to Ted and Janice to happily inquire, "Are you ready?"

They nodded eagerly, and Tam-lure touched the gold symbol on his right sleeve again three times. Then they too vanished from the room.

# CHAPTER SEVENTEEN

# A PUBLISHER
# EXPERIENCES TRUTH

*M*ark Santfield had now fully recovered all memory of his original off-world Pleiades origin as Ambassador Shon-ral, and the University of California Medical Center was about to release him after he had just undergone a fictitious health observation. The local police, and select members from the NSA faction secretly operating with the Galactic Alliance, had debriefed him for the benefit of the press. He had been inundated non-stop for three straight days by reporters from all the major television networks and newspapers. They had accepted the fabricated cover story Mark relayed to them about how he had suffered from amnesia for nearly a week, after surviving a lightning strike while camping in the mountains.

Agent Jacobson, the special NSA agent that took Mark from the Crystal's cottage home to the hospital, was standing next to him handing back his wallet and other personal effects that were kept safe to make the amnesia cover story convincing.

"What's your next move?" he asked Mark.

"Hmm . . . that's a good one, but I think I should first let my publisher off the hook by showing up alive to hand him the long overdue manuscript of my next book. What's contained in its pages will help prepare the public for the day when Galactic Alliance representatives show up here in great numbers to help this world make the transition to become one of its members. Can you imagine how this negative world will be transformed?"

"Mr. Ambassador, I can only speculate," he replied respectfully. "But there is one thing I've always wanted to do since I was just a boy. Can I go to the stars and visit other worlds?"

Mark nodded smiling, finished straightening his tie, slipped on his new suit coat, and then enthusiastically replied, "Agent Jacobson, I can promise you that over the next few years the transformation of the Earth back to a normal world of benevolent human beings will take place. Then you and the rest of Earth's human population can visit other worlds in many exchange programs of learning. You will be involved in uplifting exploration, and new enlightening experiences. Yes, Agent Jacobson, you will get to live your dream far beyond even your wildest expectations. I do deeply appreciate and thank you for all your help. I know you will be monitoring my movements for security reasons from now on, and I hope we cross paths many times over the next few years. Now, I have to catch a cab. Goodbye my friend."

Smiling in wonder, Agent Jacobson shook Mark's hand and then escorted him out of the hospital room. A few minutes later, they walked side by side out of the hospital lobby, and Agent Jacobson waited until Mark caught a cab. Then he took a special cell phone from his pocket and said something into it. A moment later, a dark blue late model four-door sedan pulled up beside him with a fellow female agent at the wheel. He jumped into the front passenger seat and they pulled away.

Mark walked into a modern twelve-story building in Beverly Hills a half-hour-later with the manuscript tucked under his arm. He took the elevator to the fiftieth floor and entered the Waymeyer Publishing Company offices through the double-wide ornate oak doors. Chairman and CEO Dan Waymeyer was impatiently standing in front of the receptionist's desk with his hand out palm up, insinuating that Mark should immediately hand over the manuscript. The very pretty receptionist in her mid-twenties looked up and smiled cutely at Mark from behind her boss's back.

"Mark, it's about damn time you came here to deliver that manuscript," he stated firmly, and eyed him with an expressive rebuke. "I watched the news about what happened to you, how you were found and finally recovered your memory. Damn lucky break if you ask me. I'm relieved to see you in one piece."

Mark reached to place the manuscript in Dan's hand, playfully yanked it back just to see the grimace on his face, and then dropped it. Dan grabbed it out of the air and read the title page, turned it over, and then scanned down the list of chapter titles before he looked back up concerned.

"Now wait a damn minute. Do these chapter titles actually reveal what they imply?"

"You bet your ass they do," replied Mark, "and there's much more to it than what's on the pages of my second book. I plan to expand it considerably through the editing process before it's finalized and released."

"Please come into my office," requested Dan, and he nodded with a roll of his eyes toward the pretty secretary sitting behind the reception desk. "There's something important I need to discuss with you, in private."

Mark could not help but notice an unmistakable concern deepening on Dan's face that was beginning to show signs of fear as they walked to the end of the long polished oak wood floor hallway. They stopped in front of a set of double clear glass doors with bold gold letters painted across them which read: Waymeyer Publishing Group—Mr. Dan Waymeyer, Chairman & CEO. They headed through the doors and stopped again to face each other beside two lush blue leather guest chairs arranged in front of Dan's very expensive looking huge dark wood desk. A taller and more lavish leather chair was behind it. Mark looked away to gaze through the floor to ceiling corner office windows at the expansive overview of the city of Beverly Hills, and the mountainous hills beyond it and looked back.

"Mark are you out of your mind or do you just have a death wish?" Dan blurted out, suddenly hot under the collar.

Mark did not flinch and continued to stare back at his senior editor and publishing company owner.

"Don't be concerned about the content even though every word in it is true, and there's more, ever so much more, you need to know. When this book is published, you, your wife, your offspring and their children, as well as every employee working here will be protected from any harm in ways you couldn't possibly imagine at this moment."

"What ways could possibly protect us from the tyrants you claim are operating a powerful second hidden government with the assistance of their diabolical extraterrestrial allies?" inquired Dan.

"Dan, listen to me," Mark requested calmly. "I'm not who you think I am. I'm not from this world, although this body is."

Dan flushed red in the face, cleared his throat, and then angrily replied, "Damn it Mark, are you telling me you're now on some kind of psychic mumbo jumbo kick, and you're claiming to actually be a walk-in from outer space?"

Mark still did not flinch while he steadily gazed at his apprehensive publisher and replied, "There isn't time for me to try and convince you of anything I'm telling you. Only direct personal experience of your own will convince you and answer all your questions. Do I have your permission to prove, without a shadow of doubt, that everything I'm telling you is the undistorted truth?"

"What do you mean?" Dan snapped back nervously.

"Will you come with me to discover for yourself just how deeply everyone has been lied to on this planet?" Mark asked. "Do you want to safely know the real truth behind all this for yourself?"

"You're kidding, right?" replied Dan, even more perplexed than before. "Are you saying you can get me aboard a flying saucer or something like that?"

"That's exactly what I'm saying," replied Mark confidently. "Wouldn't you like to know you're about to publish a book that's part of a vast plan to free this world once and for all time, from madmen who have been running things from behind the scenes while unconsciously heading our world to destruction?"

Dan looked at Mark with deep worried lines of consternation etched into his face. Mark reached up and touched the pendant hidden under his shirt and it flashed once. Dan's tight shoulders suddenly dropped, and he relaxed with a shake of his head. Then he looked at Mark with newfound courage.

"Mark, you better be right about this," he firmly stated, pointing his finger at Mark's chest.

"My friend," grinned Mark, "you're about to go on the greatest adventure of your life."

He reached up and grabbed the pendant hidden under his shirt in his fist, and it instantly lit up, radiating subtle rainbow-colored rays throughout the office. Dan's face began to show he was being deeply uplifted as an expression of childlike wonder began to form. A moment later, both of them were encased in a bright upward whirling vortex of light and they vanished from the office.

They rematerialized aboard Monti's Scout ship, and Dan looked around the control room amazed before his eyes came to focus on Monti, who was just starting to stand up from behind the console.

"Welcome, Mr. Waymeyer. I'm known as Monti," he cordially stated. "I am a human being from another world that belongs to an ancient benevolent organization known as the Galactic Inter-dimensional Alliance of Free Worlds, and we're the good guys."

Dan was smiling back, spellbound by Monti's slightly larger than average sky-blue eyes and the uplifting vibrations emanating from his benevolent face. He was also surprised he innately understood that Monti was benevolent, and that was that. Then he looked to Mark for more answers.

"As I said, you're about to go on the greatest adventure of your life," restated Mark.

Dan was speechless at first, and then without realizing he was actually expressing his thoughts, blurted out with gusto, "Wow! I mean . . . oh my God, WOW! You were telling the truth the whole time, and I thought I was just publishing another money-making conspiracy theory novel. My God . . . oh my God. Should I . . . uh . . . well what do we do now?"

"How would you like to visit one of our mile-long flagships hidden in the rings of Saturn?" replied Monti kindly. "There you can discover for yourself the truth about what is covertly happening hidden behind the scenes on your world, and what's about to take place there for the great benefit of all the people."

Mark nodded and winked encouragement, "Monti can have you back here in half a day, but you will be a completely different man by then, and a far wiser person."

Dan rubbed his sweating palms on his pants, but he was no longer concerned for his own welfare. All fear had left him, and he felt better than he had felt at any time in his entire life.

He looked at Mark and Monti, and then replied with the excited zeal of a ten-year-old on his first camping trip, "Oh my God, I would like that very much. Let's do it!"

"You'll be in good hands for the next six hours. Monti will see to it that you are discreetly returned to your office back on Earth, and don't worry about your secretary Suzanne. She will not realize the hours have passed so quickly when you walk out of your office before closing time. I promise, you will never forget the wonder of the experiences you are about to have, and thanks for trusting me. Now Monti will send me to an important destined meeting with the President of the United States."

Dan gazed at him mystified, but Mark reassured him, "Dan, remember I said I'm not who you think I am. Officially, I am actually Ambassador Shonral from the Galactic Inter-dimensional Alliance of Free Worlds to Earth's leaders and people. Now, I need to get the President permanently free from the Trilotew Ambassador's control and the hidden second world government. We'll meet up after that momentous deed is done."

Monti calmly interjected, "Mark, you should know I received an update an hour ago from Commander Tam-lure and Second Commander Una-mala regarding Janice and Ted. They said Henry took Janice to meet Ted at the Griffith Observatory. Then she and Ted drove to his home and beamed to a secret government underground installation in Arizona. However, the members did not accept the message Janice gave them, and when two Trilotew agents disguised as known members attacked them, Janice used the pendant and it worked perfectly. They are both safe. One hundred members of the secret hidden worldwide governing Council and several dozen attacking Trilotew soldiers are now permanently free from the terrorizing influence of their former perverted subconscious programming. Implementation of *The Seres Agenda* is now underway."

"That's wonderful news, Monti. Although I really expected it to go well."

Monti continued on an up note, "You should also know that Janice and Ted are assisting Tam-lure and Una-mala with the full rehabilitation of the Council members and the Trilotew soldiers. Perhaps you would like to join them there after your mission to the President is complete."

Mark smiled and nodded for Monti to proceed. Before Dan could ask another question, Monti touched a control, and Mark dematerialized in another bright upward whirling beam. Dan looked at Monti to ask him a question, but changed his mind with a shake of his head, and then smiled with childlike trusting acceptance instead.

"Monti, my good man, take me to your leader," he jovially commanded, and laughed, feeling extraordinarily good.

"That's supposed to be my line, friend," Monti shot back, and he laughed with Dan.

Dan shrugged his shoulders and smiled eagerly as Monti touched several other controls, and the projected energy view screen appeared above the console.

"I thought you would like to experience a perspective of Earth from where we are now aboard this ship," added Monti with a mischievous gleam in his eyes.

Blurred images cleared on the screen, and Dan was amazed to discover he had become an astronaut aboard an extraterrestrial spacecraft orbiting high above the beautiful blue-green water covered jewel of planet Earth. He could see far below through a break in the clouds all of California, part of Oregon, and all of Nevada and Arizona.

Monti just smiled when Dan looked back spellbound. Then he placed both hands into the guidance controls' hand impressions.

The Scout ship had been hovering invisibly camouflaged in a slightly higher molecular frequency or parallel dimension in a stationary orbit just outside Earth's atmosphere. It gradually faded back into full visibility. The blue aura surrounding the hull pulsed brighter, and the ship darted in a blur of light into the depth of space.

# CHAPTER EIGHTEEN

# THE PRESIDENT AT CROSSROADS

*P*resident of the United States, Martin McCoy, was standing by the curved Oval Office windows gazing out over the well-manicured green lawn and flowering rose bushes. A golden-white flash brightened the room from behind him, and he jumped around, startled to behold Mark Santfield smiling back at him.

"Who the hell are you?" demanded the President nervously.

"I'm Shon-ral. However, I am actually the official Ambassador from the entire Galactic Inter-dimensional Alliance of Free Worlds to you, and the rest of the duly elected world leaders. In other words, Mr. President, I'm here to help you out of the jam you're in with the Trilotew, and with all the misguided secret world government members."

A moment later, the beam weapons concealed inside the Oval Office walls at twelve different locations suddenly opened fire on Mark with thick radiant green beams. The pendant hidden under his shirt instantly flashed to life, emanating a transparent golden spherical shield that surrounded him. The sizzling green beams hit the luminous sphere, deflected back to the walls and vaporized all the concealed weapons into oblivion. The smoke quickly faded and vanished; leaving burned round foot-wide holes in a dozen places in the walls and ceiling.

The energy shield surrounding Mark vanished, just as Trilotew Ambassador Grotzil materialized behind him, slowly reaching out to strangle Mark with the long sharp nailed fingers of both his reptilian hands. He suddenly lunged forward to grasp Mark's neck, but the glowing pendant hidden under Mark's shirt immediately emitted two fiery red rays that darted around both sides of his body to instantly burn the Ambassador's hands into blackened stumps at the wrists. The shocked Trilotew Ambassador backed away screaming in agony, while Martin helplessly looked on aghast at all that was unexpectedly happening before him. Mark spun around, grasping the pendant under his shirt with his clenched fist, and two widening blue beams of energy darted from it to envelop the Ambassador's entire body in a halo of rainbow-colored light. The Ambassador, still screaming, watched as his hands miraculously rematerialized unharmed. He gazed astounded down at them and smiled with great pleasure. Then he looked up at Mark and bowed gratefully before him.

He was beginning to discover his subconscious evil nature was now gone, and he asked very much amazed, "What did you do to me?"

"I didn't do this to you," Mark said. "The special Ray that accomplished what you are experiencing is a gift to the entire Galactic Alliance, the Trilotew, and all life. It comes from a far, far higher dimension beyond the entire physical universes. You are now experiencing your true nature. If you are willing, after you return aboard your ship you can discover the suppressed truth about how your white-winged relatives from a parallel dimension captured your entire culture so long ago. They genetically perverted all of you to carry out their evil intentions throughout this galaxy before the Galactic Alliance stopped them. Are you willing to be set free?"

Ambassador Grotzil started to cry and smile for the first time in his life, as his hardened facial characteristics softened before Mark's and the amazed President's eyes.

"Wait a minute," interrupted President McCoy, "I recognize you. You are the Mark Santfield that wrote that conspiracy theory book. How did you get into this office, and what are you doing to the Trilotew Ambassador?"

Mark turned and kindly smiled at the President then replied, "Mr. President, I was sent here by the Galactic Alliance to make you aware that you have been under the subversive technological brainwashing of the Trilotew to carry out their mission to not only enslave this planet, but also utilize the world's populace as a food source. This is the same kind of perverted genetic programming another more monstrous race used to capture the ancient Trilotew ancestors over five-hundred-thousand-years ago. Since then, the Trilotew have been automatically carrying out that genetically altered subconscious program, without awareness of the fact that back then, special friends of the Galactic Alliance from the Andromeda galaxy permanently removed that terrible race from this galaxy. Mr. President, you are suffering from the effects of a subconscious projection control device this Trilotew Ambassador is carrying in his pocket at this very moment."

Martin's mystified face revealed this was beyond his understanding, and his skeptical fear was unmistakable. Try as he might, he also discovered that he could not make his body move. Mark boldly walked up to the Trilotew Ambassador and reached into his pocket to pull out a circular black metallic disc with a dozen multi-colored buttons on its polished surface.

Mark handed the device to the Ambassador and calmly stated, "Now do the right thing, and set President McCoy free from the effect of this vile thing."

To the President's dismay, Ambassador Grotzil graciously accepted the device. Then he touched several buttons on its surface that flashed on, and Martin blinked several times, shaking his head as if he was trying to clear a fog from his thoughts.

Amazed, he looked up and stated, "Oh dear God, I remember."

He angrily gazed at Grotzil and hotly demanded, "What the hell did you do to the millions of this planet's citizens when you took them off-world?"

The dejected Ambassador was deeply embarrassed and his green face turned beet-red as he lowered his head in agony of despair. Mark stepped toward the President and stopped again to patiently wait while he continued to hold the pendant under his shirt in his clenched fist. A moment passed, and the pendant lit up, projecting a wide beam of transparent rainbow light that enveloped Martin from head to toe. His angry expression melted away as he became aware of a new understanding of all that was done to the Trilotew so long ago by their wicked invading white-winged cousins. Then he discovered he could move again and gazed at the despairing Ambassador with real compassion for the first time. He fearlessly walked up to Grotzil and looked up at him, then placed a friendly hand up on his shoulder.

Ambassador Grotzil slowly lifted his head, and as his sad reptilian eyes looked down to meet President McCoy's benevolent stare, he proclaimed, "I was not in control of what we were doing to your people. In the name of Prime Creator, I now remember everything. How could we have become such monsters?"

He looked away toward the windows overlooking the White House lawn as tears continued to flow freely down the now softer features of his reptilian face.

"You are once again your true self," proclaimed Mark as he reached out and placed a consoling hand up on Grotzil's other shoulder. "That's all that will be required of you from now on. Return to your ship orbiting the planet, and you will discover something new has been added there as well."

As Grotzil looked down at him with a slight glimmer of hope in his forlorn eyes, Mark continued, "You will find a very special golden pyramid is now aboard your vessel. Your crew is already starting to go through this same experience. Join them, and then pay a visit to all the other Trilotew aboard all your other ships, and in your hidden Earth bases. You will then experience for yourself how this Ray will go with you and be passed onward, until your entire race on all your collective worlds are free forever from the awful ancestral genetic programming they endured for so many thousands of generations. In a short time, your race will become a benevolent boon to the entire Galactic Alliance, and your citizens will be welcomed to join us in our efforts to free up many other world systems from this type of nightmare madness."

Grotzil actually discovered he was quite pleased with the prospect but then humbly replied, "We would deserve, under any other circumstances, to be destroyed for all the evil we've done. However, I realize even as you do that we too are to accomplish something far more constructive in the great collective of life in the universe. I will never forget this meeting and your kind words to me. I owe you my eternal allegiance to help emanate the new energy Ray that comes from those mysterious pyramids you spoke of, and I will dedicate the rest of my life to that end. You have my undying thanks."

He looked down at the President standing before him, who was gazing up with kind eyes, and he sadly stated, "Mr. President, many of those humans who were taken off-world are probably dead. Know that I am truly sorry. I am certain some are alive, kept as slaves or for other evil deeds. I promise you on my life that I will find any survivors and return them to you. Please trust me with this."

As the now greatly changed Supreme Illumined High Lord Ambassador Grotzil of the Trilotew looked at the world through hopeful eyes for the first time, President Martin McCoy reached up to clasp forearms with him in friendship. Smiling compassionately, the President nodded again, and Grotzil reached down and clasped his forearm.

"Please do that as a priority before you do anything else," insisted Martin. "It will not satisfy the great loss to the families who will never see their loved ones again, but if I'm reading Mark correctly, all of the people of Earth will receive this new enlightening energy coming from these pyramids in the very near future. No doubt, the anger and hatred they will all aim toward your race when they first learn the truth about your hidden existence on this planet, and what was done to some of their relatives and friends, will quickly be replaced with knowing benevolent understanding by the wondrous new Ray."

For the first time, Ambassador Grotzil expressed a greatly relieved smile.

"Ambassador Shon-ral, is it?" inquired President McCoy, gazing at him. Mark nodded and the President continued, "Please accept my deepest apology for having conspired with the Trilotew to have you killed. As you know, I also did not realize what I was doing. From now on, I will do all I can to see to it no one will interfere with your latest book upon its publication, and you have only to ask any favor of me. If it's within my power as President, I will see that it is done."

"It wasn't your fault your predecessors got caught in their own lust for supremacy, secrecy, and dominance over the rest of humanity after World War II," replied Mark, kindly gazing at the President. "The Trilotew were manipulating their budding thirst for power to make inroads to bring the secret world government under their seductive control. Since you now understand this, all is well. The benevolent neutralization of the misguided, looming annihilation of the Earth has begun. Mr. President, you must also understand that if the Trilotew had continued their secret operations, the consequence, known without a shadow of doubt from galactic history, would have been the unexpected and unanticipated misuse of your secret weapons. The subsequent destruction of the entire planet Earth would likely be the result. The Trilotew would then have simply abandoned this planet to embark on a quest to conquer some other world. All that has now changed forever.

"Our next big problem will be to safely extricate the remaining hidden world government members from the hypnotic control they are under and send home any remaining Trilotew who are present among them. I must leave you now, but remember you will have an unseen protection around you, as will Trilotew Ambassador Grotzil. From this moment on, both of you can go forward doing what you know to be right, and negative forces will have no power to stop you in any way. Will that meet with both your approvals?"

"Yes, indeed it does," replied Martin and Grotzil happily nodded. "I've been so depressed lately," continued Martin. "But now everything has changed for the better, and you will always have my grateful thanks. You will be welcomed back here at anytime. Goodbye for now, my friend."

Mark smiled at President Martin McCoy and Trilotew Ambassador Grotzil, and they smiled gratefully back.

The newly transformed Trilotew Ambassador then reverently bowed before the President and humbly said, "I will now return to our command ship, then contact the fleet Commander of our hidden bases under the great Amazon jungle in Brazil, and our Commander deep in the Congo jungle of Africa. I believe the Trilotew warriors there will need some changing before they rejoin our ships orbiting the poles of your planet."

He touched a button on his hand-held device, and a spiral of energy whirled around him before it teleported him away.

"It's time for me to return aboard my friend's Scout ship," stated Mark, looking at the President. "I will be in touch. Farewell."

He grabbed his pendant again and touched it six times. Then he too vanished before the astonished eyes of the President.

Mark reappeared aboard Boun-tama's Scout ship, pleased with his recent accomplishment and declared, "Boun-tama, my friend, President Martin McCoy of the United States, and Trilotew Ambassador Grotzil of the Trilotew, are now finally freed from tyranny. *The Seres Agenda* is officially underway on Earth."

Already jubilant, Boun-tama stood up from behind the console smiling. He walked over to Mark and clasped forearms with him.

"Well done Ambassador Shon-ral. Well done indeed," he enthusiastically proclaimed. "A new day is finally dawning throughout the universe. I will relay your success to Monti, Janice, and the others. However, we must also remember that a spy remains hidden somewhere within the ranks of the Galactic Alliance. Once this news gets out, the Trilotew will make their next move. We will be discreetly watching them to expose the spy."

"Boun-tama, that is a relief. Everything is proceeding as planned. Now if you would be so kind, perhaps it would be good if I returned to meet up with Janice to carry out our supposed romance and marriage back on Earth, and I must get my next book published. Do you think Mrs. Crystal, I mean Lean-tala would mind your being late for dinner?"

Boun-tama laughed and Mark laughed with him just to vent relief from all that had happened to unexpectedly transform his life.

Boun-tama remarked a few moments later, "Janice is back at the Mt. Shasta base with her foster Earth father, Ted. We can be back there in under a half-hour, and I'm certain they will both have their own stories to tell."

"You can be sure of that, my friend," confirmed Mark. "From what I understand, they also had a long day."

Back at the White House, the now gratefully transformed President Martin McCoy turned away from gazing out through the Oval Office windows at the well-kept verdant grounds. He picked up the phone handset on the desk and paused to briefly reflect on the wonders that had just occurred. He then punched a button, put the receiver to his ear and commanded, "Susan, contact all the Joint Chiefs and the entire cabinet, have them come to the White House immediately. Then get my wife on the phone."

"Yes, Mr. President, right away," replied his young sounding secretary on the other end of the line.

# CHAPTER NINETEEN

# THE TRILOTEW ARMADA TRANSFORMS

wo Trilotew Medium Galactic Destroyer Class ships, charcoal-black and a half-mile long with a characteristic red light enshrouding the oval hulls, were rapidly moving down through the upper ionosphere of Earth's atmosphere. Far below them, hidden somewhere in the Arizona desert, was their intended target—one of many hidden combined classified United States government and Trilotew underground bases. Elongated triangular fighters, bat-wing shaped with red ionized light tightly hugging their hulls, were keeping pace with their command ships in two triangular formations.

For two years, the lead command flagship was stealthily stationed in orbit over the North Pole, while the identical command ship was stationed over the South Pole. Now, they were about to try and cover up their sinister presence on Earth.

Aboard the flagship was the arrogant High Divine Imperial Commander Yalgoot, sitting in a wide high-backed obsidian textured command chair. His long, forked tongue darted in and out of his jaws while he gazed with arrogance at six other subordinate Command Officers. The four male and two female officers and six warriors were sitting at stations that encircled his command console. They were monitoring three-feet-square view screens, suspended at eye level from long black metal poles, extended down from the arched ceiling, twenty feet above their heads. Sharp nails at the end of their reptilian fingers were deftly activating many multicolored Trilotew caricature symbol controls, displayed underneath clear two-feet by three-feet control boards—similar to thin LCD (liquid crystal display) TV screens.

Commander Yalgoot gazed steadily at a particular younger male warrior sitting directly opposite him.

"Lieutenant Shogmot," he angrily yelled in the Trilotew growling language, "order our escort fighters to disperse in a wide staggered pattern, thirty-thousand-feet above that desert base. Have them ready to launch the Matter Disintegrator bombs on my command."

The thinner cowering officer instantly lowered his eyes, bowed his head, and yelled back, "At once, oh most High Divine Imperial Commander Yalgoot!"

Then he touched a luminous Trilotew symbol on the console in front of him in the middle of a dozen parallel vertical rows of varying sized control symbols.

The two groups of fifteen escort demon fighters in triangular formations slowly moving alongside their massive parent vessels, turned downward in unison at a forty-five-degree angle aimed toward a wide desert area located in the southwestern United States. The red ionized light encompassing their hulls flashed brighter, and they sped away from their command ships toward the Earth, leaving in their wake swiftly dissipating spectral light trails.

Back inside one of the bridge command control rooms, located on each end of the Galactic Alliance flagship, unique events were also quickly unfolding. Commander Jon-tral and Second Commander Sun-deema were standing behind the center of the ivory-textured, fifty-feet-wide control console covered with luminous controls. A dozen other Command Bridge personnel were still sitting to each side of them along the length of the console that curved along the rounded end of the ship's hull. They were intently monitoring the instrument panels and view screens connected end-to-end along the top of the console that curved behind the twelve horizontal oval view portal windows. The dozen interlinked view screens revealed a wide continuous view of Earth's upper atmosphere. The two Trilotew command warships were clearly visible, descending below the light cloud cover fifty-thousand-feet above the State of Arizona. Monti and Mark's publishing company guest CEO Dan Waymeyer had arrived aboard, and they were standing just behind the two Commanders to observe unfolding events.

"You mean you people are about to attack those ships?" Dan inquired nervously, as he looked to Commander Jon-tral for confirmation.

"Their attack on the hidden underground base has started, but our four much larger undetected command ships are now beginning to surround the two enemy warships," answered Jon-tral. "However, we do not intend to cause them harm or destroy them, if it can be helped." Then he kindly requested to Sun-deema, "Please change the view screen mode to the split-screen view."

She nodded and touched a golden spherical control on the console in front of her. The six rectangular view screens to the right of the central point of the curved console changed to view the thirty Trilotew Demon Scout fighters. All the enemy escort ships were beginning to break from their triangular formations spreading out over a wide area. They stopped to hover approximately thirty-thousand-feet above the same desolate desert area in Arizona.

"The time has come for us to move the flagship back to Earth," stated Commander Jon-tral. "However, Mr. Waymeyer, after this emergency operation that is about to take place above your own home world is resolved, you can undergo a very uplifting enlightening experience aboard this ship. But first, you can bear witness to the kindness we will impart to the Trilotew, although they would not have hesitated to viciously annihilate all humans, and their own warrior soldiers in that secret base under the floor of the desert." He looked down at the man sitting behind the console directly to his left and kindly commanded, "Pilot Shul-non, take the ship through the vortex to Earth, and establish a high orbital position in the atmosphere above the battle area."

The long blond-haired Caucasian man in his early thirties looked up and replied enthused, "We're already moving Commander."

Dan tried to smile, but was unable to hide his nervousness about the seeming unreality of his off-world experience with extraterrestrials, and he stuttered, "Uh . . . w-wha . . . what are you going to do with me?"

"Do not be at all afraid," replied Sun-deema with a deep kindness that made Dan unconsciously smile back at her. "You will soon recall all that was purposefully kept from you, and remember who you really are beyond just this one lifetime. Your intelligence will also greatly increase, and you will be uplifted in many other ways."

"Oh . . . well then that's uh . . . that's a good thing," he replied, and smiled as best he could under the circumstances.

The massive cylindrical flagship ship was already moving up out of its stealthy hiding place among the icy rings of Saturn. The blue anti-gravity aura surrounding the hull brightened, and the ship moved swiftly away from the planet. It quickly disappeared inside the inter-dimensional vortex opening in space.

The flagship was already emerging several minutes later out of the other end of the invisible vortex opening just outside of Earth's atmosphere. It quickly settled into a geosynchronous orbit above the southwestern United States. The occupants could clearly see this through the observation windows far below the ship through a break in the cloud cover.

The two half-mile long Trilotew command ships came to a sudden stop side by side, high in the upper atmosphere directly over the secret underground desert base.

Trilotew Commander Yalgoot sternly eyed his intimidated younger officer as he angrily shouted, "Lieutenant Shogmot, order our Demon Scout fighters to attack that base with their Matter Disintegrator bombs timed to go off a mile below ground in the central meeting chamber. We must destroy any evidence of our Trilotew presence there immediately."

"At once, oh most High Divine Imperial Commander," replied Shogmot standing up at strict attention behind the other side of the console.

He reached to touch another illuminated caricature symbol on the control console but hesitated, and ever so humbly inquired with downcast eyes, "Oh most Supreme Imperial Commander, what about our soldiers down there? Should we beam them out first?"

"Do as I command at once or you will experience the agony of dying in a fiery blaze of heat and light along with those stupid humans," growled Yalgoot, menacingly squinting his violet eyes through their red vertical cat-like slits. He began to hiss, darting his long forked tongue in and out of his jaws and growled, "Do not question my orders ever again . . . s-s-s-s. Do you clearly understand me, Lieutenant . . . s-s-s-s-s?"

"Yes, most Supreme Divine One. I will order the attack at once."

Shogmot snapped his jaws shut and slumped down in his own smaller high-backed black chair on the opposite side of the control console. Then he reached over with his shaking long sharp nailed forefinger and touched another illuminated symbol.

He leaned slightly over to speak into the transceiver and crisply stated, "This is Lieutenant Commander Shogmot. By order of Most High Divine Imperial Commander Yalgoot, set your Matter Disintegrator bombs to explode at a one-mile-depth below the ground, cluster-targeted for the main meeting chamber, and launch them immediately. Do it now before beaming out our warriors or your lives will also be forfeit."

The pale red halo surrounding all thirty Demon Scout ships suddenly brightened, and they simultaneously shot whirling red fireball projectiles from the rounded clear quartz tips at the front points of their elongated triangular hulls.

An instant later, thirty blue energy beams in a spherical pattern surrounding the Trilotew Scout ships ripped through the air and penetrated each red fireball, melting them into swiftly vanishing vapor. Before the attacking Trilotew Scout ships could fire again, sixty swiftly materializing Galactic Alliance Scout ships appeared encompassing them. The blue light surrounding each ship brightened and green beams shot from the outer edge of their hulls harmlessly passing directly through the center of the hulls of all thirty Trilotew ships. The beams instantly interconnected beyond them to rapidly form a green spherical grid pattern in the atmosphere surrounding the enemy attackers. The space between the grids instantly filled with green light, creating a transparent sphere. Several of the enemy ships started to move to flee their captors, but the red light enshrouding their triangular hulls suddenly shut off, leaving them suspended in the air.

"No, it's not possible," grumbled a female Trilotew warrior pilot aboard the lead Trilotew ship at the very center of the Demon Scout fighters. She touched one of the symbols on her console and shouted, "It's a trap! The enemy was waiting for us. They cut off our power. We cannot maneuver. What are your orders?"

Higher in the atmosphere aboard the primary command ship, Commander Yalgoot was now beside himself with anger and was standing up frothing at the mouth.

"Both command ships open fire immediately on those puny Galactic Scouts . . . s-s-s-s-s. Destroy them all now . . . s-s-s-s-s."

Both large command ships hovering parallel to each other, began firing massive red fireball energy weapons down at the Galactic Scout ships at incredible speed out of opening circular portals along the bottom length of their curved hulls.

The roaring sizzling energy projectiles had not gone a hundred feet when powerful golden energy beams intercepted all eighty red fireball weapons, and they just faded away. The four, mile-long Galactic Alliance Command ships materialized in positions surrounding the enemy ships half their size from above and below their parallel positions, emanating the wide golden energy beams. Before the enemy mother ships could return fire, the re-directed golden beams hit the hulls of both enemy ships, and like liquid light, the golden energy roared over their hulls to surround each one in a single wide transparent oval. The golden beams widened the oval light spheres until they joined and completely encompassed both Trilotew command ships, and the red anti-gravity power surrounding their hulls vanished.

"First Lieutenant Shogmot, self-destruct our ship immediately!" screamed High Commander Yalgoot frothing with venomous anger, "and order our second command ship to do the same. We will take them all out with us. Do it at once!"

Shogmot hesitated and started to open his mouth, but Yalgoot screamed louder, "Perish then, cowardly fool!"

He yanked out an elongated handgun from his black leather side holster and fired it at Shogmot. The Lieutenant screamed in agony, while the molecules of his body burned away into fiery vaporizing atoms. The remaining officers jumped up from their chairs in astonishment as the maddened Yalgoot menacingly waved his gun at them.

"Do any of you wish to ignore my orders?" he viciously growled, and the closest female officer walked up to Shogmot's station, touched several luminous symbols on the control console, and the lights dimmed inside the Command Bridge.

"Those Galactic Alliance meddlers will be extinct in five more seconds," stated Yalgoot with devilish glee. "Do not fear, warriors of the Empire. We will be well-remembered with high honor back on the home world, and the Emperor himself will honor our families."

He closed his eyes to wait for annihilation but nothing happened. As he slowly opened his eyes, the power to the entire bridge suddenly turned off.

A three-dimensional projection of Galactic Alliance Commander Jon-tral appeared above the circular command console between all the remaining Trilotew officers kindly stating, "Do not be afraid Trilotew warriors. We will not harm any of you. The time has come for you to be set free from the terrorizing subconscious programming and gene manipulation that was forced upon your ancient ancestors to control them long ago, that was passed on generation after generation."

Commander Yalgoot was now frothing anger, and he fired his weapon at the projection. The beam harmlessly passed through the image to blast a foot-wide burning hole in the control panel at the back of the room.

The large golden pyramid in the center of the Galactic Alliance Flagship flashed an expanding circle of golden light out through the hull. The expanding energy hit both Trilotew command ships and slowly dissolved inside them.

Yalgoot was about to fire at the projection again, but an invisible force stopped him. He was now terrified and unable to move, while he watched reluctantly as thousands of tiny golden teardrop shaped lights appeared, softly dropping from the ceiling like falling snow. Most of the drops passed through everything in the bridge control room to vanish through the floor. To his great astonishment, and that of his remaining officers and warriors, the luminous drops hitting their bodies vanished inside their reptilian flesh, and their more coarse physical features gradually softened. Their scale-covered torsos transformed into smooth green-scaled skin, and Commander Yalgoot's anger washed away. Then he actually smiled, quite pleased for the first time from a deeply pleasure-full experience.

"Now you know, Trilotew Commander," continued Commander Jontral from the projection. "You and your warriors are now freed from the vile subconscious programming your white-winged cousins forced onto your ancient ancestors. They genetically suppressed and then controlled your entire race over five hundred thousand years ago."

Just then, large spheres of white transparent light appeared above all the Trilotew officer's heads, and they all looked up to observe scenes of horror, murder, and every imaginable terror depicted before them.

"You must each choose now if you want that monstrous brainwashing removed from you forever. Know that this new energy Ray is a gift from a reality far beyond the lower worlds of time and space. The transforming uplifting effects you are each experiencing, and what you are beginning to remember, cannot be reversed by any power or being residing in the lower world systems."

Yalgoot and his officers and warriors groaned in terror, just as the horrifying images within the spheres above them dissolved into white light and the spheres faded away.

Commander Yalgoot humbly lowered his head and asked, "You mean we are no longer under the dominating power of the Emperor or his secret terror soldiers?"

"You are all now free from any outside control by anyone, including your Emperor. Even his ancestor's twisted technology passed on to him to brainwash you all under his control will no longer affect any of you. During your journey back to your home world, other officers and soldiers aboard their ships will contact you. Know this energy Ray will pass through you into them, and they too will be set free. On the day you arrive back on your home world, your Emperor and his staff will undergo this very same great change. From now on I will call you friends of the entire Galactic Inter-dimensional Alliance of Free Worlds."

The once mighty High Commander Yalgoot actually started to cry with real relief and emotion from the complete removal of the subconscious tyranny he and all Trilotew had been suffering under since the most ancient of times in their racial memory.

The female Trilotew Captain aboard the lead Trilotew Scout fighter, suspended without power in the atmosphere, was now greatly transformed. She was sitting down in the black chair behind the circular control console humbly smiling with her now refined and softened reptilian features. The same projection of Jon-tral, only smaller in scale was also before her. She too was experiencing and hearing all that her Commander was going through.

Yalgoot was still crying tears of joy when he looked up at Jon-tral's projection to ask, "You would do this for us, when you know we would have destroyed you all without mercy?"

"While I'm speaking with you," began Jon-tral, "what has very recently become known throughout the membership of the entire Galactic Inter-dimensional Alliance of Free Worlds will surface within your awakening consciousness. This great truth is the ancient Trilotew, and other totalitarian races aligned with them half-a-million years ago, had no choice but to follow the subconscious terrorizing genetic programming placed in them. After the white winged Trilon-Kal discovered a way to cross over from their very negative parallel dimension into this dimension they conquered your race. After that, they had your ancestors initiate a long destructive war with the Galactic Alliance. Eventually, with the secret aid we received from highly evolved friends residing in what Earth people call the Andromeda galaxy the Galactic Alliance forced them out of this dimension, and then permanently sealed them inside their own hellish dimension. Your ancient Emperor then signed a treaty with the entire Galactic Alliance membership to end the very destructive war he started. It was only recently that we discovered from the gift of this new Ray the enlightening understanding that your entire collective races still had the genetically altered program running on automatic deep inside your subconscious minds. They reprogrammed the DNA of your race so their twisted diabolical nature would be passed-on generation to generation.

"Our own ancient ancestors mistakenly thought the Trilotew were only using this outlawed brainwashing technology to dominate the races they conquered. They did not realize the same misused technology had also reprogrammed your DNA. A very long line of your Emperors have continuously reinforced this tyrant nature upon your entire race because they were also genetically subjected to it generation after generation. You can now understand how this twisted insanity is about to permanently transform for the great uplifting benefit of all life in this galaxy. In fact, this is beginning to take place throughout the vast creation of the entire multi-dimensional universe."

Yalgoot looked up to see what only moments ago he thought was merely an enemy that was good only for enslaving or eating, and his green face reddened with shame—but it did not last long. A wave of gold light appeared, coming through the metal walls of the bridge control room in circular expanding waves. They harmlessly passed through the Trilotew officers' bodies to continue through the hull of the ship into space.

"Commander Yalgoot, that shame you feel was also part of the original suppressive genetic programming. As we speak, it is dissolving away forever. You will soon remember that long ago, your entire race was not carnivorous. In fact, they were once highly evolved loving beings that were our friends, and great constructive contributors to the entire Galactic Alliance."

"Now I know," replied Yalgoot, as he gazed directly into Jon-tral's eyes in the projected image. "What you have done for us will never be forgotten. We owe you an eternal allegiance of friendship."

Jon-tral nodded and happily added, "We have another surprise for you and your warriors, Commander. If you and your officers are willing to discover more, I request that you all beam yourselves into your largest storage bay near your launch bay facility ten feet away from the center of the chamber. There you will all find something extraordinary."

Commander Yalgoot began to experience the eager enthusiasm of a fascinated child, and he looked questioningly for the first time at his male and female warrior officers gathered around him to seek their permission to go forward. They were already eagerly smiling back at him, and the once mighty terrorizing Commander Yalgoot now smiled wide with them for the first time in the Spirit of true friendship.

"We will meet with you there," he replied to Commander Jon-tral, relieved.

The projection of Commander Jon-tral vanished, and Yalgoot nodded to his formerly intimidated officers and warriors, who were now standing before him confident and fearless. Yalgoot leaned down and touched several lit beaming symbols on the console, and a moment later everyone on the bridge vanished in an upward whirling light.

They reappeared from the same whirling light standing near the center of a large rectangular storage facility. Directly behind them was a closed wide oval entry door located in the bottom center of the long right sidewall of the rectangular storage bay. Sealed gray plastic-like containers, with smooth rounded ends tied down with red woven ropes, were neatly stacked in a dozen parallel rows three-feet-tall, against all four walls. The open free-space centered within the storage bay was unused. Sitting in the exact middle was a fifteen-feet tall golden pyramid. Its seamless walls appeared to be translucent to all the gathered Trilotew, and they began to unconsciously smile with pleasure while they continued to gaze with childlike wonder at the new addition to their storage bay. The faint golden light radiating into the room from the top, bottom, and four sides of the pyramid was uplifting them.

Commander Jon-tral and Second Commander Sun-deema simply appeared, standing between them and the pyramid kindly smiling with the palms of their right hands held across their hearts in a respectful salute. Yalgoot boldly stepped forward and returned their salute with a nod and his hands held crisscrossed over his chest. The other Trilotew soldiers gathered behind him repeated the gesture.

"Commander Yalgoot, my wife Sun-deema and I would like to introduce you and your fellow Trilotew gathered in this chamber to the new Ray that comes from a pure dimension far above the physical worlds. I mentioned this but it bears repeating. The radiant energy emanating from this device has already liberated each one of you from the tyrannical control that has subconsciously haunted your race to be destructive for over half a million years."

Sun-deema kindly continued, "This great gift will now take us all beyond our physical bodies to re-experience our true energy forms as beings of light with knowing awareness that is, and always has been, beyond the physical nature of things. Are you ready for the greatest adventure beyond imagination?"

Yalgoot eagerly gazed at his fellow Trilotew warriors, who were just as eagerly looking back and he replied, "We are all beyond ready. Please help us remember who we really are once again."

Jon-tral nodded in the direction of the mysterious radiating pyramid, and the light emanating from it intensified ten-fold, causing them all to shield their eyes from the powerful golden illumination. Expanding circular golden energy waves began to emanate out into the room from the top, and from all four sides of the pyramid. It appeared to be comprised of millions of pastel golden teardrop shaped lights that harmlessly passed right through all their bodies and out through the walls of the storage bay chamber. Each one of the Trilotew, including Jon-tral and Sun-deema, were now expressing sublime uplifted freedom and knowing bliss.

A moment later, an eight-feet-tall statue of a bare-chested man standing in the center of a wide white stone bowl, supported by a foot-wide by four-feet-high round white stone column, appeared visibly outlined inside the pyramid through the front triangular wall. The bald bronze-skinned human appearing male was wearing two golden bracelets on each of his strongly built upper arms. A white skirt extended from the waist down to just above his bare feet. He was standing upon a raised disc centered in the bottom of the white bowl with an ornately carved scalloped rim. The radiant glow emanating from his face rendered any distinct facial features not clearly discernible. His arms held down at his sides with palms facing forward were pouring from them an even brighter glistening golden-white liquid light to continuously keep the bowl filled. The luminous liquid continued pouring over the entire rim in a smooth sheet to vanish through the metal floor, headed for unknown destinations. It was similar to the drawing power of flower pollen to bees, and the Trilotew found they were slowly walking toward the fountain.

"Fellow beings living within our great Prime Creator," continued Jon-tral, "although this liquid light looks like glowing water, know that it is actually a new expanding consciousness liberating Ray that comes from the higher worlds down into this physical universe. The process is beginning to permanently remove all fear and emotional suffering from all the worlds of creation. A new way has finally been created to take the place of fear or evil as a way to prod beings to evolve into their co-creative place among Prime Creator or the source behind and supporting all life."

"Real truth within this golden field of energy cannot be kept from you," encouraged Sun-deema, smiling. "You are all now feeling the natural pull to drink from this nectar. Once you do, you will forever leave your dismal tortured past behind. Each one of you will then remember your benevolent constructive place among the stars. Fearlessly go forward, new friends, and remember who you really are."

Commander Yalgoot approached the fountain first as it passed right through the front wall of the pyramid and sat itself on the chamber floor. An ornate golden cup appeared in his hand, and he gazed at it smiling with wonder. Then he carefully dipped the cup into the fountain, lifted it to his reptilian mouth, opened his jaws, and poured the liquid down his throat. The effect was immediate. The radiant liquid visibly moved throughout his body until it began to softly emanate a golden aura. Then the other Trilotew drank from the fountain with the same result.

"Now fellow beings from afar," added Sun-deema, "the time has come for you to remember what was taken from you so long ago. Countless lifetimes were lived by you in repetitive rounds of births and deaths with no memory each time of who you were or where you came from previously."

"Now it begins," Jon-tral stated confidently.

All of their bodies simply began to dissolve into identical looking transparent bodies made of thousands of radiant blue teardrop shaped lights. A moment later, brighter foot-wide energy spheres appeared, rising out of their heads to stop a foot above their bodies, radiating a light as bright as the golden light coming from the pyramid. Each Atma, soul, or pure spherical energy being was comprised of a white central core, surrounded by luminous colors spanning the spectrum from a white core to a violet exterior in successively widening concentric spheres or layers of teardrop shaped lights. A golden outer layer was softly radiating around them. The true selves of Jon-tral and Sun-deema, hovering above their transparent physical bodies, appeared slightly larger and brighter than the true Atma forms of the Trilotew.

All of the Trilotew then began to clearly hear Commander Jon-tral telepathically state, *My fellow beings living within the great Prime Creator, here in this state of true being, truth can no longer elude any of us. Look about you, and you will discover you can now clearly see in any direction or in 360 degrees all at once if you so desire. Commander Yalgoot, do you remember this hidden truth now?*

*Yes, yes . . . yes, yes we all remember now,* excitedly replied Yalgoot's excited telepathic voice, almost breathless with enthusiasm. *Oh great Prime Creator, how could we have lost so much? This is beyond anything any one of us ever hoped for or imagined. We are finally free. We remember who we really are. Like you, in our true form we are eternal energy beings experiencing lifetimes, often in differing forms, to discover our true destiny to become consciously aware, co-creative benevolent lords of creation in harmony with the one omnipresent radiant source of all life and all that is. We are here to contribute new ways for Prime Creator to constructively expand through our personal journeys of exploration and experimentation in the grand universe.*

Sun-deema's sweet telepathic voice confirmed, *Yes, my Trilotew brothers and sisters. Now you know the truth again. Except, this time no force or beings that exist anywhere in the vast multi-dimensional creation can ever take this from you again. What took place here today is irreversible. The constructive expansive change coming to the entire creation is permanent. This great awakening of the One behind all life to expand creation again is now taking place within each one of us.*

Jon-tral then added one last true blessing to the Trilotew's extraordinary unexpected and unanticipated turn of events.

*This change is now complete. However, you will all be remembering so much more in the days and months ahead each time the inspiration wells up within you to drink from this fountain.*

The fountain then lifted up a few inches off the floor and floated over to the front face of the four-sided golden pyramid. Then it passed right back through the translucent wall to slowly fade from view. For a moment, they could all see its faint glowing outline within the pyramid, before the golden side facing them brightened to hide what was inside.

The Atma, or true spherical energy beings of everyone, moved back down inside their transparent physical forms, and their bodies returned to their normal solid physical appearance. Everyone in the room was now literally glowing with faint pastel golden auras that swiftly moved inside their bodies.

"You and your men aboard your two command ships, and those warriors aboard your Scout support fighters are now considered friends of the Galactic Alliance," stated Commander Jon-tral gazing at Yalgoot. "Contact your fellow Trilotew in the hidden bases on Earth, and this new Ray will also transform them. They will go through the same experience that each of you just went through. In essence, you will take this new freedom and greater awareness with you back home. We will now release your ships from the power neutralizing effect of this Ray. As you may have intuitively sensed, the ability for us to neutralize your weapons, and the power aboard your ships, did not come from any new weapons technology we developed. This all happened by the grace of this new gift operating through our activated weapons consoles. It bears repeating that this new way of doing things comes from those realms that exist in parallel dimensions many, many levels beyond time and space. This is not now, nor will it ever be, a power that any race can use at any time to control or dominate any other race. No thing or any being in the entire creation can change or control this new Ray. No doubt, you will find this out on your own."

Sun-deema declared, "What you have all experienced here today is freedom for the first time, which comes directly from the awakening and consciousness expanding new way of the Ancient One or Prime Creator. The source of all life is beginning to administer creation for the far greater good of all that is. Now be at peace, gather up your fellow Trilotew soldiers, and take your ships home. Along the way, this new Ray will set free all other Trilotew you contact. As each one of you now inherently knows, one day even your Emperor will go through this same experience. We did not harm your disguised Agents in the secret desert base or the soldiers you sent there. We safely sent them to our mountain base located in northern California, and they have already gone through what you are experiencing. We will now send them back to your ships."

Jon-tral touched the golden pin symbol attached to the right chest area of his command suit, and it flashed once. A moment later, he and Sun-deema simply vanished from sight. Commander Yalgoot then touched a button on his wrist device, and all the Trilotew were sent away from their now sacred pyramid storage chamber in an upward whirling transporter light.

They re-materialized back inside the bridge control room, and Yalgoot casually walked over and sat down in his command chair. He took a deep peaceful breath, and then smiled as he gazed with gratitude at his patiently waiting, serenely smiling officers and warrior soldiers.

Back deep inside the Galactic Alliance Mt. Shasta base, Commander Tam-lure and his Second in Command Una-mala, were standing near a much larger central teleportation station. He looked down at a blinking light on the control console next to the female technician, and then looked back up at the several dozen lined up Trilotew soldiers who were continuing to pass by them to briefly clasp forearms in committed friendship. Each Trilotew soldier walked behind the console and took their place standing beside others, who were already standing on the teleportation pad. Ambassador Shon-ral's cousin Moon-teran, and her foster father Ted Carter, were standing beside each other just behind Tam-lure and Una-mala to observe unfolding events. They were smiling with compassionate understanding toward the Trilotew warriors that would have either killed or eaten them alive a short time earlier. After all twenty-four Trilotew soldiers stepped onto the pad, the base commanders saluted them with their right palms held across their hearts. The highest-ranking Trilotew squadron commander saluted them in return, and Jon-tral nodded his head again toward the female teleportation technician. She smiled and touched a control. A moment later, all the Trilotew soldiers were teleported away.

One dozen of the Trilotew soldiers materialized in High Commander Yalgoot's bridge control room between the other officers and bridge personnel. Commander Jon-tral's holographic projection appeared before them above the control console.

"Commander Yalgoot," he kindly stated, "the other dozen of your soldiers that were in our mountain base have been sent to your sister command ship. When you are ready, you can meet diplomatic members of the Galactic Alliance by standing before one of the golden pyramids, and then just ask to make contact. Please go in peace with the friendship of the entire Galactic Inter-dimensional Alliance of Free Worlds. Farewell for now."

Jon-tral's holographic projection faded away, and the truly grateful High Trilotew Commander Yalgoot gazed at his officers and warriors serenely smiling back at him for the first time. They were free and aware of all that he now knew.

Outside in the atmosphere, the power neutralizing golden sphere of light enshrouding both Trilotew command ships, and the green light encompassing all thirty elongate triangular Demon Scout ships vanished. The red aura of their own anti-gravity power reappeared around all their hulls, and the Demon Scout ships reformed into two triangular squadrons comprised of fifteen ships in each group. Each squadron then flew back up toward their respective command ships breaking from their formation to enter, one at a time, through an opening rectangular launch bay centered in the bottom of the oval cylindrical hulls. The two command ships slowly moved straight upward another thousand feet and stopped, then darted off in different directions headed towards stealthily hidden bases located somewhere under the Earth's surface.

The four much larger Galactic Alliance ships remained in place, while all sixty of their support Scout ships separated into four squadrons that flew back up beside the central hull of each parent vessel. One at a time, each Scout ship turned transparent just before it entered the launch bays of their four command carriers. The four mighty Galactic Alliance Emerald Star cruisers then darted up out of the atmosphere and into space to join the flagship moving in a geosynchronous orbit far above the planet.

# CHAPTER TWENTY

# FROM TYRANTS TO ANGELS

$\mathscr{B}$ase Commander Tam-lure was standing beside Una-mala, and Moon-teran was standing to the right of them in front of the teleportation console. They were deep inside the secret Mt. Shasta Galactic Alliance base in northern California.

Teleportation technician Trel-una, still seated behind the console, looked up at them and stated eagerly, "Commanders, Ambassador Shon-ral has returned from visiting the President of the United States aboard Boun-tama's ship. He just triggered the teleportation beam back to us."

Mark appeared a moment later out of the whirling, bright beam standing upon the circular platform and smiled confidently back at them. Moon-teran ran up the three steps to the platform and joyfully embraced him. They walked arm in arm back down the platform steps and up to the base Commanders.

"Well, Mr. Mark Santfield," she began, gazing cutely at Ambassador Shon-ral with a hand on her hip, "How will you juggle being married to two women from the same planet at the same time?"

"Well, Janice Carter," he replied fondly back to his home world cousin Moon-teran, "I guess we'll both have some very careful explaining to do when we get home to our own families."

"You two have had quite a busy day," remarked Second Commander Una-mala. "Perhaps now would be the right time for you to journey back home for a short time to reunite with your true families again."

"Yes, and we can arrange for both of you to undergo the DNA replacement therapy we told you about," encouraged Tam-lure. "It will transform your Earth bodies into your original Norexilam four-stranded-DNA human forms. We will have the DNA samples stored on your home planet sent to the Transport Carrier ship once it arrives in orbit. You can then go through the transformation together aboard ship. It will only take twenty-four hours to complete, and then you will be reunited with your loved ones."

Too moved for words, Mark and Janice nodded. They were holding back tears of joy over the prospect of actually reuniting with their own dear ones after so many terrifying years. At the same time, they were telepathically picking up on the intense but disciplined emotional longing to be reunited that was emanating from their families across a distance more than five hundred light-years away.

Now fully aware of his true identity disguised as author Mark Santfield, Ambassador Shon-ral told Commander Tam-lure thoughtfully, "We both came to help in whatever way we can with the uplifting transformation of Earth's hidden government leaders and the Trilotew soldiers you beamed to this base."

"We already perceived you both felt that way," Tam-lure remarked kindly. "However, they already stood before the radiant pyramid, and now they know who they really are."

"You would be amazed at the complete transformation they went through to regain their true benevolent natures," added Una-mala. "Their former terrible subconscious fear-based implants, engrams, and aberrations are no longer driving them to dominate and destroy. All the Trilotew here are eager to get back to their respective worlds. They want to witness how this transforming Ray will manifest upon their home planets to set free all the rest of their people."

"Come with us for a short time, and you can both experience this amazing event for yourselves," requested Tam-lure. "Then we will send you back to your home planet."

"Lead on, Commander," replied Mark.

Janice remarked curiously, "Back at the hidden desert base, the Trilotew had already started going through the transformation, but I would really like to experience what they are like in their fully restored natures."

Tam-lure and Una-mala appeared pleased as they headed out of the teleportation chamber through the triangular exit. Ambassador Shon-ral and Moon-teran simultaneously recalled how they recently falsely believed their identities were the Earth humans Mark Santfield and Janice Carter. They gave each other a knowing glance and then eagerly followed the Commanders.

They soon entered the main conference room inside the secret Mt. Shasta base and stopped with the Commanders to gaze at the multitude gathered there. To them it was now a truly odd sight to witness one hundred of the former self-righteous tyrant leaders of Earth's hidden covert government freely mingling with several dozen of their own black-ops protection soldiers and nearly the same amount of Trilotew officers and soldiers. Everyone appeared to be happy; openly sharing excited conversations that permeated the entire room with vibrantly transformed life.

First Officer Zorbok, who had first walked up to Janice and Ted back at the Arizona base after the Ray through Janice's pendant changed him, approached them. He bowed respectfully with both his long, clawed hands held crisscrossed over his chest.

"I see now that you two are actually non-Earth humans," he stated curiously.

"You are quite correct," Moon-teran replied. "Both Ambassador Shon-ral and I come from a planet beyond what Earth astronomers call the Pleiades star group. Seven of these stars are visible from Earth in the night sky away from city lights."

Zorbok's now gentle violet reptilian eyes with vertical red slits showed surprise, and he inquired, "You, Mark Santfield, are actually the Ambassador for the entire Galactic Inter-dimensional Alliance of Free Worlds?"

Mark smiled and nodded.

"But we tried with all our might and resources to kill you, and that I truly regret."

"You are free now from what was controlling your conscious will," replied Mark. "Know that I look forward to serving the Galactic Alliance in the near future as a negotiator between your worlds and the entire Galactic Alliance."

The Trilotew officer appeared quite pleased, and he bowed again at Shon-ral and Moon-teran. Then he turned and walked away to join several other Trilotew soldiers who were engaged in a jovial conversation with Tam-lure and Una-mala.

Mark looked at Janice to say something, but three approaching former tyrant leaders of Earth's secret worldwide government interrupted him. All three men were wearing expensive suits with the golden symbol pin of their secret organization attached to their lapels. Mark noticed it was a rectangular gold pin, embossed with a raised white alabaster pyramid and single radiant eye suspended above the apex. Two of the men were of medium height, one aged around forty with his black hair swept back over the top of his head, and the other older, slightly rotund bald man appeared to be aged about seventy years.

The third taller, dashingly handsome middle-aged man with wavy brown hair and a handlebar mustache stepped closer to Mark and Janice and respectfully stated, "Hello, my name is Harold Van Tipton. This is Jameson Rockefeller." He nodded toward the older bald man. "And this is Jason Armontel." He nodded toward the black-haired man. Both humble men standing behind him smiled as he continued. "We want to thank you for freeing us from the terrible subconscious implants the Trilotew placed in us to arrogantly dominate others. We also want you two to know we will use all our financial resources and our positions within the secret government to heal the Earth. Please believe that we are very sorry for having conspired with the Trilotew to command our combined agents to have both of you killed. We would have deserved it if the Trilotew had succeeded in taking over Earth and then viciously killed us. That you would subsequently care to liberate us from their sinister control has taught us a great lesson. What really matters is our reawakened true nature to respect all life."

As Ambassador Shon-ral, Mark smiled and replied, "I believe each of you now know why we endeavored to free you without harm, and I will confirm what you recently discovered yourselves. Your already warped passion for covert power and monetary control over your fellow Earth inhabitants twisted your spiritual reason. That made all of you easy targets for the Trilotew agents. First, they subconsciously fanned your lust for power to artificially bloated heights. Then it was relatively easy for them to get you to consider creating an alliance with them. All they had to do was promise your predecessors they would eventually gain total control of the entire Earth and all its citizens. They further encouraged compliance with their wishes by using their hidden hand-held controlling devices, to misdirect your intuitive insight from determining right from wrong. In other words, they shut down your intuitive perceptions that would warn you of their treacherous covert motive to take over the Earth with absolute ruling terror. The Trilotew probably killed certain members of your secret organization not present at the hidden desert base when Janice and Ted arrived. They would have replaced them with Trilotew disguised by a device that makes them look, act, and talk like them. Each one of you would have been next in line to be eaten alive and replaced with Trilotew lookalikes, probably within just a few more weeks if we had not intervened."

Harold smiled genuinely at Mark's words, for his malevolent former self was no longer in his subconscious to make him feel ashamed or embarrassed, and he extended a hand.

Mark gladly shook it, and then Harold added, upbeat, "We know you are actually Ambassador Shon-ral, and we want you to know that from now on you and the entire Galactic Alliance will have at your disposal our committed grateful assistance to help free up the rest of the world leaders and all the people of Earth." He looked at Janice and inquired, "Moon-teran is it?" She nodded, and he continued. "I can't imagine how horrible it must have been for you to grow up on Earth with all memory of your true self from another world suppressed."

"All of us are now restored once again to who we really are, and that is good enough for me," she replied kindly and smiled at him.

"Thank you, Moon-teran," he acknowledged, relieved. Then he looked at Mark and humbly asked, "How can our entire organization and resources help you now?"

"After you and your associates here are returned to your desert base, call all your members worldwide to come together for a meeting of extreme importance. Many will come. However, the Trilotew who already took over the identities of some of your secret members will refuse, and they will plan your demise. Know that there is no need to fear them. Each of you is now an emissary of the new consciousness freeing energy Ray emanating from special fountains within golden pyramids. Two are already in operation on the bottom of two of Earth's deepest oceans, and a third one is deep inside a mountain in the Himalayas. Wherever you go from now on, any being that may cross your paths will go through the very same transformation you just went through. This will always occur before you or your families can be harmed."

Base Commanders Tam-lure and Una-mala approached, and Tam-lure added kindly, "All of your members that we brought here will be watched over by Galactic Alliance observers from now on. We are dispatching many more Scout reconnaissance ships to monitor the Trilotew that remain hidden in various locations on Earth. We will be ready for them when they attempt their next move."

Una-mala added, gazing at the three transformed men, "We have already assigned a number of Galactic Alliance representatives to discreetly watch over your families when you are engaged in any future government activities. Once each of you have finished the complete deprogramming, you will have full use of your innate benevolent intelligence, and you will remember the many lives you lived to be standing here today. Then we will beam you back to your desert base. Know that from now on, Tam-lure and I will be in constant contact in one form or another."

The three men beamed gratitude as they shook hands with Commander

Tam-lure, Second Commander Una-mala, Mark, and then Janice. Then they walked away to give the good news to their ninety-seven other associates standing in various places around the chamber.

Una-mala glanced at her husband, he glanced back, and she turned to Ambassador Shon-ral and Moon-teran and said, "And now at least for a short time, you two have the opportunity to return home to go through your DNA transformations to regain your former original physical natures. We can have you back at your home world in under a day's travel time."

*Finally,* Mark and Janice telepathically stated together.

"The smaller three-hundred-feet-long Transport Carrier you saw stationed in front of the command complex when you first arrived has returned," remarked Tam-lure, "and I have instructed the Captain to leave within the hour. Will that be acceptable?"

"We are in your hands, Commander," replied Mark.

"I have other matters to attend to with Commanders Jon-tral and Sun-deema aboard the flagship regarding Earth and our approaching fleet," continued Tam-lure with an enthusiastic smile. "Thousands of Galactic Alliance Emerald Star cruisers, including a number of the ten-mile-long intergalactic class cruisers are already on the way here. More will arrive in a second wave behind them. This should give you two at least several weeks to be reunited with your anxiously awaiting families, before you will be temporarily needed back here. Una-mala will escort you to the ship. For now my friends, farewell."

He held his right palm over his heart and nodded. Mark and Janice returned the gesture, and he walked away.

Janice heard her Earth father's voice calling excitedly from behind them. "Janice, dear daughter, it's so good to see you."

She and Mark turned to see him walking into the conference and recreation room at a hurried clip. Ted looked more vibrant, and many years younger, as he walked up to his daughter and stopped to fondly gaze into her eyes.

She heard him continue telepathically to her amazement, *Dear foster daughter from far away, it's really me. I remember more about my true self. As you have guessed, I also recovered some telepathic ability after they reactivated several of my genetically suppressed genes. It is just so amazing. My God Janice, all of Earth's people are asleep. They have no idea how suppressed the entire human race has been for so many thousands of years.*

Moon-teran threw her arms around her foster father with tears trickling down her cheeks, and they hugged long and tenderly.

She let him go and then smiled up at him.

*Dearest foster father of the entire universe, this is beyond words for me. You look many years younger.*

He gazed lovingly at her for a moment and then turned toward Mark to say, "Mark, I mean Ambassador Shon-ral … I … well … I don't know how to say this. Because of you, I have been set far more than free. I remember a number of other lifetimes I spent on this planet blindly seeking power and fortune, but I did not originally come from Earth. Like you, I too came from the stars during another colonization period after one of the earlier polar shifts a million years ago."

"I'm not who you should credit for that miracle," replied Mark, smiling back at him. "The gift of the special Ray emanating from many dimensions far above this physical universe accomplished that. If my own people had not located me on Earth after the publication of my first book, we would not be having this conversation. Now that you are back to who you really are, I am quite satisfied with how you so carefully raised Janice, I mean my cousin, Moon-teran. Now we can finally be returned to our former home planet forms and to our own families very soon."

"If you will be so kind as to follow me," said Una-mala with a wink, "we will get you two back home, and the long wait will finally be over. Ted, you may wish to go through a more thorough past life awakening aboard the flagship before you return to Earth. Then you will be prepared to help awaken your fellow hidden-government members."

"Commander Una-mala, I would like that very much," replied Ted, "and thank you for all the kindness you have shown me and all the others here in this amazing Mt. Shasta base. My colleagues and I are quite anxious to get back to the business of freeing all the people of Earth, with Galactic Alliance guidance and assistance of course."

"Then by all means, we will not keep any of you waiting a moment longer," Una-mala replied graciously.

She waved her hand toward the exit from the chamber, but before she took a step, Tam-lure returned at a quick pace, concerned, and announced, "Dear wife, I regret to say our friends' trip back home will have to be temporarily postponed. Our monitoring ships have picked up Trilotew conversations coming from their hidden base deep in the Amazon jungle. It has been confirmed the Trilotew now have control over both the Chinese and the Russian leaders, and they have just compelled them to arrange a coordinated preemptive nuclear strike against the United States."

"Oh, my husband," replied Una-mala, blanching, "they must have been contacted by the Trilotew General we set free aboard one of their fleet cruisers. We both know this new Ray cannot work through a communication link or transceiver unless one is near the intended contact. Only a completely freed being operating with the Ray passing through them from a pyramid source can bring about a benevolent change in others."

"After being set free," continued Tam-lure, "the Trilotew General and their own Ambassador must have contacted their remaining two Commanders on Earth through their ship's console. If they tried to arrange a face-to-face meeting with those two remaining twisted Commanders without their Emperor's direct order, they would refuse to allow it. Knowing the Trilotew, they would conclude that somehow the Galactic Alliance had forced the General and the Ambassador to be traitors or driven them insane. The two remaining Commanders operating underground in those two countries would have immediately called for reinforcements from home. Most certainly, an armada of Trilotew warships is already on the way. We will have to work fast if we want to avoid much destruction."

"I have an idea," Mark stated enthusiastically. "Janice is still wearing her pendant under her clothes, and I'm authorized to transmit the Ray from the pyramid on the flagship through my pendant directly to anyone standing before me." He gazed eagerly at his cousin, but she appeared sad, and he asked, "Dear Moon-teran, I know this delay will be hard, but we must practice patience for the benefit of all. Are you willing?"

She looked away sadly for a moment in thoughtful reverie and then looked back, smiling.

"Mr. Ambassador, forgive me," she began, now courageously upbeat. "I let myself momentarily indulge in a selfish yearning to see my family again, but I let go of it. I'm with you."

"Oh good, that's a relief. I felt the same thing, but we are so close to freeing the people of this planet. We know many of them trapped here for countless lifetimes are actually our own people who came to explore this world long ago. Dear Cousin, we must see this through to completion. Otherwise how could we rest in bliss with our families back home?"

She nodded, and Shon-ral confidently continued imparting his plan to Commanders Tam-lure and Una-mala.

"Of course, we'll need the consent and cooperation of fleet Commanders Jon-tral and Sun-deema aboard the flagship. Can you also arrange to have the four Emerald Star cruisers operate invisibly over the Russian and Chinese Capitals?"

"Of course we can," answered Tam-lure. "I'm certain fleet Commanders Jon-tral and Sun-deema will agree."

"Then I believe—no I'm certain—we can bring to a permanent end the Trilotew role and presence on this planet," continued Mark. "When the time is right, your base personnel and all the ships we have on or around the Earth will have to be coordinated for one well-timed move."

Tam-lure and Una-mala gazed at each other, then smiled encouragingly at the direction his plan was heading.

"What have you envisioned?" Una-mala asked.

"You must be prepared to beam the remaining controlled world leaders and the Trilotew thugs controlling them to one place at the same moment, including the Trilotew already disguised as the humans they probably killed in order to take over their identities. Moon-teran's special pendant will shield us from any initial attacks they try, while the transforming Ray can pass through the pendant I wear to free them from the subconscious terror that drives their hideous behavior. Can you do it?"

"Yes, yes we can certainly do that," Tam-lure answered eagerly.

"Can Janice and I use the smaller Inter-stellar Transport Carrier ship you have landed outside this complex as a temporary base of operations?"

"Indeed, you can," replied Tam-lure.

"And we will need someone to oversee any beaming we will have to accomplish with great precision at very precise moments."

"We already have that covered," confirmed Tam-lure. "I asked our friends Boun-tama and Lean-tala to join us here in case their assistance is required, and they have probably already beamed to the base from their cottage home. I'll have them meet us at the ship, and they can oversee everything you require."

"Then once again," continued Mark, "I must state what the genius detective character, Sherlock Holmes, in the old classic Earth novels would say to his assistant before starting a crime-solving adventure, 'Watson, my good man, the game is afoot.'"

"And I'm your Watson, Mr. Ambassador," announced Janice.

"Indeed, you are, dear Cousin," Mark agreed. "Indeed you are."

"How can I help?" inquired Ted.

"You, my good man, should first get more deprogramming freedom aboard the flagship. However, before that you will want to experience a firsthand overview of what is about to take place around the planet. Then you can later communicate telepathically what took place to your fellow associates back on Earth."

Satisfied, Ted's smile slowly widened as they walked away at a fast clip.

A few minutes later, they walked out of the football field sized command structure. They crossed the boarding ramp and stopped in front of a trim muscular middle-aged man standing in front of the open hatch leading inside the Transport Carrier ship. He was clean-shaven with high cheekbones, shoulder-length wavy brown hair, and clear sky-blue eyes slightly larger than the typical eyes of Earth humans. He smiled and acknowledged the Commanders, and then Mark and Janice, with his right palm held over his heart, and they returned the gesture.

"Mr. Ambassador and Prime Scientist Moon-teran," the Pilot announced cordially, "it will be my pleasure to escort you back to your home world."

"For now, Captain Zin-tamal, that will have to wait," Commander Tam-lure interjected seriously. "Something has come up. We must use the Transport Carrier ship as an emergency base of operations for Ambassador Shon-ral and Moon-teran. I'll fill you in on our way to the flagship."

"As you wish, Commander," the Captain replied respectfully. "If you will all come aboard, we can get to the flagship in orbit around the Earth in about ten minutes Earth time."

As he turned and headed toward the oval entry hatch, Boun-tama and Lean-tala approached at a good clip from behind. They were very cheery as Mark and Janice greeted them with a warm bear hug.

"My cousin Moon-teran and I are about to help stop a nuclear war," stated Mark confidently. We're glad you're here to assist us."

"With all that happened, I didn't get the chance to properly thank you two for all you did for Ambassador Shon-ral's survival," remarked Janice, as she beamed a smile at them.

"Well," Lean-tala replied happily, "it's what we do."

"Indeed it is, dear wife," Boun-tama agreed heartily.

"I have filled them in, and they are ready to assist you," interjected Tam-lure. "We must get to the flagship as soon as possible."

As they walked through the oval entry hatch of the Transport Carrier ship, they could hear the soft deep hum of the inch-thick, pale-blue antigravity energy field and see it surrounding the ship's massive cylindrical-shaped hull. A golden light grid appeared across the opening behind them rapidly filling with materializing solid silvery metal until the hull appeared seamless with no apparent door.

The light enshrouding the cylindrical ship brightened, and it lifted straight up above the landing pad. The two semispherical launch-bay doors far overhead began to open at the top of the cavern base. The massive ship turned vertical as it began to fade into invisibility, and then it shot straight up and out of northern California's mysterious Mt. Shasta's extinct volcanic caldera to vanish in the brilliant star-lit night sky.

# CHAPTER TWENTY-ONE

# OBLIVION
# OR
# PARADISE

*In* just under ten minutes, the medium-sized Transport Carrier ship was already slowing its approach to the mile-long Emerald Star Galactic Alliance flagship. It dwarfed the Transport Carrier as it slowed to a stop to hover in a parallel position, several thousand yards from the central section of the massive inter-stellar parent vessel.

Tam-lure Una-mala, Mark, Janice, Boun-tama, Lean-tala, and Ted were standing on the teleportation platform, as Captain Zin-tamal nodded to a trim, well-built technician with curly brown hair that appeared to be in his late-twenties. The technician nodded, smiling back as he touched a luminous control on the console. A moment later, their seven bodies were dematerialized and whisked away in the whirling teleportation beam.

They reappeared at the same moment on an identical pad deep inside the flagship of the Galactic Inter-dimensional Alliance of Free Worlds. Waiting to greet them with warm welcoming smiles were Commanders Jon-tral and Sun-deema, standing directly behind a very pretty, long brunette-haired female technician in her mid-twenties.

They walked down the steps from the pad and up to the flagship Commanders, and then respectfully acknowledged them with their right palms held over their hearts.

The flagship Commanders returned the gesture, and Jon-tral stated, "This flagship and our other four Emerald Star cruisers are now stealthily orbiting the planet. We are prepared to act on a moment's notice."

"Thank you for the update," acknowledged Mark.

Jon-tral waved his arm toward the triangular exit from the teleportation chamber and remarked, "If all of you will follow us to the bridge command center, we can monitor the Trilotew movements before we engage Ambassador Shon-ral's plan."

Jon-tral and Sun-deema walked out of the room followed by Mark, Janice, Ted, Boun-tama, Lean-tala, and then Tam-lure and Una-mala.

They walked into the command bridge through the triangular hallway entrance and continued until Jon-tral and Sun-deema stopped in front of the waist-high central-command station. The long control console curved before them like a half moon below the horizontal, oval space-view windows.

Jon-tral kindly asked the beautiful young female technician sitting in front of the console gazing down at the control board, "Jin-trean, please activate the surrounding view screen."

Like a graceful swan, she lifted her head up on a long slender neck, turned to face the Commander, and replied, "As you wish, Commander, and welcome back everyone."

She turned back around and touched a control, and the end-to-end projected view screens appeared along the top of the long half-octagon shaped console. All of Asia, including Russia and China, appeared as a single large image spread across the series of screens providing an overview from a hundred miles above the planet. The image zoomed closer to gradually focus on China and then continued to zoom forward until a large government complex in Beijing came into clear focus. Then the image switched to a large interior office within the government-building complex. A slightly rotund sixty-year-old Chinese President with gray-streaked hair, black-rimmed glasses, and an expensive three-piece, blue suit was standing behind his large cherry-wood desk. A tall thin Chinese man with glaring black eyes, black wavy hair, wearing a dark-blue suit was standing right behind him. The Chinese flag with a single red star draped down from a golden metal pole behind them. A stiff, fully extended plastic Chinese flag on a small wooden stand was sitting on the middle front edge of the desk. The taller man pulled his right hand out of his suit pocket holding in his clenched fist one of the Trilotew subconscious-programming devices. He pointed it at the back of the Chinese President's head, pushed a button, and then quickly stuffed it back into his suit pocket.

Then he sneered at the back of the President's head, mocked up a smile, and stated in Mandarin Chinese, "Mr. President, you know what we must do now that we have the full cooperation of the Russian President."

The translation into English simultaneously appeared across the bottom of the view screens back on the Galactic Alliance flagship, as the silent observers continued to watch. The Chinese President blinked several times, and his blank expression transformed into a devilishly cunning grin. Then he nodded his agreement as he reached down and touched one of ten buttons on the back edge of the desk with his forefinger. The yellow wall to their right slid up into the ceiling, revealing a rectangular twenty-feet-wide and ten-feet-high LCD television screen. The solidly built Russian President in his sixties with gray hair parted on the side, wearing a black suit, came into focus. He was standing behind his large dark-wood desk somewhere in the Kremlin government complex in Moscow. Standing behind him was a taller lanky Caucasian man with penetrating dark-brown eyes and short brown hair, wearing a more modest dark suit. He was staring at the back of the President's head with malicious glee as he stuffed one of the subconscious implant programming devices back inside his suit coat pocket.

The Russian President's blank look suddenly transformed into devilish glee, and the taller man mocked up a respectful smile, then stated in Russian, "Mr. President, you know what we must do to stop the United States President from threatening our plans. We know he has left our worldwide hidden organization. Now he will attempt to destroy us with his new Galactic Alliance allies."

The translation from Russian to English also simultaneously appeared across the bottom of the view screens aboard the Galactic Alliance flagship as the Russian President asked, "Are you ready, Mr. President of the great Chinese nation?"

The Chinese President smiled back with equal malicious intent and replied, this time in English, "Yes, Mr. President of the proud Russian republic. Our generals are now in communication with your generals. The time is set for eight o'clock tonight. We are ready to launch our entire ground and space-based nuclear missile arsenals."

The Russian President proudly confirmed back in English, "We also have our orbital platforms and ground-based missile units ready for launch."

The facial expressions of everyone watching events unfold back on the bridge of the Galactic Alliance flagship revealed their intense focus to see the critical situation safely neutralized.

Mark had a sudden realization and he asked Jon-tral, "Commander, how much time does that give us?"

Jon-tral looked at the console in front of the technician, then looked back and replied, "That gives us just under two hours to stop this madness."

"Can you have two of the large fleet cruisers hovering invisibly over Moscow, and two more hovering invisibly over Beijing within the hour?" Mark inquired enthusiastically.

"Yes, we can arrange that," Jon-tral replied, curious. "But what are you suggesting?"

"Can they also be ready to beam up the Russian and Chinese Presidents, along with those two disguised Trilotew thugs controlling them at the same instant? Then can you beam them to the Oval Office in the White House in Washington, D.C.?"

"Yes, we can certainly accomplish that," replied Jon-tral, still curious.

"Can you also neutralize their launch computers on the ground and in space?" Mark inquired.

"Yes, of course," he replied confidently. "But we can only accomplish that through the command ships by using a device with that capability that was installed long ago at the Mt. Shasta base." He nodded at Commanders Tam-lure and Una-mala.

"Mark, that device back at the base can neutralize any power system or computer device worldwide," Tam-lure confirmed, "if the emergency need should arise. In fact, we were compelled to secretly use it twelve times on Earth through our Scout class ships during the Cold War between the United States and the former Soviet Union, after the fools on one side or the other actually pushed the button to annihilate the planet. During those times, we had no authorization to directly interfere with the affairs of Earth governments according to strict treaty regulations with the Trilotew. However, we all knew how often over many thousands of years the Trilotew have broken that treaty to try to gain control of one planet or another. Because of that fact, we at least had permission to stop the world super powers from destroying themselves through their uncontrollable negative passions, which the Trilotew were artificially fanning into flaming heights. The nuclear destruction of the planet's surface would have caused harm to several hundred billion beings living in a number of parallel dimensions about which the Earth scientists know practically nothing. Of course, every time either government tried to push the button to engage in nuclear war, mysterious extraterrestrial Scout ships would appear over their key launch-control facilities, and shut down their launch computers. Our Scout ships would then simply leave without interfering in any other way. Then we turned on their launch computers again with the launch-ready modes deactivated. When we're ready, this same neutralizing beam can be transmitted through our four Emerald Star cruisers hovering over Moscow and Beijing."

"To clarify several other points," continued Second Commander Una-mala, "both sides soon realized some power beyond their control was not going to allow them the insane use of their new nuclear weapons. Of course, both governments, and in fact the governments of thirty-three other countries as well, soon agreed to keep most highly classified their awareness of far more advanced extraterrestrial beings, and what they knew about their capability to intervene in their insane affairs. Subsequently, at great secret expense, nearly all of Earth's people have been kept in the dark for considerably more than the last sixty years."

Mark and Janice looked at each other, and Mark continued, "We must be ready to act the moment the Chinese and Russian Presidents attempt to actually launch their missile arsenals."

"You two should now beam back to the Mt. Shasta base to prepare the Energy Field Dampening Device," suggested Commander Jon-tral to Mt. Shasta base Commanders Tam-lure and Una-mala. "The Russian and Chinese launch computers must be shut down the moment you receive the signal from Ambassador Shon-ral."

The base Commanders nodded with their right palms held over their hearts. Jon-tral returned the respectful salute, and the base Commanders walked away.

Janice's Earth foster father, Ted, had remained silently observant of all that was transpiring, and he looked anxiously at Commander Jon-tral to request, "I would like to return to Earth with my fellow freed classified-government associates as soon as possible. With the assistance of my General Counsel Henry, I can do far more good down there than I can from up here."

"You should first finish your full deprogramming, and there is another important matter we have not told you about regarding Henry," replied Second Commander Sun-deema with an alluring smile.

"What's happening with Henry?" asked Ted puzzled, gazing back at her.

"Look behind you," she replied, and Ted spun around to see Henry walking into the command bridge through the triangular entry hallway. His beaming smile from ear to ear was unmistakable to everyone as he approached and stopped a few feet away to bow regally with a comical wide sweep of his arm.

"Henry!" Ted and Janice simultaneously exclaimed.

"Well, what did you expect?" shot back Henry, quite jubilant. "I have been through the complete deprogramming and Ted, I must tell you it is just beyond amazing how expanded your awareness of everything comes clearly into focus for the first time. I understand you have yet to finish your full deprogramming. Let me recommend you go through it right away if you really want to be effective back on Earth."

Ted, Janice, and Mark walked up to Henry, and Ted gave him an unexpectedly vigorous bear hug, swept him off the floor, and then spun him in a circle before he set him back down. Then Janice kissed him on the cheek and hugged him. Mark extended his arm, and Henry clasped it as if they were reunited long-lost brothers.

"Henry, my good man," continued Ted, elated, "it looks like our association has permanently changed for the better. Now that we know who we really are, I can only thank you for all the years of loyalty and brilliance you gave to me. Please know that I now deeply regret having kept my most important friend in the dark regarding the trap I was getting myself into ever more deeply."

"Not to worry," Henry replied calmly. "That's all behind us now. If you go through the rest of the deprogramming, which takes only about an hour, you will remember ever so much more about your true self. Sun-deema said that after that we would both be ready to return to Earth to help liberate the other hidden-government members worldwide. Now that is something I can really sink my teeth into, so to speak. What do you say?"

"Henry, dearest of friends, I will listen to your wise counsel now and do exactly that, if Sun-deema will accompany me," Ted replied happily as he looked to Sun-deema.

She was already smiling back at him like a loving mother as she walked up and confidently stated, "It would be my honor to help set you free. First, we must remove the remaining veils that are keeping you from knowing who you really are, including those that occurred before this familiar lifetime. If you will follow me, I'll escort you to the liberation chamber, as some of us now call it."

"Commander, would you mind if I borrow your wife Sun-deema for about an hour?" inquired Ted, gazing hopefully with raised eyebrows at Jon-tral.

"Go with her and get it behind you," replied Jon-tral. "When you return, Mon-tlan, or the one you know as Monti, who is on his way here, can safely escort you both back to Earth. We will also send your other associates gathered here back to the Arizona base. Will that do for starters?"

Ted smiled and gazed eagerly at Sun-deema. She motioned with her hand toward the triangular hallway exit, and he gallantly offered her his elbow. Pleased by the gesture, she regally clasped her arm around it, and they walked side by side out of the command bridge.

"Well, what do ya know?" stated Henry, surprised. "Now that's a brand new side of Ted I've never seen before." He looked hopefully at Jon-Tral and inquired, "Commander, do you mind if I go with them? I would really like to be there when the completely rehabilitated Ted shows up for the first time. I have a feeling we will have a lot to talk about."

"Go ahead and join them, but you will not be allowed to attend the actual session unless Ted wants you there," replied Jon-tral, and his smile faded. "Some of the things a person discovers through this process can be really shocking, and many people do not want others to know about it."

"Understood, Commander," Henry replied anxiously. "I'll offer to be there for him as a friend, if he wants one."

Henry spun around and walked at a quick clip toward the triangular hallway exit. Commander Jon-tral gazed after him until he disappeared down the hallway, and then he smiled appreciatively in reflection of Henry's newly awakened wisdom.

Boun-tama and Lean-tala had remained silently observant of all that had transpired during the previous half hour, and they glanced knowingly at each other.

Then Boun-tama urged Mark and Janice, "If we are to get you two to the White House in Washington in time to succeed with this plan, we must return to the Transport Carrier now."

"There's never a dull moment around here," remarked Janice.

"That's an understatement if ever there was one," added Mark as he threw his arm around her shoulder and gave her a squeeze for courage. Then he continued confidently, "Well friends, let's get this done once and for all time. Please lead the way."

Boun-tama gazed at his lovely wife and offered her his arm. They too walked at a quick pace out of the control room, followed close behind by the eager Inter-stellar Diplomat Shon-ral and his equally eager cousin, Prime Scientist Moon-teran.

They were in a jovial mood, and a few minutes later they rematerialized back aboard the Transport Carrier ship standing upon the teleportation pad. Captain Zin-tamal was waiting to greet them standing behind the semicircular control console.

"Welcome travelers," he stated serenely. "Maybe now we can take the ship to a place where we can actually accomplish something. I assume we are heading to Washington, D.C. in the invisible frequency, cloaked in a higher parallel dimension."

They walked off the pad and up to Zin-tamal, and Boun-tama replied, "Yes Captain, the moment has finally arrived. We must get this ship hovering over the White House as quickly as possible."

"I can have us there in a stationary hovering position in under ten minutes, if the need is great," the Captain replied confidently.

Mark stepped toward him and stated, "Captain, once the ship is in position, Boun-tama and Lean-tala will coordinate our beaming to the President's Oval Office in the White House. When his military advisers tell him the Russian and Chinese homelands are about to launch an all-out nuclear war against the United States, I'll make certain he doesn't prepare a retaliatory strike." He took a deep breath and looked to Boun-tama and Lean-tala, then continued, "I will keep the transceiver pin on my coat lapel open so you two can monitor events as they unfold."

"I hope after this day is over," added Janice, "there will be some sort of worldwide peace to build upon in the coming months. Lean-tala, may I ask when the massive open disclosure and worldwide landing of the Galactic Alliance fleet is scheduled to take place?"

Lean-tala looked at her husband for approval; he nodded, then she looked back at Janice and Mark and answered, "After all the Trilotew secretly operating on Earth are transformed and they are departing for their own world systems, the much larger aspects of *The Seres Agenda* will be openly brought into operation. Via a worldwide TV transmission, the President of the United States will stand beside the man the people know as Mark Santfield and announce that you are actually Ambassador Shon-ral from the Galactic Inter-dimensional Alliance of Free Worlds. He will state you are here to officially announce to the world that extraterrestrials exist. Then sparks will fly all over the planet."

"After the TV broadcast," Boun-tama elaborated, "you two will be free to take your vacation back on your home world to finally be reunited with your anxiously awaiting families. The Galactic Alliance Grand Council also hopes that you will both return to Earth as emissaries of this new consciousness-transforming Ray. Your presence on Earth will help to safely bridge the great constructive changes that will happen to the people all over the planet at an accelerating rate. Enormous benevolent environmental and political transformations will also be taking place worldwide. I believe you get the big picture."

*Yes, dear friends, we do,* Janice and Mark replied telepathically in unison with solemn nods of their heads.

"Captain Zin-tamal, get us hovering over the White House," Boun-tama commanded.

The Captain eagerly spun around and headed off toward the bridge control room, and they followed close behind him.

The Transport Carrier arrived to hover in the slightly higher frequency of a parallel dimension five-thousand-feet above the White House. It was radiating its usual pale-blue antigravity aura around the cylindrical hull, but no radar picked them up, and no one on the ground could see anything in the clear blue sky that day over the capital of the United States.

Lean-tala was standing next to Boun-tama behind the teleportation control console. They placed their right palms over their hearts, smiling encouragement, and nodded their best wishes. Mark and Janice standing on the pad returned the gesture, as Lean-tala touched the illumined golden spherical crystal on the console. The control brightened, and the two emissaries to President Martin McCoy of the United States dissolved in the upward-whirling teleportation light.

They rematerialized from the same whirling light standing upon the official eagle symbol woven into the rug in front of the President's desk, just as an astonished President Martin McCoy was getting up from his chair. Repairs to the burned holes in the Oval Office walls were completed.

"Oh my God, what's happening Ambassador Shon-ral, and who is that with you?" blurted out the nervous President.

Mark motioned with his hand for the President to calm himself and replied, "Mr. President, the United States is about to be attacked by the combined nuclear forces of both Russia and China, but do not be afraid. We are about to neutralize their launch capabilities."

A loud, frantic knock on the Oval Office door interrupted them, and Secretary of Defense Daniel Samuelson barged into the room, out of breath. He stopped in his tracks, surprised to see Mark and particularly Janice, and then asked distrustfully, "What in blazes is he doing here?"

"Don't worry about him, Daniel. I invited him. Now, quickly tell me why you're here," ordered Martin.

"As you wish, Mr. President. Our early-warning satellites detected that both the Russian and Chinese nuclear missile arsenals have been placed in a launch-readiness mode, and our primary agent in Russia just informed us their generals have been ordered to make a preemptive strike against the United States at any moment."

"Daniel, for your own well-being I want you to remain here to experience what's about to take place. Make sure the door is locked behind you," the President commanded calmly.

Though confused, Daniel turned around and walked back to the Oval Office door then locked it and returned for some answers.

Janice carefully observed Daniel's nervousness as he began to back up slowly against the Oval Office door. She touched her pendant under her blouse, and it briefly flashed. Daniel suddenly stopped and shook his head as if coming out of a trance.

He gazed, amazed, at Janice, Mark, and the President then asked, "What's happening to me? I suddenly feel so good, and now I remember that I never trusted the Trilotew Ambassador every time he came here to visit you, Mr. President. However, whenever I endeavored to speak out, I suddenly found myself agreeing with whatever he was saying. He must have done something to me or to both of us."

"It's all right, Daniel," Martin reassured. "We are now free from the brainwashing they put us both through."

"But I thought we were supposed to be allies with the Trilotew," shot back Daniel, still mystified.

"Daniel, what does your heart tell you now?" Janice inquired.

"It's clear we were being manipulated by those reptilian monsters. They meant to do us all harm. I'm certain of that now," he stated angrily, and then his anger suddenly transformed into compassion. "The Trilotew must also be compelled to behave that way by subconscious drives they cannot control or stop." He looked to Mark to confirm his suspicion and asked, "Could that be correct?"

Mark walked over and put a consoling hand on Daniel's shoulder and replied, "My friend, you are beginning to regain your own innate intuitive wisdom. Just go with it."

"Trust your own feelings, Daniel, while you patiently observe what is about to happen," Martin quickly insisted, and Daniel nodded that he understood.

"Mr. President and Secretary Samuelson, please let me introduce my cousin Moon-teran from our home planet. She is here to assist me with the events that are about to unfold around the world, but we must act quickly."

"I don't follow you," replied President McCoy, concerned. "What must we do?"

Mark continued calmly as he walked back over to Janice. "With your permission, I must now contact the Galactic Alliance flagship to stop the Russian and Chinese launch computers in time. May I proceed?"

Before the President could answer, the pin on Mark's lapel flashed three times. He reached up and touched it, and he heard a telepathic communication.

*Ambassador Shon-ral, can you and Moon-teran hear me? This is Commander Jon-tral aboard the flagship.*

193

# CHAPTER TWENTY-ONE

"Yes, I hear you clearly," replied Shon-ral.

"We both hear you," confirmed Moon-teran.

*In thirty seconds, it will be 8:00 p.m.*, continued Commander Jon-tral, *the designated time for Moscow and Beijing to launch their missiles. Both the Russian and the Chinese Presidents have just given the green light for their top military generals to order the combined preemptive nuclear strike. I just ordered the Emerald Star fleet cruisers invisibly hovering over Moscow and Beijing to stand ready to receive the energy-dampening beam from the Mt. Shasta base. We are ready. Stand by to hear Tam-lure's voice.*

A moment passed, and then Mark and Janice telepathically heard, *Can you two hear me? This is Commander Tam-lure. Una-mala is standing here beside me, cheering you on.*

Mark and Janice glanced at each other, and Mark replied aloud, "Yes, we both clearly hear you. We are ready to receive our unexpected guests. I will count down from five. Then activate the device to shut down their launch computers and signal the fleet Commanders to teleport them all here in shielded energy spheres. Moon-teran will signal you to release them from their surrounding shields after the Ray neutralizes their negative-subconscious drives. I'm beginning the count now … five … four … three … two … one."

At that moment in Moscow and Beijing, both Presidents simultaneously ordered their top generals to launch their missiles through a special direct phone link. Standing behind their respective Presidents, scowling with devilish glee at the backs of their heads was a Trilotew disguised as a taller human.

The top generals deep inside the command and control bunkers of both countries simultaneously turned a single gold firing key to launch their entire missile arsenals stationed on the ground and on orbiting satellite platforms.

However, one finger just a second ahead of them was already touching a luminous, clear red crystal on the central control board deep inside the Mt. Shasta base.

An identical triangular red crystal atop a silver pole extended a dozen feet above the extinct volcanic caldera floor of Mt. Shasta turned on. A six-inch-thick beam of red wavering light shot from it up through the sky into space to hit an identical crystal at the end of a pole extended from the curved hull of one end of the mile-long Galactic Alliance flagship. The beam passing through this crystal split into four beams that darted at the speed of light back down into the atmosphere. They passed through identical crystals at the ends of poles extended from each end of all four Emerald Star cruisers hovering above Moscow and Beijing, and continued down into the Russian and Chinese underground launch-command facilities.

The two generals in their respective bases did not see the red beams invisibly vibrating at a higher frequency as they penetrated their launch control computers and instantly shut them down. Both frustrated angry generals picked up a phone to contact their Presidents.

Having overheard the Generals' flustered messages to their respective Presidents, both disguised Trilotew were now frothing venomous anger. They simultaneously ripped the phones from the hands of both Presidents and then started to gleefully strangle the backs of their necks, but their hands suddenly went limp and they let go with terror etched across their faces.

Both Presidents and their disguised Trilotew overseers suddenly found themselves encased in transparent golden energy bubbles that faded away.

In France, England, India, Pakistan, and several other nuclear capable countries, the same phenomenon was taking place. Transparent golden energy bubbles instantly surrounded their stunned leaders, and their equally stunned disguised Trilotew overseers, just before they faded from sight.

In the Oval Office of the White House, many transparent golden energy bubbles containing the now angrily fuming leaders were reappearing all over the room. The human disguises camouflaging the Trilotew hovering in bubbles next to each of them suddenly melted away in vanishing puffs of black smoke, revealing their true bipedal reptilian natures.

Janice stepped up beside Mark, and they both reached inside their clothes and pulled out their special pendants hanging from the gold chains, then held them up at chest level. They respectfully lowered their heads, just as both pendants lit up with radiant white light. Waves in repeating concentric circles began emanating from them to harmlessly pass right through the beings encased inside the energy bubbles, and through everyone else in the room, then out through the walls of the Oval Office. The angry expressions of the Presidents of Russia and China and the other leaders transformed into uplifted joyful bliss none of them had ever experienced before in their lives. The coarse, green-scaled skin of the Trilotew agents began to soften as their facial features became more elegant and benign. Apparent to everyone else in the room was the devilish glare of their oval violet eyes with vertical cat-like red slits as they transformed to gentler, loving natures.

President Martin McCoy walked around his desk and stood equidistant between Mark and Janice.

He raised his right hand in a peace gesture toward the other eight transforming government leaders, and to the Trilotew encased in their transparent golden energy spheres, then calmly announced, "Fellow leaders from around the world, and their Trilotew associates, be at peace here in the Oval Office. As you must know by now, no harm will come to you. All of you are being set free from the terrible subconscious-implanted programs that were driving you to act in an insane, destructive manner."

The Chinese President gazed back at him and replied timidly in Mandarin, which everyone heard translated into their language by the mysterious uplifting Ray, "But we were trying to annihilate you and your country. Now this makes no sense, and I don't understand how we could have acted this way."

"Yes, he's quite right," agreed the Russian President enthusiastically in Russian, which everyone also clearly heard stated in his or her own language. "We were driven to annihilate you by the hideous Trilotew we stupidly trusted to gain more power."

A general agreement was voiced in a mix of rambling chatter excitedly coming from the other world leaders hovering a foot above the floor in their individual energy spheres. The sad, downcast eyes of their former devilish Trilotew programmers were now apparent to Mark, Janice, and President McCoy. They waited for the general clamor to die down, and then Mark touched his pendant hanging from its gold chain again. One pulsing, radiant, soft golden light poured out of it like an expanding waterfall comprised of tiny golden self-effulgent teardrops that penetrated and dissolved inside everyone in the Oval Office. They were all greatly uplifted to a momentary speechless state of profound insight and understanding. The Russian President was the first to speak with newfound compassion to his former Trilotew controller floating next to him.

"Shaoulnoom, it wasn't your fault. You could not stop what you knew was wrong with every fiber of your being."

Shaoulnoom's deep, regretful sadness suddenly lifted, and his newly freed consciousness gazed for the first time through benevolent eyes at the Russian Earth human he had wanted to eat alive the moment he finished using him.

"You would say that to one that would have destroyed you only moments ago without remorse?" Shaoulnoom inquired.

"Do you now know the true nature of your being as I do my own?" asked the Russian President, smiling kindly at him.

Shaoulnoom thoughtfully lowered his reptilian head and then looked back up, beginning to smile, and replied, amazed, "Yes, yes I see it now."

"Why did you give all of us this great gift of freedom?" he asked, looking at Mark.

"No, my friends, I did not do this," replied Mark, gazing at all the world leaders and the Trilotew. "This special uplifting and transforming Ray does not originate from me. This gift comes to all of us from a reality that exists in a far, far higher dimension above the entire physical universe. The liberation of consciousness you are all experiencing is now beginning to spread throughout creation. It is not just for the Earth humans, the Trilotew, or any one planet or people. Each of you will soon further awaken to all that is within you, which had been suppressed in lifetimes so long ago. You will begin to innately know that evil, an experimental artificial emotion brought into creation in the great distant past to prod beings to evolve, is being permanently retired and replaced with this wondrous consciousness freeing energy Ray. Now the time has come to remove the protective energy shields that surround each of you. They were only there for your protection during this change."

"This is my cousin, Moon-teran, from my home world," declared Mark as he looked at Janice. "Here on Earth you all know her as Janice Carter, the daughter of your classified second-government Chairman Ted Carter. She is also here to assist you as a channel of this wondrous, transforming Ray."

Janice smiled at everyone in the room. Then she touched the gold pin on her lapel three times. All the transparent golden energy spheres surrounding the world leaders and their former Trilotew captors dissolved away a moment later, and their feet, suspended a few inches above the floor, gently touched the carpet.

The freed government leaders were immediately inspired to gaze with compassionate, knowing eyes at their former Trilotew tormentors, only to discover the Trilotew were also gazing in a knowing, compassionate manner back at them. All subconscious terror, hate, and lust for dominance over others was now gone.

"Since our true benevolent natures have been returned to us," announced President Martin McCoy as he stepped forward and indicated Mark with his hand, "let me introduce Ambassador Shon-ral to you, who is also known as the author Mark Santfield here on Earth. He is the official emissary of this new consciousness-freeing Ray to Earth and to all Trilotew everywhere. The entire Galactic Inter-dimensional Alliance of Free Worlds he represents will be assisting all of us from now on to straighten out this damaged world. If this new Ray had not been brought into existence as a gift from far beyond the physical universe, we would most certainly have destroyed this planet with the compulsive insistence of our former Trilotew associates."

The coarse, hardened, scaly-skin characteristics of all the Trilotew were continuing to transform, becoming more appealing, and their sinister violet eyes with red cat-like vertical slits were actually now radiating benevolent natures.

The now gentle face of the Trilotew Shaoulnoom blushed and he exclaimed to Mark, "Ambassador Shon-ral, our superior Commander Gonshockal, hidden in an underground base complex deep in the jungles of Brazil, will quickly discover he can no longer command any of us to be destructive or act in any sinister covert manner. He will assume the attempted control of Earth has somehow failed, and you should know he most certainly would attempt to set off a special bomb he brought with him to this planet in case of failure. Our Supreme Emperor himself ordered this. Such a device would blow the planet apart from the core outward, and it would become another asteroid belt circling in the orbit of a planet like the one between the planets you call Mars and Jupiter. He will set a delayed timer and then attempt to escape the planet aboard the special inter-stellar transport he has stationed at the base."

"Thank you, Shaoulnoom, for telling me this," Mark replied gently. Then he touched the gold pin on his coat lapel and asked, "Boun-tama and Lean-tala, did you get that?"

*Yes, we have it all recorded,* they telepathically replied together.

Boun-tama continued, *The information has been sent through to base Commanders Tam-lure and Una-mala and to Commanders Jon-tral and Sun-deema on the flagship. They report they have tuned into this Supreme Commander Gonshockal in the Brazilian jungle, and they are moving the flagship to hover invisibly above the hidden base.*

"Wow … I could hear them in my head," remarked President McCoy, surprised.

"Yes, I heard them too," stated the amazed Russian and Chinese Presidents.

Then the other world leaders who were gathered in the Oval Office proclaimed in amazement that they too could telepathically hear them in their heads.

"I see your natural telepathic abilities are already resurfacing," confirmed Mark. "That is excellent. Now you will all be able to help vastly improve this planet and its people in the days to come. Before we send all of you back to your respective countries, I have a surprise for the Trilotew that are present here." Mark touched the gold pin on his lapel twice and said, "Okay, Commander Tam-lure, send him here."

*He's on the way,* replied the clear telepathic voice of the Mt. Shasta base Commander.

A moment passed, and the Supreme Illumined High Lord Ambassador Grotzil materialized from a whirling teleportation beam directly in front of Mark, Janice, and President McCoy. His benevolent gaze swept the room coming to rest briefly, one at a time, upon the other transformed Trilotew.

"My fellow Trilotew, our entire race has been suppressed for over five hundred thousand years. As a result, we have been one of the worst tyrant races in the galactic history. Now that is all behind us. I have gone through a more thorough deprogramming, and certain genes purposefully turned off in our race long ago are now reactivated. This process is beginning to take place within all of you here. You can come to the Mt. Shasta base, and each of you can experience the great return to our true kind, generous natures. Will you come with me?"

The other Trilotew standing in the room beside their former world-leader captives nodded solemnly and grinned.

Grotzil turned to Mark, Janice, and the President of the United States and said, "Now that we Trilotew have been set free from the subconscious over-control of our perverse tyrant Emperor, we will always be ready to assist the Galactic Alliance in any way we can. There is only one more problem to solve, and that is our still vicious Imperial Overlord Fleet Commander Gonshockal in Brazil. However, I understand from Commanders Tam-lure and Una-mala that Commanders Jon-tral and Sun-deema aboard the Galactic Alliance flagship are en route as we speak to resolve that problem. All the Trilotew in this Earth sector will return to our home planet once that is accomplished. We can then observe firsthand how the mysterious fountains within the golden pyramids, which recently appeared aboard our two main battle transports, will transform our powerful overlords and the more powerful Emperor."

He reached out his reptilian arm, and Mark firmly clasped it. He repeated the friendly gesture with Janice and President McCoy and then respectfully bowed to them with both of his long, sharp reptilian hands crossed over his chest. All three returned the respectful gesture. Then Grotzil turned around to face his fellow liberated Trilotew, bowed to them in the same manner, and they happily responded in the same way.

"Now you will soon know what I know," stated Grotzil as he stood back up, "and each of you will remember just how many lifetimes you have already lived in tyranny to finally come to this point of freedom. Come with me, my fellow Trilotew."

He touched the device on his wrist, and all the Trilotew in the Oval Office faded away with him in another whirling teleportation beam.

"It's time for each one of you to be returned to your own countries," announced Mark, gazing at the world leaders staring back at him with childlike wonder. "Please have your respective military leaders stand down and tell them what happened was only a test. Know that a Galactic Alliance representative will soon be in contact with each of you and with your top military personnel. Then you can all go through the complete deprogramming back at the Mt. Shasta base. None of you will be gone more than a day to complete the procedure. When you return, you will discover a much deeper profound wonder of life has surfaced that is beyond what you can now imagine. Know that I wish each of you only the very greatest goodwill. Farewell."

Mark touched the gold pin on his coat lapel five times, and the world leaders faded away in another bright beam of light.

"President McCoy, a number of Galactic Alliance specialists have arrived at the Mt. Shasta base," remarked Janice. "If you can spare a day off from your busy schedule, we can take you with us back to the base where you can go through your own complete deprogramming. Other genomes in your DNA that were genetically turned off long ago in your ancient ancestors will be reactivated there. You will have a hundred percent use of your brain, recover your photographic memory ability, and much that was buried spanning many lifetimes over millions of years will resurface. This will greatly help you to bring about the same wondrous change in the rest of humankind in the days and months ahead. Then I believe you will want to deliver the truth to the entire populace of the planet via a worldwide television broadcast. From now on, you will be able to count on the combined support of your fellow hidden world leaders."

President McCoy sighed, took a relieving breath, and concurred, "Yes, I gathered that from what just happened here, and I would like to go through the full deprogramming."

He looked over at Secretary of Defense Daniel Samuelson, who had wisely remained silent during the entire episode in the Oval Office, smiling with childlike wonder back at them. The President walked up and threw his arm around Daniel's shoulder, as if they were actually best friends.

"Well, my friend, we won't be able to look at each other in the same way from now on. What I mean by that is, now we both know I am not actually your superior. My guess is in a relatively short time we won't need governments on Earth anymore like we have today, or money for that matter, and we will not want them."

"I was hoping you were also seeing what I was imagining," replied Daniel, relieved. "We will have a lot to do from now on."

"Daniel, I trust you can handle things for a day without me," the President stated confidently. "Please let my wife know I'll be away on a special mission for the night and that I'll be back tomorrow. I will go with Mark and Janice now, and when I come back it will be your turn."

Daniel smiled respectfully.

"I'm ready if you two are," President McCoy stated, looking at Mark and Janice.

"We will have the Commanders at the Mt. Shasta base return the President sometime tomorrow," Mark confirmed, and then he touched the gold pin on his lapel six times.

A moment passed, and then Mark, Janice, and the President were dematerialized in another bright beam, leaving the astonished Secretary of Defense alone—but greatly changed. Daniel's smile widened as he hurried out of the Oval Office.

Mark, Janice, and the President rematerialized back on the pad aboard the Transport Carrier ship, and Boun-tama and Lean-tala were waiting to graciously greet them.

"What's the status of the remaining problem in South America?" inquired Mark.

"The flagship is now hovering, invisibly undetectable, five-thousand-feet above the hidden Trilotew jungle base complex in the remote Brazilian jungles," seriously replied Lean-tala. "Rolling lush tree-covered mountainous hills and waterfalls surround the underground facility in the most dense jungle area, and there is no outward sign of any entry or exit to the base. It is well camouflaged."

Boun-tama touched the transceiver control on the console and reported, "Captain Zin-tamal, they are now safely back aboard ship, along with the President of the United States. How fast can you get us to rendezvous with the flagship hovering above the Brazilian jungle?"

"We will arrive there in approximately fifteen minutes," answered Zin-tamal. "Come up to the bridge, and all of you can watch the arrival."

"Mr. President, Ambassador Shon-ral, and Prime Scientist Moon-teran, I sense it's important you are present over Brazil when things unravel," Boun-tama stated intuitively. "Please follow me."

He appeared confidently serene as he took his wife Lean-tala's hand, and they all walked out of the teleportation chamber.

# TICKING
# TIME BOMB

Commander Jon-tral had his hands full back in the Galactic Alliance bridge-control room. He was monitoring the enlarged image of the angry Trilotew Imperial Overlord Fleet Commander Gonshockal, utilizing the secret Galactic Alliance Deep Penetration Observation Magnifier. The image displayed extended across the entire interlinked projected view screens in a gradual curve above the semi-circular control console. Gonshockal appeared to be taller, more muscular, and more vicious looking than the hundred officers and warrior soldiers under his command, who were feverishly moving back and forth behind him. He was standing in front of the circular command station at the back of the stadium-sized underground cavernous base, exuding an arrogant air of dominating power. A hundred-feet-long, oval shaped Medium Fast-Attack Destroyer class spacecraft, supported by four cup-shaped support struts, was landed a hundred feet further away in the center of the smooth cavern floor. Four parallel rows of twenty blue-white triangular shaped lights, hung from foot-long metal poles attached to the rough rock ceiling, were brightly illuminating the ship and the interior of the cavern.

Two merry men's voices approaching from the background broke Jon-tral's concentration on the view screens, and he turned around to see Ted and Henry chatting away as they walked side by side out of the triangular hallway into the bridge-command section. Second Commander Sun-deema, following close behind them, quickened her pace and passed them by to walk up and stop next to Jon-tral. Then she carefully gazed with her husband at the enlarged image display of angry Trilotew Overlord Commander Gonshockal spread end to end across the view screens.

Ted and Henry eagerly hurried around the control console to gaze through the oval observation windows. They were instantly spellbound by the wondrous breathtaking overview of lush green equatorial rainforest covered rolling hills that receded to the horizon in every direction, five thousand-feet-below the hovering flagship. Jon-tral smiled at Sun-deema as he took her hand, and they returned their gaze to the view screens. Ted and Henry walked over to them to observe continuing events taking place inside the underground Trilotew base.

The irate Overlord Gonshockal began to rant at four shorter Trilotew officers standing at strict fearful attention before him.

"Lieutenant Trondshopa, you were responsible for recapturing Ambassador Grotzil and my two generals so they can be reprogrammed away from Galactic Alliance interference," Gonshockal spouted venomously with his forked tongue flailing out of his mouth, sending spittle into the face of the terrified warrior before him. Then he screamed out, "Miserable human lover, the sentence for failure is death!"

Gonshockal leveled a long triangular handgun at Trondshopa and pulled the trigger. A searing green energy beam hit Trondshopa in the chest, and he screamed as his body melted into a puddle of evaporating atoms on the floor. The other three officers stood back, aghast at Gonshockal's actions as he leveled the gun at the Trilotew to his right.

"Why should I spare any of you miserable failures, especially you, Lieutenant Skondrilm?" demanded Gonshockal, still irate.

Sweat was dripping off Skondrilm's green scaly brow as he replied timidly, "Oh most glorious leader, they used some kind of new weapon upon our advance Scouts. It turned them into human lovers on the spot. If we had not retreated back here at once, we would not have returned."

Gonshockal angrily pushed the end of the pointed barrel of the weapon into Skondrilm's face to pull the trigger, but managed to just contain his outrage and backed off.

"You speak the truth. I tried to talk Ambassador Grotzil and both fleet battle cruiser Generals out of their insanity when they contacted me. They tried to tell me some Galactic Alliance gibberish about subconscious compulsive drives our distant white-winged cousins placed into our ancestors in the distant past. I was so irate at their voices coming through the transceiver I leveled my gun at it and melted the com-link into oblivion. You three get down below and set the timer on the Matter Disruption Implosion Bomb to go off in one hour. I want this miserable planet turned to rubble five minutes after we take the transport into space to join our reinforcements. They are on their way here from the home system. Now get moving, and report back to me when it's done."

The three remaining terrified officers bowed and saluted him with their clawed hands held crisscrossed over their chests. Then they hurried a few feet over to a round opening in the cavern floor and climbed down a black ladder.

"How could I have ever done other than I did back there on our psychologically and genetically imprisoned planet Earth?" Ted inquired eagerly, looking for answers from Commander Jon-tral, and he shook his head in amazement at how he could ever have been the way he was before his true self and true benevolent nature had fully re-surfaced.

*I thank Prime Creator that you, and the gracious Sun-deema, were here for us,* Ted continued telepathically, gratefully trying out his new telepathic wings of freedom. *We would have been lost without your intervention.*

"Oh … that was very clear," commented Jon-tral aloud, quite pleased. "Your natural telepathic ability has been fully restored."

"He had quite a rough session," stated Sun-deema, "but as you can see, he came out of it just fine."

Ted grimaced as he briefly recalled his full deprogramming experience, and then he smiled at the awareness of his new liberated state of consciousness.

*Yes, it was wild,* he calmly continued telepathically. *Long ago, I was from the planetary group beyond the Pleiades from which you two came. Those white-winged devil cousins of the Trilotew captured me on my way to Earth during one of our colonizing scientific expeditions to the planet. Back then I was the Commander of one of our medium-sized reconnaissance and exploration vessels when it was attacked by overwhelming forces. The white-winged Trilon-Kal, as they called themselves, captured alive the few of us they did not kill at once during the brief encounter. First, they subconsciously implanted us with terrorizing control images. Then they took us to Earth as their slaves to maintain the secret bases they had established in the equatorial jungles that far more abundantly surrounded Earth at that time.*

*They were planning long-term slavery for the future of all political prisoners they had captured, by implanting them with the compulsion to incarnate over and over again on Earth completely unconscious of all that came before in previous lifetimes. I learned from Sun-deema that those monsters turned off certain genomes on our DNA, leaving us able to use only six to ten percent of our brains, and our lifetimes were shortened to grow old and die before ninety or at maximum slightly over a hundred years. Thank you for patiently listening. I needed to get it completely off my chest by relaying part of what was uncovered during my final session. My dear friend, Henry, was there to help me through it all. I know he went through his own hell because he was my best friend back then, and one of those captured alive who was put on Earth to be a long-term slave.*

"Commander Jon-tral," he continued out loud, "may I say the wonderful loving being that is your wife really helped me get through all the terrorizing, vicious death implants those cruel reptilians put me through. From now on, I will forever be available to help both of you and the Galactic Alliance."

Henry was smiling proudly after telepathically overhearing Ted, as Sun-deema graciously nodded and with an exuberant smile said, "It was an honor to help set you free, my fellow traveler through time, space, and so many lifetimes."

"We will help both of you recover much more in the coming days and months, and during the next several years while Earth's people are being liberated," added Jon-tral. "Many of them are like you and Henry. They originally came to Earth during past colonization experiments to reseed human beings and other life forms after one of the planet's many cyclic polar shifts. The planet is due for another one, but this time it will not take place. The new Expansion Ray and a host of many mighty beings you know nothing about are in the process of changing the mechanics of Earth and this solar system. Earth's cyclic polar shifts are being permanently retired, along with evil as an experiment in the lower worlds of time and space."

"Do you mean our world and its people will begin to experience normal human life again with thousand-year life spans just like you do on your worlds?" asked Henry, perking up.

"Yes, that and much more," answered Sun-deema. "You two may not realize it yet, but you are both now able to use one hundred percent of your Earth human brains, and the genomes on your DNA that control normal human longevity have been permanently reactivated. You will naturally serve as prototype channels of this new transforming energy or consciousness-liberating Ray. Your first mission is already part of your awakening natural benevolent natures.

"Mon-tlan should be here any moment. His new assignment is to assist you two with the endeavor to liberate all your hidden secret second government members from their Trilotew programming. Then all the combined financial and political power you collectively have amassed can help liberate all the other human beings living on Earth today and assist with the repair of the damaged ecology of the planet. We will transform all automobiles and other devices that utilize dangerously polluting fossil fuels, as well as all harmful radioactive materials into safe, useful products. Teleportation stations and a completely non-polluting source of energy in the universe will take their place. This energy source is never actually used. It simply passes through the advanced devices to motivate travel and other needs."

"Hello everyone," came the cheerful voice of Monti from behind them as he walked into the bridge control room.

"We were just talking about you, Special Officer Mon-tlan," remarked Sun-deema.

"Oh really, that bad huh?" replied Monti refreshingly elated, and they laughed at his quirky humor.

"It's good to see you two again," remarked Monti, gazing at Henry and Ted. "I mean who you really are. We are not so much different now as human beings."

"I remember you now," replied Ted. "You were one of the Captains under my command way back toward the end of that terrible war with the white-winged Trilon-Kal."

Monti blushed and replied, "In that lifetime I was one of the few that escaped in a Scout ship out on patrol, when the overwhelming attack on our reconnaissance and exploration transport ship began. I am sorry to say those of us who survived believed everyone else was killed. After the Trilon-Kal were finally defeated, they were compelled to return to their hideous parallel dimension, and they were locked within it with the assistance of our secret friends from Medulonta, or what Earth people call the Andromeda Galaxy. I lived to a little over one thousand, one hundred years in that lifetime. I have been reincarnating ever since on my home world with all memory of my former lives intact. You and Henry now know this is the way for normal human beings to continue to evolve, in order to expand their consciousness toward one day becoming a truly capable co-creator with the one source behind all life, which we call Prime Creator."

"It's good to have you back, Mon-tlan," interrupted Commander Jon-tral, "but I must curtail the amenities for now. Time is very short before that Trilotew Overlord Commander down there tries to destroy Earth and escape. He just set the timer on their Matter Disruptor Implosion Bomb located on a lower level of the jungle base. We have less than an hour now to destroy it and capture him, or Earth will be gone. I have explained to Ted and Henry that you will take them back to Ted's house and remain with them to assist with the deprogramming of the rest of the hidden second-government leaders worldwide. You must proceed now."

"Ted, you and Henry should also know Mark and Janice, and United States President Martin McCoy, are en route to us now," added Sun-deema. "The President will finish his full deprogramming aboard this flagship, and we will return him the next day. Mark and Janice are coming to assist us with the split-second timing that must take place in just under an hour."

"You mean I won't get to see my daughter before we go?" asked Ted, frowning.

"There isn't enough time for that now," Jon-tral replied kindly. "However, you will see her again after the Trilotew problem is resolved on Earth. Then Ambassador Shon-ral and Prime Scientist Moon-teran will return to their home planet to be reunited with their own families for a short vacation. I trust you understand they are all anxiously waiting to see them again."

Ted thoughtfully lowered his head and then elated, lifted it back up and remarked, "Yes, yes I understand perfectly what must happen. It's all so clear now."

"It sure is, my friend," confirmed Henry.

"We want you and Henry to wear a special pendant suspended from a gold chain tucked under your clothes," continued Sun-deema. "It connects directly to the pyramid aboard this ship. You will know what to do with them when the time comes."

She reached into a pocket on the side of her uniform and pulled out two golden pendants. They depicted a golden pyramid above a silver galaxy with three blue stars set in a triangular pattern just above the pyramid's apex. She handed them to Ted and Henry. They placed them around their necks and grasped the beautiful pendant symbols to gaze fondly at them, then stuffed them down inside their shirts.

"Well new friends, Ted and Henry," encouraged Monti, "it's time to get aboard my Scout ship and race back to your estate, Ted."

Ted and Henry hugged Commanders Jon-tral and Sun-deema, and Ted wiped joyful tears from his eyes before he stated, "Monti, my good man, lead the way."

Monti placed the palm of his right hand over his heart and nodded to Jon-tral and Sun-deema, and they nodded back.

"Shall we, gentlemen?" encouraged Monti with a sweep of his left hand toward the triangular hallway exit, and they walked away just as Ted excitedly initiated a rapid-fire conversation.

"Well Monti, my friend, will we receive training to pilot Scout ships? I would really enjoy that because it would fulfill an old childhood dream of mine to pilot spaceships to the stars."

"Oh right, me too," stated Henry. "I've been wondering about that ever since I remembered my true self."

"As a matter of fact," chuckled Monti, "that will be part of your further training curriculum in the months to come. You are in safe hands. We will have a lot of fun mixed with business, as you Earth people say. On the way to Ted's estate, we can discuss what to accomplish next with your new mission."

They disappeared down the triangular hallway with Jon-tral and Sun-deema looking back at them like pleased parents, before they turned back to observe the view screens.

Monti's Scout ship left the launch bay a few minutes later, gradually appearing visible again as the molecular time-rate was lowered just outside the central section of the flagship. The pale-blue light enshrouding the hull pulsed brighter, and the ship darted in a long upward arc headed away from the Brazilian jungle back toward the North American continent and Ted's mansion estate, located high above Beverly Hills, California.

The Galactic Alliance Transport Carrier, with Mark, Janice, Boun-tama, his wife Lean-tala, and United States President Martin McCoy aboard, darted into view from the distant sky, then slowed down. It faded into transparency as it headed toward the flagship, then stopped to hover alongside the giant vessel before it passed right through the massive ship's hull to land on the launch bay floor.

The glow around the craft blinked and went out. The five occupants were soon hurrying down the ramp extending from the middle of the hull below the open hatch. President McCoy briefly glanced back to notice how the Transport Carrier was very similar in appearance to the mighty flagship, but much smaller in scale, as they continued walking at a hurried clip over to the bi-directional walkways. They stepped upon the one moving toward the far left triangular exit from the hangar, and it whisked them away.

Back in the command bridge, Jon-tral touched a lit control on the curved console located between two seated technicians. The displayed image of Gonshockal walking toward his dark gray Fast-Attack ship landed in the middle of the cavern floor switched to the clear image of the lower underground level of the base. The three Trilotew officers Gonshockal ordered to set the timer on the outlawed off-world bomb were working around a solid four-feet-square green stone cube. Sitting atop it was a barrel-shaped blue metal canister. Dozens of different-colored lit controls curved across the barrel's middle circumference in three concentric rows. The taller officer touched a series of them, and they began to blink repetitively, gradually speeding up. All three nervous, sweating Trilotew officers gazed askance at each other and then raced back up a nearby spiral black metal ladder.

The three officers reappeared, climbing up to the top of the ladder, stepping one by one back onto the main cavern floor, and then stopped together in a sudden panic. They could see the pale-red antigravity light already enshrouding their oval Medium Fast-Attack Destroyer ship, and they bolted in a frantic race toward it. The last of the hundred base personnel ran up inside, and the wide boarding ramp withdrew up inside the hull. The wide oval door slid closed, just as the three frantic officers stopped a few feet away. They watched in horror as the ship lifted off the floor of the cavern and sped toward the camouflaged thick-vine-covered oval opening exit from the hidden base. The doorway covered with thick jungle growth dropped toward the jungle, and the ship raced out of it, gaining speed; then it darted in a long upward curve into the sky.

"The miserable murderous coward," exclaimed Sun-deema. "He's leaving behind his own officers just for spite at the loss of his despicable mission to Earth."

"Yes, dear wife, that has always been their way. I am beaming the three officers to the Chamber of Prime Creator aboard the flagship."

The three bewildered Trilotew officers standing in the cavern base appeared relieved as they unexpectedly beamed away in whirling golden light.

They reappeared standing in front of the glowing golden pyramid aboard the Galactic Alliance ship. Before they could react, the pyramid began emitting pulsing concentric waves of golden-white energy that harmlessly passed through their bodies. Their fear vanished as smiles of exhilarating joy began to register on their softening reptilian features.

"Now we will bring an end to the Trilotew terror campaign on planet Earth," stated Jon-tral back in the command bridge. "The rest will come later."

Sun-deema smiled as she touched a deep-blue spherical targeting control to lock it on in preparation for activation—it lit up.

Down in the sub-level of the jungle cavern base, the three concentric rows of lights across the timed barrel bomb resting on the cube stand suddenly sped up.

"The Energy-To-Matter Conversion Beam is locked on," stated Jon-tral. "This is it, dear wife. On my mark, touch the control to neutralize all power aboard Gonshockal's retreating ship. It's just exiting Earth's atmosphere.

Ready … and … now."

She touched the golden pyramid shaped control on the console – it brightened next to the spherical targeting control. Jon-tral touched the spherical control to activate it – it pulsed once.

The massive Galactic Alliance flagship slowly materialized into view from its stealthy higher frequency projecting a thick, blue light beam from one end of the giant cylindrical ship humming down through the air to the thick jungle growth to vanish below the ground. At the same instant, a thick golden beam shot from the opposite end of the flagship darted up into the clouds.

The three concentric rows of colored lights surrounding the ticking barrel bomb suddenly stopped, and the bomb imploded a moment later in a brilliant fiery white light that started to explode violently back outward, just as the blue beam shot from the flagship hit the top of the explosion. The beam sucked the expanding force of the blast backward into itself, rapidly widening as it turned the entire underground base into melting molecular white light. In moments, all materials used to build the sinister base swiftly transformed the entire cavern back into the original natural state that existed there before the perverted Trilotew took it over.

The beam withdrew from the jungle back up into the hovering flagship, and the mighty ship turned vertical. The pale-blue antigravity light enshrouding the hull brightened, and the ship darted straight up into space following the golden beam it was still projecting from the other end of its cylindrical hull.

The oval shaped Trilotew Medium Fast-Attack Destroyer ship with the pale-red aura hugging its hull had stopped in space high above the planet's equator. An inter-dimensional whirling escape portal to a parallel dimension opened several hundred yards in front of the ship that started to move inside it, but the radiant thick golden beam shot from the Galactic flagship darted up out of the atmosphere to strike the middle of the hull. In a second, the golden light spread to encompass the escaping enemy craft, and the luminous red antigravity power surrounding it vanished in the encapsulating golden force field. The open vortex to another dimension dwindled to a point of light and faded from view, leaving Gonshockal's dark-gray cylindrical ship suspended powerless in space. The Galactic Alliance flagship darted out of the atmosphere, slowed dramatically, and stopped to hover in space parallel to the Trilotew warship. The beam emanating from the end of the flagship hull shut off, leaving the golden light surrounding the enemy ship in place.

Gonshockal was now beside himself with anger. He was hissing with his long, forked tongue darting in and out of his jaws, while repeatedly touching the LCD-type controls on his command console, but everything was dead. He gazed at his helpless bridge-command crew and pointed his hand weapon at them in a sweeping gesture. Then he pulled the trigger, but a mysterious force suddenly yanked the gun from his tight grip, and it stopped, suspended in the air several feet in front of his face.

It turned around to face the triangular point of the clear barrel at his head, and Gonshockal threw his long-fingered hands up in front of his face in dire panic and screamed, "No … no … please don't kill me."

The gun vanished just as the forms of Commanders Jon-tral and Sun-deema appeared within a projected three-dimensional image between Gonshockal and his bridge-support crew.

"How dare you," spouted Gonshockal, mocking up courage to counter his obvious cowardly behavior. "Do you know who I am? What happened to our power? Let us go or face all-out war with the Trilotew Empire worlds."

"I am Commander Jon-tral of the Galactic Inter-dimensional Alliance of Free Worlds. Cease all hostility and you will not be harmed," he commanded compassionately.

"I know who you are, human devil," Gonshockal shot back, while the dozen dumbfounded male and female officers and warriors standing at various stations in the Trilotew command bridge watched in terror.

"In a moment, you will all understand the error of your ways. We will help set you free," Sun-deema stated kindly.

"Your outlawed Matter Disruptor Implosion Bomb has been neutralized," continued Jon-tral, "along with your illegal base in the jungle. As of right now, all Trilotew activity on or about the Earth is permanently retired. We have neutralized the bomb you set off in an attempt to destroy the planet. You have failed. However, we will not harm any of you for your vile deeds. Although I can't say that for your own officer you murdered back there in the jungle base."

"Do something now or you will all be sent to the frying pits back home," Gonshockal screamed viciously at his bridge crew.

The warriors in the bridge-control room could not move.

At that moment, Mark and his home world cousin, Moon-teran, along with Boun-tama, his wife Lean-tala, and President McCoy walked into the Galactic Alliance flagship command bridge from the triangular hallway.

They hurried up to Jon-tral and Sun-deema, and Mark inquired anxiously, "What's our status?"

"The bomb this mad Trilotew timed to destroy the Earth was neutralized back into pure harmless energy the moment it detonated," replied Jon-tral, "and we used it to turn their base back into the original pristine jungle state it was in before they arrived. Gonshockal's neutralized escaping transport is now floating in space, suspended without power. As you can see, one irate reptilian lunatic is helpless, along with a hundred Trilotew on his ship. Now it's up to the new Ray emanating from the pyramid in this flagship."

"Commander Gonshockal, I am Ambassador Shon-ral from the Galactic Alliance," began Mark, addressing the Trilotew Overlord Commander displayed on the interconnected view screens. "Your presence on Earth today, and in fact any future plan the Trilotew have for the planet is permanently suspended. Although it is certain you would have killed everyone on the planet without remorse or care, we will not harm you or the warriors under your command. What is about to happen will set you free from a tyrant subconscious program that has been dominating your race for half a million years."

"No . . . no . . . no, let us go or war is upon you all," Gonshockal spouted back fearfully—he had never shown signs of any fear before in his life for anyone or anything, other than in front of his far more sinister Emperor back home.

Mark looked at Janice, and they both reached up and touched the pendants hanging from the gold chains around their necks. They simultaneously flashed a bright golden-white light.

Deep inside the flagship, the radiant golden pyramid began to pulse concentric waves of circular golden light, comprised of thousands of tiny teardrop lights, out through the walls of the chamber into space and into the hull of the Trilotew carrier.

The metallic walls of the oval control room on Gonshockal's ship began to rain the tiny teardrop lights from every direction until the entire bridge filled with them. Then they shot into the chest of Gonshockal and all the other Trilotew standing throughout the bridge in a transfixed state of bewilderment. A warm pastel pink radiance began to glow in their chest areas, spreading throughout their entire bodies before it turned golden white and moved above their heads to form into transparent spheres of light. Many subconscious controlling death implant memories began to appear within the spheres that compelled the Trilotew to gaze at them. Their coarse reptilian characteristics softened, and Gonshockal breathed a sigh of pleasureful relief. For a reason none of them understood, they all simply knew to silently ask this new Ray to remove those implanted demonic false natures. Starting with Gonshockal, the terrifying images of torture and terror dissolved away forever. All the transparent golden-white spheres then faded away, but that was not the end of their beginning transformations.

"What … what's hap … happening to us?" Gonshockal nervously stuttered, voicing the same concern the other Trilotew officers were experiencing standing around the oval control room.

"You are beginning to rediscover your true selves, and your original true natures," answered Jon-tral from the projected image in front of Gonshockal. "This is the way you were before your ancient white-winged cousins genetically altered your true Trilotew form. They diabolically implanted the subconscious minds of your distant ancestors over five hundred thousand years ago, and then used them as slaves that they compelled to terrorize many races on other worlds for their selfish ends. If any refused, they would horribly suffer from the subconscious controlling images they had programmed into them."

Mark looked at Janice again, and they touched their pendants. This time they emitted a bright white flash, and Gonshockal and the hundred other Trilotew simply vanished.

They instantly rematerialized standing in concentric circles around the special pyramid chamber aboard the flagship. Gonshockal found himself closest to the pyramid as Jon-tral, Sun-deema, Mark, and Janice appeared between him and the other Trilotew, who were now free from fear, terror, and any desire to harm others.

"Behold," proclaimed Mark, indicating the glowing pyramid with his hand.

A moment passed, and the faint outline of a radiant statue standing in a fountain began to appear within the pyramid through its four slanted walls that were becoming transparent. The fountain levitated right through the front pyramid wall and then expanded to fifteen-feet-high. The Trilotew, filled with wide-eyed wonder, were too uplifted to be afraid. They could see the statue of a bronzed bare-chested bald man, wearing a white cotton-like skirt extended from the waist to just above his bare feet, and two gold bracelets around his upper muscular arms. He was standing in the center of the curved white stone bowl set upon a round white stone pillar. The golden-white liquid light issuing from his open palms, held at his sides facing forward, was pouring down into the full bowl to evenly drop over the entire rim like a smooth radiant curtain to vanish through the floor.

A Ray of light suddenly shot from the heart area of the majestic statue into the heart area of everyone. A moment later, all the Atma, or true spherical Soul forms, of the Trilotew and the humans lifted out of the tops of their heads. They were comprised of teardrop-shaped golden droplets of light built in layers from a white central core through the light spectrum to a violet exterior, surrounded by a pale-golden aura.

Jubilant cries of amazement emanated from the telepathic voices of all the Trilotew as the telepathic voice of Gonshockal cried out, elated, *Oh Prime Creator, I remember now. How could we have fallen so far? Now we remember, but I was trying to destroy all of you. For you to show such compassion for us is beyond understanding. I thank you, Commander Jontral and the Galactic Inter-dimensional Alliance of Free Worlds, for setting us free from our diabolical leaders back home.*

The true Atma, or Soul, of everyone then reentered their physical bodies, and Shon-ral replied aloud, "Now that you are all your natural benevolent selves again, I can officially welcome you as friends, instead of enemies, of the entire Galactic Inter-dimensional Alliance of Free Worlds for the first time in over five hundred thousand years."

"You are all welcome to meet with us and many of the other personnel aboard this Galactic Alliance flagship in our main reception and observation lounge," added Sun-deema kindly. "Know that each of you have a very bright future."

Gonshockal and the other Trilotew respectfully crisscrossed their hands over their chests and bowed as they vanished from the pyramid chamber of Prime Creator.

They reappeared again standing in more spread-out positions around the Galactic Alliance flagship reception and observation lounge. The North American continent on the beautiful blue-green, ocean-covered planet Earth loomed large through the oval observation windows in the near background of space. Several dozen of the flagship's personnel entered the lounge through the triangular hallway and then spread out to walk up and introduce themselves to the Trilotew who were happily waiting to greet them.

Meanwhile, Monti's Scout ship sped further down into Earth's atmosphere, fading into invisibility. It vanished as it briefly punched a downward whirling hole in a fluffy cumulus layer of clouds, and soon slowed its rapid descent heading toward the high mountainous hills above Beverly Hills, California.

Clearly displayed on the view screen aboard Monti's ship was the city of Los Angeles and surrounding suburbs. Ted and Henry were utterly fascinated by the images of the city they were seeing zooming ever closer as the ship slowed until it stopped to hover above Ted's ten-acre estate. Then it slowly lowered down again and stopped just above the well-manicured lawns and flowering plants near a large swimming pool at the back of Ted's home.

The Scout ship faded back into visibility, hovering just a foot above the

214

early morning dew-covered emerald-green lawn. The well-manicured grass continued another hundred feet up to the Olympic sized swimming pool and poolside bungalow located in the backyard of the Tudor-style mansion surrounded by Greek-style green granite pillars. Then the ship lowered and softly landed upon the three triangularly positioned semispherical pods extended down from under the ship's hull. The pale-blue light surrounding the ship shut off, and the seam of the vertical oval door appeared, and the door retracted inside the hull. The ramp slid out of the hull below the opening and lowered to the grass, just as Monti stepped out of the ship. He headed down the ramp, followed by the very exuberant Ted and Henry. They walked a few feet away from the ship's hull and stopped to talk.

"Monti, I have a plan to run by you and Henry," stated Ted, raising his eyebrows expressively.

"What you're imagining will work," Monti remarked confidently, to Ted's surprise.

"Oh, you saw what I was imagining," remarked Ted with a chuckle.

"So did I," stated Henry.

"Do you think it's safe to use the Trilotew teleportation device hidden in my office?" inquired Ted.

"The remaining Trilotew are being transformed, and I'm certain we can use it without risk," answered Monti. "Do you know what capacity it can handle?"

"I was told by Gorsapis and Zushsmat it could send up to twenty-five individuals at one time. We could bring all four hundred remaining worldwide hidden government members to the Grand Reception room in the mansion. They can comfortably stand together there, and then with our new link to the transforming Ray they too can be set free to be benevolent evolved human beings once again." Then Ted looked at Henry and instructed anxiously, "Monti and I will get to the teleportation unit to begin beaming each group to the reception room, and you could remain there to greet them with the Ray coming through your pendant."

Henry smiled enthusiastically with acceptance of his part in the plan.

Ted gazed curiously at Monti and asked, "Can you help me lock the teleportation unit onto them at various places around the Earth, if I give you their names and approximate locations?"

"Ted, I'm already ahead of you. The ship's sensors can pinpoint their individual vibrations, and the ship's central computer intelligence can relay their coordinates. We can then input them into the teleportation computer in your office and transfer them to the reception room."

"Dear friend, Henry, you must be ready to activate the pendant Sun-deema gave you to link to the pyramid Ray the moment they arrive. They will be bewildered and angry, and some will have Trilotew hand weapons. Their subconscious implants will compel them to attack first and ask questions later. Each arriving group of twenty-five must be treated the same way until we get them all gathered together at one time."

"I'll contact Commanders Jon-tral and Sun-deema telepathically to update them about our plans on our way to the house," stated Monti.

"Well then, my friends, we better get moving," encouraged Ted, and they started walking over the grass along the right side of the pool walkway, headed toward the double-wide French glass doors at the back of his two-story mansion.

Henry and Monti picked up their pace to walk on each side of him. On the way, Monti touched the gold symbol pin on his coat lapel three times, and he began to send a telepathic communication.

*Commanders Jon-tral and Sun-deema, I'm reporting in with an update. I will now send you the complete visual of our plans to liberate the rest of Earth's hidden-government leaders.*

*Well done, Mon-tlan,* he heard Jon-tral telepathically respond. *Sun-deema and I have clearly received your plans. Proceed, and let us know the moment the first phase of their transformation is complete. We will be ready to take them to the next level after that.*

*Dearest and oldest of friends, you have our thanks for all you have done,* Sun-deema gratefully stated.

Back on the flagship, Jon-tral, Sun-deema, Mark (Ambassador Shon-ral), Janice (Prime Scientist Moon-teran), and President Martin McCoy were now beginning to cordially entertain the once-tyrant Overlord Gonshockal. The ninety-seven other officers and warrior soldiers were standing around the flagship's large reception and observation room with over four dozen of the ship's personnel, jubilantly discussing many topics with their former Trilotew reptilian enemies.

Gonshockal respectfully crisscrossed both his hands over his chest and bowed before Commander Jon-tral, Sun-deema, Ambassador Shon-ral, and Moon-teran. He rose back up smiling with joyful tears running down his face.

"We are now free to once again be the benevolent beings we were so long ago," he stated, and then his gentle eyes expressed genuine remorse and lowered. "I mercilessly destroyed one of my best officers down there in the jungle base. He didn't deserve to be the target of my insanity."

Sun-deema reached up and compassionately placed a gentle hand on Gonshockal's shoulder and encouraged, "That could not be helped, for your actions were beyond the control of your true nature that was still suppressed. You can best serve your people now and help repair the damage they have caused through history by walking among them. Be filled now with the joy of your awakened true self, and this wondrous consciousness liberating Ray will travel with you."

Jon-tral observed Gonshockal lifting his head back up with pure joy radiating from his benevolent reptilian being.

"Commander Gonshockal," he continued cordially, "this is the official Galactic Alliance Ambassador Shon-ral. This is his Prime Scientist cousin, Moon-teran, and this is President Martin McCoy of the United States of America."

"Oh yes, I know of you, Ambassador, but you were known to me as Mark Santfield. I had my agents monitoring your movements in hopes of having you captured or killed. Now I truly regret those actions."

"We are no longer enemies, Commander Gonshockal," replied Mark, smiling, "and now I can sincerely call you a friend. I also look forward to assisting with our future relationship as the Galactic Alliance Ambassador to your home world systems."

Gonshockal nodded his thanks and looked to Moon-teran, then curiously stated, "I also know of you, Moon-teran. However, I knew you as Janice Carter, the daughter of the Chairman of Earth's hidden government. We were using you to get to him over the years, and for that I am also truly sorry."

"As terrorizing as this whole thing has been over many years, I know now it was all worth it," she replied gently. "I do not hold you personally responsible. Shon-ral and I will be reunited with our own families soon, and for that alone I could not be more grateful."

"Thank you, Moon-teran, from all of us. We will forever be in your service wherever and whenever you may need us," replied Gonshockal, and he bowed courteously and then turned to face President McCoy.

"Mr. President, let me say I'm truly happy you are now free of all our Trilotew terrorizing brainwashing. You probably know I did not know what I was doing. I was unable to stop myself."

"That's all behind us now," Martin encouraged happily. "We are once again free to be our true selves, and I'm quite pleased with our new relationship. I'm also equally relieved the old one is gone forever."

"You are most kind, Mr. President, to say that to me now, for I would have had you killed when we were done with you. Now I am unable to imagine contemplating such a twisted thing for any other living being. For that miracle I will be forever grateful."

"Wherever you go, you will experience this gift Ray beginning to free all those who come across your path," encouraged Jon-tral. "You are now considered my friend, Sun-deema's friend, and a friend to the entire Galactic Inter-dimensional Alliance of Free Worlds."

Gonshockal smiled wide, then pondered a new sudden realization and stated urgently, "You should know a fleet of a hundred battle cruisers are on their way here because I signaled for them as emergency backup right before I was set free."

"Thank you for sharing that with us," replied Jon-tral. "Our own massive fleet is monitoring their movements. Thousands of ships stationed throughout this solar system are now invisibly operating in a higher parallel reality, and many more are on the way. All the fleet cruisers are carrying the new pyramid with the new Ray it emanates. They will free your fellow Trilotew aboard those one hundred ships before they can cause any more damage or harm to life. Now we will send all of you back to your ship. After you arrive aboard, you will discover something new there. One of the new golden pyramids is appearing aboard your transport as we speak, and you will intuitively know where to find it. The special Ray will go with you on your return trip to benevolently neutralize any weapons technology or harm your people or your Emperor may attempt to employ against you. Your crew and families on your home worlds now have special protection. Depart knowing that each of you will experience for yourselves how the golden pyramid aboard your ship will multiply itself. At the right time, they will appear aboard all one hundred of the ships that are on their way to this solar system with the intent to cause harm. Several Commanders from our fleet will contact you on your way to rendezvous with your approaching fleet. Now go in peace with the friendship of the Galactic Alliance."

Several dozen of the other grateful Trilotew officers and warriors in the room drew close to Gonshockal as he gratefully crisscrossed his hands over his chest and bowed. Then Gonshockal and all ninety-seven of his fellow Trilotew repeated the gesture again.

Jon-tral, Sun-deema, and the many Galactic Alliance ship's personnel returned their own respectful gesture with their right hand held over their hearts and a gentle nod of their heads. Then Commanders Jon-tral and Sun-deema raised their right hands up with the palms open at shoulder-level facing the Trilotew, and they simply vanished.

# CHAPTER TWENTY-THREE

# A FREEDOM
# SO RARE

$\mathcal{T}$ed opened the back door to his mansion, flicked on the living-room lights, and walked inside with Monti and Henry. They walked across the living room and through a doorway leading inside the front entryway. Then Ted and Monti hurried over to the fountain of the female angel statue standing on the raised square granite platform in the center of the three-feet-wide blue granite bowl between the twin staircases. Water spewing down from her palms was reflecting the light coming from the overhead chandelier like sparkling diamonds, and rainbow colors were radiating out into the room. To Henry, the hundred teardrop shaped lead crystals, which were hung from chained-together gold-metal frames in concentric circles diminishing downward in size, appeared like a glittering upside-down Christmas tree. Ted and Monti glanced at each other and headed up the right staircase. Henry continued to watch them until they entered Ted's office through the door centered at the back of the balcony between the staircases. Then he hurried into the Grand Reception room through the twin set of folded-back accordion style French glass doors. He walked across the deep-blue granite floor and stopped at the left side of the large green granite fireplace to await the teleportation of the first group of hidden-government members to the royal sized room.

Up in Ted's office Monti was already entering the first set of coordinates into the Trilotew teleportation control console hidden inside the room behind the now wide-open camouflaging bookcase.

"Okay Ted, I have the first group of twenty-five members locked into the teleportation unit's computer memory," stated Monti, and he gave Ted a thumb-up sign that he was ready to proceed.

"Well then here we go," Ted replied courageously, and he grabbed the gold pendant symbol suspended from the gold chain around his neck.

Down below in the Grand Reception room Henry's gold pendant hanging from its gold chain around his neck flashed a gold light once, and he grabbed it in his right fist.

Back up in the office Ted's pendant flashed gold light once through his tightly closed right fist, and he nodded to Monti, who touched the illumined semispherical teleportation control on the Trilotew console.

Henry's eyes opened wide in anticipation as his pendant began to emit a steady, faint golden glow, and then twenty-five of the world's remaining astonished hidden-government members, comprised of men and a dozen women ranging in age from their mid-thirties to late seventies, appeared huddled together in a tight circle a few feet away from him. His eyes then lit up with recognition of one of the taller women in the group. It was none other than the snobbish and very wealthy Cynthia Piermont, the member of the secret-government Council he had been asked to escort to Ted's party, before he discovered Ted was actually Chairman of the entire classified secret government.

Two of the taller men in their late forties suddenly pulled Trilotew handgun weapons from their suit coat pockets. They aimed them at Henry to fire but instantly discovered they could not move a muscle as concentric circles of golden-white light began to emanate into the room from Henry's brightly glowing pendant. The pulsing energy waves, comprised of the tiny golden teardrop-shaped lights, flowed like a river of thousands of horizontal raindrops to harmlessly pass right through the bodies of all the men and women, and their astonished expressions transformed into childlike smiles of wonderment. The two taller men holding the Trilotew guns out at arm's length watched, astonished, as the weapons turned into white light and vanished in a puff of dissipating mist. Suddenly everyone could move again. The two taller men lowered their arms and gazed gratefully at Henry.

"Welcome to your Chairman's house everyone," stated Henry, proudly grinning back at them. "You are all being freed from the twisted negative drives the Trilotew implanted into your subconscious minds. Your distorted behaviors created by your tyrant Trilotew overseers caused you to act as their emissaries to negatively dominate your fellow human beings on Earth. They would have killed all of you and your families after they were finished covertly using you. You should know now that your former Trilotew mentors responsible for that brainwashing have been transformed back to their true benevolent natures by this same special energy Ray each one of you is experiencing. They are now headed back to their home worlds as we speak, and our planet is about to be permanently, dynamically transformed."

Transparent golden-white spheres appeared above all their heads, and Henry watched all of them look up to behold inside each sphere many subconsciously implanted terrorizing images that were driving their diabolical actions. Then, one by one, the vile images dissolved into white light and the spheres faded away.

Henry touched his glowing pendant and began to send an enthusiastic telepathic message to Ted upstairs. *The first group has successfully arrived, and they have experienced the new Ray. Their subconscious-controlling implants are gone, and they are now returning to their true naturally benevolent human natures right before my eyes.*

*That is good news,* Ted replied telepathically.

*I have received the coordinates for the next group,* interjected Monti. *Are you ready to have them beamed over?*

*Quite ready, Monti, my friend,* replied Henry.

Monti continued telepathically, *Have the first group remain standing where they are, and I will send the second group of twenty-five Council members to you. They will arrive standing in a tight circle to the right side of the fireplace. Here they come.*

The successful teleportation of all four hundred worldwide hidden-government Council members to the Grand Reception room in Ted's mansion was soon completed. Then Monti and Chairman Ted Carter, with his pendant still glowing faintly, walked side by side back down the right staircase and into the Grand Reception room to join all of them.

Ted placed his hand over his heart and nodded, then respectfully beamed a benevolent smile at all of them and stated, "Fellow governing Council members, you are all now aware of the reason you were brought here with no forewarning. We most certainly could not ask your permission while the Trilotew subconscious terror images controlled you. Here in my home, you are all welcome now that you are beginning to experience your true human natures or your true selves that have been deeply suppressed for years beyond count."

While Ted was talking, Henry was gazing fondly at Cynthia. Though middle-aged, he had to admit she remained quite lovely with her shapely figure and long, silken-black hair. Then he noticed she happened to again be wearing the expensive diamond-and-emerald necklace hanging down over the open front of her low-cut blue-and-black silken dress. She stepped away from the older, shorter white-haired woman standing at her left side to speak to the Chairman.

"Mr. Chairman, how could this have happened to all of us? We started out with such good intentions for the planet, and then those demon reptilians twisted everything we were originally trying to accomplish."

"Cynthia Piermont, you have been a good and loyal Vice Chairman and a good friend. I know it's hard to accept at first, but you know it's all true," Ted answered solemnly, and he glanced around the room at the entire group of men and women. "Now I can reveal the truth to all of you because you will be able to perceive it in a knowing manner through the new consciousness-liberating Ray. If the Galactic Alliance had decided not to intervene at this time in the perverted affairs of our world, the treaty-breaking interference of the Trilotew would eventually result in the destruction of the entire planet. Fellow Council members, you will not be able to return to hate, anger, and other misguided negative ways because all the Trilotew stationed on or around Earth have now undergone this transformation back to their original benevolent natures. That nature is the same that their ancient ancestors expressed before their white-winged Trilon-Kal cousins suppressed them a half-million years ago.

"We now have the great opportunity to accomplish wonders working alongside the specialists who are on their way here from the Galactic Alliance. When they arrive, every man, woman, and child on our planet Earth will know without a shadow of a doubt that human and other advanced benevolent extraterrestrials exist throughout the galaxy. Highly proficient Masters of every specialized skill will assist us to completely transform the entire surface of the planet by using a form of non-polluting limitless energy in the universe. They will also help free the human race of all known diseases and reactivate certain genomes on the DNA to enable everyone to once again utilize one hundred percent of their brains, instead of merely six to ten percent. In addition, they will significantly expand your lifetime to a thousand years or more, after they reactivate several longevity-age clock genomes purposefully suppressed in our ancient ancestors and genetically passed on generation after generation. The one hundred Council members that were convening with Janice and me back at the underground Arizona facility have already experienced this Ray. Now, at last, all other worldwide members are being set free."

Cheers from everyone went up like a rolling, thunderous, liberating tide across the room, and Vice Chairman Cynthia Piermont, standing closer to Henry, remarked blissfully, "It's just beyond amazing. I am actually beginning to have insight into the deeper hidden co-creative purpose for life. I'm simply astounded I couldn't see it before." She paused to muse about something and then timidly tried sending out the telepathic thought, *Can you hear me, Chairman Carter? I want to help any way I can with all the wealth and position I have to free up all the people of Earth, and I know all the others feel the same way.*

*I most certainly can hear you, my friend*, replied Ted, and he continued aloud, "and I'm delighted that you, Vice Chairman Piermont, and each one of you are already regaining your natural telepathic ability. That will make what we must do in the days to come much easier and far more efficient. We have a lot of work to do to prepare the world for a joint worldwide broadcast that will take place at the appropriate time by duly elected President of the United States Martin McCoy. Ambassador Shon-ral and his cousin, Moon-teran, representing the entire Galactic Inter-dimensional Alliance of Free Worlds, will be present, along with the now benevolently transformed Ambassador Grotzil of the Trilotew. I will also be there as Chairman to represent our secret-government Council and announce to all the world's people that there will be no more secrets.

"Together from the White House we will reveal the truth about our secret worldwide government and how we came into existence by the unethical actions of our forebears. More details than that are not necessary to disclose at this time. You can all now understand the significance of what I am saying to you. We are about to be fully exposed. However, be aware the people of Earth will swiftly come to know that your former tyrant natures are gone. With Galactic Alliance assistance, they will also come to know we are now irrevocably dedicated to utilize our great combined financial and political resources to completely transform the entire Earth and help set free everyone living on it in vastly improved ways. In addition, do not forget the special liberating Ray each one of you are experiencing right now will also be made available throughout the world to all our fellow human beings and to all life on the planet. We will not be alone."

Ted gazed at Monti. "This, my fellow Council members, is Mon-tlan, or whom we like to call Monti, and he is my new trusted friend," Ted stated respectfully. "He is a Special Mission Representative of the entire Galactic Alliance from a star system beyond what we on Earth refer to as the Pleiades star group, and he is here to help us through this worldwide change."

All the transforming members gazed at Monti with grateful childlike wonder.

"Well … I sense it's safe to say that both myself and the extraterrestrial humans that live on far more elevated pollution-free worlds no longer appear to be much different than yourselves," stated Monti, smiling at them. "Now that your true natures have been liberated, I can tell you that thousands of Galactic Alliance ships are on their way here. After they arrive, each of you, and all the people of Earth, will receive assistance from a vast host of off-world beings that are very adept at every imaginable advanced discipline. Openly provided will be cures for every disease, greatly extended longevity, antigravity outer space and parallel dimension travel technology, as well as very advanced ecological, biological, and geological sciences, to name just a few. We will help prepare this world and its people for official admittance into the Galactic Inter-dimensional Alliance of Free Worlds. Will that do for starters?"

Vice Chairman Piermont replied happily, "I know I speak for all of us when I say that we are . . . oh how can I put this . . . well beyond passionately committed to free up the entire world. We actually have a true creatively constructive purpose in life now, and most importantly all fear and dread for the future has vanished from us. We are looking forward to once again being benevolent contributors to this vast and wondrous universe we live in."

Monti delightfully placed his right palm over his heart and slightly bowed.

"I believe you all know my General Counsel, Henry Throckmorton," said Ted as he looked at Henry. "He will be my trusted right hand to all of you to help us carry out this new most important mission we all now share together."

Henry smiled toward the group and noticed Cynthia was gazing affectionately at him. Then he realized he was gazing fondly back at her, and Ted noticed their affection. He beamed his hearty best wishes to them with a subtle smile.

"In the days and months to come," continued Monti, "you will all be taken aboard the Galactic Alliance flagship to go through more thorough deprogramming of the Trilotew brainwashing. After that, each of you will remember ever so much more about the nature of your true selves as spherical energy beings we call the Atma, or what you Earth humans refer to as Soul. You will also begin to realize just how many lifetimes were already spent evolving in order to be in this room at this moment to go through such an unexpected dynamic change for the better."

"We wish you and your families only the very best," added Ted. "Now we better send you all back to your various locations around the world before it becomes any more strange to those who may have witnessed your sudden departures. Each of you will simply intuitively know what to say and do from now on. Henry, Monti, or I will soon be in touch with you in one form or another. By the grace of the special liberating Ray itself, we will now send you back to your respective locations on Earth in a more direct manner. Farewell."

Ted placed his right palm over his heart and nodded. All the other Council members in the room were inspired to return the gesture in sincerity. Then Ted and Henry simultaneously touched the gold pendant symbols hanging from the gold chains around their necks, and they both flashed once. A moment passed, and all four hundred secret-government Council members simply vanished from the room without requiring the use of the hidden Trilotew teleportation device up in Ted's office.

"Well, my friends," commented Monti to Ted and Henry, "we are in the thick of it now."

Both Ted and Henry paused to ponder the meaning of Monti's odd statement, and then softly laughed with him as they both telepathically picked up on the uplifting nature of his dry sense of humor.

# CHAPTER TWENTY-FOUR

# THE MIGHTY SERES RETURN

*M*ark's publisher, Mr. Dan Waymeyer, was sitting behind his desk atop the twelve-story Waymeyer Publishing building, gazing out through the large surrounding corner windows at the small mountainous ridge-line above Beverly Hills, California. He was nervously tapping a pencil on top of Mark Santfield's latest book manuscript for which he had just finished the final edits, when the phone on his desk rang.

He was impatient when he picked up the handset and snapped, "What is it, Suzanne?"

She politely replied, "Pardon me for interrupting you, Mr. Waymeyer, but Mathew McConnell is holding for you."

Dan rolled his eyes and said, "Go ahead and put him through." Then he paused and asked, "Yes Mathew?" He listened and shot back hotly, "No . . . we've already been over this. I want Mark Santfield's new book set for worldwide release on the first of next month." He listened to Mathew's beginning response and then cut him off, "Yes, yes Mathew, I'm well aware we have to spend several million more for the marketing campaign at such short notice than probably any other book in history. I ordered it. Were you listening back at the book-release scheduling meeting? Look, as I stated then, this book is going to be the most monumental ground-shaking success of any publishing company on the planet. What's that? No, I can't elaborate now, but like I told the entire executive staff, what will officially be revealed worldwide regarding the truth about what's coming to our planet that's revealed in Mark's second book will put sales right through the roof. Hell, we'll be very hard pressed just to come up with ways to keep books supplied to the retail stores and online. I just finished the final manuscript edit, and I will send it down to you in the next few minutes. Then finish the final galley proof and get the print-ready draft on my desk by tomorrow evening. Trust me on this, Mathew. Don't think about it, just do it. Use the entire editing staff to get it done if you have to, and I'll authorize any overtime." He listened more intently and then replied, "Good … good, all right then. Call me here or at home anytime just as soon as you have it ready. Remember I want the television ads, the trade-magazine ads, and the Internet campaigns tied together like clockwork for release to the public in two weeks. All the major bookstores have already committed to the timing because of the unique full-sized LCD-display monitors and video promotion about Mark's second book we are providing them, at no cost. Now get on it, Mathew, and there will be big rewards and promotions for everyone working here." He paused to listen and replied anxiously, "Yes, yes, inform all the employees their efforts will be well worth it. Okay then, call me later."

He hung up the phone and stood up. Then he walked over to the surrounding wide corner windows to gaze out thoughtfully over the city and up at the mountainous hilltop crest line above Mulholland Drive, hidden from view. Then he stated softly, "This world and all the people on it are in for quite an unexpected shock. There will be no turning back now, thank God."

Up on the Galactic Alliance flagship stealthily hovering in orbit above the North American continent were Mark and Janice, standing next to each other, gazing down through the oval observation windows at the beautiful planet they knew most people living on its surface took entirely for granted.

"You know, dear Cousin, I suppose I'll miss this world of strife and constant turmoil while we're gone," remarked Mark, a little melancholy.

"I was feeling the same way, but I remember my husband and children now as if I had left them only yesterday," Janice replied.

In reverie, Mark continued, "Having lived the lives of two people from two different worlds at the same time has at the very least expanded our creative horizons beyond what anyone would have expected."

Janice turned to him and gently placed a hand on his arm, then added softly, "You know, Mr. Ambassador to the whole incredible unexpected universal change for the best in all creation, there will be no returning to the way things were. By the grace of Prime Creator, our loving natures have been expanded to encompass the entire Earth world, our own home planet, and now it's beginning to embrace the whole multi-dimensional creation."

Mark nodded solemnly and silently looked back at the Earth, spinning slowly on its axis. Then he voiced his thoughts, as he began to imagine the tremendous changes coming to the entire Earth planet and its people.

"We should bring our families from the home world to Earth while it's being completely liberated and transformed. They would have profound experiences of a lifetime."

Telepathically picking up Mark's vision, Janice began to see Earth's new future unfolding and she commented thoughtfully, "All the suffering and all the pain of our former tortured lives seems so unimportant now, compared to what we have become. Yes … we should bring our families back here to see the entire planet and people transformed from utter unconscious terror to the brilliant light of a new day."

Commanders Jon-tral and Sun-deema walked up behind them, pleased about something. They too had tuned into the future vision for Earth's transformation coming from the mysterious liberating Ray that filled their lives with ever-expanding awareness. In truth, at that very moment, the limitless overflow of its liquid-light presence was passing through them to all life for the great uplifting benefit of the entire creation.

"*The Seres Agenda* is beginning to unfold across the face of the Earth, and everywhere else in the universe," Sun-deema stated sweetly.

Jon-tral added, "We are in the very heart of the greatest expanding benevolent change in what the Earth people call the Supreme Being, or what we know as Prime Creator. None of us can yet see all the incredible uplifting events that are now coming. At least we do know this is the end time for evil as an experiment, and not the Armageddon of destruction so many people on the Earth are hell-bent on imagining. Those perverse attitudes will melt away like a fog in the morning sun when the Expansion Ray also touches their lives. Now that we are all on the same page in this dynamic change, I believe the time has come for Captain Zin-tamal to finally take you two back home to be reunited with your families. The captain, crew, and ship are waiting in the launch bay."

Mark and Janice didn't reply, for the moment was too profoundly deep in truth, trust, love, and joy for what all life would soon be experiencing, and they just hugged both Commanders in turn like the true brothers and sisters of the one Prime Creator they had now fully become in their hearts.

Both Commanders placed their right hands over their hearts and nodded respectfully. Mark and Janice returned the true gesture of wise understanding and then started to walk away.

They had not gone ten feet when Sun-deema's sweet voice called to them,

"We'll be awaiting your return with your families to help out with the great many changes the Earth humans are about to go through."

Mark and Janice stopped and turned, smiling, before Mark commented curiously, "You both already know about our family plans."

Smiling wider, Sun-deema continued, "And you will need to be here when the President of the United States makes the worldwide announcement about all that was covered up."

"You should also know by now, we were not spying in on your private conversations," remarked Jon-tal. "With the new Ray, truth is true for all or it's not true at all."

The four of them laughed softly, knowing no more secrets and no covert thoughts or imagined negative scenarios remained within their beings. They no longer had subconscious minds within their now greatly expanded benevolent human natures.

*Farewell,* said Mark and Janice in telepathic unison, expressing deeply compassionate understanding.

*Farewell,* replied Jon-tral and Sun-deema in return, expressing the same depth of expanding love for all life.

The cousins turned around and walked solemnly out of the observation chamber.

Jon-tral began to gaze into Sun-deema's loving eyes as only a true lover can for his beloved trustworthy wife, and she gazed in knowing union back at him. He threw his arms around her slender waist and drew her near. Then they kissed passionately, long and tenderly. When they parted, they gazed together for a few moments down through the wide oval observation windows at the lovely blue-green, water covered Earth planet in contemplation of its future. Hand in hand, they turned around and walked out of the main gathering and observation room of the mighty Galactic Alliance flagship.

Captain Zin-tamal greeted Mark and Janice happily at the boarding ramp that led into the medium-sized inter-stellar Transport Carrier, and then escorted them inside.

The glowing three-hundred-feet-long cylindrical ship lifted up above the launch bay floor a few moments later, turning transparent as it moved right through the hull of the massive flagship.

It stopped for a moment in space several thousand yards away, and the pale-blue light enshrouding the ship projected a white swirling spiral of light from the front of one end of its curved oval hull to open an inter-dimensional, whirling, violet vortex tunnel. The ship shot in a blur far beyond the speed of light into the mysterious energy tunnel, and the vortex whirled closed and vanished.

Mark and Janice were reclining in comfortable white formfitting chairs similar to the one they both sat in inside the deprogramming chamber aboard the flagship. Their conversations were jovial now, mostly about their excitement at the prospect of reuniting with their families at last. They had been traveling through the inter-dimensional vortex for nearly a full day, and the ship was now more than five hundred light-years from Earth, beyond the Pleiades star group. It was nearing their home planet Norexilam in the Starborn Cluster.

Another whirling violet vortex appeared opening in a far distant space amidst a brilliant cluster of several dozen young, hot blue-white stars. The Transport Carrier shot out of the opening and almost instantly slowed to a stop, as the vortex behind it whirled closed and vanished. The luminous blue hull pulsed brightly, and the ship sped away toward a nearby planet that was similar in appearance to the blue-green, water-covered jewel of planet Earth.

It was soon orbiting the planet in a geosynchronous orbit above the equator. Three large mountainous continents centered over the equator extended a considerable distance above and below the planet's northern and southern hemispheres. Two more continents were over the north and south poles, but they also appeared to be lush with verdant plant life with no polar ice caps covering them. Deep, emerald green oceans surrounded and separated the three landmasses.

Several dozen large saucer shaped transports were flying in and out of the planet's turquoise-blue atmosphere from numerous points around the globe, headed in many different directions. One approached the Transport Carrier, turning transparent as it moved through the hull into the central section of the ship.

Captain Zin-tamal approached the cousins, who were merrily chatting away, and stated courteously, "Ambassador Shon-ral and Prime Scientist Moon-teran, we have arrived at Norexilam. One of the larger Courier Scout ships has docked in our launch bay. Your original DNA samples are with one of the advanced biology scientists. She will assist both of you with the DNA-reversion process."

Mark and Janice got up, and Mark replied, "Thank you, Captain Zin-tamal. We are most grateful for your assistance."

Janice gave him a kiss on the cheek and said, "You told us your family is also waiting for your return down on the planet. Will you be able to go see them now as well?"

"I have planet leave coming, if that's what you are asking," Captain Zin-tamal replied kindly. "I am anxious to see them, but not as anxious as you two must be after all the years of separation you went through on Earth." He smiled. "Fortunately, the time-space differential that occurs when we travel through the inter-stellar vortex from Earth to here means they only had to wait a relatively short number of months since your departures. Know that I will be standing by with the Transport Carrier whenever you need me."

*Thank you*, replied Mark and Janice in telepathic unison, and they walked with the Captain out of the lounge area.

A short time later, a trim, middle-aged woman, shorter than Janice, with long brunette hair and a striking adorable smile, was walking toward them along a long light-beige oval corridor.

"There she is now," Captain Zin-tamal said, and he stopped. "I have something to attend to so please introduce yourselves."

He smiled at her and then walked away in the opposite direction.

*So, you two have finally returned to us from the land of the lost. Somehow I knew one day you would turn up*, the woman stated telepathically as she walked up and stopped by them in the center of the long corridor, carrying a small rectangular silver case clutched in her left hand. "I'm Prime Biologist Shanal-teal," she continued cordially using her voice. "It was my privilege to be selected to bring the samples of your original DNA which we fortunately preserved before either of you departed on those dangerous missions to the planet Earth."

"You look very familiar to me," Janice stated curiously. "Have we met before?"

Shanal-teal replied, pleased, "Why, of course, dear Moon-teran, we have. I was one of the lead development biologists on your parents' team that spearheaded the DNA-reversion procedure. Your Prime DNA Biologist parents, Kantal-teran and Fimala-tanis, were best friends with my husband and me before they tragically translated from this life in that unexpected meteor collision with their exploration ship. I understand the ship was hovering stationary with the shields coincidentally down for repair when that meteor hit. I suspect to this day that the Trilotew had something to do with it. You were very young at the time."

"I remember you now," Janice responded, briefly gazing away in reflection. "You often came to our home in the Jubilanton Forest after my parents failed to return from that week-long journey away from me. My father's brother and his wife had no children, and they raised me after my parents perished."

"Now they are great scientists in their own right, advancing the speed and efficiency of our inter-stellar cruisers," commented Shanal-teal.

"I never knew my parents," interjected Mark, a little forlorn, with a shrug of his shoulders.

"I know, but I did know them," Shanal-teal replied solemnly. "Your father was one of the greatest Ambassadors the entire Galactic Alliance has ever known. That is, until that previous terrible Trilotew Emperor betrayed and killed him and your High Council-member mother. She traveled with him to their awful ruling planet on the fateful day under a flag of peace."

"I remember the events now," said Mark, briefly gazing away again in reverie and he winced at the memory. "Our flagship orbiting the planet retaliated and destroyed the Emperor and half their capital city before it retreated back to Galactic Alliance territory. The brief but devastating battles that began after that nearly plunged the galaxy back into an all-out inter-stellar war like the one we left behind five hundred thousand years ago."

"Ambassador Shon-ral, the Galactic Alliance owes you a great debt of gratitude," Shanal-teal interjected encouragingly. "You are most certainly taking it beyond your father's footsteps now. After you took his place, I know that Ambassador Shon-dema and your mother Coral-shana would have been very pleased with how you orchestrated our current treaty with the new Trilotew Emperor, despite his diabolical character. Now you are the official Galactic Alliance Ambassador to prepare the way for our fleet to arrive and save the people of Earth and the planet from certain annihilation. It was a sore loss to all of us when you vanished without a trace en route to Earth, but we are beyond delighted you and Moon-teran have safely returned to us."

"Thank you for that, Shanal-teal," Mark replied, smiling kindly at her. "I can see you are exactly the right Norexilam scientist to take us through this process. How long has it been available?"

"We were nearing completion of the DNA-reversion process after Moon-teran disappeared, and shortly after you vanished we succeeded," she replied. "We were driven because too many of our citizens were being covertly intercepted over the years by those Trilotew monsters to be used as programmed tools for their vicious missions. Many of the citizens we retrieved were operating unconsciously in suppressed human bodies on other worlds, and we were able to successfully change them back to their original advanced human physical forms using the new DNA-reversion procedure. Since then, we have installed special chambers aboard several of our large Scout ships, medium and large inter-stellar transports, and the very large Emerald Star cruisers.

"As you know, a traitor high up in the Galactic Alliance was tipping off Trilotew spies. On your way here, I received a report from the Galactic High Council in the central Novissam system. They finally discovered the traitor. It was one of the High Council members. The Trilotew had previously captured his wife and then used her as bait to get her husband to reveal travel schedules of very select Galactic Alliance citizens like you, Ambassador Shon-ral, and you, Moon-teran. Otherwise, they promised to devour her alive while he watched. They made him secretly meet with their disguised spies, and afterward he was under their control through those outlawed implantation devices.

"We secretly liberated him from their grasp and caught the spies that captured his wife. They experienced the liberating Ray, and then helped us track down his wife with Special Forces that raided their hidden base on a remote planet. They captured the dozen Trilotew that imprisoned her there, and then set them free from their subconscious brainwashing. The High Council member's wife, found chained to a crude wall, was badly mistreated and near death, but the new Ray saved her life and liberated her from their vile subconscious-implanting madness.

"Dear Moon-teran, my team was only able to finish the DNA-reversion experiment shortly after your disappearance because of the brilliant advances your parents had already completed before their so-called 'accidental' demise. When we get enough of the Trilotew liberated from the twisted implants that direct them, we will likely discover they were actually behind your parents' deaths as well."

Janice nodded gratefully.

"There is much more to this tale, dear friends," Shanal-teal continued seriously. "After the pyramids started to manifest on several primary Galactic Alliance worlds, a ten-feet-wide glowing sphere of radiant light appeared in the main Council Chamber on the central Galactic Alliance world of Zetranami in the Novissam system. It appeared comprised of thousands of teardrop-shaped self-effulgent lights built in layers of the spectrum from a white central core to a violet exterior, surrounded by a golden aura.

"Before anyone could speak, the radiant sphere transformed into an eighteen-feet-tall human from the mysterious ancient Seres race. He was elegant beyond any being anyone had ever witnessed with his glistening long, blond hair, slightly pointed ears, and blue eyes emanating a subtle radiant wisdom so deep words fail to describe it. Like a legendary Greek God of old from Earth's history, he was wearing a golden knee-length gown and simple sandals. Tucked under his long right arm was a three-feet-long, two-feet-wide, and two-inch-thick book with golden-white, thin flexible metallic pages and a blue metallic cover.

"No one had seen one of the Seres in over a billion years, and he was described as being radiantly beautiful, beyond any concept of handsome, with a soft golden light radiating around his body. His presence alone transformed the Council in under a minute, and they understood the purpose of the pyramids. The liberating new Ray emanating from the fountains within them is now bringing about the unfolding great change in the galaxy."

She reached inside her gown with her other hand and pulled out a small, clear spherical crystal with a red faceted gem in its center, then held it out in her open palm.

"This crystal storage unit was sent to the most wise leaders from all of the Galactic Alliance worlds. Then, one mysteriously appeared in my open hand. It contains the visual and voice recording of that event with the Seres Ambassador. The odd thing is, I understand he spoke in Galactic Standard. However, those in the meeting chamber could all simultaneously hear him speak in their own native tongue. There is no explanation for the phenomena at this time. I'll play it now, and you will both be brought up to date."

This new revelation deeply moved Mark and Janice, and Mark remarked, "I knew they were behind this to some degree. I sensed they were returning but could not be sure. This changes everything for the better. I have the great privilege of being the Galactic Alliance Ambassador in this galaxy at this time. My destiny is to meet the Seres Ambassador one day. He will have much to share with everyone. We are most fortunate to be alive at this moment in eternity."

Shanal-teal nodded at the crystal sphere device, and a cone of golden light shot into the hallway revealing a three-dimensional projection down the corridor. The Milky Way Galaxy appeared, and then the image zoomed closer revealing the labeled Norexilam Planetary System located near the galactic center. The image zoomed closer again to the fifth planet from their sun labeled Central Planet Zetranami. Then the massive circular High Council Chambers on Zetranami appeared. Tall Greek-style white stone pillars surrounded the inner circumference of the deep-blue walls of the chamber. Five thousand Council members wearing white silken slip-on footwear and their customary white robes with the gold sash around the waist were present. They were all seated in their comfortable white leather-like chairs arranged in fifteen circular tiered seating levels, under the wide clear overhead dome below a golden cloudless sky.

A radiant sphere of transparent golden-white light appeared before them, hovering above the round key-speaker stage centered below the fifteen-tiered circular levels, and all the alarmed Council members jumped to their feet. A soft energy instantly emanated from the sphere causing them all to be at peace, and then the eighteen-feet-tall Seres human male formed from the sphere. With a deep melodious voice, he began to address all five thousand Council members representing over four hundred and fifty million advanced space-faring world systems.

"This benevolent High Council has done all it could for so many hundreds of thousands of years to bring sanity and truth to all those who are living in your member worlds, since our departure from your dimension so long ago. The new Ray from Prime Creator also recently elevated our awareness in our higher protected parallel dimension. Golden radiant pyramids emanating the new Ray first started appearing among us, and we began to realize we have a new responsibility to help you in this reality become free from evil as an experiment in the lower worlds for all time. Our old selfish view to leave you all behind to struggle through your own way to a higher expanded awareness has been washed from our beings. Since then, much more of our true benevolent characteristics have surfaced.

"The gift of this new Ray from the lofty dimensional realm of Prime Creator, or the Ancient One, in a fineness of vibration far above our own, is permanently retiring evil as a prodding tool to encourage growth throughout creation. Something far better in creation is taking its place. The lower universes that have been fixed and finished with good and evil concepts dominating them are about to become unfixed and unfinished so they can change for the better. They are about to finally become reflections of the more greatly expanding love for all life that is also now taking place above the void, well beyond even the fifth main creative dimension. This Ray originates from the lofty ocean of majestic Light and Sound where dwells the source behind and supporting all creation, which we call Prime Creator.

"I am Seres Ambassador Torellian to your physical universe and this prototype galaxy where the golden pyramids and the fountains within them emanating the Ray are manifesting. I brought this gift of *The Seres Agenda*. It contains active new manifesting directions for the mighty change that is taking place. In the days to come, this book will help transform all that exists. You are all destined to become fully awakened trusted co-creators with Prime Creator or Gods amongst the Great One itself, even as we are. The time has finally come for this great expansion to all life.

"Know that the Seres race is about to return to this galaxy and to that planet referred to as Earth by its inhabitants, for it was one of the first worlds where we seeded human life over fifty million years ago after the dinosaur age on that world had come to an end. Planet Earth's cycle of one-hundred-and-eighty-degree polar shifts every one hundred thousand years, that usually destroys most of the life on its surface, made it necessary to constantly reseed that world with human beings and animal and plant life from other planets. This has unfortunately resulted in it being the most suppressed of human worlds for far too long. That planet's cyclic polar shifts are about to permanently end with the help of far more advanced beings we of the Seres race refer to as the Silent Mentors. They control the mechanics of the multi-dimensional universe and serve as direct manifesting channels of the new Ray that makes this great transformation to this and other galaxies possible for the first time. I must apologize for our race having been so long away from assisting you to greatly expand your awareness. The time has come for you to begin to play in much more expanded ways here and in the far higher realms where the new Ray only recently began to appear. We will contact you again when we are ready. Farewell."

The mighty Seres Ambassador placed the large blue metallic covered book on the floor of the Council Chamber. Everyone there could clearly see *The Seres Agenda* title etched upon its surface in large golden letters. Torellian nodded to all five thousand members with a wide benevolent smile, then transformed back into the radiant sphere and simply faded away.

Even through the recorded projection, Shanal-teal, Ambassador Shon-ral, and Prime Scientist Moon-teran were profoundly moved by the Seres Ambassador, and they simultaneously took a relaxing breath, let it out, and then blinked several times from the amazing revelation presented by the ancient majestic being.

"Well I believe you two will agree," continued Shanal-teal with an uplifted voice, "that was the full update of the recent most monumental historical event you missed during your absence. I must now get you both back into your original physical natures. Then you can rejoin your families, who happen to know you are on this ship in orbit above them right now. We must not keep them waiting a moment longer than necessary. Please follow me to the Medical Bay."

Mark and Janice eagerly followed Shanal-teal who portrayed a barely subdued renewed zest for life as she began to walk further back along the corridor in the direction from which she had come.

# CHAPTER TWENTY-FIVE

# THERE'S NO PLACE
# LIKE HOME

They walked together into the fifty-feet-long smooth white walled cylindrical Medical Bay containing unfathomably advanced crystal control panels, diagnostic instruments, and reclining treatment chambers. Shanal-teal stopped halfway inside and turned aside to enter another room through a triangular doorway opening. Four empty, transparent oval containers, built parallel to each other waist-high at ninety-degree right angles, lined the nearby curved white wall. A curved four-feet-wide control panel to their right lined the adjacent quarter wall of the chamber. Another three curved medical diagnostic control panels lined the other three quarter sections. Although the light in the chamber was bright, there was no apparent light source.

Shanal-teal smiled at Mark and Janice and stated, "This is where you will be restored to your original advanced human bodies. We call the device that controls the horizontal enclosures a DNA Transverse Molecular Reconstructor, and this is the transverse procedure room of our newly designed Medical Bay.

"You will both be suspended, floating in one of these antigravity suspension and DNA-reversion tubes, and then a highly oxygenated fluorocarbon emulsion converted into a specially designed breathable gas is injected into them. A precise sonic or sound frequency sent through the gas will compel the Atma, or your true spherical energy forms, to leave your physical Earth bodies. Then from above the chambers, you will both be able to witness the transformation of your Earth human bodies to your original advanced Norexilam human characteristics and capabilities.

"We do this to eliminate the intense pain you would otherwise experience over the next twenty-four hours if you remained inside them. The change occurs on a sub-atomic molecular level at one time, including reactivating the genomes that will allow both of you to live the normal human lifespan of a thousand years or more. You will also regain one hundred percent use of your brains, recover your natural photographic memory ability, and many other more advanced characteristics of your former Norexilam lives.

"Please step into the individual dressing closets you can see to the left side of the four oval chambers. Take off your Earth clothes and slip into the special flexible formfitting body-suits inside. They conduct the Transverse Carrier Waves containing the imprinted patterns of your original advanced four-stranded DNA genome codes into your Earth bodies. Inside these chambers, a golden checkerboard-patterned light grid or matrix will surround your bodies and the process will begin. The two-stranded Earth-human DNA helix will recombine with the genomes of your original four-stranded DNA helix. You will be able to consciously observe the Earth human bodies being restructured into your more advanced human forms."

"Cousin, I'll see you on the other side," Janice stated whimsically, but she was still feeling a little nervous.

"All right then, let's get this done, Cousin, and behold each other as we once did before this whole Trilotew madness intervened," Mark replied confidently and they followed Shanal-teal up to the two dressing closets.

She opened the oval doors, and the cousins stepped inside. They emerged a few minutes later wearing the sheer formfitting single-piece slip-on gowns that shimmered with changing iridescent colors as they moved in the light.

Shanal-teal touched a blue rectangular control on the console, and the clear canopy top halves of the closest two oval chambers swung up and stopped parallel to the wall at ninety-degree angles to the floor. The containers lowered for easy access, and then Mark and Janice stepped inside them and laid down face up. The lids closed over them and sealed with a soft suctioning *hiss-s-s*.

"Are you both ready?" asked Shanal-teal.

They both nodded, and she touched a lit pink rectangular crystal and it brightened. The subtly pink transparent gas quickly filled both containers, while Mark and Janice continued to breathe normally in the new atmosphere Shanal-teal then turned on several square golden controls, and the inside of both chambers were instantly filled with seven horizontally stacked rectangular layers of small checkerboard-patterned light grids. The layers then harmlessly interpenetrated their entire physical bodies, remaining extended another four inches above their torsos, and Mark and Janice began to drift into an aware trance-like physical sleep state. The encompassing golden grid pattern then suspended their bodies up to float in the center of the chambers.

Shanal-teal opened the small silver case she was carrying and lifted out from the molded sockets in the bottom two sealed transparent vials containing a clear liquid. She opened the square lid on the console and inserted both vials into two of the four silver cylinders that projected up out of the compartment. The cylinders automatically lowered back down, and the lid closed. Then she touched a small blue triangular control next to the compartment containing the vials, and it turned on, radiating a pulsing blue light. The grids encompassing the bodies of Mark and Janice began to flash on in very complex light patterns. Then they sped up until just a brilliant steady luminance remained.

A moment passed, and the true Atma energy spheres of Shon-ral and Moon-teran appeared exiting upward out of the heads of both bodies. They passed right through the clear closed lids of the chambers and stopped above them to float side by side.

*Moon-teran?* Shon-ral called telepathically.

*I'm here, Shon-ral,* she answered.

*Can you hear us, Shanal-teal?* Shon-ral asked anxiously.

*Yes, I hear both of you, but my physical eyes cannot see you.* She looked down at the instrument panel and continued. *The screen monitor on the instrument panel is now showing me your true energy forms hovering above the chambers. The DNA-transverse procedure will now automatically begin.*

The skin covering the faces of Mark Santfield and Janice Carter began to ripple slowly like tiny ocean waves, first up and down and then from side to side. Their craniums, eyes, facial bones, jaw lines, ears, noses, hair color and texture, skin color, and other discernible characteristics began to morph into their former recognizable forms. Shon-ral's and Moon-teran's original, far-more-advanced Norexilam human body characteristics, which they had treasured before the Trilotew viciously destroyed them, began to appear.

Time swiftly passed for them, while they experienced their true Atma energy spheres hovering outside their physical forms. Then they turned their focus down on their suspended sleeping bodies to discover they were looking at the exact physical characteristics of their formerly destroyed but far more advanced Norexilam bodies.

Shanal-teal walked back into the DNA-transverse laboratory at that moment and stated confidently, "The process has finished. You two should now get back into your new home world bodies."

The golden grid light pattern lowered their bodies to the bottom of both chambers and shut off, just as the subtly pink gas within them dissolved and vanished. The true Atma forms of Shon-ral and Moon-teran lowered back down through the clear lids of the oval chambers and faded inside the heads of their advanced human forms. A moment passed, and they opened their eyes just as the lids to both chambers unsealed with a quick *s-s-sip* and opened.

Shanal-teal smiled at them and then helped them climb out of the lowering chambers. When they were standing on their feet, they looked at each other, and their gaze of astonishment was unmistakable.

"Moon-teran, is that really you?" asked Shon-ral, delighted to hear his own more deeply attractive, vibrant home world male voice.

"Shon-ral, is it true, are we really back?" she asked, amazed at the return of her original angelic home world voice.

They embraced and held each other at arm's length, ecstatically smiling from ear to ear. Of course, their more radiant clear eyes were now slightly larger than most human eyes on planet Earth, and their own original voices sounded more resonant than Earth humans have yet experienced.

"I told you two we perfected the technique," proclaimed Shanal-teal. "Now you are finally ready to rejoin your families."

Shon-ral and Moon-teran gazed at each other to share a private thought, and then Shon-ral remarked, elated, "Shanal-teal, you are a saint. It's truly amazing."

"You have saved our marriages and our families from much suffering," added Moon-teran, equally elated.

"Nonsense," she humbly shot back, "I was just doing my job. You know, what I love doing anyway. It was my privilege to do this for you two, and to borrow an Earth slang word I further proclaim … damn it, I would do it again in a heartbeat."

They both cracked up laughing with Shanal-teal as she opened one of the cabinets and pulled out two sets of new clothes.

"I thought you would be more at home with your own home world clothes. I had your families provide these for your momentous return. Now get dressed, you two, and the joyous reunion can begin. I can then return planet-side to rejoin my husband, Tamal-shan. You would like him. He's Prime Scientist in inter-stellar vortex and parallel-dimension physics, and he's even more of a kidder than I am."

Her smile widened as she pictured him back at their home, somewhat impatiently awaiting her return. Then she headed out of the Medical Bay, and the Norexilam cousins eagerly followed.

Ambassador Shon-ral and Prime Social and Historical Trend Scientist Moon-teran, now fully conscious of their restored true natures, were soon dressed. He was wearing the exact same Galactic Alliance Diplomat's single formfitting silky white attire he was wearing the day he left on that ill-fated mission to Earth thirty-one years earlier. Moon-teran was wearing the same beautiful casual spring blue-and-green silken formfitting dress and the comfortable blue silken slip-on shoes she wore thirty-one and a half years earlier, just before she left on her supposed six-month scientific mission to Earth.

They were sending picture memories telepathically to each other while en route to the ship's teleportation beaming platform. They recalled many details of what their advanced normal human planet was like, compared to the deranged functioning of the purposefully misguided Earth people.

They began to reflect together that long ago very advanced human civilizations living on eighty-seven worlds circling their parent stars in the Starborn Cluster had disbanded their centralized cities. They actually had the cities dissolved on a molecular level and reformed back into the natural harmonious environments that existed before the cities were constructed. They created gorgeous flowering gardens, parks with beautiful waterfalls, and natural pathways with vast areas of remaining terrain that all citizens could enjoy. The buildings they did manifest were architectural works of art made of special non-corrosive alloys, large naturally appearing laboratory grown crystalline spires, and organic fibrous materials that were all created from combining various molecules together under controlled conditions. None of the materials came from mining the land or harvesting the verdant forests and abundant fauna around their world.

The individual home of each family was an expression of their artistic imagination with at least twenty acres of allotted land per family dwelling. They each had their own power-supply device to furnish all their needs and teleportation beaming units to send food, trade goods, and people to and from the science and manufacturing facilities or to visit friends anywhere on the planet. No fences between properties existed on these worlds' systems, and no one sought to possess another person's property or station in life. Their governing Council members were selected from only the wisest enlightened people to act as the planetary citizens' representatives in the small government complexes built within the art, science, cultural, and manufacturing centers. However, no one lived in these small, centralized city complexes. Everyone teleported to and from their homes to a given destination, and their homes were liberally spaced around the planet ecologically built in harmony with the environment. Since the people were telepathic and only worked for the pleasure of creating for the benefit of all life, their Council members truly represented the combined decisions of all their people when it came to implementing any change within their societies.

They long ago solved all non-polluting energy requirements, after they discovered an unlimited power source woven through the magnetic fields around their planets and the galaxy to drive their spacecraft. They invented ways to pass this latent energy through their devices and out the other end without depleting anything or causing harm to their planetary environments.

This unlimited energy source, coupled with the citizens' lives being free from the drudgery of working in ways to survive that were contrary to their creative natures, resulted in great leaps forward in medical and many other sciences. They neutralized all environmental pollutants and simply switched off any genetic genome code on the four-stranded helix of their human DNA found to be responsible for any disease. Eventually, they eliminated the possibility of the occurrence of any kind of disease. All microscopic life on their worlds that preyed upon more evolved life forms were swiftly neutralized, and their human life spans were increased to well over a thousand years or longer, if the individual had a purpose for extending the vitality of a particular body. Though rare, any failing organs could be grown from a person's own DNA and replaced in their bodies without invasive surgery. Matter transformation consoles took care of that by the instantaneous removal of the failing organ and replacement of it with a healthy, newly grown one without invasive surgery.

As a race, they had finally collectively attained their full higher sanity as naturally evolving benevolent human beings. War had been retired over five hundred thousand years earlier at the end of the last official inter-stellar conflict with the Trilotew. After that, the tyrant totalitarian race, and those few space-faring civilizations aligned or controlled by them, continued to be a thorn in the side of the Galactic Alliance. They remained a constant reminder that aggressive, insane beings still roamed the stars. In some ways, the ever-present potential for conflict also held back the entire Galactic Alliance from attaining higher states of consciousness. Now the citizens were joyously relieved that potential threat was finally coming to a neutralized permanent end with the unexpected introduction of *The Seres Agenda* and the new Ray by Seres Ambassador Torellian.

They finally understood that the key to this greater expansion was in some way intertwined with the survival and uplifting transformation of the distant suppressed people on planet Earth. They further discovered, during long ages past, many of their own people were subconsciously trapped and put on Earth, then compelled to reincarnate there, remaining completely unaware of their former higher human lives on other worlds. However, until *The Seres Agenda* and the new liberating Ray from the luminous fountains within the pyramids came into their lives, they had no way to safely liberate the Earth world. They did their best to maintain ongoing treaty breaking policing actions to keep the diabolical Trilotew and their associated space-faring cultures from dominating or destroying the people of Earth.

Of course, the Galactic Alliance had remained fully capable of defending itself with advanced weapons, which they kept state of the art out of the sheer necessity to continuously police any tyrant threats. However, their strict use was for self-defense purposes only. In fact, they were able to develop certain capabilities far beyond what the vile Trilotew reptilians could imagine. They had not deployed them out of their compassionate love for all life. Even so, the Trilotew and their allies still represented a serious threat because of a healing technology the Trilon-Kal had stolen from a peaceful culture they dominated long ago and then perverted to trap the Trilotew race. The affected Trilotew then signed the first treaty with the Galactic Inter-dimensional Alliance of Free Worlds after their defeat in the Great Galactic War. After that event, they constantly sought to secretly raid any world not already a part of the Galactic Alliance to retrieve any advanced weapons technologies they could discover. Their Emperor back then forced the Trilotew scientists to devote themselves to refining more deadly weapons. The combined sciences of the Galactic Inter-dimensional Alliance of Free Worlds always managed to keep one step ahead of them. They held the Trilotew at bay with a constantly maintained vigilant surveillance and enforcement of the treaty for over five-hundred-thousand years.

Most of the benevolent human, humanoid, and other beings living on more than four-hundred-and-fifty-million inhabited Galactic Alliance worlds had never been prey to the evil practices of totalitarian monsters from other world systems. They were able to safely develop past their earlier industrial stages by expanding their collective consciousness to experience knowing the purpose for their benevolent existence as beings. They had crossed over into that higher vibration or threshold of expanded understanding that allowed them to respect the freedom of others to explore how they wanted to creatively contribute to the betterment of all life. This they practically accomplished by collectively encouraging and supporting each individual from the time they were infants. They inspired something uniquely creative to develop within each child so that as adults they could present new creations of great benefit to their societies.

Permanently removed from their subconscious minds were all conflicts over territory, personal wealth, and dominating drives for individual glorification and gratification at the expense of others. The collective free choice of well over two hundred billion human, humanoid, and other benevolently evolved races living throughout the Galactic Alliance had agreed. They reached a harmonious unselfish way of thriving with each other by refining and expanding their respect for all life, and continued to create more efficient ways to improve everyone's well-being.

Eventually anything that was needed for the fulfillment of their lives toward greater enlightenment, artistic development, scientific inventiveness, personal housing wishes, clothing, clean healthy food, and any other necessities for living an abundant life were taken care of by the very refined development of highly efficient non-polluting automated facilities.

No one had to make a living just because of their birth on those worlds, and there was no taxation of any kind. They were all raised from the cradle into adulthood, being genuinely encouraged to excel only at what they loved doing. As adults, those citizens that worked in any particular field of endeavor volunteered to supervise their own area of expertise. They would actually only engage in any necessary manual labor with others of like creative natures because of their passionate love for what they were working to accomplish.

It was to this kind of normal human world that Ambassador Shonral and Prime Scientist Moon-teran finally returned, a planet the people of Earth would certainly see as paradise. Two golden-white upward whirling teleportation beams whisked them from the pad aboard ship to two different specific locations on the planet's surface. They were now beaming as pure energy to the smaller matter teleportation chambers located in each of their family homes. Every family enjoyed this wondrous interconnected worldwide transportation system on the advanced human planet of Norexilam, which was located beyond what the Earth astronomers call the Pleiades star group.

Moon-teran materialized from the whirling teleportation beam standing on the pad in the back of her specially designed, smooth ivory-white-textured six-thousand-square-feet geodesic home. Her strikingly handsome middle-aged husband Donum-tuma, with his long brown hair touching his shoulders and slightly cleft chin, was a few feet away standing with their two daughters and son to each side of him. The slightly taller eleven-year-old Yoral-telan, with wavy blond hair and dimples, and her nine-year-old sister Vera-tima, with wavy brunette hair and a contagious smile, were beautiful girls that would grow up to be beautiful women who would rival their lovely mother—although they would never express their beauty in competitive ways like adults back on the Earth planet do so frequently to obtain their desires. Their seven-year-old boy Danim-tama was handsome like his father with identical long brown hair, and no covert nature existed in his being.

Tears spontaneously poured down the cheeks of both parents coming from a joy so deep in knowing the connection that existed between them. It stretched even beyond time and space to finally reunite them again as she stepped down off the pad. The children ran up to her and threw their arms around her waist as she squatted down, embraced, and repeatedly kissed each one.

"Mother…Mother…Mother," the three ecstatic children repeated excitedly.

"Dearest Yoral-telan, Vera-tima, and Danim-tama, I have missed you so," replied Moon-teran, crying tears of joy.

They huddled together in the depth of their hearts that now beat as one, and when she finally stood back up, the children remained hugging her waist. Her patient husband stood there, staring in wonder at her radiant beauty he so much missed during the vast time and space that held them separated for a year and a half in his time, and thirty-one and a half years Earth time for her. Donum-tuma gently approached his wife, not quite knowing what to do next.

Then he telepathically stated with deep caring respect, *Beloved Moon-teran, I can't imagine what it must have been like growing up again in another life on that planet, but know that your loss to me was far greater than all the treasures of the universe.*

With tears streaming down her face, Moon-teran's widening joyful smile expressing an agony of anticipation of being in his arms, once again connected to him. His matching smile of anticipation beamed back an almost palpable loving energy that even the children could perceive as they stepped back from them in awe. They observed both parents hesitate for a moment, before they leapt into each other's arms, crying and laughing. He lifted her up and swung her off the ground in circles, while the children spontaneously jumped up and down, giggling with delight and clapping their hands. Then Donum-tuma passionately kissed Moon-teran for the first time since their long separation from each other.

That kiss was one for the history books. The sweetness of their committed dedication to each other, and their gratitude for life, was about to go far beyond their physical bodies. Their true spherical Atma, or Soul energy, suddenly floated up out of the tops of their heads, while their bodies remained below in a kissing swoon. The enlightened children stopped their excited play to gaze above their parents' heads, for they could see their true Atma selves. The children's pure, wide-open eyes in a deep gaze of profound awe and wonder of the special moment would stun almost any human being living on Earth, had they witnessed it. The white light radiating between them increased in intensity, and their two separate Atma spheres gradually moved into each other to become one slightly larger and more luminous sphere. The tiny teardrop-shaped lights that comprised the structure of their spheres built in layers from a white central core through the spectrum of colors to a violet exterior, surrounded by a pale, golden aura, was doubled inside the one slightly larger sphere they had become.

Waves of the finest golden energy mist began to pulse from the larger sphere out into the room. The three children stood there, bathing in the profound experience their fully illumined parents were sending them as an example of a true parental bond, and the intrinsic value it held for all life because of its committed experiential nature. They were expressing their well being now to all life, not just for their own family members. The elevated awareness of their true eternal natures was now emanating the new Ray of unsuppressed love that is always for the uplifting benefit of the entire universe and everything in it.

The wonder of their united sphere slowly separated again, and the two spheres remained for a moment hovering a few feet apart, before they re-entered their kissing, swooning bodies by fading back into the tops of their heads.

The children suddenly broke out giggling and performed jubilant dancing antics and then laughed with delight, clapping their hands while their blissful, tightly embraced parents stopped kissing. They turned their heads to gaze lovingly at their three children with opening arms, and the children ran into their closing embrace.

*Mother...Mother...Mother,* shouted all three ecstatic children, this time in telepathic unison.

***Oh Moon-teran, my heart was so yearning in an empty room without you here,*** Donum-tuma stated telepathically, much relieved, with his deeply melodious quivering inner voice.

Smiling through tears of joy, she replied, ***My heart was glowing ever warmer in an agony of anticipation the closer we came on our return to the home planet, and to you my husband.***

Donum-tuma wiped tears of joy from his eyes and then replied sweetly, fondly gazing down at the smiling upturned faces of their children, *Beloved young ones, your mother has finally returned to us. She is home at last.*

She sighed, wiping tears from her eyes, and then sweetly added with gratitude deeper than the sky, *Dear Donum-tuma, there is no place like home. Oh, Prime Creator of all, there just is no place like home.*

He took her hand, and she squeezed his fingers tightly, expressing the firmness of their inner connection. They began to reflect in unison that their kindred but still suppressed fellow human beings back on Earth should be experiencing what they now knew about their true natures. Then she rested her head on his shoulder as they walked through an oval opening at the back of the teleportation room to enter the main living-room area.

Their three vibrantly happy children rushed past their parents, who stopped to gaze at the large wide oval indoor swimming pool. Moon-teran looked up fondly through the gentle curve of the transparent semispherical canopy that crowned the top third of their luxurious home in the country, and he followed her gaze. She stood there drinking in with her eyes the magnificent vibrations of peace and harmony, and then her gaze slowly swept around the pool and living room area of their tranquil home.

On the far side of the pool, centered in the surrounding living room under the overhead dome, were several steps that led up to a modern, open kitchen. A number of other rooms extended from each side of the kitchen around the circumference of the upper half of the dome. Living-room sofas, chairs, and clear-glass-like-topped tables adorned the wide, blue stone floor surrounding the pool. Four spiral metal staircases, positioned at four equidistant points around the interior circumference of the dome, also accessed the bedrooms on the second level. An advanced form of fiber-optic lighting, recessed underneath three overlapping concentric circles of one-feet-wide, ivory-colored panels, surrounded the lower half of the clear overhead canopy. The hidden lights illuminated everything as if they were outside under the natural light of their planet's twin suns.

Moon-teran returned her gaze to her happy husband and rested her head on his shoulder again. Just then, the children who had changed into bathing suits ran together and jumped into the beautiful pool with the surrounding rim set with glistening gems of many colors. They began a happy splashing play by throwing a floating blue ball back and forth in appreciation of each other. Competitive natures for gaining or winning over another were not apparent in their loving, gentle actions. The fully aware children truly appreciated the great gift from Prime Creator of knowing they were together for each other's benefit

Then Moon-teran began to reflect on how fortunate they were to live on a normal human world. With her inner vision, she recalled how they resided in a beautifully lush country setting not far from one of the twelve worldwide governing complexes with their science labs, art, and cultural buildings every citizen enjoyed on their home world of Norexilam. Then she lit up with an overflowing joy she had never imagined existed in her suppressed life growing up as Janice Carter back on Earth.

Having also envisioned all she was seeing, Donum-tuma gently took her hand and kissed it. Then they casually walked together outside their home through a clear, vertical oval door that automatically opened, sliding inside the surrounding circular eight-feet-high smooth ivory-colored wall.

They had stepped into a botanical garden paradise. Multi-tiered waterfalls laced the wonderfully landscaped flowering rock gardens. Trees far bigger than the great redwood and sequoia trees along the northern coast and inland mountains of northern California back on Earth were growing in well-selected places, interspersed through the wonderland of nature in harmony with itself. The lush gardens extended into the distant acreage toward the snow-crowned blue-gray mountain range. Perhaps twenty miles away, they curved like a half moon across the horizon under the twin golden-bronzed suns. The slightly smaller radiant orb was just above the top of the crest of the mountain range, and the radiant larger orb was to the right of it, higher up in the deep-turquoise-blue sky. Faintly crimson-and-lavender-tinted clouds laced between them on several levels were slowly moving from west to east.

There were plants the size of an adult person with broad green leaves like prehistoric giant Earth ferns, and wide gold and violet flowers blossoming from ten-feet-tall dark-green stalks. Soft bright-green moss covered the many paths that wound throughout the garden splendor.

Small chirping birds were singing complicated beautiful tunes through long thin beaks extended from lovely violet heads. They looked similar to birds on Earth, except for their rapidly flapping wings. They were fluttering merrily back and forth, briefly stopping to hover over a large flower to dart a long sticky tongue down behind the shimmering phosphorescent six-inch-tall stamens, dripping with nectar. The curved, overlapping, four-inch-wide, teardrop-shaped flower petals spread around the stamens like a fan. The full iridescent spectrum of pastel-feathered plumage on several dozen birds flying by overhead subtly blended together down their twin long fan-shaped tail feathers. The two sets of beautiful wings, one above the other, were beating together like a dragonfly. Their aerodynamically streamlined bodies became more apparent when a mated pair briefly landed on a branch, and they started to sing a different beautiful melody to each other. The slightly smaller female exhibited her more delicate feminine characteristics by spreading out her two slightly longer tail feathers like twin Japanese fans. The pair flew away again with their two sets of wings rapidly beating as fast as a hummingbird back on Earth.

Later that night, the parents gratefully tucked the three children into their soft oval beds in their individual rooms on the second floor and snuggled them close. Then Donum-tuma and Moon-teran went to their bedroom and climbed into their big oval bed. It was ideally located, centered at the top of their living dome between the smaller rooms that surrounded the second-floor level. They lay side by side to appreciate the breath-taking celestial view of the night stars under the clear overhead canopy. If any Earth person suddenly arrived to see the radiant depth of stars, and numerous colorful nebulae that adorned the night sky of their world, they would be stunned beyond words. They would not believe their eyes as they watched the pale-blue, pale-green, and pale-red moons orbiting the planet at various positions across the heavens. It would all seem like a dreamy fantasy after their instant arrival back on Earth.

The two reunited lovers were soon reaching the peak of their intimate passionate ecstasy when their true radiant spherical Atma selves unexpectedly propelled out of their bodies to hover side by side above their swooning physical forms. Their telepathic cries of release began to create blinding concentric waves of white light that pulsed outward in all directions. The waves then quickly faded away, just as a whirling, golden-white inter-dimensional tunnel opening appeared above them. Their two radiant spheres merged into one brighter and slightly larger sphere that darted up into the tunnel of light.

A third of the way around the planet, on one of the other three equidistantly spaced continents centered over the planet's equator, stood another elegantly designed domed home. It rested on several dozen lush, green moss-covered acres. The nearby light green, mile-high waterfall, illuminated by the phosphorescent mineral rich water with a soft moonstone-like sheen, was tumbling over the top of a higher crescent valley below the rolling lush-forested snow-free mountain ridge. The powerful water was cascading across a lower three-tiered cliff face to the valley, where it joined a river winding in a snake-like pattern through the distant countryside. The twin suns were now high in the sky above this mountain range. It just happened to be located on the same latitude as that of the taller snow-covered mountains a continent a third of the way around the planet's equator near Moon-teran's home.

This unique three-geodesic-domed home complex built in a triangula pattern was interconnected by transparent glass-like triangular walkways Crowning two of the domes were clear transparent canopies. The third on had a smooth ivory-white smaller turret dome topping it that looked like i might conceal some kind of advanced astronomical telescope or other stella observation equipment.

Assortments of multicolored vegetables cultivated in crisscrossing row beside many bushy fruit trees were growing inside the triangular area betwee the three domes. The acreage surrounding the domes was immaculatel landscaped, laced with many circulating multi-tiered rock garden waterfalls Verdant flowers, much larger and more prolific than in any Earth garden, wer artfully growing in and around them.

The interspersed forest trees were ten times larger than the tallest gian redwood or sequoia trees back on Earth, but the resemblance to Earth varietie was uncanny. Some of the tree trunks with crimson-red bark were seventy five-feet-wide at or near the ground and several-thousand-feet-tall. The eight to-twelve-feet-thick branches near their base extended straight out from th massive trunks nearly twenty feet before they gradually curved up at ninety degree angles.

In the distance beyond this particular home spread out a thick forest of th giant trees with more geodesic-domed homes built upon the massive branche in gradually ascending levels. Spiraling-upward transparent, triangular corridor that connected them together were like those that linked together Shon-ral' three-geodesic-domed home complex back in the valley near the mile-higl waterfall.

It was to this house that Ambassador Shon-ral arrived as he full materialized on the teleportation pad in the chamber on the far right sid of the primary living dome, under the clear overhead canopy. His beautiful trim wife Lorun-eral, appearing to be in her mid-thirties, was standing nearb with her long, golden-blond hair flowing down her back. She was wearing th very same soft white dress that shimmered in the light like a moonstone as sh moved, that she wore before he went to Earth on his ill-fated mission. She ha been anxiously awaiting his return with their two eager, lovely children for full year, undergoing the agony of dearly missing his absence from their lives.

The handsome eight-year-old boy, Shan-dreal, and beautiful ten-year-ol girl, Taluna-tala, who resembled their parents' characteristics to a fine point ran to him as he stepped off the pad and squatted down to embrace and kis them.

"Father…Father…Father," the ecstatic children repeatedly cried out.

"Oh, my beloved Shan-dreal and Taluna-tala, I have so dearly missed you," exclaimed Shon-ral through tears of joy.

While they both hugged his neck and kissed him back, he gazed up at his wife just as she stepped toward them with tears running down her cheeks through a smile of anticipated joy deeper than the clean clear sky around their planet, and he was awe-struck. Her radiant beauty now surpassed his deepest recollections of their previous bond of love for each other and for the gift of their two wondrous children. The tears finally sprang from his eyes as he stood up and embraced his graceful wife, who rose up on her tiptoes like an Earth-world ballerina. Their two children hugged their hips and then stood back in wonder with their mouths open to observe the deep reunion that was taking place.

Shon-ral picked his wife up a foot off the floor and swung her around, kissing her. She placed the long, slender feminine fingers of her hands behind his head and neck to tenderly cup his head in her palms. At that moment, their children broke out joyfully clapping and giggling, and then they began jumping up and down.

*Father…Father…Father,* shouted the two ecstatic children, this time in telepathic unison.

Their parents continued to passionately kiss even as he gently set her feet back down to the floor. To the children, time suddenly appeared to stand still as the pure Atma spheres of their parents appeared, ascending above the tops of their heads. The children stepped back in awe of what they were witnessing. The eternal essences that were the real Shon-ral and Lorun-eral hovering above the heads of their physical bodies gradually moved toward each other until both spheres perfectly blended into one slightly larger, more radiant sphere of light. The white luminous cores of their beings began to radiate with increasing intensity until a warm golden energy mist pulsed out into the chamber. It uplifted the children, impressing them with the refined honest nature of their parents' pure love for each other, for them, and for all life everywhere. The children's wide joyful eyes grew larger with anticipation, and then they broke out with more giggles, laughter, hand-clapping, and jumping up and down. The radiant spheres of their parents gradually separated and hovered back over the heads of their kissing bodies before they faded back down inside the tops of their heads.

Shon-ral and Lorun-eral parted to gaze fondly down at their knowing children, and the youngsters happily ran into their opening arms. A few minutes later, the harmoniously reunited family walked gracefully together through the oval opening leading into the living-room area of their home under the transparent canopy. Shon-ral began to appreciatively survey the majestic home, loving wife, and children he had to leave behind thirty-one Earth years earlier.

The entire family then calmly walked past the large oval swimming pool and smaller circular pool beside it into the triangular opening leading along the clear-sided forty-feet-long triangular walkway. They gazed along the way at the vibrant food garden growing outside in the triangular land between the walkways that connected the three-geodesic-domed home complex together.

They passed through another oval opening at the other end of the walkway to enter their kitchen dome filled with very advanced appliances, beautiful blue and green stone counter tops, and sinks and food preparation areas built below the cabinetry with the octagon-shaped doors that encircled the kitchen under the clear curved dome. Then they continued to the other side of the kitchen dome to pass into another triangular hallway, and they were soon walking into the third dome.

There Shon-ral paused to gaze with zeal up through the round transparent second-floor level to fondly appreciate the very special tube-shaped astronomical telescope device attached to the center of the floor. It was two-feet-wide and twenty-feet-long pointing at an upward angle toward the curved closed sliding hatch to the outside. A horizontal and vertical axis mounting system supported the telescope. A double terminated four-inch wide by four-inch high and two-feet-long clear quartz crystal protruding from the end of the tube was attached by a three-legged, gold metal tripod pointed at the middle of the closed hatch.

Shon-ral looked away, and they walked together over to a clear vertical oval doorway similar to the one in Moon-teran's home. It automatically opened, silently sliding inside the eight-feet-tall ivory-white wall surrounding the lower level of the dome. The two children ran playfully out through it to the outside, and their delighted parents walked out after them.

Just outside the astronomical dome, they stopped again to gaze at the nearby waterfall and the giant forest trees with the many domed homes built ever upward in the strong branches. Their astronomical dome was facing the direction of their serene gaze at the waterfall and their running children playing before them in the glorious landscaped garden paradise.

As Lorun-eral looked up lovingly into his eyes, she telepathically stated with great relief, *Oh, how I thank the great Prime Creator behind all life for your return, dear husband. You are finally home with us.*

He kissed his wife again and replied with sublime humble gratitude while gazing lovingly back down into her beautiful green eyes, *Dearest wife, all I can say is there is no place like home. Oh, dear Prime Creator of all, there just is no place like home on any other world in the universe.*

After their two children were in bed and snuggled close in their rooms on the second floor, Shon-ral and Lorun-eral climbed into their own big round bed in their large round bedroom centered under the top of the clear curved sleeping canopy. They lay back to view the breath-taking celestial view of the night stars, colorful nebulae, and the three pale-blue, pale-green, and pale-red-moons orbiting their planet. They thought about how elevating their simple experience at that moment would be for any of the people back on Earth, after such a liberating gift of life is freely available to them.

They were soon intimately entwined for the first time in thirty-one Earth years for Shon-ral. For Lorun-eral, one year had passed now that he was back in his original advanced human body. Just as they reached the peak of their passionate intimate ecstasy, the Atma spheres of their true selves suddenly propelled out of their swooning bodies to hover close together above the bed. The telepathic cries of release no one but they could hear filled the air, as their two radiant orbs merged into one larger brighter sphere creating brilliant circular light waves pulsing in all directions. A whirling, golden-white inter-dimensional portal or tunnel opening appeared above the slightly larger united sphere, and it darted up into the tunnel of light.

A mighty ocean of brighter whirling light, filled with millions upon millions of orbs identical to what they had become, soon appeared before them, moving like a galaxy around a more brilliant massive bulging nucleus in the immense deep-blue-surrounding void of some ethereal space. They were now in a far, far higher reality, and their sphere shot into the immense distance toward the galaxy-like nucleus center of the mighty ocean of light. They were being moved forward by a deep humming sound mixed with a hauntingly beautiful, alluring ocean of breath-taking male and female voices singing in round drawn-out-tones the original primordial sound "HU" on many harmonic levels in perfect pitch. Their united sphere soon reached the center of the massive light and then vanished deep inside its thunderous power.

Together as one light, they began to speak telepathically to each other, just as their light sphere emerged inside another deep-blue void with one identical but massively larger and more radiant sphere in the distance. It was hovering peacefully before them in the very center of the mysterious void.

*Oh Shon-ral, where are we?* Lorun-eral humbly asked, her quivering telepathic voice creating a pulsing light within their sphere that matched each uttered word.

Shon-ral replied with his own quivering telepathic voice, *Lorun-eral, dear heart, we are now in the high realm of Prime Creator. I do not know how I know this, but it is true.*

*Oh my, what's happening to us?* she replied, a little frightened.

*Feel my courage, my love, and do not be afraid,* replied Shon-ral with his light sphere continuing to pulse with each word spoken. *We are exactly like Prime Creator, but on a much smaller scale, and we are here to learn.*

The voice of Prime Creator, or The Ancient One, was deeply melodious and filled with the secrets of the center of eternal creation itself. It too pulsed from within its massive center, but each word created ecstasy in the combined light sphere of Shon-ral and Lorun-eral, and they separated back into two spheres hovering close side by side.

*Beloved ones,* began its smooth elevating deep vibrant voice, *you have come home at last. You are here to understand more about the purpose for the new Ray that was sent to your physical universe, and what this means for the far better enlightenment of every Atma or eternal being throughout the many mansion worlds in the multi-dimensional universe. This new understanding will awaken within you now.*

A wave of misty white light so high in hue the finest tinge of gold could just be made out laced throughout it, shot from the center white core of Prime Creator to the center white cores of Shon-ral's and Lorun-eral's true selves. Both spheres expanded slightly larger, and their light intensity increased several times greater, while the misty wave continued into the distance beyond the deep-blue void.

*Now you know,* spoke Prime Creator's majestic vibrant voice once again.

*Yes, dear Prime Creator, now we know,* their inner voices solemnly proclaimed in perfect unison.

*Be at peace and freely create with this new liberating Ray, for it will forever bring constructive change to the lower dimensions. All fear or what many beings refer to as evil is being forever retired from all the worlds of time and space. Return now and enjoy this moment in eternity. Know that your futures are very bright indeed.*

*Can we return here?* asked Shon-ral and Lorun-eral in telepathic unison.

*You will both return here many times to ever expand your awareness capabilities envisioned throughout your uplifting benevolent co-creative futures. Now you must go back. To stay here longer would result in the loss of your physical bodies on your home planet, and you would not then be able to carry out your part in the unfolding Expansion Ray mission that is uniquely yours to enjoy by right. All is well.*

Their two separate spheres merged into one again, and then it shot downward in a blur of light at incredible speed. The radiant sphere sped right back down out of the open whirling inter-dimensional vortex, to hover above their bodies that were now peacefully asleep with arms wrapped around each other. The vortex vanished, as the radiant sphere separated back into two slightly smaller orbs. Then both spheres descended back down inside their bodies through the tops of their heads, and grateful smiles appeared on their sleeping faces.

# CHAPTER TWENTY-SIX

# THE CALL
# TO
# EXCELLENCE

The weeks went by for the cousins on their beautiful home world of Norexilam. Their normally highly refined human love for their world had been significantly elevated, evolving into a deep abiding love they knew was a privilege to express in waves of goodwill to all life throughout the multi dimensional universes of Prime Creator. Their fellow citizens knew where this uplifting energy was coming from, and they knew why it was now radiating across the face of their world. They had all known about the loss of Ambassador Shon-ral and Prime Scientist Moon-teran, and about their amazing recovery and return from their devastating ordeal on the troubled Earth planet. Now they were all silently rejoicing, for they were beginning to go through an ever greater transformation after a dozen of the mighty golden pyramids appeared in the botanical parks located within each of their twelve government, cultural and science development centers. In just several days, the Ray radiating from them had refined every man, woman, and child on their world even further. They had all become dedicated together in their collectively awakened goodwill to see that Earth would finally be set free from the tyranny that had plagued it for countless ages. The energy coming from all of them was emanating back through the chain of pyramids stationed across time and space all the way to planet Earth. That alone, they knew, would do more to uplift that planet's suppressed people than anyone could possibly imagine in the days, weeks, months, and several years that were to follow.

Then one day the fountains hidden within the pyramids emerged from them to permanently sit themselves down in the very center of each botanical wonderland. The irresistible liberating white-golden light, in the form of a drinkable liquid, continuously poured from the palms of the mighty male statue standing in each of the white stone bowls. What happened to the people on Norexilam after that can be best revealed by the phenomenal event that took place after the eighteen-feet-tall Seres Ambassador Torellian unexpectedly contacted Ambassador Shon-ral and Moon-teran one bright twin-sun-filled day.

They were both puttering around alone outside in their home gardens on their respective continents just for the pleasure of solitude and peace it afforded them, when the mighty being appeared before Shon-ral radiating a clearly visible soft golden light from around his entire body. Shon-ral's wife and children had teleported away earlier to visit the nearest art and science center located several hundred miles from their home.

*I knew that one day we would meet,* Shon-ral stated telepathically, expressing rather more elation than usual at that moment, while the very tall, ancient majestic immortal being towered above him.

Although he appeared like a youthful male in his thirties, Shon-ral knew the Seres race had immortalized their physical bodies before they disappeared from the galaxy a billion years ago. At that moment, he recalled they had originally seeded all human, humanoid, and other life throughout the many galaxies of time and space before they mysteriously vanished. He knew the Seres had evolved to greater heights in that distant past than the refined humans who presently lived within the Galactic Inter-dimensional Alliance of Free Worlds.

*You are now one of us, although you may not yet be aware of this fact,* replied the deep melodious inner voice of the Seres Ambassador with a loving nature that almost literally lifted Shon-ral off his feet.

Shon-ral was about to say something but held back as Torellian continued to enlighten him with the purpose of his visit.

*We are not now so different. You are about to begin to discover you have an eight-stranded DNA helix structure in your molecular makeup, instead of four. You and your wife Lorun-eral, and your cousin Moon-teran and her husband Donum-tuma, are gradually being transformed. This great change will not be noticeable to your fellow citizens on Norexilam just yet. However, this new body type will allow the Atma that is the real you to operate through it in ways you cannot yet imagine. I am committed to helping you and Lorun-eral through the transformation of this great gift given to you by Prime Creator during your recent visit. The full awareness of this will come in time.*

*I am also here on another matter. I have spoken with the Galactic Alliance High Council. They requested that I ask you and Moon-teran if you would both return to Earth this day. The President of the United States on that world, newly liberated Trilotew Ambassador Grotzil, and Chairman Ted Carter of the secret worldwide government are about to announce to all the people of Earth the truth about all that has been kept from them. There could be great unrest, and perhaps even rebellion among the confused masses. To avoid this, it will be necessary for you and Moon-teran to be present there to transmit to them what you both went through to awaken from the torturous suppression you endured for so many years. After the most important speech in Earth's entire history is given to them, radiant pyramids will begin to appear, while you and Moon-teran are inspired to share more about what is unfolding on their world. When this is taking place, you will both serve as examples for all the people. The new advanced human prototypes both of you have now become will provide them with a glimpse of what they will experience in the near future. Once they have the understanding of what you went through, all fear, anger, hate, and other subconscious terrorizing implants driving their lives will be given up and turned back into the pure primordial omnipresent force that supports and sustains all that exists.*

Shon-ral was smiling in a compassionate depth of understanding he never knew before. He began to actually see the tremendous worldwide transformation that was coming to planet Earth to awaken the people, now that the Ray had benevolently neutralized the insane tyrants' characters.

He looked up at the graceful Seres Ambassador and said, using his voice, "Now I clearly see what you have been saying about the entirely unexpected events that are coming to the people of Earth."

"Will you return?" Torellian asked humbly, using his vocal chords, and he unassumingly waited for Shon-ral's response.

"Yes, of course I will," replied Shon-ral without hesitation, "and I am certain Moon-teran will agree."

Torellian smiled, and the soft angelic light emanating around his entire body brightened.

*Then all is well,* he stated as if he were actually relieved. *The truth you and Moon-teran will radiate through the pyramids to all the people of Earth will help them remain peacefully balanced through the tremendous changes that their planet must go through to purify the environment. However, this will not be the destructive method of cyclic planetary polar shifts used to accomplish this in the past. You can also communicate to them all about the coming return of our Seres race to this universe and their planet. However, we will not make our presence known to the people there until after the planet is transformed and they have accepted being part of the Galactic Inter-dimensional Alliance of Free Worlds.*

*Moon-teran will contact you now, for I have appeared before her during this same time while she stood alone outside in her home garden. Her husband is also away with their three children on a day trip to the mountains. The ability to be in more than one place at the same time will awaken in you when the time is right. You will shortly both discover that I have already spoken with your mates, and they are comfortable with the plan to temporarily return to Earth. You will also soon realize you do not need a spaceship to return this time, and Moon-teran will be the first to utilize this important ability beginning to awaken within each of you. You will understand. For now, know that you have the goodwill and friendship of the entire Seres race, and the gift of grace from Prime Creator. Now I must depart. Farewell.*

The majestic angelic Seres Ambassador began to sparkle like a million tiny glittering blue stars and faded away. Ambassador Shon-ral walked back inside his primary domed living quarters and went into the teleportation chamber to see a blinking yellow control on the console. He touched it, and a projected view screen appeared above the console. Moon-teran's image came into focus standing in her garden, not in the expected teleportation room. She appeared radiantly happy.

"Dear Cousin, it looks like we're headed back to Earth already," she stated serenely. "I understand what Ambassador Torellian meant. I no longer need the teleportation unit to join you now. Behold!"

Her image on the view screen vanished from view, and she just as instantly reappeared standing beside Shon-ral in his teleportation chamber an ocean and a continent away. He began to express amazement but stopped as he smiled with his own sudden new understanding, and he gently grasped her hand. Then they both simply vanished again and reappeared standing side by side back outside in his garden, quietly giddy with childlike wonder.

"Cousin dear," began Shon-ral, elated, "I perceive the President of the United States is about to give that scheduled speech to the people of Earth."

"Yes, I see the liberated Trilotew Ambassador Grotzil standing beside him," replied Moon-teran, also elated.

"We're already discovering new abilities with our transformed eight-stranded DNA helix bodies," Shon-ral added curiously. "We can project ourselves anywhere now just by visualizing the destination, and the new liberating Ray will send us there, bypassing certain laws of physics that only apply to the lower dimensions."

"Perhaps we should contact the President first, before we just show up unannounced in his office," Moon-teran inquired cautiously.

"You're right," concurred Shon-ral, and he added thoughtfully, "but I must try something I'm beginning to sense we are now capable of doing or he won't recognize either of us."

"Yes, yes, you're right, Cousin. I was just sensing the same thing," she confirmed.

Shon-ral looked away dreamily, and a transparent blue energy wave passed down over his body, similar to a heat wave in the desert, to swiftly rearrange his molecules back into the body of Mark Santfield.

"Well Cousin, how do I look?" he asked and bowed regally.

Laughing back at him she replied, "Oh, it's perfect. You look exactly like Mark Santfield. Okay then, here goes.

"She looked away dreamily, and her body transformed back to Janice Carter.

"Oh, that's just superb," Mark stated delightfully. "Now how are we going to explain this to our families?"

"We don't!" she replied and winked at him. "At least not for a while if we're wise."

They laughed together in agreement.

President Martin McCoy and Trilotew Ambassador Grotzil were standing in front of the President's desk back in the Oval Office at the White House in Washington, D.C. on planet Earth, when they both clearly heard Mark's telepathic voice respectfully inquire, *Excuse my interruption, Mr. President and Ambassador Grotzil, but can you both hear me? This is Ambassador Shon-ral.*

Startled but unafraid, they both replied in unison, "Yes," and the President asked, "Where are you?"

*On our home world of Norexilam,* replied Shon-ral. *Moon-teran and I would like to join you to add our voices to the momentous announcement you are about to make to the people of Earth. I perceive that Chairman Ted Carter is not with you now. It is important that he disclose the truth about his hidden worldwide organization as well.*

"He'll be arriving any minute with Monti and Henry," commented the President. "I've been very anxious to hear from you. You are both always most welcome here. It would not be a complete announcement without you two."

*We are on our way,* Shon-ral and Moon-teran replied telepathically in unison standing in the garden outside his domed home complex on Norexilam.

*Are you ready, Cousin?* asked Shon-ral.

*I'm more than ready,* Moon-teran replied happily.

Shon-ral confidently extended his elbow to her, and she placed her arm around it and grabbed his hand. Then they both looked up into the sky with widening exhilarated smiles and simply vanished.

They reappeared an instant later right in front of President McCoy and Ambassador Grotzil, standing upon the elegant rug with the official Presidential eagle seal woven beautifully into it.

"There was no teleportation beam. How did you get here?" Grotzil inquired, surprised.

"All I can say for now is that we have acquired some new abilities. A moment ago, we were more than five hundred light-years away on our home planet, Norexilam, and now we're here," replied Mark.

Grotzil thought about what he said and had a profound realization.

"You can project between worlds on your own," he proclaimed, amazed.

"Yes, and I suspect after all your fellow Trilotew citizens living on your combined world systems are set free from their subconscious nightmare they too will discover how to accomplish this. The ability will not function if the intent is negatively covert or if it is intended for conquest or the domination of others."

The Trilotew Ambassador reflected thoughtfully on Mark's words, and then nodded and remarked, "I understand. It is as it should be."

There was a knock on the door. Secretary of Defense Daniel Samuelson opened it and walked in but stopped to stare, amazed to see that Mark and Janice had somehow arrived in the Oval Office without going through the front door.

"Welcome back, Mark and Janice," he stated sincerely, gazing curiously at them. "We've been wondering if you two would show up." They both smiled and nodded their appreciation for his warm welcome. Then Daniel looked at President McCoy and announced, "Chairman Carter just telepathically informed me that he, Henry, and Monti are about to arrive."

"Thank you, Daniel," Martin replied calmly. "You should join us. Now we can begin the news conference. Is everything ready to go?"

"Yes, Mr. President," Daniel answered confidently. "We go live worldwide in fifteen minutes."

A bright whirling beam appeared behind Mark and Janice at that moment. Chairman Ted Carter and his General Counsel Henry Throckmorton were in business suits, standing close together with Monti as the beam faded away.

"Dear daughter Janice," Ted cried out, "I really missed you."

He and Janice ran into each other's arms, and he gave her a long fatherly embrace. Then she looked up at him and said, "Dearest foster father from Earth, I have also dearly missed you."

Henry walked up and hugged Janice, and then she remarked, "Dear friend Henry, I am so very glad to see you too."

"This news conference is going to be most interesting," he declared, smiling at her and then looked at Mark. "Well, Mark, or rather Ambassador Shon-ral, what's going to happen on this planet after all the frustrated people in the world learn the truth about just how much they were lied to over the decades? They will have every right to get really pissed off."

"I was thinking the same thing," Ted concurred.

"That foreseen difficulty has been taken care of," answered Mark.

Mark gazed back at both men, at the President, at Ambassador Grotzil, and then at Monti, who appeared quite jubilant, and asked, "Monti, my friend, will you join us?"

"I would like to but not this time," he replied. "I must return to the flagship to assist with the changes that will be taking place all over the Earth after you conclude your announcement. Know that I will contact you when can. Farewell, my friends."

He touched the gold pin on his lapel and vanished in a whirl of teleportation light.

"If the people do get really pissed off as Henry said, how are we going to handle that?" inquired Ted.

"You will all see events take place on this Earth today that will stay vividly impressed within your new expanding states of awareness for eternity." Then he announced to the President, "It's time for Janice and I to reveal our true off-world natures and physical characteristics. Our Earth bodies have just undergone a genetic transformation back to our original extraterrestrial human forms, even though the Trilotew destroyed the original bodies long ago. This took place through a special process that utilized our original DNA stored back on our home world. What you are seeing before you now are the temporary molecular DNA reformations from our original extraterrestrial human bodies back to the Earth physical bodies that are familiar to you."

Mark glanced at Janice, she glanced back, and they looked away, as Ted watched in wonder as the desert-like heat wave effect appeared, flowing down over their bodies, and turned their molecular DNA compositions back into the true original human appearances of Ambassador Shon-ral and Prime Scientist Moon-teran. All the others in the room were awestruck by the change. They also could not help but notice that Shon-ral and Moon-teran had slightly larger-than-average human eyes and more youthfully refined physical characteristics. Then the amazed observers began to realize an invisible energy radiating from them was actually expanding their awareness.

"Janice, is that you?" Ted asked apprehensively.

She smiled with deep affection back at him and replied, "Yes, I am the same being you knew while I was growing up, and ever so much more. Do not be concerned. In a short time it will be clear to everyone why we are all here together."

"I believe the time has come for me to use our morphing device," interjected Ambassador Grotzil. "I will camouflage my reptilian features until the time comes toward the end of my speech to reveal my true appearance to Earth's people. We use a device that projects an electromagnetic field that tightly bends light around our bodies to make us appear like normal human beings wearing appropriate attire. I've preselected one stored in the memory of my device I like to use, but it doesn't actually change my molecular structure."

He touched the symbol on his belt buckle, and his body rippled with light while it took on the appearance of a taller, thin human male with oddly penetrating eyes, wearing a dark blue suit.

"Will this do, Mr. President?" he asked, gazing at the President.

"It will indeed," replied Martin, smiling, "at least until you reveal what you really look like as agreed toward the end of your disclosure to the people of Earth."

The pleased Trilotew Ambassador nodded.

"We've got to get moving," stated Daniel Samuelson looking down at his wristwatch. "We go live in the conference room in ten minutes.

"Lead the way, Daniel," replied President Martin McCoy, and they all began to head out of the Oval Office. Then the President stopped to relay to Ambassador Shon-ral, "I'm scheduled to speak to the nation and the world at large first. Then Ted will go on, followed by Trilotew Ambassador Grotzil. After that, things will really heat up. You and Moon-teran will address the people of Earth last as channels of the new Ray to prepare them to go through their own coming transformations."

"Understood," Shon-ral acknowledged serenely. "My cousin, Moon-teran, and I will deliver to all the people of Earth our entire experience of what we went through from the time we were both captured by the Trilotew to finally being liberated from their suppressive subconscious programming to rediscover our true highly evolved human natures. Then we will reveal our purpose for coming to Earth and the far greater awareness we both now share. But first, I believe it would be best if Moon-teran and I changed back to Mark and Janice because the people will initially be able to relate to us far better as recognizable fellow citizens."

Shon-ral and Moon-teran glanced at each other, and the transparent heat wave energy effect rippled down over their bodies to transform them back into Mark Santfield and Janice Carter before the astonished eyes of the entourage.

Mark smiled and nodded encouragement to the President, who smiled confidently and nodded in return before he turned and walked out of the Oval Office behind Daniel. Then Mark gallantly offered Janice his arm. She delightfully threw her arm through his, and they walked out of the Oval Office. The amazed Trilotew Ambassador, and the equally amazed Ted and Henry, followed close behind them.

# CHAPTER TWENTY-SEVEN

# THE EARTH WORLD TRANSFORMS

*P*resident Martin McCoy walked into the White House Press Room and up behind the podium, but there were no reporters this time. Mark, Janice, Ted, Daniel, and then Ambassador Grotzil, appearing as the tall lanky man wearing a dark blue suit, stopped together beside each other along the sidewall. President McCoy nodded that he was ready at the lead TV camera operator. The operator nodded back and then touched the headset on his left ear. He listened for a moment for timing instructions from the control booth. He held up three fingers on his right hand and silently mouthed, dropping a finger each time, "Three, two, one," and pointed at the President to let him know he was now on live television to the entire world.

"Good evening, my fellow Americans. Tonight, I am here to address you and all the citizens of planet Earth. This will be the most important speech that any President or any leader has ever given to the people of this world. A great uplifting transformation is coming to our planet, and it is finally time to reveal what the misguided leaders of many countries have purposefully kept from you for far too long. It may be difficult at first to hear this, but we came under the control of a misdirected small elite group of financially powerful men that orchestrated the creation of a second secret worldwide government after World War II. They did this with good initial intentions to create an inner government that could run the country if the elected officials were killed in a nuclear war with the former Soviet Union. After its creation, the power-mad ambitions of this group could operate completely outside of the law with the creation of the National Security Act, and they rapidly gained control of the military industrial complex.

"A short time later, they gained influential control over the true elected officials in our country, and the leaders of many other powerful nations after they secretly signed a treaty with a visiting cunning totalitarian extraterrestrial race called the Trilotew. This race offered to provide certain advanced alien technology and weaponry to the United States in exchange for being permitted to conduct supposedly harmless DNA experiments on a number of unsuspecting world citizens they claimed would not be harmed — but they lied. After the small group of power-hungry men started down the covert path of secrecy to acquire an elite controlling status over all humankind, the alien race began to take over their minds without their realizing it. They did this by using a far more advanced subconscious terrorizing control technology. Tonight, I formally announce their sinister designs upon our world have miraculously ended.

"I am also deeply sorry to report that six million citizens from our planet were secretly abducted by the Trilotew over the years, and quite a number of them have never been returned. We know the Trilotew returned some of them and killed many others, and now they will be returning those they kept alive to do their bidding. The very real alien threat to this world threatened the existence of every man, woman, and child on the planet. If something quite unexpected had not stopped their inroads to controlling our world, their continued influence would likely have resulted in the complete destruction of our planet. A great benevolent force no one expected or saw coming has now completely neutralized the evil intentions of the Trilotew, who were operating hidden behind the scenes on our planet.

"Here with me tonight to enlighten you are several very important guest speakers. Their significant part in this worldwide-televised event will become clear to you, while you listen to what they have to share. The first guest speaker will be Mr. Ted Carter. Many of you may know him as the wealthiest person on Earth. He is actually the Chairman of the secret worldwide government. He and his associates have just gone through their own liberating transformation, and he will relay what happened that will change the direction of the destructive destiny of our planet to one of amazing liberation.

"My second guest to speak will be the newly liberated and transformed Trilotew Ambassador Grotzil. He will relay how he and his Trilotew associates have also gone through an entirely unexpected change, brought about by a new liberating energy Ray that is beginning to manifest on Earth, even while

I'm speaking to you tonight. What was subconsciously driving the Trilotew race to behave in an evil covert manner for hundreds of thousands of years no longer exists. This new benevolent energy completely removed it. Rest assured, I know from personal experience that all Trilotew who were secretly operating behind the scenes have already left our planet, other than Ambassador Grotzil. He is temporarily remaining behind to relay his own experience about what is creating this great change.

"Then there are two other very important human beings with us tonight who wish to speak with you, but like Ambassador Grotzil they are not from Earth. You may know of Mark Santfield from his successful first conspiracy research book that revealed very prophetic revelations about a suspected hidden government and their involvement with a sinister extraterrestrial race. His second book just released two weeks ago has already skyrocketed far beyond the *New York Times'* bestseller list. In fact, worldwide sales are dramatically climbing through the roof, and you should know what is contained in this second book is one hundred percent accurate in every way. There is a reason for this. Mark Santfield and Chairman Ted Carter's adopted daughter, Janice Carter, are actually emissaries from a vast extraterrestrial organization called the Galactic Inter-dimensional Alliance of Free Worlds. This organization is comprised of over four hundred and fifty million human, humanoid, and other highly intelligent benevolent space faring races. They are coming here to help us make a great transition to becoming a planetary member of their organization. Mark is actually Galactic Alliance Ambassador Shon-ral, and Janice is actually Galactic Alliance Prime Social and Historical Trend Scientist Moon-teran. Their home planet, called Norexilam, is over five-hundred-light-years from Earth, beyond what we call the Pleiades star group. We finally have the answer to that great question of whether or not we are alone in the universe.

"They will directly share with every man, woman, and child on Earth what they went through starting with how they were trapped by the Trilotew, how they were finally freed from a torturous subconscious programming, how this reawakened their originally very evolved extraterrestrial human natures, and how the even greater expansion of their beings recently took place. Once they finish imparting their truth, each one of you will remember your own much more advanced human natures that were originally available on Earth before they were purposefully genetically suppressed a long time ago and then passed on generation after generation.

"Fellow citizens of planet Earth, you have all been deceived about a great many things by your governments for considerably more than sixty years. To sum things up, the military industrial complex was under the control of a secret worldwide organization that was being covertly controlled by the extraterrestrial Trilotew race, before this great change began. Now our planet and our lives are about to transform into something truly beyond wonderful. Prime Creator or the benevolent central source that sustains all life, recently gave a great gift to the Galactic Alliance. They are now openly engaged in sharing this with us. Our planet will become a space-faring member of the wondrous Galactic Alliance, and you will actually know the experience of what it is like to travel to the stars. The end of evil as an experiment, like the extinction of the ancient dinosaurs, is finally occurring on our world."

The President paused to let the profound last statement sink in to the television audience.

"I will now introduce my first guest speaker, Chairman Ted Carter of the secret world government. First, know that he and his associates have all just gone through a liberating change back to their natural benevolent natures."

He nodded, smiling at Ted who was standing with the other guest speakers along the sidewall, and then he stepped away from the podium. Ted smiled as the cameras focused on him, and he walked up behind the podium and took a relaxing breath.

Then he began solemnly, "My fellow citizens of planet Earth, I am the nominated Chairman of a Council of secretly classified men that have been collectively running the major governments of the world since shortly after World War II. However, your votes did not elect me to this position. My forebears started down that dark road of deceit and covert misdirection after World War II. They originally created their secret control at the beginning of the Cold War with the former Soviet Union to maintain a consistent level of government that would survive if a surprise nuclear attack destroyed the duly elected government officials. They truly felt they were doing the right thing.

"Then a wild card was thrown into the works. Many unidentified flying objects began to appear around the world after the first nuclear bomb tests, and soon direct secret contact with both benevolent and totalitarian extraterrestrials began to take place with certain world leaders. The highly evolved benevolent human Galactic Alliance representatives who first contacted them required that all Earth governments give up their nuclear weapons and deadly radioactive materials, before they would share any of their extraterrestrial technological wonders. The government leaders of our country turned them down because of an understandable fearful mistrust of this genuine benevolent offer. Then the Trilotew made contact, and they did not require nuclear weapons be given up even if a treaty were signed with them. However, the President of the United States back then refused the Trilotew offer because he knew instinctively it was insincere. The Trilotew Ambassador also knew the President wanted our country to remain technically dominant over any future adversary and cleverly compelled or blackmailed him into signing it.

"To elaborate, a great traumatic fear remained in our leaders after the destructive Second World War ended, and the President at the time and his generals reacted to the sincere Galactic Alliance offer in an understandably paranoid manner. However, several months later the totalitarian Trilotew emissaries with their own sinister designs upon our planet met with that President and another particular world leader to make them an offer they could not refuse. The Trilotew claimed they were willing to provide what the U.S. military industrial complex leaders wanted without requiring they first give up all destructive nuclear bombs and dangerous radioactive materials. The President refused their sinister offer at first. However, he soon stepped into a blackmail trap when the Trilotew Ambassador further stated that if the United States refused to sign a treaty with them, they would take their offer to the Soviet Union to make them the preeminent superpower on Earth. The Trilotew also compelled that past President and his generals with a subconscious implantation device to sign the treaty against their better judgment. What they did not know was another Trilotew representative was covertly in Moscow blackmailing the former leader of the Soviet Union with the same offer at the same time. They played one side against the other. This is precisely the same technique this same diabolical extraterrestrial group secretly used through their dominated extraterrestrial allies on Hitler and some of his scientists before World War II. Both benevolent and malevolent extraterrestrial races have been secretly coming to Earth at one time or another for countless ages. Yet, no extraterrestrial race has ever been allowed to dominate the entire planet by an off-world treaty stipulation for over 500,000 years.

"The Trilotew began to infiltrate and dominate the leaders of our secret government. I inherited my position from my father's position before me in what many people on Earth have labeled the Illuminati or what we call the Triumvirate World Council or just the TWC. According to Galactic Alliance scientific historians, the perversely subconscious-implanted Trilotew tyrants have been driving us in a direction that would unexpectedly end in the destruction of our entire planet.

"My fellow human beings, you will come to know for yourselves the former twisted nature of the Trilotew that orchestrated this direction, and all of our hidden secret TWC Council members, have just gone through a liberating transformation. The implanted negative drives in our subconscious minds are permanently gone, and I now have the great privilege of announcing to all of you that our hidden government no longer exists. All the worldwide members have unanimously committed their lives, and our collective monstrous fortunes, to liberate all of you in harmony with the coming uplifting transformation of our world. I have been informed that everyone, without exception, will soon have their own experience with this liberating Ray that comes from the source behind all life or whatever you may conceive that to be.

"Please hold back any anger and frustration for just a few moments longer, and each one of you will know what we now know to be true beyond any doubt whatsoever. There will be no more secrets between us. We will soon disclose everything that has previously remained hidden from you. Your recently freed, rightfully elected President Martin McCoy is now benevolently in charge, as he should be. He is now openly accepting the guidance, wisdom, and assistance of the entire Galactic Inter-dimensional Alliance of Free Worlds. Thank you for listening and for your considerate understanding."

Ted stepped away from the podium, and the President stepped back up behind it to announce, "Now it is my privilege to introduce to you Trilotew Ambassador Grotzil," and he stepped back away from the podium.

The Trilotew Ambassador walked past him and stepped up behind the podium. He appeared in his dark-blue suit to be similar to any member of the President's staff but with oddly penetrating eyes.

"Thank you, Mr. President, for your kind introduction. First, I wish to state that we Trilotew would deserve only the worst fate after what we have secretly done here on Earth. If this new Ray from Prime Creator, or the source behind all life, had not been sent here to intervene, we would have all gone up in flames."

"Fellow beings living on Earth, know that we of the Trilotew were your bitter enemies, and your fate under our control would have caused you unimaginable suffering. We were also set free from a terrible subconscious programming that we have been suffering under as a race for ages. The Galactic Alliance referred to by President McCoy recently received a new liberating power. This new Ray reverses all genetically limiting mechanisms, and removes all covert tyrannical drives implanted in races living on many world systems over the last half-million years by the Trilotew. When they brought this liberating force to Earth, we were the first Trilotew to be set free of such madness, and now the entire Trilotew race is about to become benevolent loving beings again as we once were in the far ancient past. I say to all of you, the Trilotew who were secretly operating on Earth have been set free from any desire to harm any of you or dominate your world, and they have left your planet. We are now also committed friends of the wondrous Galactic Alliance that is helping to liberate all of you, the people of Earth, so that you too can play among the stars.

"Please forgive us for the harm that we caused to the relatives of some of you that disappeared without a trace over the years. Although many of them were likely killed when we were not in control of our behavior, know their real selves still exist. It is true that many have lost their bodies. However, you will each soon discover they are still alive in their true spherical energy or Atma forms, what you refer to as Soul, and you will all see them again soon in a very special way. I know this to be true. I also have the greatest privilege to speak the truth to all of you at last. There will be no more secrets. Now the time has come to introduce all of you to my true bipedal reptilian body form. You may be shocked at first because I am not actually the human male you see before you. What you are seeing is a projected illusion. First, remember that I am now a benevolent eternal being, as each one of you will soon fully remember. Behold!"

Grotzil touched his belt buckle device twice, and the electromagnetic light projection of a tall, lanky human male dressed in a suit tightly hugging his body changed, revealing his reptilian nature.

Gasps of surprise came from the mouths of the camera operators, and President McCoy encouraged, "Don't be frightened by his appearance. Stay at your cameras. He is not harmful."

They obeyed and continued to gaze through the cameras at his vertical, red cat-like slits centered in horizontal, oval violet eyeballs, and then they surprisingly began to perceive they were emanating a gentle nature. The Ambassador's smooth green scaly skin actually appeared to be strangely elegant to them without their understanding why, even though they could also clearly see the two receding rows of sharp, fanged teeth lining the inside of his upper and lower jaws. His wide smile was unmistakably warm and friendly toward them, and the same was now true for all the people around the world seeing his true form for the first time. Ambassador Grotzil stepped aside and bowed with the palms of his hands placed crossed over his chest upon each shoulder. Then he rose back up, smiling warmly. He turned and walked away passing by President McCoy as he walked back up behind the podium.

"Fellow world citizens, please do not indulge in anger or fear, for your futures are very bright beyond even your finest dreams. Now I have the distinct privilege of introducing to you Mark Santfield, or Ambassador Shon-ral, and Janice Carter, or Prime Scientist Moon-teran, from the Galactic Inter-dimensional Alliance of Free Worlds."

The President nodded to them as he stepped away from the podium again. Then Mark and Janice stepped up behind the podium and stood side by side, smiling, then nodded their heads.

"First of all," Mark began cordially, "I want to thank all of you who purchased my second book. You will discover it is now operating as a channel of this new liberating Ray. I can also assure you, and those close to you who may not have read it, that you are all about to receive vastly more in liberating new awareness and freedom."

Janice stepped a little closer to the podium and added, "In a few moments you will all begin to experience the liberating Ray on a grand scale all over the planet. Then you will remember your true advanced benevolent natures as human beings. Long ago, you were genetically implanted with suppressive controls that have kept you from recalling the true heritage and very advanced human awareness that was once freely enjoyed."

"You should all now see us as we really are," Mark stated boldly, "now that we have been returned to our original human extraterrestrial natures that were also suppressed until recently. Your greatly unexpected destiny is to become enlightened members of the Galactic Inter-dimensional Alliance of Free Worlds and spiritually free, space-faring adventurers that can confidently state you are from the completely transformed planet Earth. Behold!"

They both stood to the side of the podium and looked away to envision the coming miraculous changes. The desert-like heat wave effect appeared, washing down over their bodies revealing the true radiant advanced human characteristics of Ambassador Shon-ral and Prime Scientist Moon-teran. Then a pulsing series of expanding circular golden energy waves began to radiate from their bodies out through the walls of the conference room.

Shon-ral's deeper melodious voice, carried upon the waves to every human being and every living thing on Earth, stated telepathically, *Experience now all we went through, starting with how the Trilotew captured us after we arrived to help the people of Earth not destroy yourselves. Then witness how we were set free from the Trilotew subconscious-brainwashing technology and observe how the full realization of our greatly expanded awareness as highly evolved human beings resurfaced. Know that all of you are about to experience this awakening for yourselves.*

From outside the White House, the concentric circles of golden energy waves expanded until they encompassed the surface of the entire planet in under a minute. People everywhere were suddenly experiencing a great uplifting feeling and clarity of awareness they had never known before. They quickly discovered that all fear, hate, bigotry, prejudice, jealously, greed, and vain religious superiority attitudes had simply dissolved away within their consciousness. People about to commit murder or shoot a weapon in conflicts taking place at different locations around the globe simply could not fathom what they were about to do. Murderers, child molesters, rapists, and thieves were free from all impulses to behave in any other way than benevolently toward all life. They all began to realize that evil as an experiment was being retired from creation because the time had finally come to replace it with something far more effective, true, necessary, and kind. This new awareness was beginning to inspire each individual to embrace the wonder of becoming a liberated co-worker with the source that supports all life, and thereafter with all beings living in the vast multi-dimensional universe.

Then twenty-feet-high luminous golden pyramids began appearing in the central parks of major cities and in ideally centrally located places in the countryside all over the Earth, until ten thousand had appeared. A short time later, childlike wonder began to dominate the entire attention of everyone around the planet. An irresistible force was drawing them to approach the pyramids in a peaceful, loving manner that absolutely amazed them.

Everyone heard Shon-ral's loving, vibrant telepathic voice encourage, *Now be at peace on this world, and enjoy together this mighty gift from Prime Creator, or the source behind all life.*

The pyramids began to simultaneously radiate a brighter light. Then the mysterious fountains with the majestic angelic being standing up inside the white stone bowls began to become visible through the pyramid walls turning transparent. The fountains then moved out of the pyramids and lowered to the ground to permanently connect to the Earth.

There stood the youthful, strongly built, bare-chested and completely bald majestic angelic statue of a man, perhaps in his mid-thirties, with light-bronzed skin. Two golden bracelets encircled each of his upper arms, and a white cotton-like skirt extended from the waist down to just above his bare feet standing upon the raised square stone platform centered in the bowl. The golden-white vibrant liquid light pouring out of his open palms held facing outward in front of his hips was streaming down to keep the wide white stone bowl filled. A round white stone column supported the wide bowl full of the luminous liquid that was flowing over the entire circumference of the outer rim, like a shimmering, smooth curtain of nectar, to mysteriously vanish in the ground. Twelve ornate golden cups hung from golden hooks appeared around the circumference of the bowl's outer rim. A flat, circular, two-feet-wide white stone seat two feet above the ground encircled the luminous liquid fountain one foot away, supported by a dozen intricately carved white stone legs.

The loving vibrant voice of Moon-teran clearly stated, *You will all know how to properly drink from these wondrous fountains to be completely set free from the subconscious nightmares that have driven your lives for countless generations. The a ltered g enomes o n y our t wo-stranded D NA helix that have limited your full potentials as human beings from surfacing on Earth are being corrected, and soon the more advanced four-stranded DNA helix will return to your conscious experience. In time, the DNA will become an eight-stranded helix, and then your creative horizons will open up beyond your most sacred dreams. Know that Shon-ral and I, and all the vast number of your fellow beings in the Galactic Alliance, wish you all only the most uplifting, enlightening goodwill.*

Shon-ral's benevolent soothing voice added serenely, *Something amazing, something wonderful is also coming to planet Earth. Thousands of Galactic Alliance star ships filled with scientists, scholars, medical personnel with cures for all disease, biologists, botanists, builders, engineers, and teachers of every advanced benevolent discipline will be landing all over the planet to assist you all in attaining your true potential. Useful benevolent products transformed from the dangerous forms of energy you now use will take their place, and teleportation units will replace your automobiles. Antigravity propulsion systems in spacecraft capable of traversing the vast distances of outer space and into many parallel dimensions will replace your polluting aircraft. These ships are also capable of freely traveling under the oceans.*

*You will become a welcomed planetary culture that can then freely explore the wonders of other worlds. You will meet the people of many advanced cultures you have not dreamed existed through prearranged exchange programs. Your children will grow up in a world of wonder free from fear after their natural creative talents are encouraged to blossom to their full potential. It is our privilege to assist all of you to go through the coming great world transformation that has in our view taken far too long to come to Earth. For now, I will just say farewell.*

Back in the White House in Washington, D.C., the combined vision of Ambassador Shon-ral and Prime Scientist Moon-teran of the planetary changes underway and yet to manifest, returned to focus in the Oval Office. Childlike expressions of amazement were now on the faces of Ambassador Grotzil, Chairman Ted Carter, President Martin McCoy, Secretary of Defense Daniel Samuelson, and the three camera operators that were experiencing wondrous changes in their own awareness.

Shon-ral and Moon-teran stepped back behind President McCoy as he stepped in front of the podium to encourage, "I don't know how many of you are actually still at a television set that have not already headed out the door on your way to visit one of the fountains. All of us in the White House somehow saw the same vision of what is starting to take place all over the Earth. We are all in this together. It is clear that our current forms of government will be retired, and money will no longer be necessary. Fellow citizens of planet Earth, we are no longer alone. Good night and may God bless the United States of America, and every other country and people, as well as all animal and plant life on our soon to be purified world. We will remember this day as the day we were reborn into a higher life of wonder. God bless you all, and good night."

The President nodded to the lead camera operator, a moment passed, and he indicated to the President they were no longer on the air. Ambassador Grotzil was now radiant with kindness, gazing with true friendship at everyone in the conference room.

"I am honored to have been a part of this change beginning to take place on Earth, and I will now return to the last of our ships waiting in orbit. I am very anxious to be among those of us who will witness what the mighty Ray coming from the pyramids will do to our fellow Trilotew living on all our empire worlds, to our military forces, and then to the Emperor. Know that I will witness the last days of our worlds ruled by an Emperor. We too look forward to becoming part of the entire Galactic Inter-dimensional Alliance of Free Worlds. Farewell, my new friends."

He bowed again with his arms crossed over his chest and his palms placed upon his shoulders. Then he stood back up, smiling from ear to ear, touched his belt buckle three times, and dematerialized a moment later in a bright golden-white teleportation beam.

President McCoy gazed fondly at Shon-ral and Moon-teran and then stated happily with newfound confidence, "We certainly have a lot to do now that really counts. "Ted, my friend," he said, quite refreshed, "I believe we should coordinate our efforts together to combine funds from all over the world to help heal this stricken planet, even though in the near future it will not be necessary. If those Galactic Alliance ships show up soon, we may not need money any more. In the meantime, we should see what the two of us and all the disbanded secret-government TWC Council members could do to clean up this planet. What do you say?"

"You're on, Mr. President," answered Ted Carter with a joyful shake of his head. "I will contact all of them and have them come to the White House. Will that do?"

"You bet your ass it will," replied Martin happily, relieved and uplifted.

*All is well, gentlemen,* Shon-ral interjected telepathically with a wide smile, and they looked back at him surprised.

*That is an understatement if ever there was one,* replied Ted Carter with his own wide smile.

*That's the truth of all truths,* Martin added happily.

The three astonished camera operators gazed in wonder at them and then stated aloud almost simultaneously, "We heard you ...in our heads!"

*You fine cameramen are already starting to remember who you really are,* confirmed Moon-teran with a wry grin, *and this is only the very beginning.* She gazed longingly at Shon-ral and asked, *Well, Cousin, are you ready to return home to rejoin our families before we get into hot water with them?*

*Well, Cousin, when you're right you're right,* replied Shon-ral, and he laughed.

*Thanks for all the hospitality. We will have to do this again sometime,* he said, looking at President Martin McCoy and Ted.

*Right, we'll do lunch,* shot back Moon-teran catching his reference to an old Hollywood cliché.

They all cracked up laughing, and after the levity died down, Shon-ral calmly stated, using his voice, "We will return when the massive fleet arrives, which is scheduled to take place in the near future. Things are going to get very interesting on this planet during the next few months, and we want to bring our families here to stay for a while. Our children would receive quite an education observing the complete overhaul and uplifting transformation of an entire world and its people. They will want to help. Cousin, what do you think?"

"Well, Cousin," she shot back jovially, "when you're right you're right."

They glanced playfully at each other, nodded a simple farewell, and looked away to visualize their families back on Norexilam. Then ...they simply vanished.

"Wow!" mused President Martin McCoy. "They really do get around, don't they?"

# CHAPTER TWENTY-SEVEN

"They sure as hell do," Ted replied wholeheartedly.

"What do ya say we get some lunch?" inquired Martin, smiling with raised eyebrows.

"I thought you would never ask, and I'm starving," answered Ted, rubbing his empty stomach.

Martin smiled at Daniel and requested, "Daniel, my friend, would you care to join us?"

Daniel smiled enthusiastically, and they walked together out of the television conference room with a newly transformed profound zest for life.

# CHAPTER TWENTY-EIGHT

# DAWN
# OF
# A NEW BEGINNING

There is no going back when what is behind has forever changed to a sublime new truth, and the world turns an entirely unexpected page to reveal a wonderland for all. The people of Earth will be left with only one query to ponder as the planet is changed in tremendous ways right before their amazed eyes, and under their feet. All over the world people will be asking each other in astounding joy, "How could this be happening?"

They will come to know they were not actually free to imagine a better world, for their imaginations were fixated on oblivion. Many people will understand they had been fervently praying for the end of the world to cease their lives of meaningless toil and fear. This was not because they had an inkling of a chance to turn around the destructive direction the planet was going. They will become aware they were not really in control of their lives because true freewill had successfully eluded them. The wonder of their newly liberated awareness will be gratitude enough because they will not be able to explain how this new Ray works.

Something beyond what they will know was not earned will liberate them, and they will begin to remember their true God-like characteristics as benevolent human beings. As startling as the new revelation will be, when they use their imaginations in the years to come, they will only create visions that will benefit all life. They will begin to see that everything—including people, animals, plants, and stones—have a presence of Atma, or Soul, an evolving nature they could never see before, not even within themselves.

A new appreciation of their pets will begin to surface, as people recall the far deeper understanding they are also committed, loving, and evolving, eternal, spherical energy beings that temporarily reside in various animal physical forms. People all over the planet will find that their former desires to kill and slaughter animals without regard to their feelings swiftly fade away. At the same time they will discover an innate ability, which will enable them to consume vibrant food for pleasure or take in any necessary nourishment, vitality, and longevity by simply breathing the air or drinking the subtle form of energy derived directly from the liberating Ray. They will know this awareness is being radiated throughout the Earth's atmosphere coming from the fountains within two giant golden pyramids sitting on the bottom of two of Earth's deepest oceans, and from a third one located deep within the Himalayan mountains. Then, one day, it will just happen.

Everyone will begin to hear each other speak inside their own beings without the need to use their vocal chords, and they will know certain genomes on their DNA double helix have been reactivated. Then the human population on Earth, including those who are suffering from various diseases, will start to recover. Soon after, they will experience their two-stranded-DNA as it transforms into the advanced four-stranded-DNA human beings enjoy on other worlds.

The massive, mile-long, cylindrical Galactic Alliance spaceships will then arrive, radiating a pale-blue light around their silver-blue hulls, while they hover in the skies all over the planet. However, no one will be afraid because fear of evil will be retired from everything living on the planet above or below the surface. More than seven billion people will be quietly beaming joy to their fellow beings aboard those magnificent spaceships, as they hover down and land in nature preserves, in fields, and in the countryside near every major city on Earth. More ships will arrive with highly trained specialists aboard, and thousands of Scout class ships will emerge from their massive parent carriers. Their Galactic Alliance pilots will maneuver them in an acrobatic dance in the skies for the delight of the watchers below, before they start landing them near every government capital center all over the planet.

The advanced human beings aboard comprised of different skin colors, shapes, and other striking characteristics will be breath-taking to their Earth brothers and sisters as they emerge from the ships to joyfully greet their equally jubilant new Earth friends. Almost at once, special molecular engineers will begin to take surveys of all the major congested cities where people had been unnaturally stacked on top of each other in small creativity-stifling spaces to which they return each day after trying to eke out a living. These technician will be using hand-held devices that look like inch-thick, foot-long transparen rods with a small deep-green sphere at the end. They are programmed to analyze and record the entire internal structures of the massive city skyscraper and surrounding facilities before they are transformed.

Teleportation chambers will be set up all over the planet. Dozens wil appear in the big cities in vacant lots, public parks, and in every small town The serene people of Earth will be telepathically encouraged to go to th teleportation chambers to beam away in groups of a dozen and reappear in vas unpopulated fields, forests, and plains that are still numerous all over the planet After that, their new Galactic Alliance friends will escort them to their waitin; natural land areas, and help them use their creative imaginations to manifes their own unique domed and rectangular energy-self-sufficient homes abou every twenty acres. The energy generators in these homes derive their powe from the electromagnetic field surrounding the planet that interconnects witl worlds throughout the universe. These gifts from the Galactic Alliance have no moving parts, and nothing in them can wear out or pollute the environmen in any way.

At least six and a half billion people will soon witness, in the sanctity o their own inner vision, the seven other prepared Earth-like planets that awai them in close parallel dimensions of the physical universe. Galactic Alliance specialists will ask which of them would like to volunteer to leave Earth to have wondrous adventuresome lives on other worlds as new colonists. Oddl; enough, six and a half-billion people or more, depending on the population a the time, will volunteer, and implementation of the massive relocation aspec of *The Seres Agenda* will begin.

*** 

Far away on another world, Shon-ral and Moon-teran appeared, standing side by side in Shon-ral's garden outside his three-domed complex on plane Norexilam. They fondly gazed at each other, hugged, and then acknowledged their understanding of each other's silent communication. Moon-teran stepped back and looked away to visualize her husband and three children. Then she vanished. Shon-ral smiled and turned to greet his loving wife Lorun-eral and their two children as they appeared walking out of the dome's entrance to welcome him back. His wife jumped into his open arms, and the two happy children watched as he joyously spun her around while they kissed passionately Then he sat her down, and the children surrounded their parents who began to hug and kiss them with an awakened depth of knowing their true natures as benevolent beings.

"Well … I'm back, and the Earth planet is finally being transformed. Dearest Lorun-eral, it is breath-taking to observe first-hand. I wish you and our children could be there to assist with this great change."

"We want to go, Father!" shouted their excited children.

"We have already talked it over, and the children and I agree," stated Lorun-eral, smiling up at Shon-ral. We want to travel back to Earth with you for an extended stay to experience the rare, monumental changes taking place there and to observe the moment when our brothers and sisters on the planet Earth are formally accepted into the Galactic Alliance."

Shon-ral was beyond pleased, and he kissed his wife with tender gratitude for her evolved insight.

"Dear children, I sensed you were ready to make the journey. Run along now and play in the pool. Your mother and I will join you in a few moments."

The young boy and girl ran back inside the dome, laughing and giggling while their parents listened to the patter of little feet running until one splash followed another as they jumped into their magnificent indoor swimming pool.

"Before we travel back to Earth," Shon-ral continued passionately, "you and I have some catching up to do. I want us to stay home for perhaps six months before we depart. I have said this before, but there really is no place like home. However, I am beginning to see we can have a second home on Earth. There the children can spend time helping out and appreciate what the Earth parents and children are going through. Beloved wife, they will have invaluable experiences that will help them reach their full potential while growing up that they could not realize in any other way. Now we should head back inside and join them. Tonight, after the children are asleep, I want us to spend quality time alone together."

They kissed again and walked hand in hand inside the living room by the swimming pool under their spacious dome.

Moon-teran simply appeared on another continent a third of the way around the planet's equator standing before her husband Donum-tuma and their three children who were eagerly expecting her return. He grabbed her into his arms, and they kissed long and tenderly, while their three children excitedly surrounded them. They soon parted to hug and kiss the children, and then their young ones walked together with them back inside the domed home.

"I'm so happy to be back home with you again," Moon-teran stated joyfully, as a single tear ran down her left cheek.

"And I have also dearly missed you, but at least this time you were not gone for long," replied her grateful admiring husband.

"Dearest husband, the Earth planet is being transformed. The golden pyramids have appeared all over the planet's surface, and the true enlightened nature of the people is awakening from a deep, unconscious, terrorizing slumber. It's just amazing what's happening there so quickly that has never occurred on any world in the entire history of the Galactic Alliance."

"Yes, I know, sweet wife. While you were away we also experienced this in our inner vision," confirmed Donum-tuma.

"My cousin and his wife are going to take their children back there," continued Moon-teran. "They wish to provide them with the great opportunity of spending part of their young lives growing up on a world of constant uplifting benevolent change. Donum-tuma, it would be good if we also had a second home there amongst those who were once from our own planetary system, before those malevolent beings forced them to reincarnate there unaware so long ago. We could help them build a bridge between worlds, and some of them could spend some liberating time back here."

"I've already talked it over with the children, and they are eager to go," he confirmed happily.

"Oh, that's wonderful," she replied and sighed. "Then all is well. As one of the Prime Scientists, I will have the unique opportunity to scientifically study and document the extraordinary rare historical changes that are taking place on Earth and in the Galactic Alliance. I would not want to miss the reward of the new awareness this will bring to the entire Galactic Alliance. You know I love you, dear husband, even beyond time and space."

"And I'm still entranced by the expanding love I always discover is still manifesting between us, dear wife. Yes, all is well. We can venture back to Earth as a family perhaps six months from now. Will that do?"

"Yes, it will do," she replied delightfully, relieved it had been so effortlessly settled.

Moon-teran and Donum-tuma blissfully walked back inside their large domed home to join their children; their arms wrapped around each other's waists, and her head rested on his shoulder.

Six months went by before the two cousins and their families were together again. They were standing in front of one of the mysterious fountains with that youthfully strong male statue pouring the luminous liquid light from his palms down into the white stone bowl at his feet. It was located on Norexilam at a point equidistant between their two domed home complexes. They were wearing their customary clothes, but they did not bring other belongings with them because they knew nothing would be required upon their return to Earth. Everything they might wish to have could be easily manifested, including artistically well-designed and entirely energy-self-sufficient second homes.

"Well, Cousin Moon-teran," Shon-ral began respectfully, "is your family ready to venture to the planet Earth?"

Excited cheers from all five children went off like an Earth rocket, and they began jumping up and down.

"Well, Cousin Shon-ral," Moon-teran replied respectfully, "we are here and we're more than ready."

Shon-ral smiled at his lovely wife Lorun-eral, who was patiently standing by his side smiling back at him, then at Donum-tuma and Moon-teran, and at all five excited children.

"Then, everyone, hold someone's hand," continued Shon-ral, "while Moon-teran and I visualize the cottage home of our friends Boun-tama and Lean-tala in the mountains in a place they call Northern California in the United States. They are expecting us, and we must not keep them waiting. Here goes." Then they both looked away in an imaginative gaze across time and space, and they all simply vanished.

They reappeared holding hands standing in the round grass field beside their jubilant friends Boun-tama and Lean-tala. Their cottage home was in the immediate background behind them.

After hugs and greetings were finished, and the kids were off playing together in the tall grass that surrounded the now unshielded and clearly visible Galactic Scout hangar, Shon-ral remarked merrily to Boun-tama and Lean-tala, "Dear friends, it's so good to see you two again."

"Maybe now you two can finally have that good cup of tea and fine meal we promised you some time back that always managed to somehow get interrupted," replied Lean-tala with zestful sparkling eyes.

Moon-teran took a peaceful breath and sighed, then stated calmly, "Sounds wonderful. We were both looking forward to spending some tranquil moments with you two this time around."

"You have really beautiful country around here," said Donum-tuma with a wide sweep of his arm at the beautiful surrounding forests. "Have you really found twenty-acre parcels for us to establish our second homes?"

"We did indeed," replied Boun-tama, smiling. "We were given several thousand acres to allocate to individual families by the United States President in full agreement with the Galactic Alliance Council, while the nearest cities are being dissolved and transformed."

Lean-tala added, bubbly with joy, "Your children are certainly going to have a good time playing in this nature wonderland. So much has changed so quickly. Boun-tama and I have missed company from our home world systems, and we are very glad your two families have arrived to join us on this transforming planet."

"If you like," encouraged Boun-tama, "Lean-tala and I can take your families aboard our Scout ship. We could give you a real first-class tour of the wonderful changes that the new Ray is emanating to the planet, and from the transforming changes the Galactic Alliance technicians and engineers are making to repair the polluted worldwide environment."

Shon-ral and Moon-teran looked at each other, and their spouses gazed at them, and then they all happily replied in telepathic unison, *That's why we came here.*

Later that afternoon the cousins, their spouses, and their combined five children were aboard Boun-tama's and Lean-tala's sleek Scout ship. It had been just six months since Shon-ral and Moon-teran had left Earth to reunite with their families. The projected view screen above the control console was revealing a true wonderland on the planet's surface. The relocation of six and a half billion people from Earth to seven other amazing Earth-like worlds in parallel dimensions was now complete. Special Galactic Alliance engineers were transforming the senseless massively congested and polluted cities back into the virgin forested lands and natural unspoiled ecology of the planet that existed before so-called "civilized" man built them.

Several hundred ten-mile-long Galactic Alliance Emerald Star Cruisers were sending thick green matter-reforming beams down over the cities to rearrange the molecules back into pure energy. The radiant light then took the form of giant transparent, white-light domed energy that rematerialized back in place the natural environment that was still stored in the planet's memory. This was true, for the Earth planet is also an Atma or living spherical energy being, who waited oh so patiently for this event to finally arrive.

The planted food-producing acres all over the planet remained in place. However, the farmers that stayed on Earth experienced the astonishing transformation of their barns and homes into individual uniquely designed spacious domed homes with indoor swimming pools. They were equipped with special food processors that could materialize whatever healthy food may be required to supplement their produce. They could also share food supplies with others if an unexpected catastrophe occurred that temporarily interrupted the shared food distribution. Each home produced pure water from the air even in the deserts and stored all they required for future use.

With the help of Galactic Alliance Botanists and food-producing Engineers, the newly enlightened farmers had transformed their farms into growing wonderlands of healthy nutrient-rich vegetables, fruits, and hydroponics facilities. They were now capable of growing food all year round, including many new varieties with much higher nutritive properties the advanced human specialists brought as a gift to the people of Earth.

The two special extraterrestrial families visiting Earth aboard Boun-tama's and Lean-tala's Scout ship perceived and observed all these changes as they continued their tour around the surface of the planet. They were witnessing changes to Earth that were exponentially increasing at a wondrous phenomenal rate. It was a thing to behold watching the Masterful advanced assistance of over ten million Galactic Alliance specialists diligently applying themselves individually and collectively to their chosen tasks.

First, they neutralized all radioactive materials and transformed them into non-harmful sources of free energy. Then they molecularly transformed all nuclear reactor buildings, nuclear bomb casings, and nuclear storage facilities into teleportation stations and spacecraft. Recombined molecules also produced advanced extraterrestrial building materials with amazing properties Earth scientists never dreamed existed. They transformed the molecules that comprised power lines and sewer systems into natural soils that stimulated accelerated plant growth. Matter recombining tanks underneath each new home transformed all human and animal waste into odorless pollution-free fertilizers. Every public art, science, and cultural facility created thereafter was for the mutual enjoyment and advancement of all the people of Earth. Galactic Alliance scientists also transformed many now-antiquated structures on the planet into useful household necessities such as toilet paper and paper towels that looked and worked even better than any former tree-based products. Once used, they were recycled into other non-polluting and non-toxic products by the household matter-transforming units.

All forms of money and taxation, as well as police and military forces, were retired for good. The people who occupied these professions naturally awakened to be happily creative contributors in ways that had been sleeping in their former suppressed selves. This was true for all the people, including those who were out of work before the marvelous change to Earth began.

The people of Earth no longer cared for such things as money accumulation, and tyrants were no longer tyrants. All the people on Earth had freely availabl all the necessities of living life abundantly, and none had to work for a livin for the right to be born on the planet. Instead, they naturally loved to toil a those necessary occupations that were already naturally dear to the true dream of their creative liberated potentials. They were also now able to use a hundre percent of their brain, discovered their photographic memory and telepathi capabilities, and their IQs rose through the roof.

Many of the five hundred million people left on the Earth were soor scheduled to go on exchange field trips with their families to other worlds and many citizens in the vast Galactic Alliance had already enthusiasticall volunteered to come to Earth just to be part of the great world change tha was taking place all over the planet. Such transformations to entire planets an their people were beyond rare. No planet had ever gone through such a swif liberating transformation after being on the brink of annihilation in the entir Galactic Alliance history dating back over five hundred thousand years.

In order to bring the overpopulated planet down to a healthy five hundre million inhabitants, a massive number of other people living on the plane volunteered and were relocated to seven prepared Earth-like worlds located ir close accessible parallel dimensions. In this way, the Galactic Alliance Scientist returned the planet's overburdened resources to a sustainable maximum health supportable ecosystem. Everyone was already gaining tremendous new insight into creation by participating in the phenomenal event.

The people of Earth had a hidden destiny to be set free from their own subconsciously driven negative imaginations, even though they had no ide this monumental liberating change was actually coming. They were all nov naturally well beyond grateful.

# CHAPTER TWENTY-NINE

# OUR
# EVER EXPANDING
# HORIZON

𝒩ow the most important story ever foretold about the wondrous new Ray that few people living on Earth today know exists is accomplished. As human beings we have only one great talent we can apply to create beneficial change here and now on Earth that we take with us after we depart this lifetime. That wonderful gift is childlike loving imagination. This eternal nature in us neutralizes destructive childish greed that selfishly gains a temporary power over others at the expense and goodwill of every living thing in creation. When it comes right down to it, the only benevolent freewill choice we really have is to choose to constructively focus the intent of our creations for the greatest constructive outcome to all life on Earth and in the multi-dimensional universe, not just for human beings but also for animals, plant life, and our environment.

What is coming to Earth that has finally been unexpectedly green-lit is not reversible by anyone or any power. This dynamically unique new revelation provided now for our great benefit discloses the hidden off-world origins of all human beings, and our planet's recently changed future destiny. As per the agreement I have with Seres Ambassador Torellian, the purposefully hidden truth revealed in the announcement of *The Seres Agenda*, the coming return of the mighty Seres race, as well as highly evolved enlightened beings from other worlds, is accomplished. We can now choose to align our imaginations with this new liberating gift Ray beginning to manifest to permanently retire evil as an experiment from creation, or we can temporarily fall prey in the meantime to negatively manipulated news on television, radio, in newspapers, and other media. For the most part, their misguided endeavors channel a negative imaginative stream designed to trap our celestial gift of imagination like a slave in the subconscious mind. This just binds our normally unlimited constructive imaginations to the very limited destructive misuse of vision toward the world's terrorizing end.

What is already here, that will only briefly remain a mystery to most of humanity living on our planet, will continue to make its presence known in ever more obvious ways. This astounding new Ray very recently brought into creation will provide every man, woman, and child with the personal liberating experience of their currently suppressed but highly evolved true selves. One day soon, all the people of Earth will know without doubt that vast numbers of human, humanoid, and highly evolved benevolent beings actually thrive in the multi-dimensional universe beyond planet Earth.

Even those people who temporarily refuse to correctly use the great secret of imagination that can lead to liberation from oppression, suppression, fear, hate, and evil as an experiment will soon experience this liberation for the benefit of all life. This new Ray is about to awaken in everyone the expanding awareness of our true benevolent human natures purposefully suppressed for far too long. Our world's negative destructive destiny is beginning to change forever because a new omnipresent force or liberating Ray from the source behind all life has finally come into existence to save us from ourselves. This new dispensation of grace is emanating into the lower dimensions to reach all the way down to good old planet Earth, and our future is wondrous beyond our wildest imaginations.

Fellow human beings, we now have the safe opportunity for once to choose wisely to use our imaginations together with this new liberating Ray. The special vibratory word "HU" that Shon-ral and Moon-teran experienced while visiting the source behind all life can now connect us to this same source, so that we can safely explore purposefully hidden truths in wondrous new ways that were not available just a little over three and a half Earth years ago. You will experience for yourself how this uplifting transforming gift is actually emanating to us from the highest dimensions of creation far beyond the lower dimensions and physical worlds of time and space. You will awaken to this new Ray as you utilize the "HU" to connect with it. Look for and be ready to behold the coming liberating worldwide change. Gaze into the skies with your heart to behold that which you have never seen before but suspected might just come true someday. Expect the unexpected, for it most certainly is coming to our world. This is certain. Let us look into the truth of what our hearts are really beginning to tell us now. We must discover for ourselves, through our own direct awakening knowing experiences, that we now have the privilege to explore and experience the grand multi-dimensional universe. After all, as human beings, we are all in this together on our beautiful blue-green, water-covered jewel of a world.

The revealing of this great part of *The Seres Agenda* for the first time is gratefully serving to spearhead our coming, entirely new, unexpected destiny—our new future. Although this book now ends, the special Ray flowing like an expanding celestial river of vibrant luminous Light and Sound through its pages remains open. Whether one knows it now or not, our future is very bright indeed.

From this moment onward, the reader will uncover more hidden truth deep within that is waiting to surface while the far…far greater adventure continues to unfold on planet Earth.

THIS ENDING

…is only the BEGINNING…

# THE SERES AGENDA
## Special Techniques to Safely
## Explore and Awaken Deliberately Hidden Truth

## By R. Scott Lemriel

# PRELIMINARY TECHNIQUES SECTION

Welcome to *The Seres Agenda*, 5th edition, containing the experientia techniques to practice in conjunction with reading the Prologue and eacl subsequent chapter. If you have not done so, it would be best if you first ge on the personal journey of reading *The Seres Agenda* book before pursuing the following special techniques. This is important because each chapter stimulate the awakening of certain dormant or suppressed higher faculties of direc knowing perception. I encourage you to be courageous, have faith in yoursel and the source behind all life, and go on this journey to safely discover the validity of this statement for yourself.

You are beginning a majestic journey; a co-creative endeavor that sets uț the conditions necessary to begin the process of having direct knowing abou the vast nature of the multi-dimensional universe. During your upcoming explorations, you will cross paths with highly spiritual space-faring beings anc the many Master teachers that counsel them. You will also discover an ever greater knowing of the expansive harmonious love operating between you anc them.

Before starting, I suggest you first accomplish a few basic preparatior exercise techniques. This way, you can experience for yourself turning on the pineal gland in the center of your brain. This gland is the direct safe link, a protected doorway, to higher perception. Then you — the individual being soul, or what many spiritually evolved extraterrestrials call the Atma (pure non-physical being) can explore the vast cosmic multi-dimensional universe by co-creating your own direct experiences with the assistance of very advancec beings or Master Teachers.

A) First, sit comfortably in a chair or lie down comfortably upon your back.

B) Begin to imagine someone or something that you love, and that you are grateful for having them in your life.

C) Next, take several deep, relaxing breaths. Imagine placing all your cares, concerns, fears, health conditions, worries, or trepidations about your life on a shelf. Just leave them all on the shelf for now. You can pick them up later if you wish after each exercise has run its natural course.

D) Take a deep breath and then on your outgoing breath send out the special vibratory word known as HU (pronounced like the name Hugh). Use a comfortable steady tone until your exhale is completed. Pause briefly in silence inside the sanctuary of your imagination to just look and listen for any sounds, lights, benevolent beings, or enlightening visions you may experience. Then send out the HU four more times, taking a relaxing breath between each one.

E) Pause briefly to reflect on any experience you may be having, and then aloud or telepathically with your imagination, send out the following statement:

**"Safely show me purposefully hidden truths on a grand cosmic multi-dimensional scale, and a much greater knowing of the expansive love within it."**

## SPECIAL NOTE #1

As you do this, understand that practicing the HU will connect you, the being, with the living omnipresent, benevolent loving force that underlies and supports all life and all that exists. This force is far beyond anything good or bad, positive or negative beings and controlling negative technologies. It is important that you have direct awakening knowing that the HU can ONLY connect you to uplifting, benevolent, beneficial experiences. It is important that you often send out this request during the practice of each of the special exercises revealed in this technique section of the book.

Negative beings, technologies, weapons on Earth or off world among extraterrestrial races, or negative beings from other dimensions cannot influence, manipulate, affect, or control the HU—or you—while you are utilizing it. You are safe and protected while practicing this special vibratory word.

This word and what it does today originates in a higher dimension far abov the physical universe. The HU did not originate among the extraterrestria races. However, they utilize it to keep from ever acquiring a subconsciou mind. In a relatively short time, anyone practicing the HU today will come t understand this with a certainty of knowing by direct experience.

## SPECIAL NOTE #2

After you have set in motion the preliminary practice above, follow th instructions provided for each chapter you wish to explore in order to begi safely experiencing the hidden truths revealed within its pages.

## SPECIAL NOTE #3

As a suggestion for your benefit, it is most effective to be consistent with chosen special technique by practicing it at the same time every day. You ma choose to do this in the daytime, or preferably at night before you go to slee This will set up a bridge of memory between where you go when you, th being, are out of your sleeping physical body each night exploring the multi dimensional universe. Everyone leaves the physical body at night, after leavin it operating on automatic in the trance state called sleep. However, many peopl have no recollection of where they travel to or what they do while they ar out-of-body exploring. Using the HU consistently will open inner spiritua sight through the pineal gland, and then each being can consciously explore th purpose for life and their much greater grand destiny.

## SPECIAL NOTE #4

Understand that the highly advanced benevolent extraterrestrials an Master Teachers utilize the HU themselves to keep from ever acquiring subconscious mind. The HU is the original vibratory word of what we o Earth call The Supreme Being, or what many extraterrestrial races call Prim Creator. When the HU crosses your path, the results are only beneficial. Also understand that control over you can only occur through what we are no aware of in our subconscious. However, do not blame the misdirected hidde leaders on Earth or tyrant extraterrestrials for this diabolical dilemma. Do no remain stuck in anger and revenge, for they too were implanted and are no longer in control of what they are doing on Earth. You will come to clearly understand this.

# SPECIAL NOTE #5

Tell yourself before falling asleep that you will remember to only open one eye upon awakening in the morning. The purpose of this is to establish a conscious connection to your higher memory and awareness, keeping it open long enough for you to recall or record your out-of-body experiences into the physical consciousness. With a little persistent practice, you will accomplish this with wondrous results.

# PROLOGUE
## (Exercise #1)

1) If you have not already done so, first practice basic preparations A through E given above.

2) Next, read *The Seres Agenda* from the top of page 7 to the end of page 9, before going on to the special exercise for the PROLOGUE given here.

3) Now, close your eyes. Imagine a special white-golden light coming up from the ground and down from a clear blue sky. See it gently penetrate all life on planet Earth, including you. Watch it begin to transform people all over the world into radiant, serene beings—previously suppressed in them—as they recover the love, appreciation, and gratitude for all life and all that exists.

4) Continue to observe as the subconsciously implanted programs that terrorize and suppress higher perceptive faculties of all human beings, including yours, rise up above your heads to vanish in the white-golden light. Continue to watch as all people, including you, begin to be wondrously uplifted. You all start to smile while your true highly evolved benevolent nature begins to re-surface with a certain knowing recall.

5) Now, send out the HU to all of the people on Earth. Then watch the world transform before your inner vision into a harmonious pristine paradise— what it was originally designed to become. Then send out the HU on each

outgoing breath for 10 to 15 minutes more, or longer if you are having an ongoing experience. Pause briefly between each HU to just look and listen to what may be happening. You will notice the phenomenon of the HU coming to a natural stop by itself. Open your eyes and take several deep-relaxing breaths.

6) Send out gratitude to the omnipresent HU, for it is beginning to guide you into the personal experience of the new consciousness-liberating energy Ray blended with it. Then just go about your day, if you practice this PROLOGUE exercise during the day. If practiced at night before bed, remember to tell yourself that upon awakening in the morning you will experience ever-increasing, crystal-clear memories of where you journeyed and what you did, while you were operating outside of your sleeping physical body exploring the multi-dimensional creation.

## CHAPTER ONE
### Taken Beyond Earth (Exercise #2)

1) As with every special technique for each chapter, begin to explore the meaning of the title of this chapter by first practicing basic preparations A through E.

2) Please read page 13, starting 1/4 of the way up from the bottom of the page with, ...Mark let his eyes caress... and continue reading to the bottom of page 21.

3) Now, send out the HU once more. Begin to imagine that you are leaving your physical body in peaceful serenity, knowing the HU is protecting you throughout the entire exploratory experience into hidden truth. While operating outside the body, if you are able to view the true self, you will discover that you appear as a radiant spherically-shaped energy. Your true self, the soul or Atma, is made of a bright white central core, surrounded by separate layers of the spectrum colors from the white core to a violet exterior. Thousands of luminous teardrop-shaped lights make up each successive layer extending outward from the core. A subtle golden glow surrounds your entire sphere.

4) Behold a beam of white-golden light suddenly surrounding your energy sphere, and see it draw you up inside a disc-shaped spaceship. See yourself

appear inside this craft in a luminous body that looks like your physical self. You are standing before a human-appearing male or female, depending on what gives you comfort, whose presence immediately uplifts you. The warmly smiling, highly evolved and benevolent human extraterrestrial standing before you has slightly larger-than-average blue eyes. The vivid blue eyes emit a depth of compassionate kindness that almost lifts you off the floor.

5) You immediately know this very wise and loving being is there to help you recover all that has been purposefully taken from you, suppressed in your subconscious mind, without your consent or awareness. The extraterrestrial welcomes you with their right hand held over the heart area, and a slight respectful nod of the head. You begin to hear inside yourself a friendly telepathic greeting and a very personal uplifting message. This message is private and meant only for you. It will be apparent that what you hear will be of benefit from this moment onward throughout your life. Now, let your uplifted joyful imagination take you where it will from here. This is your experience, so flow freely with it.

6) After your experience reaches its natural conclusion, see the white-golden light again encompass your luminous higher physical form. See it take your luminous physical body out of the spaceship, and as you change into your spherical energy form, you return to your waiting physical body that has been in a deep sleep trance like state, back on Earth. Now awaken your body and open your eyes. Take a deep relaxing breath.

7) Send out gratitude through the HU to the benevolent loving guide you just encountered. It is important to express gratitude through the HU to every enlightened being that helps you along the way to recovering all that you really are. Now go peacefully about your day if you practice this exercise in the daytime, or simply go to sleep without concern for the future if you practice this exercise at bedtime.

## CHAPTER TWO
### With Eyes Wide Open (Exercise #3)

1) Begin by practicing preliminary exercises A through E. Remember to start each special technique by first picturing or imagining someone or something you love and are grateful to have in your life.

2) The following special technique is designed to awaken in you the ability to see through the illusion of wealth and power which certain misdirected people on Earth wield to trap the masses under their elitist control. Read from the middle of page 25, starting with, ...Twenty feet up the wall... and continue to the end of page 26.

3) Now, send out the HU three times with the intent to access the new consciousness-liberating Ray woven within it. Do this in an effortless way with childlike curiosity, to see into the secrets of the universe.

4) Utilizing your imagination, see a white-golden transparent energy sphere appear before you twenty feet away. It emits a warm, glowing, uplifting energy. You feel completely protected and safe from any form of negativity. Look deeply into the luminous sphere to notice images beginning to appear inside it. These images turn into entire moving scenes. It is like watching a movie inside the sphere that reveals the truth about everything suppressed from your conscious awareness. You see right through the deception orchestrated on Earth that keep you from knowing the truth about who you are and where you originally came from before this lifetime. You are able to see the advanced, Masterful, loving, benevolent extraterrestrial and higher-dimensional teachers who wish to assist you to recover your higher knowing faculties by removing subconscious blocks.

5) Next, give permission to the HU to permanently neutralize and dissolve those terrifying control images you see within the sphere into pure white-golden light. Watch the sphere you are looking into become clear with bright white light. This takes practice. A certain protection and assistance is provided for you to eventually experience being permanently set free from these subconscious control mechanisms.

6) This is your ongoing experience of recovery and liberation; so let your true imagination flow forward to show you all that you have a right to know about your true higher nature, faculties, and your true place in the grand multi-dimensional universe.

7) When you know this safe and uplifting current journey into recovering hidden truth is concluded, take several deep-relaxing breaths and slowly open your eyes. Now send out a HU of gratitude to the entire experience you just went through, and in particular, to any benevolent Masterful Teacher beings you may have met along the way.

) Then go about your day, or to sleep if practiced at night, without worry or concern about your present situation in life or the future. Remember to keep practicing this special technique for up to 30 days, in order to have remarkable enlightening experiences. Be patient. They will cross your path.

## CHAPTER THREE
### Guests From Way Out of Town (Exercise #4)

) After completing the connecting exercises A through E, send out the HU three times, then stop to feel the serene nature of the calm it brings to you. Now read the book from the bottom paragraph on page 28 that begins with, ...He looked around the room behind them to see... and continue reading to the end of page 31. This special technique will awaken your higher faculties, so that you can experience highly evolved people both on and off-Earth without running into negative ones. As they cross your path, you will be uplifted.

:) To begin this technique, imagine that you suddenly appear in the very large ballroom of a stately mansion. Standing around the room are the world's elite, hidden government members, those who operate within a classified covert system. No publicly elected government official in the world can penetrate this system, and thus they do not realize they are leading the world in a negative direction that is covertly manipulated and not of their own choosing.

·) Because of the new Ray that is entwined and blended in the HU, you become aware that the hidden, non-elected, secret world government leaders sincerely believe their guidance of world affairs is for the best, despite negative results for so many people. However, you can see right through this illusion because you now understand they are being manipulated and subconsciously controlled by a totalitarian extraterrestrial race that does not respect human beings in any way, shape, or form. You awaken and know this is true, because no normal human being would ever do to the world and its people what they are doing. You begin to recognize the clear perception of this purposefully hidden truth awakened within you through the benevolent grace of the new Ray. This is an entirely new manifestation operating within the omnipresent vibratory word HU.

4) Continue this vision to further discover a suppressed awareness resurfacing, revealing the benevolent extraterrestrial races and the grea Master Teachers that counsel them. You will understand these beings a now engaged in the benevolent process to neutralize tyrant off-world rac and the negative technologies they used to gain a temporary control of th hidden actual leaders on Earth. Such a beneficial mission has never bee done before in the entire history of our multi-dimensional universe. Yo will come to know with certainty that the future of planet Earth is actuall very bright indeed.

5) After this co-creative journey has run its course, open your eyes an take a relaxing breath. Send gratitude out into the vast creation, to a the wondrous highly evolved beings that are committed to transformin Earth in entirely unexpected, uplifting new ways. Now go about you day or, if practiced at night, simply go to sleep, knowing that when yo awaken in the morning, you will recall in ever-deepening detail wher you go and what you do when you are out of your body exploring th grand multi-dimensional universe.

# CHAPTER FOUR
## The Mysterious Mr. Crystal (Exercise #5)

1) First, go through the preliminary exercises A through E.

2) The purpose of this next special technique is to prepare those who want th experience of having actual contact with spiritually advanced benevolen extraterrestrial human beings. They can assist you to awaken all of you suppressed higher faculties. Through these techniques, you are discoverin how to plug directly into the omnipresent living energy that sustains an supports all life and all that exists. Through this energy, you will come t understand any currently hidden truth you wish to awaken within yoursel.

3) Start reading from the bottom of page 32 beginning with, ...Janice kisse him on the cheek... and continue reading to the end of the chapter o page 34.

4) Now, send out the HU three times. Begin to imagine yourself standing b a green stone fireplace inside the expansive oval reception room of a larg

stately mansion. Although you do not understand why, the fireplace is radiating a heart opening, uplifting energy to you. It makes you smile with pleasure. You turn to look around the room and discover a special being has appeared standing beside the fireplace next to you and is looking intently into your eyes. The being's presence uplifts you even more, and you stare spellbound into the kindest emerald-green eyes you have ever seen. The eyes seem to be actually emitting a soft luminous radiance. You simply know this person is spiritually advanced and kind; you inherently understand they have your best interests at heart.

5) The mysterious being cheerfully tells you their name. It is quite unusual, and you immediately know the off-world origin of the name and the being. Ask this special person this question:

**"Will you safely show me purposefully hidden truths on a grand cosmic multi-dimensional scale, and the much greater knowing of the expansive love within it?"**

You will see the being nod and smile affirmatively.

6) There is a gold pin on the being's coat lapel that he touches three times before vanishing from sight. You remain calm, and you clearly hear the telepathic message inside your head that he will be back one day to escort you off world for a short journey. He states that he will escort you to a place where you can safely re-familiarize yourself with your dormant understanding of highly evolved extraterrestrial life, a place where you will be introduced to Masterful Teachers who exist in special protected parallel dimensions on Earth, elsewhere in the universe, and in higher dimensional realities.

7) Telepathically, send this being your thanks in one grateful HU. Know that he will hear it, as will all advanced spiritual beings in the grand multi-dimensional universe that use and tune into the HU. Then go about your day. If you practice at night, remember to tell yourself you will recall ever more about where you travel and what you do while out of your sleeping body at night. It is important to tell yourself this each night right before you go to sleep. Every technique for the chapters of this book repeats this statement, because it is easy to forget to reprogram your subconscious mind while living on such a troubled, backward, suppressed planet like Earth.

# CHAPTER FIVE
## Arriving Aboard the Mother Ship (Exercise #6)

1) Practice preliminary exercises A through E.

2) Read pages 35 through 38. Know that this technique will assist you to co-creatively imagine and bring into manifestation your own experiences. You will find yourself among advanced loving beings from other world systems aboard one of the many mother ships. Your higher true freewill is involved here.

3) Now imagine you are aboard a thirty-feet-in-diameter Scout spacecraft, standing beside the benevolent human extraterrestrial pilot described earlier in Exercise #2. If you have not practiced this exercise yet, go back and read the technique for Chapter One before continuing with this exercise.

4) Imagine you can hear the melodic vibrant voice of the extraterrestrial pilot in your head. Hear him clearly and telepathically ask if you would like to visit the mile-long mother ship that brought him to your solar system. He tells you a large mother ship is hidden in the ice rings circling Saturn. Because you know this experience will only be for your benefit, you nod consent. He smiles kindly and then sits in the white chair behind the luminous crystalline control console. You see on the holographic 3D view screen above, that the Scout ship you are in is fast approaching a mile-long cylindrical-shaped mother ship. Oval view ports eight feet apart are visible around the entire circumference of the ship. You watch amazed, as the metal hull of the parent vessel appears to become transparent before the Scout ship passes through the central section of the mother ship, and gently lands on a launch bay floor.

5) The pilot escorts you out of his ship, through an oval doorway and down a ramp. The first thing you notice are the many types of humanoid beings working around other Scout ships that have landed and come to rest in parallel rows within the vast enclosure. Your guide escorts you over to a conveyor belt moving in the floor of the massive chamber. You both step upon it and it whisks away to a triangular opening in the wall at the far end of the huge chamber. You walk through the triangular opening together.

6) Now, return to full awareness of your physical body, wherever you left it, sitting comfortably in a chair or lying on a bed, couch, or floor. Send

out one HU in deep felt thanks to your escort on this journey, and then continue your day. Have no fear for the future. If you practice this exercise before bed, remind yourself that you will remember ever more about where you go and what you do during your journey, while your body sleeps and you explore the multi-dimensional universe.

# CHAPTER SIX
## The Grand Deception (Exercise #7)

1) First, prepare yourself by opening the doorway to peer into purposefully hidden truth. Follow preliminary exercises A through E. This is vital to the success of these exercises.

2) Now, we are going to awaken deeper awareness of the history hidden from you. You will discover truth on a grand cosmic scale, and you will become aware of many highly evolved, benevolent human, humanoid, and other extraterrestrials that exist in the multi-dimensional universe. You will come to understand we are kindred spirits related to them.

3) Read pages 39 through 43.

4) Visualize or imagine that you are aboard one of the gigantic mother ships of the Galactic Inter-dimensional Alliance of Free Worlds. You are standing inside a large observation lounge. Notice the many human and humanoid personnel with different skin tones, varying from smooth ivory-white to pale-green, to dark tanned, and to smooth snake-like patterns. You see a mix of elegantly beautiful women and unusually handsome men, all appearing to be from 25 to 35 years of age, although you sense they are much older. The energy emanating from them uplifts you in ways you have never experienced before. You cannot help but smile with appreciation. Looking around the room, you notice many are sitting at consoles monitoring projected 3D view screens.

5) Focus on an oval glass-topped table centered in the wide room, then gaze at the man and woman sitting behind it. They appear radiant and healthy in their mid-thirties and are smiling widely back at you. They stand up, greeting you telepathically with welcoming words clearly heard in your head. Pay close attention to what they show you about the true nature of benevolent extraterrestrial life, and the grand deception perpetuated

upon the people of Earth. Just let this information flow within you imagination, awakening in you knowledge previously hidden. They wil show you that the cyclic polar shifts of planet Earth, which occur ever hundred thousand years, that destroy most life on the surface are in th process of being permanently ended. From now on Earth humans wil continue to evolve for millions of years uninterrupted just as advancec extraterrestrial races do on other worlds. You will know when this firs meeting with the co-commanders of this parent ship ends. Thank then both by placing your hand over your heart and nodding your head. The return the same respectful gesture.

6)  Return now to your full awareness of your physical body back on Earth Send out one HU in appreciation for meeting them, take several concludin; deep breaths, and then go about your day—or go to sleep if you practic at night before bed. Know deeply that your future is very bright indeed.

# CHAPTER SEVEN
## Parting the Subconscious Veil (Exercise #8)

1)  We begin by practicing the preliminary exercises A through E.

2)  Now, we will begin to experience exploring the implant removal proces through the - Frequency Harmonizing Mind Link Activator - device. Ir the Masterful hands of compassionate Galactic Alliance technicians, thi. benevolent extraterrestrial device is not only able to free suppressed being; from subconscious controlling implants, it can also eventually remove th subconscious mind altogether. Remember that normal human beings o other worlds do not have subconscious minds.

3)  Read page 45, starting at the middle of the page with, ...For some reason the memory from a geometry class... and continue reading to the end o the chapter on page 54.

4)  Now, imagine that walking beside you is another benevolent extraterrestria similar to the one who took you aboard his Scout ship and then to th launch bay aboard the Galactic Alliance mother ship. You both enter ; sixty-feet-wide spherical chamber and step upon a transparent floor tha equally divides the spherical structure in half. Lining the inner wall, you

see precisely shaped eight-inch-long by four-inch-wide quartz crystal spires pointing at the spherically shaped dodecahedron (12 pentagonal or five-sided faces) chamber centered in the middle of the floor. It has transparent walls and you can see a white chair in the middle of the floor through the pentagonal-shaped walls of the structure. A control console formed from half an octagon sits just outside the chamber, beside a clear quartz stairway that leads down under the structure's walls before angling upwards into the room itself. Filling the control console are multicolored faceted crystal controls. Your escort guides you down the steps and up inside the chamber.

) Your companion motions with his hand for you to sit in the chair. As you do, you are pleasantly surprised to discover the chair conforms to your body shape in a delightful way. You feel comfortable and safe as a pleasurable energy gently runs up and down your spine. The transparent pentagonal walls of the chamber light up and project transparent computer view screens. You begin to experience and see surfacing memories previously implanted in your subconscious mind. These implants have kept you from remembering your higher faculties and who you really are.

5) Artificially-implanted images begin to appear on the view screens of the chamber walls surrounding you. The images are terrorizing and you recognize they engender fear. What you begin to see in your imagination here is actually, what has been holding back your higher faculties from surfacing in your conscious awareness. For the first time in your life, you can actually see the vicious implanted images projected on the view screens in this safe, objective way. Now you hear the voice of your kind extraterrestrial guide say to you, "While you gaze at these images, ask to have them dissolved back into pure energy for your uplifting benefit." Watch the images actually move from inside you and appear in a golden energy sphere above your head. You see the torture images dissolve into the brightening white-golden light within the room, and then this golden energy quickly recedes back inside your body. You begin to recall what happened, when, and where.

7) When you feel serene, smile deeply as you sense relief and appreciation. Return to your physical body that is waiting for you back on Earth. Send out a grateful HU of thanks to your kind extraterrestrial escort. Take several deep relaxing breaths and go about your life.

# CHAPTER EIGHT
## Escape From Reptilian Claws (Exercise #9)

1) As always, before exploring the special techniques for each chapter of The Seres Agenda, practice preliminary exercises A through E.

2) This next technique is designed to set in motion your permission to have the special Ray that operates within the HU assist you in awakening your inner knowing ability, so that you can clearly and immediately discern good from bad in any being you encounter on Earth, from other worlds or from higher dimensions of life.

3) Read from the top of page 55 to the end of page 61. It is important to read these pages because contained within them are the secret stimulation to experience emerging freedom from tyranny.

4) Send out the HU three times to open the safe doorway or connection through the pineal gland in the center of the brain. Doing this opens the inner eye, known in esoteric circles as the Third Eye. This gives you ability to see 360 degrees in any direction, using the inner vision of your true spherical energy self or soul - what benevolent extraterrestrials call the Atma. Gazing into the multi-dimensional universe through the omnipresent HU allows us to understand any hidden truth with knowing certainty.

   You are accessing the primordial, omnipresent, pure living force behind all creation through using the connection tool of the HU. This time, as you access your multi-dimensional nature, imagine meeting two kind extraterrestrial human beings standing together side by side. They can be male or female. They are smiling at you, extending their hands to shake yours in introduction. Do not shake their hands just yet.

5) Briefly, gaze into their eyes. You will instantly note there is an energetic difference between them. You feel an uplifting warm glow in your chest and head coming to you from the human being on the left. When you gaze at the human being on the right, you immediately perceive this one is disguised to appear human using a device hidden from sight. You feel the hair on the back of your neck stand up and a cold chill runs down your spine. However, you have no fear, for the HU is protecting you in this experience in order to awaken your ability to tell the difference between these two beings. Now reach out and shake the hand of the benevolent human standing to the

left. Instantly the illusion surrounding the disguised human on the right vanishes, revealing he is actually a tall bipedal (upright walking with two arms and two legs) reptilian, staring at you with angry red vertical cat-like pupils in violet oval eyes.

6) Remember, a special protection surrounds you as you watch a blinding white Ray of light suddenly appear. It passes down through the head of the malevolent reptilian, enveloping it in an oval white-golden light and the creature vanishes.

7) Continue to let your imagination flow with the experience you are having until it naturally concludes. Now return to your physical life here on Earth. Send out gratitude and thanks to the highly evolved, benevolent extraterrestrial human that just befriended you, and who helped you to discern the difference between benevolent and malevolent beings despite any disguise they may be using. Ask this friendly person from another world to reveal their name to you. Know that you will hear it accurately, either right away or in a later exercise when you are ready to go further.

## CHAPTER NINE
### The Secret Mountain Base (Exercise #10)

1) Practice preliminary exercises A through E.

2) In this practice, we will explore one of the secretly established benevolent human extraterrestrial bases on Earth. You will meet kind, highly evolved personnel who can assist you to further recover the higher faculties of knowing perception that remain suppressed in your subconscious mind.

**Note:** The point behind all these special enlightening techniques is to experience being free of all doubt, fear, and uncertainty. Thus, we will start by visiting the protected hidden base inside Mt. Shasta in Northern California, USA described in the book. This exercise will focus the creative imagination, and awaken often-dormant abilities. You will practice gazing into the special vibration of HU that supports and sustains the multi-dimensional universe, in order to have direct experiences of knowing hidden truth with certainty.

3) Read pages 62 through 68, to be reacquainted with the hidden truth about one secret, protected, benevolent extraterrestrial base on Earth. Understand the dedication the personnel secretly working here have to liberate the population of Earth from Tyranny.

4) Send out the HU five times and then ask:

**"Safely show me purposefully hidden truth on a grand cosmic multi-dimensional scale, and the much greater knowing of the expansive love within it."**

We will be sending out this request numerous times during techniques listed in this book. Designed in a virtually unlimited manner, this request can bring about an ever-expanding awareness of the universe.

5) Imagine you are meeting with the male and female commanders of the Mt. Shasta base. You will notice that you immediately feel uplifted and fearless in their presence. This is because they rightly utilize a special device, a golden pin on their clothing which temporarily suspends any subconscious implants from misdirecting your higher faculties through fear, enabling you to make a true freewill decision regarding your personal liberation from suppressive beings and technologies.

6) The senior base commander telepathically asks you to go with them further inside the Mt. Shasta base. There you will begin to experience the permanent removal of the higher consciousness-suppressing implants buried in your subconscious. Let your imagination flow in a steady stream to discover the ways they assist you to recall hidden truth and experience your ever-expanding awareness. When you are finished with this journey into recalling your higher nature and freedom as a human being, return to full awareness of your physical body. Send out a HU of grateful thanks for the assistance the two base commanders gave you. Their true friendship will deepen as your knowing of hidden truth expands. Then go serenely about your day. If you practice this technique at night before bed, after it is finished, go to sleep with no concerns or fears about your changing destiny. This will help to bring wondrous results into your life.

# CHAPTER TEN
## Destined Reunion (Exercise #11)

1) We will explore further the loving compassionate nature of advanced benevolent extraterrestrial humans and other races. You will see how they treat Earth humans, and how they contact people and assist them to free their higher consciousness from suppressing implants.

2) Read page 74, starting halfway down the page with, ...Janice was now also shaking with fear... and continue reading down page 78 and through the second paragraph that begins with, ...Pleased with her newfound confidence...

3) Practice the A through E preliminary consciousness liberating techniques. Briefly pause for a few minutes to reflect on the hidden truth revealed in the section you just read, and then send out the HU three or four more times.

4) Using the inner screen of your imagination, with your physical eyes closed, imagine yourself being taken to the same special chamber that Janice experienced aboard the Galactic Alliance mother ship. Sit in the white chair that conforms to your body, refreshing it. If you suddenly feel terrified, one of them will touch a gold symbol on their clothing to temporarily suspend the terror, so you can continue to explore hidden truth until the subconscious terror implant can be removed. Then watch the transparent octagon-shaped view screen come to life, revealing much about your suppressed past and the true higher nature of your being. You are safe here. Two capable loving human extraterrestrial beings, a man and a woman, who appear to be in their late thirties, are monitoring your progress. You will come out of this experience a more liberated person, with greater inherent ability to clearly understand purposefully hidden truth with more knowing certainty.

5) Let your imagination flow where it will until this exercise has run its natural course, then simply go about your day with no concern for your future destiny. If you practice this exercise right before bed (recommended but not required), go to sleep telling yourself that you will awaken in the morning with answers to long-sought questions, and more awareness of where you were and what you did while out of your sleeping physical body exploring the multi-dimensional universe.

# CHAPTER ELEVEN
## The Chamber of Prime Creator (Exercise #12)

1) First, read from page 87 to page 90, through the end of the third paragraph that begins with, ...Also, the one you know as...

2) Practice the A through E preliminary exercises, which open a protected doorway enabling you to awaken all that was taken from you without your consent or awareness.

3) In this exercise, you will awaken suppressed higher faculties of knowing perception, your inner certainty, by exploring the consciousness-liberating Ray woven into the HU.

4) Send out six HU tones and then pause. Within the sanctuary of your own being, just look and listen in the silent place within. Be alert to see any manifestation of inner light and sound. After a few minutes, listen for the sound of running water, similar to that heard when standing by a gently running brook.

5) Now, see a spherical chamber sixty-feet-in-diameter. In the middle of the floor is a fifteen-feet-tall golden pyramid. Its four highly polished sides are glowing. A white-golden light pulses from the sides, sending out concentric doughnut-shaped circles of expanding energy. These bands of energy harmlessly pass through you as they expand out into the universe. The pyramid is radiating energy to uplift and awaken all life to its real eternal nature and wondrous true destiny. This energy allows you to see deeper and further than ever before.

6) Watch, amazed, as the sides of the pyramid turn transparent. You see inside a white fountain bowl of smooth white polished stone. A statue stands in the center of the fountain. It is a bald-headed, muscular, bare-chested man with bronzed skin, wearing a white tunic that extends from the waist down to just above his ankles and bare feet. Two round gold bracelets encircle each upper arm. The light radiating from his face is so bright you can barely make out the smooth skin of a human male in his late thirties or early forties. His hands are down at his hips open palms facing forward. A radiant liquid white light tinged with gold is pouring from his open palms in a steady stream down into the bowl, keeping it constantly filled. The luminous fluid flows in an unbroken sheet over the entire circumference of the wide white bowl. The smooth sheet of falling liquid light vanishes into

the floor below the fountain base. Twelve golden cups hang from golden hooks surrounding the outer edge of the fountain bowl.

7) With your imagination gazing into the multi-dimensional universe where this fountain exists, let yourself experience the uplifting energies of the luminous liquid light. Watch as one of the golden cups lifts off its hook, dips itself into the consciousness-liberating nectar, then moves through the air to pause one-foot in front of your face. You are peacefully serene. Allow the cup to pour the radiant liquid down your throat. Feel it flow through your being in an intensely uplifting manner, and then it begins to radiate from your entire body to pass through the spherical walls of the chamber.

8) When ready, come back to full awareness of your physical body on Earth. Take several deep-relaxing breaths, and then send out the HU with gratitude to all enlightened beings from other worlds and higher dimensions that helped protect and guide you through this experience.

9) Go about your day, knowing much is now in progress to awaken more of your higher nature and abilities. If you practice this exercise at night, right before sleep, tell yourself before drifting into sleep that you will remember more and more about where you travel and what you do during these travels in the multi-dimensional universe while your physical body sleeps.

10) Repeat this exercise daily or nightly for several weeks, up to thirty days, until results occur. You will experience some awakening of your direct knowing ability to see into the universe and perceive hidden truths in a direct manner.

## CHAPTER TWELVE
### Attacked From Two Directions (Exercise #13)

1) Before beginning this next awakening exercise, contemplate for a few moments how you are now experiencing some awareness of the new Ray, woven in the HU, is protecting you both here on Earth and while out-of-body exploring the universe at night during the physical body sleep state.

2) Read page 98, starting with the second paragraph that begins with, ...Mark and Janice were soon taking their seats... and continue reading to the end of page 101. The special Ray operating through the HU protects you in the

same way it protects the extraterrestrial humans described in this chapter. However, the energy of HU also works through special devices that can channel it.

3)  Practice preliminary exercises A through E.

4)  Set aside on a shelf all worries or fears about your present life circumstance and your future destiny. You temporarily set them aside to facilitate increased higher faculty recovery. Without fear or worry hindering you, you can more easily look into multi-dimensional creation through the pineal gland's function to see deliberately hidden truth with knowing certainty.

5)  Keep your eyes gently closed, unless you can practice creative imagination with your eyes open—some people can do this. Send out the HU six times, briefly pausing between each one to just look and listen—to perceive what may be taking place.

6)  Know that you are completely protected from any harm, negative beings, or technologies, and then imagine a tyrant extraterrestrial approaching you with intent to do you harm. Watch a thick beam of radiant white golden energy suddenly pour from your chest and strike the sinister figure causing him or her to vanish. By seeing this protective action take place through your creative imagination, you will come to deeply know that this protection will work if any negative situation, being, or misused advanced technology confronts you. Recommended: Also send out the HU before you leave your home for work or for any other purpose. This will set up a protection around you and will help you remember to practice the HU aloud when alone, or silently in your imagination if you are among others who would not understand.

7)  As always, when the journey utilizing this technique comes to a natural conclusion, peacefully go about your day with the expectation that uplifting, benevolent changes are underway, or if practiced at night, simply go to sleep. Remember to affirm that you will remember so much more about where you go and what you do while you are operating out of your sleeping physical body.

8)  If you practice this technique regularly, the Ray operating in the HU today will protect you constantly, even when you may not be able to utilize it on the spot in a troubling or threatening situation. However, it will work more

effectively if you call upon it for protection whenever you experience fear of any kind. It is not necessary to accept this statement on faith alone, for you will experience this protection for yourself over time. Much will unfold and awaken within you in the days, weeks, months, and coming years.

# CHAPTER THIRTEEN
## Deadly Government Alliance (Exercise #14)

1) This next technique is designed to help you see and know hidden truth beyond the deceptive manipulations of the hidden government members and the off-world tyrant extraterrestrial allies that influentially control them.

2) Practice the preliminary door-opening techniques A through E.

3) Read pages 102 through 106.

4) Utilizing your imagination, put aside all cares, worries, or concerns for your present situation and future.

5) Now send out the HU in a comfortable tone five times, raising the tone up in pitch a little higher each time. Briefly, pause between them to just look and listen at what may be happening, or what you may perceive. After practicing the HU the first five times, pause for five minutes to sense beyond the illusion deliberately put out into the world to keep people in doubt. Without having clarity, people become ineffective at making dynamic change for the better. Be aware that various governments on Earth today have subconsciously implanted programs that compel them to deceive the population about their knowledge of the existence of benevolent and malevolent extraterrestrial races.

6) Send out the HU five more times, then pause to reflect on affairs on Earth and off world. Stretch your creative imagination to encompass many other worlds to discover what you can see and know. Then send out the HU in a third series of five intonations. You will notice the phenomena of this exercise, as in all the exercises, comes to a natural conclusion and you just stop. Now go on about your day. If you practiced this at night, after the exercise concludes, send out the thought within the HU that you will continue to remember ever more upon awakening in the morning. You will remember where you go and what you do while you explored the universe during the sleep state cycle of your physical body.

Understand that these exercises are largely telepathic in nature between you and the omnipresent living force underlying all creation. Highly evolved beings are engaged in carrying out a new agenda to assist all people living on Earth to fully awaken their ability to see past misdirection. Members of the worldwide hidden government, compelled to keep the population from recovering their suppressed abilities, know what they are keeping from them. Understand that these diabolical humans on Earth are not in control of what they are doing, because they are also controlled. Otherwise, they would not be manipulating the world in such a destructive direction.

## SPECIAL ACKNOWLEDGMENT #1:

This is where you and I affect the greater picture, because the more awake we become to what has been hidden, the better off this planet and its people will be. We become constructive, fully aware co-creators with all beings who are assisting the transformation of Earth in unexpected, uplifting new ways. We too become conscious channels of the new energy Ray woven into the HU.

## CHAPTER FOURTEEN
### The Seres Agenda Unfolds (Exercise #15)

1) Practice the preliminary door-opening connective techniques A through E.

2) Read page 107 and onward to the end of the third paragraph up from the bottom of page 109 that begins with, ...Mark and Janice glanced... - Continue reading more if you are so inspired.

3) In this technique, we explore more deeply The Seres Agenda recently designed off-world. Its purpose is to safely neutralize the subconsciously implanted evil intent that misdirects a certain totalitarian extraterrestrial race to maintain the same type of subconscious implantation control over a classified second government. This non-elected government officially came into existence after World War II by the controlling influence of a tyrant off-world race. The permanent transformation of this world in an uplifting manner will be accomplished by neutralizing the misguided natures of these tyrant off-world beings while, at the same time, ever-increasing numbers of the people on Earth will undergo the same liberating experience. The

new Ray operating within the HU now in creation is designed to assist this change. The Seres Agenda is currently underway for the first time in Galactic history.

4) Next, send out the HU seven times, briefly pausing between each one, while you serenely reflect on what may be taking place in the silent sanctuary of your being. The transforming experiences can be very subtle. You may simply realize during the exercise that much more awareness has surfaced in your consciousness regarding the hidden truths revealed in the chapter. After a short time of reflection, continue to send out the HU until the exercise comes to a natural conclusion. You will simply just stop. Now cheerfully go about your day without concern of any kind for having any experience. You should feel uplifted because all fear will have subsided for now within you. Know that a new expanded awareness is underway that will fully surface within you when the time is right.

## CHAPTER FIFTEEN
## Misguided Secret Agents (Exercise #16)

1) Begin by practicing the preliminary connective exercises A through E to experience a peaceful uplifting energy. By practicing them, you are exercising dormant higher faculties.

2) Read the third paragraph at the top of page 118 that starts with, ...Indeed I do, Mr. Crystal... and read onward to the end of page 121.

3) This exercise is about developing more courage and the proficient ability to instantly discern a good being from a bad one, should you cross paths with one or more of them. However, do not worry, for the special protection of the Ray in the HU will always go with you now that you are aware of it.

4) Begin this exercise by sending out the HU three times on your outgoing breath. Now imagine that two smiling people approach you with hands outstretched to introduce themselves. They are offering to shake your hand. They can be two men, a man and a woman, or two women. Choose how this begins in a way that is most comfortable to you. Watch as they stop their approach six feet away to nod their heads in an apparently respectful manner.

5) Do not approach them just yet. Take a moment to briefly gaze into their eyes. You will discover that the new Ray energy woven in the HU begins to emanate from your eyes. This is like beams from two flashlights that envelop both people in a transparent white-golden energy bubble immediately freezing them in time. They are unharmed but cannot move. Now approach them and stop several feet away.

6) Gaze into the eyes of the person on your left. You will instantly feel uplifted and serene as a warm peaceful glow passes between you. Now gaze into the eyes of the person to your right. You instantly feel a cold terrorizing chill race up and down your spine as the hair stands up on the back of your neck. A radiant beam of light and a deep warm humming sound suddenly passes through you. The light from you strikes this person in the chest. A dark energy exits the top of their head and it enters a transparent white-golden energy sphere that appears several feet above them. There it dissolves, leaving only the white-golden energy within the sphere. Now you see this person, who had been intending harm, give you a genuine smile. This person telepathically thanks you for freeing them from the tyrant extraterrestrial control, respectfully nods their head and vanishes.

7) The time freeze bubble suddenly releases the benevolent agent patiently standing to your left, who then approaches you. Shake their hand. You inherently know this person is connected to the highly evolved benevolent Master teachers and wise extraterrestrial friends you have yet to meet. This person then offers to escort you on a journey to explore the grand truths about highly evolved loving beings that exist in the grand multi dimensional universe.

8) Trust in yourself and go wherever your imagination (the HU) leads you until you know the experience has come to a natural conclusion. When you come out of the consciousness-awakening exercise, if done in the daytime, simply go about your day. If practiced at night, simply go to sleep, after stating that you will recall upon awakening more about where you go and what you do while traveling outside of your sleeping body. Practice this exercise at the same time every day for 10 to 15 minutes at a time, or longer if you are achieving results, and wondrous experiences will eventually occur. Do be kind and patient with yourself and be consistent in practicing this or any of the exercises available in the book.

# CHAPTER SIXTEEN
## The Hidden Government Awakens (Exercise #17)

) Practice the preliminary connective exercises A through E.

) In this exercise we will practice and then experience leaving all anger, hatred, and emotional urges for revenge behind. This enables higher benevolent faculties and abilities to re-surface in conscious awareness.

) Read page 127, starting halfway down the page with, "Janice dear, I'm so glad you're safe," ...and continue reading through the end of the short quote on page 130 that states, ..."It was confirmation we have help, and that we are to proceed. Now, let's get there and get this done."

) Take a few moments to contemplate the deeper meaning of what you just read as it relates to your own unfolding higher awareness. Let your imagination flow where it naturally goes. Then send out the HU (the connecting link) five times, pausing between each to reflect on how Janice Carter's recent return to her true, unsuppressed, loving human nature gives you insight into this same process that you are now beginning to experience for yourself.

) Utilizing your imagination, once again send out the following directive telepathically, with genuine sincerity. Continue the HU, accessing the new consciousness-liberating Ray woven within it, as you send this thought out:

**"Safely show me purposefully hidden truth on a grand cosmic multi-dimensional scale, and the much greater knowing of the expansive love within it."**

**Special Added Technique Reminder:** As previously stated, it is important o repeat this statement at least once during the practice of each of the various echniques provided in the book. For best results, practice them at the same ime every day, if possible.

Know that when you do this, you are sending out a proclamation into the mnipresent living HU energy field of your sincere endeavor to fully awaken o all that remains suppressed in your subconscious mind. Do not be surprised f what you uncover goes beyond this one lifetime on Earth, into other worlds, imes, and dimensions.

6) Continue to send out the HU for 10 to 15 minutes, or even longer, you are having uplifting enlightening experiences, until the exercise com to a natural stopping point. Then open your eyes (if you practiced th exercise with them closed for better inner perception) and take sever deep, relaxing breaths. Send out gratitude with your HU to all spiritual advanced benevolent beings within the multi-dimensional universe wh desire to help you recover your true advanced human nature.

# CHAPTER SEVENTEEN
## A Publisher Experiences Truth (Exercise #18)

1) This time first read page 146, starting with the second paragraph fro the bottom of the page that begins with, ...Mark reached to place th manuscript... and continue reading to the end of the chapter on page 15(

2) Then put in motion the preliminary door opening exercises A through F

3) In this technique we will explore awakening discernment of whic published books, feature films, music and other media available toda are beneficial, and which actually are designed to keep a person fror recovering their true higher nature and abilities. Reflect for a few momen now on how book publisher Dan Waymeyer's ignorance of his own high faculties to know hidden truth, such as the existence of extraterrestrials, gently awakened in him by the new consciousness-liberating Ray wove in the HU.

4) Send out the HU six times, and then reflect on how Mark or his tru identity as Ambassador Shon-ral co-creates in harmony with the underlyin living omnipresent energy. This energy passes through the fully awakene awareness of his true nature and through the special gold pin attached t his clothes to greatly uplift and benefit his publisher friend.

# ADDITIONAL SPECIAL NOTE #6:

This same process is helping you gain back your full ability to know hidde or suppressed truth with certainty, no matter what situation or deceptive fals face may cross your life path.

5) Now, send out the HU one more time, and then send out loud or silently inside—imagine it—the following request:

**"Safely awaken the clear ability within me, to know with confident certainty, which books, feature films, and music available on Earth today channel special energy to stimulate the awakening of suppressed or dormant higher faculties."**

6) Continue to send out the HU for 10 to 15 minutes more or longer if you are having some profound experience. Just look and listen to what may be taking place. Let your imagination effortlessly flow onward until the exercise comes to a natural conclusion.

7) Remember to send out thankful gratitude to all the highly advanced benevolent beings, who assist you to be a free being again. Then go about your day with no concern for your future destiny, knowing your awareness is expanding in an uplifting direction. If you practice this exercise at night before bed, after it concludes simply go to sleep with the serenity and peace it releases within you. Remember to tell yourself just before nodding off to dreamland that you will recall more about where you go and what you do while you are out of your sleeping body exploring the universe.

# CHAPTER EIGHTEEN
## The President at Crossroads (Exercise #19)

1) First, read page 151 to the end of the chapter on page 157.

2) Practice preliminary exercises A through E.

3) In this special technique, we will awaken our own direct knowing about how past and current Presidents of the U.S.—and all hidden classified government leaders covertly operating behind them—are not in control of their true freewill. They too must have it restored. Their awareness of this is suppressed.

4) Take a few more relaxing breaths, then send out the HU seven times. Pause briefly between each one, and then be still for a few minutes to perceive what may be taking place.

5) Now imagine you are an invisible spherically shaped energy being. You are watching in complete safety as subconsciously controlled past and current Presidents of the U.S. begin to be set free from the tyrant over-control of non-human extraterrestrials. This race often camouflages its true physical form to appear as human. Reflect on the possibility of experiencing the permanent removal of all subconscious implant controls in you.

6) Send out the HU five more times. Notice a warm loving energy flow through you. This can be very subtle or quite dramatic, so look and listen within for the experience.

7) If you practice this technique before bed at night, when it is finished go to sleep with no worries or concerns, knowing when you wake up in the morning you will recall more about where you go and what you do while you are out of your body.

**Special Added Technique Reminder:** Tell yourself before dropping off to sleep that you will remember to only open one eye upon awakening in the morning. The purpose of this is to establish a conscious connection to your higher memory and awareness, keeping it open long enough for you to recall or record your out-of-body experiences into the physical consciousness. With a little persistent practice, you will accomplish this with wondrous results.

## CHAPTER NINETEEN
### The Trilotew Armada Transforms (Exercise #20)

1) Read page 159, starting with the second paragraph from the bottom of the page that begins with, ..."You mean you people are about to attack those ships?" Dan inquired nervously, as he looked to Commander Jontral for confirmation. - and continue reading through the end of the third paragraph on page 170 that states, ..."You and your men aboard your two command ships, and those warriors aboard your Scout support fighters are now..." - If you are so inclined, continue reading to the chapter's end.

2) This technique will assist you to awaken full knowing awareness of a depth of universal compassion and understanding. These qualities you must have to be set free from all suppression caused by subconscious implant programming.

3) As a reminder, first put all concerns of your life, current or future, on a shelf in your imagination. Close your eyes, if they are not already closed.

Begin to see into the multi-dimensional universe through the third eye which links to the pineal gland in the center of your brain. You will become increasingly aware of how effective this is as you consciously implement this connection.

4) Send out the hidden truth-awakening special vibratory word HU five times. This connects you to the new consciousness-liberating energy Ray. It will manifest from the center of your being through your physical body and will enable your own direct knowing experiences.

5) Utilizing your imagination from a safe invisible perspective, watch several reptilian tyrant extraterrestrials suddenly begin to transform before you. See their more coarse cruel natures soften and change into benevolent physical characteristics. Most particularly, you will notice this change in their eyes.

6) Know that this new Ray within the HU actually works through your imagination. The purpose is to begin to transform your own personal world in a permanent, uplifting manner. As this new energy Ray does this within your own being, it also works through you to facilitate the process of transforming our entire planet and its human population in an unexpected uplifting manner.

7) Let your imagination flow further with the HU, liberating more of your higher faculties of knowing perception and ever-expanding love for all that exists. In this way, we become exactly like the Source behind and supporting all life and all that exists.

8) Go about your day in confidence and peace regarding your future. If you practice this exercise at night, after it naturally concludes remember to tell yourself that you will remember your out-of-body journeys upon awakening in your physical body in the morning. Then just go to sleep without concern for any problems or how they will be resolved.

## CHAPTER TWENTY
### From Tyrants to Angels (Exercise #21)

1) This technique will help you recall even more about what is below your conscious awareness suppressed in the subconscious domain. This is

prophetic in that it reveals the manner in which The Seres Agenda schedul
to transform hidden government leaders and tyrant extraterrestrial
is underway. During the days, weeks, months, and years that follow,
complete transformation of planet Earth and its people will be the resul
of this. There is no need to accept this on faith alone, because you wil
experience this for yourself, unless you have already come into a knowing
understanding of this.

2) Read page 174, starting with the second paragraph from the bottom tha
begins with, ...Tam-lure and Una-mala appeared pleased... and continu
reading through the third paragraph on page 179 that starts with, ..."I'm
not who you should credit for that miracle," replied Mark smiling back a
him. - If you are so inclined, read to the end of the chapter.

3) Send out the HU three times to start things off, briefly pausing betweer
each one to sense what may be taking place.

4) Imagine a beautiful place in nature you have experienced on Earth, or i
you can, on another planet. Next, envision a beam of light transports you
aboard a mile-long Galactic Alliance mother ship. See several formerly
misdirected hidden government members standing beside two peacefu
Trilotew reptilian soldiers in one of the central meeting chambers. They are
smiling, having just been set free of all controlling terrorizing subconsciou
implant programming. You are here to witness how they now treat each
other. You observe their kind manner and deep, genuine profound respec
after the transformation. Now see yourself just as liberated as they are
Respectfully nod your head to them, and then shake the hands of both th
human and the bipedal reptilian extraterrestrials (upright walking reptiliar
beings with two arms and two legs). Know that this experience is actually
the near future destiny for you and all of them.

5) As this experience comes to its natural ending, remember that you are
beginning to undergo a benevolent alteration and the future is brigh
indeed. Send out gratitude in the HU to thank all positive Masterfu
beings you have met or will meet who are assisting you to have uplifting
wondrous transformations.

6) Go about your day without fear, or go to sleep if this technique is practiced
at night, knowing you will have recovered more knowing certainty abou
purposefully hidden truths upon awakening. Also, remember the specia
technique of opening only one eye at first, to maintain a link to where you

were and what you experienced during your out-of-body travels. Open the other eye after you finish a thorough review of the experiences in your awakened physical consciousness. Then record them in a notebook or audio recording device and go about your day.

## CHAPTER TWENTY-ONE
### Oblivion or Paradise (Exercise #22)

) Practice preliminary exercises A through E.

) This technique is about fully realizing the ONLY right way to constructively utilize the creative imagination: it is to use the imagination for purely benevolent outcomes for your current life, your future, and the recently changed future destiny of planet Earth.

) Read page 185, starting 1/3 of the way down the page with, ...Jon-tral kindly asked the beautiful young female technician... and continue reading until you understand that a free, liberated being utilizes the manifesting energy of their creative imagination to bring into creation only benevolent or enlightening conditions for all life. For your benefit, you may wish to read to the end of the chapter on page 201.

) Send out the HU as many times as needed until you feel serenely centered and focused. Then imagine how you would feel and what you would know, were you a liberated being consciously operating your higher faculties of knowing, free from all controlling, terrorizing subconscious implants. Then imagine how free you would be in the universe without the limiting burden of a subconscious mind. Many human beings that live in harmony on millions of other planetary systems have no subconscious minds. Let your imagination flow until you see your life transformed with knowing certainty in wondrous, unexpected, irreversible ways. Co-create this with your imagination, bringing power to it by pouring love into your vision. Remember always that this great change for the better in your own life also serves as a vehicle assisting your fellow human beings to be set free in the same way.

) Continue to send out the HU and once again send out the following request in your imagination, with confident expectation of results:

"Safely show me, purposefully hidden truth on a grand cosmic mult
dimensional scale, and the much greater knowing of the expansive lov
within it."

6) Send out gratitude in one last HU to the universe after this experience ha
run its natural course. If practiced at night before bed, after it concludes g
to sleep, knowing you will remember more about your out-of-body trave
while your body remains in the trance state called sleep. If practiced in th
morning or daytime, after it concludes go about your day in a cheerfull
expectant manner.


# CHAPTER TWENTY-TWO
## Ticking Time Bomb (Exercise #23)

1) Read page 211 from the second paragraph up from the bottom that star
with... At that moment, Mark and his home world cousin Moon-teran... an
continue reading halfway down page 214 to the end of this paragraph tha
starts with, ...They reappeared again standing in more spread out positior
around the Galactic Alliance flagship reception and observation lounge.

2) Practice the special preliminary exercises A through E.

3) This technique is designed to assist you in awakening your higher facult
to clearly discern the hidden truth about why evil cannot be permanentl
defeated through war. It will just resurface in some other place and tim
because of a basic law of physics in the lower dimensions. This law state
"For every action there is an equal but opposite reaction." If we attack ev
by force with the intent to destroy it, evil will always react as a sore lose
and destroy many innocent lives, even entire worlds before it attempt
to escape certain looming defeat. This is true unless evil undergoes
benevolently neutralization before things escalate to this point.

4) Begin by sending out with the first HU this request:

"Safely show me purposefully hidden truth on a grand cosmic multi
dimensional scale, and the much greater knowing of the expansive lov
within it."

Then send out the HU two more times and pause after each to look and listen within the private sanctuary of your creative imagination, noting any insights or knowing intuition you may experience.

5) For the next few minutes reflect on what you read in this chapter regarding how the benevolent neutralization of the Trilotew's negative subconscious drives took place. The Galactic Alliance personnel understood the negative subconscious drives in the Trilotew drove them to behave in an evil manner. A far more diabolical race placed the terrorizing controlling implants in the subconscious minds of their entire race over 500,000 years earlier. Because this more perverse race also altered certain genomes in Trilotew DNA, generation after generation passed on the perverse control implants. It was only possible to remove this terrorizing suppressive technology when the new Ray operating in the HU crossed their paths.

6) Now, send out the HU again for 10 to 15 minutes, briefly pausing between each one to reflect on allowing this awakening knowing truth to work in your own experience. Imagine seeing it benevolently neutralize evil without causing negative repercussions. This use of the HU gives only beneficial uplifting results after neutralizing evil. The existence of evil was an experiment that never accomplished what was originally intended, by negatively cattle-prodding beings to evolve in better directions. When you practice the HU, you are actually raising your understanding of the proper use of the great gift of the creative imagination. You become part of the solution instead of continuing to create the problem.

7) Let your imagination flow if you are having an experience in your inner vision. Let it run its natural course. Then go about your life with the confident knowing that you are co-creating a bright future for yourself, your loved ones, the entire planet Earth, and the future destiny of the entire multi-dimensional universe.

## CHAPTER TWENTY-THREE
### A Freedom So Rare (Exercise #24)

1) Practice preliminary exercises A through E.

2) Read page 220, starting 1/3 of the way down the page with, ...Henry's eyes opened wide... and continue to the end of the second paragraph on Page

224 that begins with, ...Vice Chairman Piermont replied happily, "I know that I speak for all of us..."

3) The special technique for this chapter will explore and awaken awareness to perceive how an elitist group of hidden, subconsciously controlled, non-elected government leaders are about to go through the process of becoming benevolently transformed. They will be set free, along with everyone else on Earth, from the covert implants which currently compel them to act harmfully towards their fellow human beings on Earth, falsely believing their actions are justified. The consciousness-liberating Ray that operates through the omnipresent HU is also simultaneously beginning the process of liberating every human being on Earth. Be clearly aware that this undertaking involves many millions of benevolent extraterrestrial human, humanoid, and other highly evolved beings to carry this out without destruction - without an Armageddon of world calamities.

4) Now, send out the HU seven times with all your passion to fully awaken your knowing regarding purposefully hidden truth. Then pause to look and listen, receptive to the light and sound flowing to you and through you to the entire world for the benefit of all life.

5) Connect once again into the deeper loving and wise nature of the HU by imagining someone or something you love and for which you experience gratitude. Then telepathically (with your imagination) send out the following request by taking a brief pause to read it from here:

**"Safely show me the ability to directly connect to the Ray within the HU and ever more greatly awaken the knowing experience of the new Ray's consciousness liberating qualities. Show me what is now underway in the universe and hidden behind the scenes on Earth that has begun the process to permanently liberate covertly suppressed people worldwide."**

6) Now softly and with kind intent send out the HU another seven times, briefly pausing between each to look and listen for any deeper awakening understanding of hidden truth you may be recalling. You will come to know ever more about the majesty of the grand multi-dimensional universe that you previously could not remember.

7) After your journey has run its course in a way you perceive is natural, come back to full awareness of your physical body. Take several deep-relaxing breaths. Send out gratitude to the HU for all its help in remembering your

true higher human nature and abilities. Then go about your day or go to sleep if you practiced this technique at night before bed, knowing you are beginning to awaken to the wonders of creation in the multi-dimensional universe.

# CHAPTER TWENTY-FOUR
## The Mighty Seres Return (Exercise #25)

1) Read the entire chapter from pages 226 to 236. This is important because it will be beneficial not only now but also increasingly in the near future.

2) This special technique will help you explore the wonder of the benevolent loving Seres race, and the great host of spiritually and technologically advanced beings of the Galactic Inter-dimensional Alliance of Free Worlds. They are all committed to help the new Ray operating within the HU to liberate the people and all life on planet Earth. Remember this process has already begun. It will make its presence more openly known in the days, weeks, months, and years to come.

3) We begin by imagining the beautiful things on planet Earth, the waterfalls, lakes, beautiful forests, birds and animal life, the clear blue sky, and the stars at night. Recall that you are a loving being and that you are grateful for their presence in your life.

4) Once again, put all concerns for you current and future situation in life on a shelf in your imagination. Send out the HU aloud on each outgoing breath, or silently within the private sanctuary of your inner imagination. Continue to send out the HU until you come to a natural stop. Now begin to imagine meeting the tall Seres Ambassador Torellian, as described in the book. Imagine him standing before you, emanating a glowing, uplifting radiant light. Listen with gratitude to what he says telepathically to you through the protected open link of your imagination. Hear his clear, deep melodious voice that uplifts you, giving new insight and expanding understanding of your true higher nature. Become aware of the wondrous nature of the Seres human race, and vast numbers of loving citizens that belong to the entire Galactic Inter-dimensional Alliance of Free Worlds. You will understand that the people of planet Earth are destined to soon become fully awakened members of this Galactic Alliance.

5) Listen further as Ambassador Torellian tells you that many Master teacher in the grand universe will begin to make their presence known to you He assures you that the previously set programmed destiny of your life i greatly changing for the better.

6) After the experience has run its natural course, thank Ambassador Torellia and any other benevolent beings you may have met during these exercises Then go about your day with gratitude with expectation of wondrou events to come. If you practice the exercise at night before bed, go to slee illumined with the same wondrous expectations of events yet to come.

# CHAPTER TWENTY-FIVE
## There's No Place Like Home (Exercise #26)

1) Read from the beginning of page 237 to the end of page 255.

2) This chapter reveals what the true highly evolved nature of a human bein is really like, after they are given back all that was covertly taken from them without their will or consent, by hidden tyrants. A protected channel i opened that begins and then accelerates the awakening or rememberin process.

3) After you have explored the deepest of hidden truths revealed in this chapte begin to ponder your true destiny. One day you will know for yourself th experiences that Ambassador Shon-ral and Prime Scientist Moon-tera (Mark Santfield and Janice Carter) went through in *The Seres Agenda* t recover their true selves' higher abilities and serenely wise natures.

4) Put into operation your own connection to the new Ray within the HU b practicing preliminary exercises A through E.

5) Send out the HU six times, briefly pausing between each one to loo and listen for any light and sounds that may occur in your private inne sanctuary. You have the ability to see into the vast multi-dimensiona universe with the inner or third eye of your true self, or Soul, whic benevolent extraterrestrials refer to as the Atma.

6) Now, using your creative imagination, telepathically send out the followin three statements, one at a time, either aloud or silently. Say them wit sincerity, reading each until you remember them or their meaning.

"Safely show me at night my true origins on other world systems and in higher dimensions while I am out of my sleeping physical body exploring the grand multi-dimensional universe."

"Assist me to experience my real higher nature, what I was and wisely knew before I came to this planet and began incarnating with all former memory occluded and suppressed in physical Earth human bodies."

"Reveal ever more deeply during my dreams my experiential background in the multi-dimensional universe."

) Next, send out the HU nine times, briefly pausing between each one. When done, reflect on the three statements above before continuing to send out the HU for ten to fifteen minutes or longer if you are having any awakening recall experiences.

) Once this experiential technique comes to a natural stopping point, telepathically send out the following statement. Read it with sincerity right from this paper.

"I am ready to go on a fully aware journey to Prime Creator, to the source behind and supporting all life in the grand multi-dimensional universe. I know that I am capable of recalling the experience of what really am and my higher true co-creative destiny with the benevolent Prime Creator, what people on Earth refer to as the Supreme Being. I am also ready to temporarily leave my physical body to journey home in order to return to my body again as a free being, who can help bring about the uplifting transformation to planet Earth, its people, and the entire lower dimensions of the grand multi-dimensional universe."

) When you are done, send out the HU one more time in gratitude, with full expectation of such experiences when the time is right. Then go to sleep knowing you will awaken with a more expanded awareness. If you choose to practice this entire technique in the daytime, after it has naturally concluded, simply go about your day without concern for your future or the future of planet Earth. Both destinies are changing for the better and they are very bright indeed.

# CHAPTER TWENTY-SIX
## The Call to Excellence (Exercise #27)

1) Read the chapter from page 256 to the end of page 264.

2) Remember, you are utilizing the hidden truths revealed in this chapter t become aware through these techniques of your own direct experience wit the consciousness-liberating Ray blended into the HU. You can actual. accomplish this if you practice exercising your creative imagination to s into the deeper secrets of creation.

3) Practice preliminary exercises A to E and set aside all concerns for you current situation in life and your future destiny. Put them on a shelf i your imagination for the duration of this exercise.

4) Then send out the HU six times in a row, pausing to listen and look insic for any sounds, lights, visions, or open doorways that may appear befoi you.

5) Begin to imagine for a few moments what you would be like, and th bright depth of what you would wisely know with certainty, when you ai able to benefit all life, including your own. Then imagine going throug the great transformation that Shon-ral and Moon-teran went throug with the assistance of the Seres Ambassador Torellian. This being, a ver ancient, fully aware channel of the Source, the HU, or Prime Creatc provided Shon-ral and Moon-teran with additional strands to the advanced extraterrestrial human DNA. Imagine having the freedom an trustworthy consciousness as a co-creative channel of the omnipreser living force, being able to use that energy to remove implants and set you fellow beings free in a wondrous, uplifting, transforming manner.

6) When you sense this exploration into experiencing purposefully hidden trut has run it natural course, come back fully to your physical body awareness

7) Send out the HU six more times in a row, then pause to reflect on th overall experience. Know that when conditions are right, you will hav the experiences of awakening knowing certainty, regarding purposefull hidden truths because of what you have set in motion co-creatively wit the HU through your imagination.

8) Before going to sleep, tell yourself that you will remember more abou your out-of-body journeys in the morning, after you begin to awake

your sleeping physical body. If you choose to practice this technique in the daytime, do it at the same time every day for up to 30 days. You will experience astounding results.

# CHAPTER TWENTY-SEVEN
## The Earth World Transforms (Exercise #28)

1) Practice preliminary connective experiential exercises A through E.

2) Read from page 265 to the chapter's end on page 277. In this exercise, you will begin to recall your co-creative part in the uplifting worldwide transformation that is currently underway.

3) Now read the following statement, and then look within for a few moments in silence with your eyes closed, reflecting on its deeper hidden meaning. Expand your imagination to gaze into the vast area this covers.

**"Safely assist me to recall and know with certainty the true freewill co-creative part I am meant to contribute to the uplifting underway changing destiny of planet Earth and the grand multi-dimensional creation."**

**Note:** How a being (the Atma) utilizes their creative imagination determines if their direct knowing perception is liberated or suppressed.

4) This next special technique opens a protected doorway through which we can travel to safely explore purposefully hidden truth and recover our true nature as benevolent co-creators with Prime Creator. When we contact the omnipresent living Source behind and supporting all life, we recover our ability to know how to constructively utilize our creative imagination. The special vibratory word HU allows the new consciousness-liberating Ray to begin to set us free. It also provides the protection to practically achieve this accomplishment. However, each one of us must directly experience this in order to really understand and know this is true.

5) Begin this exercise by sending out the HU twelve times. Then stop to look and listen within the revealing silence of the private sanctuary of your creative imagination. Know that loving, uplifting, benevolent beings and events are assisting you during this journey to recover the full right use of the gift of your creative imagination. This happens in serene natural ways

to help us recover our higher nature, and abilities suppressed below our conscious awareness in the subconscious mind.

6) Next, go over in your imagination what you read in this culminating chapter of the book and its core purpose. Remember that tyrants, either on or off world, are not in control of the diabolical things they do. Understand that their subconsciously driven compulsive negative nature are beginning to go through the neutralizing process in a way that does not involve worldwide death and annihilation.

7) Send out the HU twelve more times, then pause to briefly reflect on what you may be experiencing or perceiving. Now imagine gazing with gratitude into the white-golden light emanating from a fountain within a golden pyramid. Listen to the higher sound frequency that accompanies the light. Now observe one of twelve golden cups, hanging from golden hooks surrounding the white stone bowl levitate up off a hook. It dips itself into the fountain full of white-golden liquid light. This nectar is pouring from the open palms of the statue, a bronze-skinned man standing in its center. The cup floats through the air and pours the liquid light into your open mouth. This form of the HU energy contains the consciousness-liberating Ray as liquid light. Drinking this soothing energy radiates light throughout your body, and out in all directions to be of benefit to others.

8) After this exercise comes to a natural conclusion, send out one more HU in gratitude to the Source behind all life, and to the majestic benevolent beings who assist your return to your true higher human nature. Then go about your day knowing your current and future destiny is very bright indeed. If you practice this technique at night before bed, remember to tell yourself silently that you will remember upon awakening more about what you did and where you went during your explorations into hidden truth in the grand multi-dimensional universe.

## CHAPTER TWENTY-EIGHT
### Dawn of a New Beginning (Exercise #29)

1) Read from page 278 to the end of the chapter on page 286. Feel and inwardly know you are becoming aware of what is subtly taking place for you on planet Earth, in wondrously unexpected ways.

2.) Utilizing this loving Masterful technique, we will explore the true destiny of all human beings on Earth. Today, most deliberately misled people operate by the influence of false terrorizing programs that were placed in their subconscious minds and no longer understand their creative, imaginative faculty. Under normal circumstances, people would operate with benevolence and wisdom to support all life. Currently, the great majority of people experience a compulsive drive to send out extremely limiting, opposing visions of both constructive and destructive outcomes for their life and this planet we live on. During these exercises, you are endeavoring to awaken through your personal explorations of the HU, the way to take back command over negative subconscious influences. Your destiny is to eventually experience them permanently neutralized and removed.

3.) Next, send out the following statement by reading it right from this page:

**"Safely provide the awakened knowing experiences of who I really am as an evolved being, and what my true higher co-creative destiny really is in harmony with the omnipresent HU, Prime Creator, or the Source behind all that exists. Help awaken my true higher nature and abilities to wisely utilize them for the uplifting constructive benefit of all life on planet Earth and in the grand multi-dimensional universe."**

4.) Now send out the HU continuously for 10 to 15 minutes, or longer if you are experiencing serene uplifting energy, or if you are seeing through the imaginative third eye into a place within the grand multi-dimensional universe.

The HU is assisting you to let go of any bigotry, prejudice, hate, and feelings of revenge or anger. Deep down we all know such negative qualities have no place in us or among the vast host of free beings that wish to help everyone on Earth know with certainty who they really are. Your destiny is to become a free, capable, trusted, consciously aware co-creator with them and the new Ray in the HU or Prime Creator—the source behind all that exists.

We can experience what it is like to ride in spaceships of highly spiritual and technologically advanced people from other worlds. This is available for you to do. If you want to meet with Masterful Teachers from many other worlds and from higher dimensions, you can. The one requirement is that you ONLY utilize the imagination to create what is of benefit to all life.

5) Let your loving imagination flow like a glistening river. Experience an expanding joyful light and sound within the consciousness-liberating Ray woven in the omnipresent HU. Eventually you will begin to recall lifetimes lived on other worlds and higher dimensions before this lifetime on earth. Since it is true that no human being originally evolved on Earth, we are all visitors to planet Earth from other worlds and higher dimensions.

6) Send out the HU nine times with grateful goodwill to all life on planet Earth, off world, and even to misguided tyrants hidden behind the scenes.

7) When this exercise comes to a natural conclusion, go about your day with knowing certainty your programmed life destiny is changing for the better. Feel and know that what is discreetly taking place on Earth now will continue to increase in wondrous unexpected ways. Know that you are awakening from a long deep dream of subconscious suppression to enter the bright light and sound of the new Ray operating through the special vibratory word HU.

8) Continue to put into operation this special technique every day at the same time for up to 30 days to have uplifting, wonderful changes in your life. Some experiences of higher dimensions are subtle, others are much more dynamic, but all awaken your abilities to know purposefully hidden truth in ever expansive ways. Pay attention to how you emotionally feel after each exercise. Take time to imagine a bright wondrous future for yourself, your loved ones, and the entire planet.


## SPECIAL ACKNOWLEDGMENT #2:

After each exercise concludes, regardless of what you may or may not yet recall, realize that your co-creative inner work is assisting the process to actually bring into manifestation right here on Earth a very unexpected but bright future indeed.


## CHAPTER TWENTY-NINE
## Our Ever Expanding Horizon (Exercise #30)

1) Read this brief chapter from pages 287 to 289.

!) Send out the HU five times, briefly pausing between each one. Reflect on how the new Ray operating through the HU can reveal aspects of our true higher nature. Know the complete strength it has over all forms of negative situations, beings, and misused extraterrestrial technologies.

) When you have some insight into this, telepathically speak aloud or silently the following two statements:

"Safely provide ongoing direct experiences with benevolent Master Teacher beings in the grand multi-dimensional universe. Show me the freeing right use of higher extraterrestrial technologies that operate within he grand multi-dimensional universe for the uplifting benefit of all that exists."

"Awaken within me the greater conscious knowing awareness of my abilities to co-create beneficially for the uplifting good of all life in harmony with the benevolent Master Teachers, whose recently greatly expanded mission is to liberate suppressed beings on planet Earth and on all worlds, through the new Ray operating in the HU."

) Send out the HU five more times. Then send out four more rounds of the HU five times, if you are having enlightening experiences and want to continue. Let the session run its natural course. As usual, you will simply know when to stop.

;) If you choose to practice this technique at night before going to bed, go to sleep after it is concluded, knowing that upon awakening, you will recall more of what you were doing and where you were during your out-of-body travels.

**Special Added Technique Reminder:** Remember to first open only one eye when you wake up after the night's sleep. Once both eyes open, the link to your exploration of the grand multi-dimensional universe shuts off and the memory quickly fades. This is true, unless you first review with one eye closed what was taking place while you were out of your body exploring. In this way, he link remains long enough for you to record in the physical consciousness the experiences of where you were and what you were doing while out of the body exploring.

# SUMMARY:

## FOOD FOR INNER REFLECTION
## AND CONTEMPLATION

Nearly every human being on Earth today is to some degree manipulate covertly into using their imagination to create both heavenly and hellis manifestations. Each day, people unconsciously send out visions of constructiv good and fear-based images of looming destruction. This subconsciou compulsive behavior, implanted in the electromagnetic energy fields tha surround people's bodies, compels them to use their creative imaginations i opposing directions. This neutralizes their higher faculty ability to manife: wondrous consciousness-freeing creations on Earth. It dilutes their focus o what is beneficial. This is a clever technique covertly implemented throug the misuse of advanced technology by tyrants from other worlds. Currentl these hidden controllers see Earth and its people as chattel (property) tha they want to dominate for destructive selfish purposes. The wondrous proce to permanently remove this type of diabolical nonsense in a safe manner underway, so that the higher faculty of knowing perception is fully recalle regarding the nature of one's rightful creative destiny within the mult dimensional universe.

## HOW THE SUPPRESSION OF
## A BEING IS CARRIED OUT:

This is accomplished by subjecting a human being, without their conser or later recall, to artificially created, primary terrorizing subconscious prograr implants that keep them from recovering the awareness of who they were, an what they really knew before this lifetime on Earth. Another method compe: the being to repeatedly reincarnate on Earth with no memory of what cam before each lifetime. In this way, no guard towers or soldiers guarding th victims are necessary. Implants subtly whisper encouragement to the victim t hate, to seek revenge, and to seek out and find those tyrants that trapped them subtly giving them the terribly negative desire to tear the tyrants to pieces. Th splits the normally constructive imaginative function of the consciousness i half or into opposing forces, rendering the victim easily controllable.

# THE SOLUTION:

The solution to this problem is simple; however, it takes self-discipline to bring it into manifestation. By consciously connecting directly to the new Ray in the omnipresent power of the special primordial vibratory word HU, all temporary negative conditions begin to be permanently neutralized. Beings who are free of the implant trap in the universe hear our HU, and they assist us in achieving our own freedom. When we recall enough of our true higher nature, we begin to neither listen to nor follow negative destructive impulses. This begins the process of liberating the individual, the being, the Soul, or the Atma from the deliberate, hidden subconscious trap that is laid out for the people on planet Earth. Every individual actually has always had power over all negativity, implants, harmful extraterrestrial technology and malevolent beings, even if they currently can no longer remember or believe this with any confidence. Utilizing the HU, over time, gives us recall of our higher knowing confidence, and certainty of what we know. The HU removes destructive doubt and fear, created long ago to hinder us from using our creative abilities in constructive new ways for the benefit of all life.

# GLOSSARY OF
# CHARACTERS AND TERMS

## Characters:

**Agent Jacobson** - He is the NSA agent working with the benevolent Galactic Alliance, who helps Mark to secretly integrate back into Earth society as Mark Santfield.

**Alec Johansson** - He is the local Deputy Sheriff, (under Sheriff Pat Donyfield), of a small northern California town near the cottage home of Dan and Mary Allison Crystal (Boun-tama and Lean-tala).

**Boun-tama (Boon-tah-mah)** - He is an advanced extraterrestrial human secretly stationed on Earth. He is Mon-tlan's associate known by the cover name Mr. Dan Crystal or Mr. Crystal.

**Corel-shana (Cor-el-shah-nah)** - She was Ambassador Shon-ral's mother who arrived on the Trilotew home world to accompany her husband to get an agreed treaty signed with the Trilotew Emperor, who then betrayed and killed her and her husband.

**Cynthia Piermont** - She is the snobbish, very wealthy Vice Chairwoman under Chairman Ted Carter of the worldwide secret second government.

**Dan Crystal or Mr. Crystal** - This is the Earth cover name for Boun-tama, who is married to Mary Allison Crystal - the cover name on Earth for Lean-tala.

**Dan Waymeyer** - He is the Chief Editor and CEO owner of Waymeyer Publishing and Mark Santfield's publishing agent.

**Daniel Samuelson** - He is the United States Secretary of Defense.

**Danim-tama (Dan-him-tah-mah)** - He is the seven-year-old son of Moon-teran and Donum-Tuma.

**Donum-tuma (Don-oom-two-mah)** - This is Moon-teran's handsome middle-aged husband on her home planet, Norexilam.

**Dun-tal (Doon-tall)** - He is an extraterrestrial human male Lieutenant aboard the flagship of the Galactic Inter-dimensional Alliance of Free Worlds.

**Elon-tal (E-lawn-tahl)** - Lieutenant Elon-tal is a control board and view screen operator in the Mt. Shasta base.

**Fimala-tanis (Fee-mall-ah-tan-iss)** - She was Moon-teran's Prime DNA Biologist mother, before she was killed with her husband aboard their Galactic Alliance deep exploration research ship. A mysterious meteor collided with it right after the stationary ship's protective energy shield surrounding the vessel was down for repair.

**Gonshockal (Gone-shock-all)** - He is the Trilotew Imperial Overlord Fleet Commander located in a secret underground base deep in the jungles of Brazil.

**Gorsapis (Gor-sahp-iss)** - He is a nine-feet-tall bi-pedal reptilian extraterrestrial from the malevolent totalitarian Trilotew race.

**Grotzil (Graht-zeal)** - His official title is Supreme Illumined High Lord Ambassador of the Trilotew.

**Harold Van Tipton** - He is a tall, middle-aged but dashingly handsome man with wavy brown hair and a handlebar mustache. He wears an expensive Italian suit. He is one of three men in the hidden second worldwide government who first approaches Ambassador Shon-ral in the secret Galactic Alliance Mt. Shasta base to thank him for helping them become transformed by the new Ray, along with ninety-seven other hidden government members.

**Henry Throckmorton** - He is Mr. Carter's general counsel attorney.

**Jameson Rockefeller** - He is a bald, slightly rotund man of medium height, about seventy years of age, who also wears an expensive Italian suit. He is also one of three men in the hidden second worldwide government who approach Ambassador Shon-ral (Mark Santfield) in the secret Galactic Alliance Mt. Shasta base to thank him for helping them become transformed by the new Ray, along with ninety-seven other hidden government members.

**Janice Carter** - She is Mark Santfield's fiancée on Earth, who is actually Ambassador Shon-ral's advanced extraterrestrial human cousin known as

337

Prime Social and Historical Trend Scientist Moon-teran from the Galactic Inter-dimensional Alliance of Free Worlds.

**Jason Armontel** - He is a middle-aged trim man of medium height with thick black hair neatly combed back over the top of his head, that also wears an expensive Italian suit. He is also one of three men in the hidden worldwide Government that approaches Ambassador Shon-ral (Mark Santfield) in the secret Galactic Alliance Mt. Shasta base to thank him for helping them become transformed by the new Ray, along with ninety-seven other hidden government members.

**Jin-trean (Jinn-tree-ann)** - She is a lovely young human extraterrestrial technician aboard the Galactic Inter-dimensional Alliance of Free World flagship.

**Joanne** - She is a close college friend of Janice Cater.

**Jon-tral (John-trahl)** - He is the extraterrestrial human Commander of a mile-long cylindrical or cigar shaped flagship of the Galactic Inter-dimensional Alliance of Free Worlds.

**Kantal-teran (Can-tall-tear-ann)** - He was Moon-teran's Prime DNA Biologist father, before he was killed with his wife aboard their Galactic Alliance deep exploration research ship. A mysterious meteor collided with it right after the stationary ship's protective energy shield surrounding the vessel was down for repair.

**Lean-tala (Leen-ta-law)** - She is Boun-tama's wife, whose cover name on Earth is Mary Allison Crystal.

**Lorun-eral (Lor-oon-air-all)** - She is Ambassador Shon-ral's wife back on his home planet Norexilam beyond the Pleiades star group.

**Mark Santfield** - He is Janice Carter's fiancé on Earth, who is actually an advanced extraterrestrial human being known as Ambassador Shon-ral from the Galactic Inter-dimensional Alliance of Free World. His home world Norexilam is located in the Starborn Cluster beyond the Pleiades star group.

**Mary** - She is also a close college friend of Janice Cater.

**Mary Allison Crystal** - She is the wife of Boun-tama (alias Dan Crystal), who is actually an advanced extraterrestrial human known as Lean-tala.

**Mathew McConnell** - He is the head editor of Waymeyer Publishing owned by Mr. Dan Waymeyer.

**Mon-tlan (Mawn-tlann)** - His official title is Special Officer Mon-tlan. He is a highly evolved human extraterrestrial spaceship pilot from another world beyond the Pleiades star constellation. His nickname is Monti.

**Moon-teran (Moon-tear-ann)** - She is the advanced extraterrestrial human historical and sociological scientist, officially known as Prime Social and Historical Trend Scientist Moon-teran or Prime Scientist Moon-teran, from the Galactic Inter-dimensional Alliance of Free Worlds. Known as Janice Carter on Earth, she is actually Ambassador Shon-ral's cousin from beyond the Pleiades star group. Her home world Norexilam is located in the Starborn Cluster beyond the Pleiades star group.

**Oceanans (O-she-ann-ons)** - They are the benevolent humanoid people of planet Oceana, who are relatively tall and trim, have pale blue skin and slightly pointed ears, and that evolved with their ability to breath on land or under water with tiny unobtrusive gill slits at the back of their chins by the top of their necks. They are much more enlightened than Earth humans, and they emit an uplifting vibration that any person on Earth would find to be beautiful - like tall benevolent Elves.

**Pat Donyfield** - He is the local Sheriff of a small northern California mountain town near the cottage home of Dan and Mary Allison Crystal (Boun-tama and Lean-tala).

**President Martin McCoy** - He is the President of the United States.

**Razjewl (Razz-jewel)** - He is the Trilotew Second Officer revealed to be overtly operating inside the secret underground, classified, second worldwide government.

**Seres (Sey-Reys)** - These majestic, highly spiritually evolved eighteen to twenty-feet-tall extraterrestrial human beings seeded human and humanoid races throughout the many galaxies long ago, before they vanished from galactic history. They very recently decided to return.

**Shan-dreal (Shawn-dree-all)** - He is the eight-year old son of Ambassador Shon-ral and his wife Lorun-eral back on their home planet Norexilam.

**Shanal-teal (Shawn-ahl-tee-ahl)** - She is a Prime Biology scientist from Shon-ral and Moon-teran's home world.

**Shaoulnoom (Sha-ool-newm)** - Disguised as a human being, he actually the Trilotew controller of the Russian President.

**Shon-dema (Shawn-dee-mah)** - He was Ambassador Shon-ral's father the previous Galactic Inter-dimensional Alliance of Free Worlds Ambassador He and his wife arrived on the Trilotew home world to have an agreed treaty signed by the Trilotew Emperor, who then betrayed and killed them both.

**Shon-ral (Shawn-rahl)** - He is the advanced extraterrestrial human Ambassador of the Galactic Inter-dimensional Alliance of Free World known on Earth as Mark Santfield. He comes from beyond the Pleiades star constellation. His home world Norexilam is located in the Starborn Cluster.

**Shul-non (Shool-none)** - He is the Pilot Shul-non of the Galactic Inter-dimensional Alliance of Free Worlds flagship.

**Skondrilm (Skawn-dree-alm)** - He is also a Trilotew Lieutenant under Gonshockal's command in their hidden underground base deep within the jungles of Brazil.

**Sun-deema (Sun-dee-mah)** - This is First Officer or Second In Command Sun-Deema, who is Jon-tral's wife aboard the Galactic Inter-dimensional Alliance of Free Worlds flagship.

**Susan** - She is President Martin McCoy's personal secretary.

**Suzanne** - She is the secretary and receptionist for Dan Waymeyer, CEO owner and Chief Editor of Waymeyer Publishing.

**Taluna-tala (Tao-loona-talla)** - Back on their home planet Norexilam she is the ten-year old daughter of Ambassador Shon-ral and Lorun-eral.

**Tam-lure (Tam-loor)** - He is the benevolent extraterrestrial human Commander of the secret Galactic Alliance extraterrestrial base inside Mt Shasta in northern California.

**Tamal-shan (Tahm-al-shawn)** - He is the physicist husband of Shanal-teal on their home world Norexilam.

**Ted Carter** - He is the father of Janice on Earth, the richest multi-billionaire, and Chairman of a hidden classified second worldwide government.

**The Silent Mentors** - They are the most evolved mysterious beings in creation who take care of keeping everything in balanced order in the many parallel and higher dimensions: the stars; planets; galaxies; and in general, all the balanced mechanics of creation. They have unlimited power and freedom, can come and go to any place or anywhere in creation from the highest dimension to the lowest in the blink of an eye, and can take any form they wish without being detected if they choose. The mighty Seres have direct contact with them, for they are the ancient Mentors of the Seres race.

**Torellian (Tor-el-ee-un)** - He is the eighteen-feet tall mighty Seres Ambassador from the most highly evolved and most ancient mysterious human extraterrestrial race that seeded all human and humanoid races long ago throughout the many galaxies.

**Trel-una (Treeal-oo-nah)** - She is a young human female teleportation technician at the Mt. Shasta base.

**Trilon-kal (Tri-lawn-cal)** - They are the white-winged reptilian race from a parallel dimension that invaded our dimension over five hundred thousand years ago, conquered the genetically related Trilotew, and then used them to start a galactic war. They were defeated by the Galactic Inter-dimensional Alliance of Free Worlds with secret help from friends in the Andromeda galaxy known by benevolent extraterrestrials as Medulonta – our nearest galactic neighbor.

**Trilotew (Tri-low-two)** - They are a race of malevolent eight to ten-feet-tall, bi-pedal totalitarian reptilian extraterrestrials, who do not respect human beings.

**Trondshopa (Trond-show-pa)** - He is a Trilotew Lieutenant under the command of Gonshockal in their hidden underground base deep within the jungles of Brazil.

**Una-mala (Oo-nah-mahl-lah)** - She is Second Commander Una-mala and Tam-lure's wife, who also oversees the secret extraterrestrial Earth base inside Mt. Shasta.

**Vera-tima (Vera-tee-mah)** - She is the nine-year-old sister of Yoral-telan and younger daughter of Moon-teran and husband Donum-tuma back on their home world Norexilam.

**Yalgoot (Yee-owl-goot)** - He is the High Divine Imperial Commander Yalgoot aboard the Trilotew flagship – one of two Destroyer Class spaceships secretly hovering above each of Earth's poles.

**Yoral-telan (Yor-all-tell-on)** - She is the eleven-year old daughter of Moon-teran and husband Donum-tuma back on their home world Norexilam.

**Zin-tamal (Zin-tuh-mall)** - He is the pilot officer of the three-hundred feet-long, Medium Transport Carrier ship from the Galactic Inter-dimensional Alliance of Free Worlds.

**Zorbok (Zor-bock)** - He is the Trilotew First Officer revealed to be covertly operating inside the secret underground U.S. desert base of the classified second worldwide government.

**Zushsmat (Zoo-shmaht)** - He is a more than eight-feet-tall bi-pedal extraterrestrial from the malevolent (evil) totalitarian Trilotew race.

# Terms:

**Atma** - This is the Galactic Alliance of Free Worlds term for what people on Earth call Soul. They know this to be the eternal, deathless, true energy spherical form of all living beings.

**DNA Transverse Molecular Reconstructor** - This recently perfected extraterrestrial device developed by scientists from the Galactic Inter-dimensional Alliance of Free Worlds, can transform the suppressed two-stranded DNA of human beings on Earth back into the normal four-stranded advanced human DNA. Four-stranded DNA is common among millions of other human populated world systems. Also referred to as the DNA Reversion Process, the device can transform the unique human DNA characteristics of one world, to that of the human DNA characteristics of another world.

**Energy Field Dampening Device** - This technology from the Galactic Inter-dimensional Alliance of Free Worlds can shut down, without damage, electronics or computer systems anywhere on Earth, to prevent a nuclear war should the need arise. During the cold war between the United States and the former Soviet Union, it was secretly very effectively used twelve times to prevent this catastrophe after both sides, for one reason or another, actually pushed the button to destroy the world.

**Energy-To-Matter Conversion Beam** - This Galactic Inter-dimensional Alliance of Free Worlds' device can neutralize any explosion or exploding device including nuclear bombs. It can transform the energy back into the natural terrain, landscape, plant and animal life that existed in the area.

**Frequency Harmonizing Mind-link Activator** - This off-world Galactic Alliance device is very effective in removing subconsciously implanted three-dimensional mental image pictures containing sight, sound, smells, motion, tactile sensations, and every possible negative imagery that can compel an individual to forget who they are and behave in an abnormal manner.

**Frequency Modulators** - The device connected to the back closet inside the cottage home of Boun-tama and Lean-tala shields the doorway entrance to the hidden teleportation pad located in a slightly higher molecular frequency, or parallel dimension. It also lowers or raises the molecular frequency or time rate of human physical bodies from one parallel frequency to another.

**Galactic Alliance Deep Penetration Observation Magnifier** - Th advanced technology allows the observer to undetectably peer through an material barrier or the underground, to observe what is there.

**Galactic Alliance Courier Scout Class Ship** - They are large one hundred-feet-in-diameter and thirty-feet-high long-range transport ship They are capable of carrying over one hundred people and much more carg than the smaller thirty-feet-in-diameter Scout Class transport and defensiv interceptors. They are capable of traversing greater distances between sta systems than the smaller Scout Class ships, without needing to be recharged.

**Galactic Alliance Emerald Star Galaxy Class Spaceship** - These massiv ships of the Galactic Inter-dimensional Alliance of Free Worlds can be on mile-long to over ten miles in length. They are cigar or cylindrically shape mother ships or parent vessels with smooth flattened top and bottom hulls. Th Interstellar Emerald Star Class spaceships have special anti-gravity propulsio drives that give them the ability to operate in planetary atmospheres, und oceans, in parallel dimensions, and to travel between planets, to stars system or anywhere in our galaxy in a very short period of time, as well as to and from other galaxies.

**Galactic Alliance Inter-stellar Medium Transport Ships** - These ar 300 to 900 feet long, slightly flattened cigar or cylindrical shaped interstella capable spaceships of the Galactic Inter-dimensional Alliance of Free World They have anti-gravity propulsion drive systems that give them the capability t travel between the stars and the vast distance of outer space in our Milky Wa galaxy in a very short time. They can also travel between parallel dimension within our galaxy, within planetary atmospheres and under oceans.

**Galactic Alliance Scout Class Spaceships** - These Galactic Inter dimensional Alliance of Free Worlds' defensive spacecraft, are thirty-feet-in diameter, disc shaped, with three convex semispherical pods facing downwar in a triangular position on the bottom of their hulls. A characteristic pale blu antigravity light enshrouds their hulls when they travel between lower an upper parallel dimensions in the physical universe, in planetary atmospheres under oceans, between worlds, and under certain conditions, between sta systems.

**Galactic Inter-dimensional Alliance of Free Worlds** - This is the larges nd most prominent benevolent organization of independent worlds systems nd space travel capable races in our Milky Way galaxy. It is comprised of 1ore than 450,000,000 inhabited planets in just ¼ of the galaxy and it has a armonious relationship with the more advanced benevolent races that inhabit he Andromeda Galaxy, known by extraterrestrials as Medulonta—our nearest alactic neighbor.

**HU** - This is the original most ancient name or vibratory word from he source behind and supporting all life and all that exists. Masterful beings ot native to Earth brought this tool here from beyond the lower worlds of reation. An individual utilizing it will consciously become aware of their rue nature as the Atma or Soul that forever exists in or out of bodies. The tma most often leaves the body through the pineal gland utilizing the HU to afely explore purposefully hidden truths in the multi-dimensional universe. t expands the innate capacity to love with respect for all life. To HU, get omfortable and imagine love for someone or something, then send out the IU aloud or silently in a comfortable tone for 10-20 minutes a day. Amazing esults will follow.

**Maldec or Maldek (Mall-deck)** - A very long time ago, a special bomb lew apart the inhabited planet Maldec and it became the asteroid belt circling n an orbit around the sun of our solar system between the planets Mars and upiter.

**Matter Annihilator Bombs** - They are Trilotew energy ray spherical ombs that bury themselves deep underground and then implode, creating a lisintegrating effect on the molecular bond of all matter within a mile wide adius of the intended target. It turns matter into energy that quickly dissipates, eaving nothing but a semispherical hole in the ground.

**Matter Disruptor Implosion Bomb** - If set off, this oil barrel sized Trilotew implosion bomb will blow apart an entire planet.

**Mayan Calendar (Ma-yen)** - This pertains to the ancient Maya (Maeh) culture or people: a major pre-Columbian civilization of the Yucatan 'eninsula that reached it peak in the 9th century A.D. They produced nagnificent ceremonial cities with pyramids, a sophisticated accurate prophetic nathematical calendar system, hieroglyphic writing, sculpture, painting, eramics, and gold icons and jewelry.

**Medulonta (Med-you-lawn-tah)** - This is the name extraterrestrials fro the Galactic Inter-dimensional Alliance of Free Worlds have for the Androme( galaxy—our nearest galactic neighbor.

**Morphing Device** - This Trilotew device is built into their belt buck symbols and tightly bends light around their reptilian bodies to make the appear shorter in stature than they actually are, as human beings with norm appearing human eyes and appropriate clothing. However, it does not alt their molecular structure or DNA, and it is not capable of hiding their inher( attitude of looking at human beings like cattle they wish to kill or eat alive ( the spot, if they did not restrain themselves.

**Norexilam (Nor-ex-eal-am)** - This is Shon-ral's and Moon-teran's hon planet beyond the Pleiades constellation. It is located more than 500 light yea from Earth in our Milky Way galaxy.

**Novissam System (No-viss-sam)** - The star and solar system nearer to tr galactic center of our Milky Way galaxy that has the central governing world ( the Galactic Inter-dimensional Alliance of Free worlds circling around a brigr white-blue star in the fifth planetary orbital position. The many races in tr Galactic Alliance also refer to this as the central Novissam system.

**Oceana (O-she-anna)** - This mostly water covered planet, with a atmosphere very similar to Earth's, has several large island masses near ( centered over the equator. It exists in our Milky Way galaxy in a slightly high( parallel dimension of the physical universe.

**The New Prime Creator Expansion Ray** - This is the new consciousne uplifting and transforming Ray that was very recently brought into existenc emanating from the omnipresent, omniscient and omnipresent source behir and supporting all life. It emanates from the highest realm many dimensior far beyond the lower worlds of time and space. Recently brought into existenc the Ray permanently removes implants and retires evil as an experiment o Earth, in our galaxy, and eventually throughout the many parallel and high( dimensions of creation. No power or being can compromise, control, alter ( use it in any negative manner. It functions only one-way.

**Transverse Carrier Waves** - These special frequency carrier waves contai the imprinted patterns of the original advanced four-stranded human DN, genome codes.

**Trilotew Demon Scout Interceptors** - The slightly elongated triangular and slightly bat-wing shaped hulls of these spaceships are thirty-feet-long, measured from the two rounded pointed ends at the base of its triangular shape to the third rounded pointed apex. They are antigravity powered reconnaissance, transportation, and offensive attack interceptors. Similar to Galactic Alliance Scout ships, they have three convex semispherical pods pointing downward from the bottom hulls. Their hull surface glows pale-red when they fly in outer space or in planetary atmospheres. They can travel under oceans, between worlds, between lower parallel dimensions of the physical universe, and under certain conditions between star systems.

**Trilotew Fast-Attack Destroyer Class Spaceships** - These Trilotew heavily armored oval shaped fast-attack spacecraft are one-hundred-feet-long and used in very destructive hit-and-run missions.

**Trilotew Medium Galactic Destroyer Class Spaceships** - They are massive oval-shaped charcoal-black Trilotew mother ships nearly half a mile long with a characteristic luminous red ionized antigravity light enshrouding their hulls. They are about half the size of the mile-long Emerald Galaxy Class ships of the Galactic Inter-dimensional Alliance of Free Worlds.

**Waveform Transmitters** - This once benevolent device, perverted by Trilotew scientists long ago, transmits controlling implants into a victim's subconscious mind. The Trilotew then gain initial influential control over their intended victims.

**Zetranami (Zee-trah-nom-mee)** - This is the central world of the Galactic Inter-dimensional Alliance of Free Worlds located nearer to the galactic center of our Milky Way galaxy in the Novissam star system.

# About the Author

Photo by: Jungle Jim (Behrens)

After over forty years of extensive experiential research, R. Scott Lemriel has finally put forth this first published hidden-truth revealing book, *The Seres Agenda*, from among four completed book manuscripts. This published book created for the purpose of sharing this uniquely transforming and uplifting adventure with his current and future readers, is now here on Earth.

Lemriel was originally inspired to write *The Seres Agenda* for the benefit of his readers, based upon many awareness-expanding events that occurred during his childhood while growing up and throughout his adult lifetime. They involved a series of experiences with the UFO and extraterrestrial phenomena, journeys via fully conscious out-of-body travel into parallel and higher dimensional realities, as well as numerous excursions along the past time track. These adventures eventually revealed a hidden history of Earth and our solar system that subsequently helped to confirm the depth of suppressed truth he was uncovering. In addition, the music compositions and productions he developed throughout his life from his early twenties continue to kindle the fire which drives his ongoing explorations into knowing ever deeper hidden truth by direct experience—in contrast to believing or theorizing.

Today, his continuing journeys into our vast multi-dimensional universe and his unique uplifting music continue to serve as an inner channel of inspiration to further explore and awaken ever-so-much-more about our true nature as knowing, eternal beings.

Lemriel is genuinely passionate about sharing eye-opening enlightening experiences and unusual encounters he gratefully received while uncovering cleverly hidden truth. For the first time, he discloses how our planet is about to be unexpectedly, benevolently transformed in the near future instead of destroyed because of a recent off-world decision that was finally made concerning changing Earth's current destructive destiny. He takes the reader on a personal journey to discover the reality of UFOs or advanced alien spacecraft, extraterrestrials both benevolent and malevolent, the true nature of the everlasting Soul; its non-destructible energy form that people from other worlds call Atma, and the reality of the existence of parallel and higher dimensions.

He further reveals to his audience what he discovered about our Earth's most important missing ancient history and discloses how he experienced much about the depth of purposefully hidden truth from the guidance of many off-world Master Teachers the majority of human beings dwelling on Earth today do not know existed at any time.

Lemriel gratefully acknowledges his mother for being the first person to read and experience the revealing depth of the transforming truth-revealing channel the pages of this book represent. She discovered, greatly surprised, much about her son she never knew or even imagined, because he kept silent about his uplifting, extraordinary life-changing experiences—until now.

Originally from Salt Lake City, Utah, where Lemriel spent the first six years of his life, he spends a lot of his time writing about his continuing explorations into hidden truth through his ongoing out-of-body journeys and direct experiential explorations into the UFO and extraterrestrial phenomena. The culmination of his passion for writing numerous books and screenplays, musical compositions, and his current endeavors with feature film and episodic TV story development, coupled with a series of uniquely distinguishing awakening lifetime events, places him as a conduit on the coming horizon for grand new transforming adventures to be opened up to the worldwide book reading public.

You can explore the YouTube.com videos of the author's personal presentations he conducted at International UFO/Extraterrestrial Disclosure conferences held around the world, several promotional videos about the *The*

*Seres Agenda* and The Parallel Time trilogy books, as well as many radio show interviews with him as a guest author/speaker, and various overviews of his feature film projects and feature film related music productions at his easily accessible and very unique website found at: www.paralleltime.com. You will also find two special recordings of his voice sending out the special vibratory word HU to access deliberately hidden truth on a grand cosmic multi-dimensional scale and discover the much greater knowing of the expansive love within it. The books, videos, radio interviews, music productions, and website link are also accessible through a search on Google by title, the author's official Washington, D.C. library of Congress copyright pseudonym, R. Scott Lemriel, or his legal name R. Scott Rochek. Links to the website are also on YouTube, Vimeo, Facebook, LinkedIn, Twitter and other social media outlets.

Lightning Source UK Ltd.
Milton Keynes UK
UKHW012332200819
348297UK00001B/105/P